Microsoft®
Windows®
Script Host 2.0
Developer's Guide

Günter Born

PUBLISHED BY
Microsoft Press
A Division of Microsoft Corporation
One Microsoft Way
Redmond, Washington 98052-6399

Library of Congress Cataloging-in-Publication Data
Born, Günter, 1955-
    Microsoft Windows Script Host 2.0 Developer's Guide / Günter Born.
      p.   cm.
    Includes index.
    ISBN 0-7356-0931-4
    1. Microsoft Windows (Computer file) 2. Computer software--Development. I. Title.

QA76.76.O63 B644 2000
005.4'469--dc21
                                                                    00-036127

Printed and bound in the United States of America.

1 2 3 4 5 6 7 8 9   QMQM   5 4 3 2 1 0

Distributed in Canada by Penguin Books Canada Limited.

A CIP catalogue record for this book is available from the British Library.

Microsoft Press books are available through booksellers and distributors worldwide. For further information about international editions, contact your local Microsoft Corporation office or contact Microsoft Press International directly at fax (425) 936-7329. Visit our Web site at mspress.microsoft.com. Send comments to *mspinput@microsoft.com*.

Acquisitions Editor: Ben Ryan
Project Editor: Sally Stickney
Technical Editor: Marc Young
Manuscript Editor: Ina Chang

For Mom and Dad,
for all their love, care, and patience

Contents

Introduction   XV

Part I   Introduction to the World of Script Programming

Chapter 1   Introduction to Windows Script Host   3

WHAT YOU CAN DO WITH WSH SCRIPTS   4
A Few Remarks About VBScript and JScript   5
UPGRADING TO WSH 2   5
CREATING AND USING SCRIPTS   7
Creating Your First Script in VBScript   7
Creating the Same Script in JScript   9
Executing WSH Scripts   10
Submitting Arguments to a Script   14
The New .wsf File Format   19
Including External Files   20
Using Type Libraries   20
Debugging Features   21

Chapter 2   Development Tools and Techniques   23

CREATING SCRIPTS   23
Using Script Templates   24
EDITING SCRIPTS   26
Invoking Script Editors   26
INSTALLING AND UNINSTALLING ACTIVEX CONTROLS   34
Registering a Control   34
Uninstalling a Control   35
DEBUGGING SCRIPTS   36
Tracing Your Programs   37
Using the Microsoft Script Debugger   39

Contents

Chapter 3 **Introduction to Programming with Objects**   **45**

OBJECTS   **45**
A Simple Object   46
The Object Model   46
Collections   47
Methods   48
A Practical Example   49

AVAILABLE OBJECTS   **49**
Getting Information About Objects, Methods, and Properties   50

Chapter 4 **Introduction to VBScript**   **51**

BASIC FEATURES   **51**
Statements, Continued Lines, and Comments   51
Constants and Variables   54
Operators   63
Control Structures   67
Loops   69
Functions and Procedures   71

ADVANCED FEATURES   **80**
Error Handling   80
Regular Expressions (in VBScript 5.0 and Later)   82
Classes (in VBScript 5.0)   85
Using the *With* Statement (in VBScript 5.0)   89

Chapter 5 **Introduction to JScript**   **91**

WHAT IS JSCRIPT?   **91**

THE STRUCTURE OF A JSCRIPT PROGRAM   **92**
Comments   93
Statements   93
Constants   94
Variables   94
Escape Sequences in Strings   98

OPERATORS   **99**
Assignment Operator   100
Comparison Operators   100
Calculation Operators   100

Increment and Decrement Operators 101
Logical Operators 102
Operator Precedence 103

CONTROL STRUCTURES **104**
if Statement 104
Conditional Operator 105
for Loop 105
for...in Loop 107
while Loop 107
do...while Loop 108
switch Statement 109
break and *continue* Keywords 110

FUNCTIONS AND OBJECTS **110**
User-Defined Functions 110
Built-In Functions 111
Objects 111
Arrays 112

Part II **Interactive Scripting**

Chapter 6 **Creating Simple Dialog Boxes in WSH** **117**

USING THE *ECHO* METHOD **117**
Using *Echo* in VBScript 118
Using *Echo* in the Command Prompt Window 119
Using *Echo* in JScript 120
Using a Line Feed with *Echo* 121

USING THE *MSGBOX* FUNCTION IN VBSCRIPT **122**
Defining the Icon and Buttons in a Dialog Box 125
Setting the Focus on a Button 127
Determining Which Button Was Used to Close a Dialog Box 128
Example: A Welcome Login Message in VBScript 130

USING THE *POPUP* METHOD **134**
Using *Popup* in VBScript 137
Another JScript Example Using *Popup* 138

Contents

Chapter 7 **Working with WSH Objects** **141**

USING THE *WSCRIPT* OBJECT **141**
Retrieving WSH and Script Properties 142
Retrieving Language Engine Properties 145
Accessing Script Arguments 147

ACCESSING ENVIRONMENT VARIABLES **152**
Accessing Environment Variables in a Script 152

CREATING AND RELEASING OBJECTS **165**
CreateObject vs. *GetObject* 167
Using *DisconnectObject* 168

LAUNCHING OTHER PROGRAMS FROM A SCRIPT **170**
Launching Notepad from VBScript 173
Launching Calculator from JScript 174
Paths Containing Blanks 175
The *Quit* Method 176
Using the *Run* Method to Execute MS-DOS Commands 180

Chapter 8 **Retrieving User Input in WSH Scripts** **183**

INVOKING AN INPUT DIALOG BOX IN VBSCRIPT **183**

INVOKING AN INPUT DIALOG BOX IN JSCRIPT **186**
A WSH 2 Solution: Combining VBScript and JScript 186
Using the *prompt* Method from Internet Explorer 188

Chapter 9 **Working with Forms** **195**

USING INTERNET EXPLORER TO CREATE AN ABOUT DIALOG BOX **195**
Using the *showModalDialog* Method to Display an HTML File 196
Displaying the About Dialog Box Using VBScript 199
Displaying the About Dialog Box Using JScript 201

USING INTERNET EXPLORER AND WSH TO CREATE A FORM **202**
HTML Code for the Form 202
Displaying the Form 203
A JScript WSH Script for Displaying the Form 207
Displaying a File Selection Dialog Box 209
Improving the Form 212

Part III Power Scripting

Chapter 10 Creating Shortcuts   225

SHORTCUT BASICS   225
Using the *CreateShortcut* Method   226

SHORTCUTS: BEYOND THE BASICS   231
Using the *SpecialFolders* Object   231
Creating a Shortcut on the Desktop   238
Creating a Shortcut on the Start Menu   242
Creating a Shortcut Using Arguments   248
Reading Shortcut Properties   253
Updating a Shortcut   259
Creating a Shortcut to a Web Site   263

Chapter 11 Using Advanced WSH Features   267

RETRIEVING THE USER, DOMAIN, OR COMPUTER NAME   267
The JScript Implementation   269

CONNECTING TO A NETWORK PRINTER   270
Printer Mapping Using *AddWindowsPrinterConnection*   271
Printer Mapping Using *AddPrinterConnection*   272
Removing a Printer Mapping   276
Listing All Mapped Printers   278
Setting the Default Printer   279

MAPPING NETWORK DRIVES   281
The JScript Implementation   284
Logon Scripts   286

ACCESSING THE WINDOWS REGISTRY   286
Accessing the Registry in WSH   288
Accessing the Registry in VBScript   290
Run-Time Error Handling for Registry Access   293
Checking the Existence of a Key   296
Techniques for Registry Access in WSH   299
Enumerating Registry Keys and Values   305
Accessing the Registry Remotely   307
Changing the Windows 98 Installation Path   309
Hiding the Last User Name at Logon   311
Retrieving the Workgroup Name in Windows 98   312

Contents

Chapter 12 **Using File System and I/O Commands**   317

  THE *FILESYSTEMOBJECT* OBJECT MODEL   317
    Creating a *FileSystemObject* Object   318
    Methods of the *FileSystemObject* Object   319

  ACCESSING DRIVES   320
    Listing All Drives on a Machine   320
    Showing Drive Properties   325

  ACCESSING FILES AND FOLDERS   331
    Listing All Subfolders in a Folder   332
    Creating, Moving, Renaming, and Deleting Folders   335
    Listing All Files in a Folder   343
    Retrieving File Attributes and Dates   347
    Copying and Deleting Files   355
    Backing Up Folders   359

  ACCESSING TEXT FILES   365
    Reading from a Text File   365
    Pitfalls of Using Dialog Boxes and
      Browser Windows to View Text Files   368
    Writing to a Text File   376
    Appending New Text to an Existing File   380
    Replacing Text in a File   382

  USING THE BROWSE FOR FOLDER DIALOG BOX   385
    Using *BrowseForFolder* to Select Folders   386
    Using *BrowseForFolder* to Select Files   391

Chapter 13 **Controlling Windows and Applications from Scripts**   397

  DELAYING SCRIPT EXECUTION   397
    Using the *Sleep* Method to Reduce the CPU Load   398
    Using a Delay to Solve a Problem with Asynchronous Processes   399

  ACTIVATING AN APPLICATION USING THE *APPACTIVATE* METHOD   401
    Pitfalls of Using the *AppActivate* Method   404

  USING THE *SENDKEYS* METHOD TO SIMULATE KEYSTROKES   406
    Using *SendKeys* in WSH 2   406
    Manipulating Two Applications Using *SendKeys*   410

CUSTOMIZING WINDOWS USING LOGON SCRIPTS 413
Setting Up a Logon Script 413
Using Global Logon and Logoff Scripts 415
Using Startup and Shutdown Scripts 416
Startup and Logon Scripts in Windows 95 and Windows 98 417

Chapter 14 **Programming Techniques and Tips** **419**

RUN-TIME ERRORS 419
Handling Run-Time Errors in VBScript 419
Handling Run-Time Errors in JScript 420
Raising a Run-Time Error in VBScript 421

PATHS AND DATES 421
Getting the Script's Path 421
Getting the Current Directory 422
Setting the Default Folder 423
Getting the Current Drive Name 423
Calculating Date Differences 424

LONG FILENAMES, THE AT COMMAND, AND SYSTEM CALLS 425
Using the Windows NT Scheduler to Execute WSH Scripts 425
Using Long Filenames in Scripts 425
Using the *Run* Method to Execute System Calls 426
Locking a Windows 2000 Workstation 429
Invoking the Copy Disk Dialog Box 430
Invoking the Format Dialog Box 431
Invoking the Screen Saver Property Page 432
Calling Control Panel Modules 432
Using the *Run* Method to Handle Network Mappings 434

USER DIALOG BOXES AND OUTPUT 434
Using Tabs and Line Feeds 434
Displaying Console Input and Output 435
Writing to a Line and Reading from It 437
Piping Program Output 439
Using Files for Streaming 440
Logging Script Output 443
Printing from a WSH Script 446

Contents

FILE HANDLING   **447**

Checking Whether a File or Folder Exists   447

Checking Whether a Folder is Empty   448

Checking Whether an Access Database Is in Use   448

Copying a File   449

Renaming a File or Folder   450

Searching for a File   452

Listing All Shortcut Files   452

PLAYING SOUND   **454**

Using Internet Explorer to Play Sound   455

THE WINDOWS SHELL   **457**

Testing the Shell Version   458

Arranging the Desktop Windows   459

Opening Folder Windows   461

Accessing Windows Shell Dialog Boxes   462

CALLING A DUN CONNECTION   **465**

Part IV Appendixes

Appendix A **WSH Resources on the Internet**   **469**

Appendix B **Script Security**   **471**

PARTIALLY DISABLING WSH   **471**

PREVENTING AUTOMATIC EXECUTION OF WSH SCRIPTS   **472**

SECURITY SETTINGS FOR WSH SCRIPTS   **475**

CONCLUDING REMARKS   **479**

Index   481

Acknowledgments

Windows Script Host (WSH) was a long time in development, as was this book. First, I want to applaud Microsoft's developers for their long-awaited, great product. They've created a powerful tool for programming at the operating system level.

Many people inspired me with their questions, suggestions, tips, newsgroup postings, and samples. Special thanks to Michael Harris, Ian Morrish, Clarence Washington Jr., and others who generously shared information with the WSH newsgroups. Their ideas were helpful to me as I learned about script programming. Also, Andrew Clinick's articles and Mike Whalen's tips were, for me, like the Rosetta stone. Additional thanks, by the way, to Andrew and Mike for reading the entire book before it went to print and providing many useful suggestions.

I couldn't have completed this book without the help of many people. My special thanks to Thomas Pohlmann, who undertook the adventure of publishing the first edition of this book in Germany. He believed in doing a WSH title even after a number of other authors had thrown in the towel. I also want to thank Thomas Braun-Wiesholler and Ben Ryan, my acquisitions editors at Microsoft Press Germany and in the United States, respectively, who gave me a chance to publish the revised edition of this book. Even though my manuscript always exceeded the page limits, they never lost their patience with me. Applause and special thanks to my editors at Microsoft Press: Ina Chang, Sally Stickney, and Marc Young. They spent many hours editing and polishing my text. Without their involvement, the English version of this book would never have seen daylight. I'd also like to thank the many other people, too numerous to mention, who were involved in the project.

Finally, I'd like to thank my wife and my children, Kati and Benjamin, who supported me as I worked on the book.

Günter Born
May 2000

Introduction

When Microsoft Windows 3.1 was released, I had hoped that it would come with an operating system–hosted script language. Other operating systems did provide such languages, but Windows 3.1 had only the old-style MS-DOS batch files. For a number of reasons, I didn't want to use third-party solutions such as PowerBASIC and Rexx. After Microsoft Windows 95 became available, I used Microsoft Visual Basic, Visual Basic for Applications (VBA), and HTML scripts from time to time. In 1998, while I was writing the Microsoft Windows 98 handbook for Microsoft Press Germany, I discovered that Windows 98 had a new feature called Windows Scripting Host (WSH), which provided two scripting languages: Microsoft Visual Basic, Scripting Edition (VBScript), and Microsoft JScript.

Later that year, I began writing the *Microsoft Windows 98 Power Toolkit* for Microsoft Press. I wanted to cover WSH extensively in the book and explain how to use scripts to automate such tasks as backing up files, mapping network drives and printers, and showing user dialog boxes. However, I couldn't find any documentation about WSH, and the help files that were shipped with Windows 98 didn't cover script programming. The Windows Script Host Reference was basically just a white paper, and the books and Web sites I consulted dealt only with HTML scripting using VBScript and JScript. So I started investigating the WSH samples that were shipped with Windows 98, visiting Microsoft's scripting site, and writing my own WSH samples.

I struggled to figure out which objects to use in a given situation, how to get information about properties and methods, and how to implement a script in either VBScript or JScript. Debugging my first scripts was a painful process. WSH 1 reported mostly cryptic run-time error messages in line *x*—or else the script simply didn't do what I expected. (At the time, I didn't know how to use the Microsoft Script Debugger in a scripting environment.) After receiving a run-time error message, I would load the script again and again into Notepad, count the lines manually to find the faulty line, and try to amend the code using a trial-and-error approach. After a few hours, I decided that this approach couldn't possibly be the right way to do script programming.

Once I started visiting WSH newsgroups, I found that other people were having the same problems. Newsgroup participants such as Ian Morrish, Clarence Washington Jr., and Michael Harris shared a great deal of useful knowledge, but I still needed more details, especially about advanced programming. I had written books about VBA programming and HTML scripting, so I was familiar with Internet sites dealing with HTML scripting and ActiveX programming. From these sites, I learned that some editors supported script programming, and I learned how to use the script debugger and tools such as the Object Browser in Visual Basic to find out more about objects and their methods and properties. I was able to increase my productivity significantly and create scripts in a relatively comfortable environment.

At the outset, I had used the typical "macro programmer" approach—I tried to combine simple statements to create a script program. Sometimes this approach worked, but often I was bombarded by syntax and run-time error messages. I also missed powerful statements that I could have used to copy files, launch programs, retrieve user input, and so on. In the WSH newsgroups, some people recommended third-party tools and languages that promised a rich collection of statements. I knew from past experience, however, that if a language provides a rich collection of statements, that language is difficult to learn and to use.

Using my VBA programming experience as a foundation, I began to explore the philosophy behind scripting. I learned that you don't need statements "buried" in a scripting language for tasks such as reading script arguments and copying files because WSH gives you access to all COM objects installed on a system. So a script can use the features offered by such COM objects to handle its tasks. You can also add new COM objects to a system, which increases the number of scriptable functions without changing the underlying scripting language. If an object provides spell checking, for example, you can simply use that object in a script. Once I became more familiar with WSH, I found it to be the hottest technology from Microsoft in recent years. WSH is the glue that combines objects (for example, a Microsoft Office spell checker, a word processor, a browser, and a mail system) into a new, customized application. You can implement a sophisticated application quickly and easily, using just a few lines of script code.

By this point, I had collected a lot of material, gained some experience, and written many samples. I had also written a brief section on WSH in the *Microsoft Windows 98 Power Toolkit*. At the 1998 Frankfurt book fair, I met with Microsoft Press acquisitions editors Thomas Pohlmann and Stephen Guty, and the idea for a WSH script programming title was born. Six weeks later, my German manuscript was ready. The first edition of the book was published in January 1999. It was the first WSH 1 book published worldwide. In the spring, the first WSH 2 beta version was released. We decided to wait until the release of Windows 2000 before going ahead with a WSH 2 book. I spent the additional time investigating WSH 2 and other hot technologies such as ActiveX Data Objects (ADO), Active Directory Service Interfaces (ADSI), and Windows Management Instrumentation (WMI). I also wrote an article series for WSH beginners in a computer magazine, created the WSH Bazaar on my Web site, and spent many hours visiting the WSH newsgroups to learn more about the troubles that script programmers were experiencing.

The material I collected was enough for two books—this one, for beginners and intermediate users, and a volume for advanced users that deals with scripting technologies. Microsoft Press will publish the second book, *Advanced Development with Microsoft Windows Script Host 2.0,* later this year. That book is for advanced script programmers who want in-depth coverage of the topics covered in this introductory volume. *Advanced Development with Microsoft Windows Script Host 2.0* will explain how to use additional objects to extend your scripting capabilities. Special topics, such as the XML structure of .wsf files and many undocumented hints that pertain to those files, will be covered. Also included will be explanations of how to use additional tools such as the OLE/COM Object Viewer or the Object Browser to find out more about objects and their methods and properties. Along with other useful techniques, you'll learn how to access Microsoft Office applications from WSH scripts and how to use objects such as Microsoft Excel spreadsheets, the Office spell checker, Microsoft Word documents, and Microsoft Outlook features. You'll also learn how to read and write to databases from scripts by using Microsoft Access or ADO. The book also explains how administrators can access ADSI from WSH scripts to maintain user accounts, services, or shares. You'll learn about the new technology Web-Based Enterprise Management (WBEM), and its Microsoft implementation called Windows Management Interface, and you'll find out how to use scripts to access networking and machine information and to cancel running processes. You'll also discover how to write ActiveX controls by using Visual Basic 5 Control Creation Edition (CCE) to access Windows API functions, create ActiveX forms, access the Clipboard, control the CD tray, and much more. I'll delve into the source code of several ActiveX controls used within this book in much greater detail. Whereas *Microsoft Windows Script Host 2.0 Developer's Guide* teaches you what you need to know to begin scripting with WSH, *Advanced Development with Microsoft Windows Script Host 2.0* will provide you with the information you need to become an expert WSH programmer. You'll learn the programming tricks professional developers use to help get the most out of WSH.

WHO THIS BOOK IS FOR

If you're an experienced script programmer who's been using WSH since its introduction, you should go straight to *Advanced Development with Microsoft Windows Script Host 2.0. Microsoft Windows Script Host 2.0 Developer's Guide* is for everyone else who's interested in WSH, including the following:

- System administrators who want to implement automated solutions for managing user accounts, backing up files, and so on, and who want an introduction to script programming

- Power users who want to customize their Windows systems and automate certain tasks using a script language

- Programmers who want a rapid introduction to WSH programming and who are looking for ideas and sample code to help them understand what others are doing with WSH

- Managers who want to know what WSH is for and how to use WSH scripts to improve the productivity of their systems

THE SCOPE OF THIS BOOK

This book isn't a complete reference to all scripting-related topics—it's a primer that begins with simple step-by-step instructions. Also, because most power users and system administrators know a bit about batch and macro programming but aren't familiar with object-oriented programming, this book provides an introduction to using objects and programming in VBScript and JScript.

After reading this book, you should know what WSH is for, you should understand the basics of VBScript and JScript, and you should be able to write your own scripts using the methods and properties of objects that WSH provides.

You can read the book from cover to cover, but you don't have to. You can concentrate on the parts or the chapters that suit your level of interest or your immediate needs.

The book is divided into four parts. Part I, "Introduction to the World of Script Programming," deals with the basics. If you've never programmed, I recommend that you start by reading this part. Chapter 1 introduces WSH and explains how to execute scripts. You'll learn about various script engines, and you'll find out how to submit arguments to a script program, how to use switches, and how to set script properties. Chapter 2 introduces tools that simplify script development. You'll learn how to use script editors, how to install ActiveX controls, and how to debug a script. If you've never done any object-oriented programming, you should look at Chapter 3, which explains what objects, methods, properties, collections, and object models are. Chapter 4 introduces VBScript, and Chapter 5 introduces JScript.

Part II, "Interactive Scripting," explains how to write scripts to obtain user input and display the results in dialog boxes and forms. Chapter 6 introduces the methods and functions for viewing results in dialog boxes, including the *Echo* method, the VBScript *MsgBox* function, and the *Popup* method. Chapter 7 explains how to use WSH objects. The samples use the *WScript* object to read script and language properties, to examine arguments submitted to a script, and to access environment variables. You'll learn how to create and release object instances within a script and how to use the *Run* method to launch programs from a script. Chapter 8 explains how to use the VBScript *InputBox* function to create an input dialog box and how to extend JScript to compensate for the missing *InputBox* function. You'll see samples that use Microsoft Internet Explorer objects to extend your scripting capabilities. Chapter 9 goes further in explaining how to use Internet Explorer objects to create dialog boxes and input forms.

Part III, "Power Scripting," introduces more objects. Chapter 10 deals with using WSH scripts to manage shortcuts on your Windows Desktop and on the Start menu. Chapter 11 looks at advanced WSH tasks such as retrieving the user, domain, or computer name. It covers printer and drive mapping in networking environments and accessing the Windows Registry from WSH scripts. Chapter 12 explains how to use the *FileSystemObject* object to deal with drives, folders, and files. For example, you'll learn how to enumerate files and folders, query drive properties, and back up files using scripts. Chapter 13 covers WSH 2 features that allow you to delay script execution, play sound, and run several applications from a script. You'll learn how to switch an application window to the foreground and how to simulate keystrokes by using the *SendKeys* method. Chapter 14 offers a collection of script programming techniques, tips, and tricks. Among other tasks, you'll learn how to obtain the current path, shut down Windows, print, and use the Windows shell from a script.

Part IV, "Appendixes," contains two appendixes. Appendix A lists WSH resources you'll find on the Internet. Appendix B, on script security, includes timely and up-to-date information and strategies for making your Windows systems more secure against WSH script viruses.

SAMPLE FILES AND OTHER TOOLS

Throughout this book, you'll find samples that you can type in or load from the companion CD. The samples are divided by chapter and are in subfolders named \Chapter01, \Chapter02, and so on in the \WSHDevGuide folder. The companion

CD's user interface allows you to browse through the samples, or you can use the setup program to install the samples on your local hard disk. Choose Run from the Start menu, and type *D:\Setup.exe* (where *D:* is the name of your CD-ROM drive) to expand the sample files into a directory structure that identifies the chapters. For example, the sample files for Chapter 3 are in \WSHDevGuide\Chapter03.

On the companion CD, you'll also find other helpful tools and files, including Windows Script Host 2. The CD also contains the WSH 2, VBScript, and JScript programmer's references and help files. Open the file Start.htm in the root folder of your CD to enter the user interface. You can then use the browser to navigate through the CD's content.

> **NOTE** Keep in mind that you can seriously damage your system with scripts. Always back up your system files and other important files before you attempt to modify and use scripts that will alter your files, the Registry, and system settings. Use the book's samples at your own risk, particularly if you plan to modify them in any way. Neither Microsoft nor I can provide you with scripting support, so make modifications cautiously.

FURTHER READING

The following sources contain additional information helpful for WSH script programmers. I recommend that you first read the following Microsoft documents:

- **Windows Script Host Reference** A help file on WSH objects and their methods and properties that also includes a WSH tutorial. This reference is located on the book's companion CD.

- **VBScript Language Reference** The definitive reference for VBScript issues. This help file also contains a VBScript tutorial and a *FileSystemObject* object tutorial. The help file containing this reference is on this book's companion CD.

- **JScript Language Reference** A help file that documents the JScript syntax and all methods and properties provided by the language engine. It also contains a JScript tutorial and a *FileSystemObject* object tutorial. This reference is located on the book's companion CD.

SYSTEM REQUIREMENTS

Using this book requires a Windows system (Windows 95, Windows 98, Windows NT with Service Pack 4, or Windows 2000) with Windows Script Host (version 2 recommended) already installed. Some samples require Microsoft Internet Explorer (version

4 or later). The tools to write scripts are supplied by Windows (an editor, for example) or are located on the book's companion CD. You might need to download some from the Internet.

ADDITIONAL INFORMATION

Every effort has been made to ensure the accuracy of this book and the contents of the companion CD. Microsoft Press provides corrections for books at *mspress.microsoft.com/mspress/support*.

If you have comments, questions, or ideas regarding this book or the companion CD, please send them to Microsoft Press at mspinput@microsoft.com or at the following mailing address:

Microsoft Press
Attn: Microsoft Windows Script Host 2.0 Developer's Guide Editor
One Microsoft Way
Redmond, WA 98052-6399

To get in touch with me regarding the book, please visit my Web site at *www.borncity.de*.

Again, please note that scripting support is not offered through any of the above addresses.

Part I

Introduction to the World of Script Programming

Chapter 1

Introduction to Windows Script Host

Versions of Microsoft Windows before Windows 98 provided almost no help for automating such tasks as backing up files and carrying out routine system administration tasks. Of course, you could use the old MS-DOS batch (BAT) files in the MS-DOS Prompt window to perform certain tasks, such as copying files. But BAT files can contain only a simple sequence of MS-DOS commands (only simple branches and no real looping functionality, among other drawbacks) and don't support dialog boxes and message boxes. In Windows 3.1, you could do a little more with the macro recorder to record and play simple keystrokes and mouse clicks, but the macro recorder didn't allow programming.

The search for a more powerful way to handle these automation tasks led users to seek out third-party solutions, such as PowerBatch or programming environments such as Delphi, Microsoft Visual Basic, and Microsoft Visual C++. But many Windows users found these solutions unacceptable because they were neither simple nor free.

Because Microsoft Office provides Visual Basic for Applications (VBA) and because Web authors know scripting languages such as Microsoft Visual Basic, Scripting Edition (VBScript), and Netscape's JavaScript, it was only a matter of time before Microsoft provided a scripting tool for Windows operating systems. This tool is Microsoft Windows Script Host (WSH), which falls under the umbrella of Microsoft's Windows Script technologies.

WSH is a stand-alone host that enables you to execute a script file directly at the operating system level. For example, you can invoke a script from a command-line interface or you can double-click a script file in Windows Explorer. WSH is handy for many administrative tasks that require little or no user interface. It is far more versatile than old MS-DOS batch files because JScript and VBScript are powerful scripting languages that have full access to WSH objects and any other available Automation objects.

NOTE Before version 2, Windows Script Host was known as Windows Scripting Host. In this book, I'll refer to both versions as WSH.

WHAT YOU CAN DO WITH WSH SCRIPTS

You can use scripts in many ways to customize your Windows system. Here are some of the tasks you can automate using scripts:

- Back up or restore files on your system. (This capability is particularly handy if you need to save only a few files from your machine to a network server.)

- Shut down or restart Windows with a mouse click. You can also use a script to add special shutdown or startup tasks, such as backing up certain files after closing applications or logging a user's name after booting the system. (The ability to log information via scripts is especially useful in Windows 95 and Windows 98; in Windows NT and Windows 2000, many logging features are built in.)

- Integrate applications and their data. For example, a script can launch an Office application, load and process a document, print it, and close the application. Using scripts in this way, you can "associate" a document with any application you choose.

- Manage system administration tasks such as adding, updating, and removing user accounts in Windows NT and Windows 2000. You can use a WSH script to automate all these tasks by using the Active Directory Service Interfaces (ADSI) provided with Windows NT and Windows 2000.

- Directly access the Windows shell through suitable objects (to create shortcuts or map network devices such as drives or printers).

- Read environment variables or retrieve information about Windows.

- Launch programs and control Automation objects.

- Display dialog boxes that inform the user about the program status or retrieve user input.

- Access the Windows shell and Windows application programming interface (API) to control windows and other applications.

A Few Remarks About VBScript and JScript

WSH, which ships with Windows 98 and Windows 2000 (and comes in a downloadable version for Windows 95 and Windows NT 4), comes with two programming languages, VBScript and JScript. VBScript uses the same syntax as Visual Basic; it is actually a subset of Visual Basic. JScript is Microsoft's implementation of ECMAScript, the vendor-independent programming language based on JavaScript.

These two programming languages are all you need to enter the world of script programming. However, Microsoft designed an open interface for WSH so that third-party vendors can integrate their own language engines to support other languages such as Perl, Tool Control Language (Tcl), and Rexx.

UPGRADING TO WSH 2

WSH 1 first shipped with the Windows NT 4 Option Pack. WSH 1 is also part of Windows 98, but if it isn't active, you must install it as an additional Windows component. WSH 2 is an integral part of Windows 2000, so if you have Windows 2000, you don't have to take any further action to install WSH 2.

To check whether WSH is installed on your system, you can simply browse a folder that contains a .js file, a .vbs file, and a .wsf file (for example, using Windows Explorer). If the icons shown for the files match those in Figure 1-1, WSH 2 is installed. If the icon for unknown document type is used for the .wsf file, WSH 1 is installed. If all files are shown with the icon for unregistered file types, WSH isn't installed.

VBScript.vbs JScript.js WSHfile.wsf

Figure 1-1 *Icons and filename extensions for script files*

VBSCRIPT VS. VISUAL BASIC/VBA AND JSCRIPT VS. JAVASCRIPT

If you've programmed in Visual Basic or VBA or have prepared scripts in VBScript or JScript for HTML documents, writing WSH scripts in VBScript or JScript shouldn't be a problem, but you do have to keep a few things in mind:

■ Visual Basic programs can be compiled into EXE files, but this functionality isn't available with WSH. In WSH, you must keep all scripts in simple text files with extensions such as .vbs, .js, or .wsf. WSH uses Windows Script engines to interpret the content of a script file directly, so you can prepare your scripts using a simple text editor (such as Notepad).

■ VBScript and JScript (which ship with WSH 2) don't include language constructs, such as the *Declare* statement in Visual Basic and VBA, that allow access to external functions and procedures. VBScript doesn't include routines for extended run-time error handling (such as On Error GoTo *label*). Neither VBScript nor JScript supports explicit data type declarations; instead, they treat all variables as *Variant*s.

■ The object model provided by WSH differs from the one provided in Internet Explorer. For example, the *window.document* object isn't supported from WSH for user output.

■ Because the WSH environment doesn't provide an extended user interface (as Internet Explorer does), the WSH object model doesn't expose any user-interface events (such as *onclick* in HTML scripts). However, WSH does support event handling, as you'll see in subsequent chapters.

To update Windows 95, Windows 98, or Windows NT 4 to WSH 2, you must install WSH manually. The companion CD includes a version of WSH 2 for each of these operating systems. You can also download the most recent WSH files (free of charge) from *http://msdn.microsoft.com/scripting*.

NOTE For Windows NT 4, you must also install Service Pack 3. To use WSH in Windows 95 or Windows NT 4, you should have Internet Explorer version 4 or later installed. To run WSH 2 with Internet Explorer 3 in Windows 95, you must install DCOM. See Microsoft's Web site *http://msdn.microsoft.com/scripting* for further details.

WSH AND LANGUAGE ENGINE VERSIONS

You should know which WSH version you have installed as well as the version of the language engines it uses to execute the scripts. Microsoft has released several language engine upgrades since version 3.1 (shipped with WSH 1). Version 3.1a fixed a few bugs. Visual Studio 6 shipped with version 4 of the language engines. Internet Explorer 5 includes version 5 of the language engines, which contains bug fixes and also extends the language features. Microsoft also offers a downloadable version 5 of the language engines as a separate upgrade (at *http://msdn.microsoft.com/scripting*).

WSH 2 is part of Windows Script 5.1, which also includes version 5.1 of the VBScript and JScript language engines. The version 5.1 language engines can be used with Internet Explorer versions 4 and 5 and IIS versions 3 and 4.

CREATING AND USING SCRIPTS

Are you ready to create and use your first script? To begin, we'll create a simple program that displays a dialog box with the message *Hello, world* so that you can see the basics of script programming and how a script executes.

Creating Your First Script in VBScript

To create the simple dialog box shown in Figure 1-2, you need only one line in VBScript:

```
WScript.Echo "Hello, world"
```

Figure 1-2 *A simple dialog box*

But how do you create the script file? For this simple script, all you need is Notepad. Simply follow these steps:

1. Launch Notepad.exe and enter the statements shown in Figure 1-3. The *WScript.Echo* statement is the most important part of the code because it creates the dialog box.

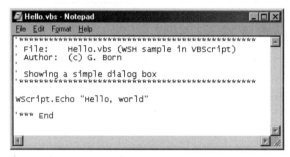

Figure 1-3 *Your first VBScript program*

2. Save the contents of the editor window to a text file on your hard disk. You can use any filename (such as *Hello*), but the extension must be .vbs.

    NOTE   I recommend that you use the .vbs extension for VBScript files. This file type is registered automatically for WSH. If your script files use other filename extensions, neither version of WSH can recognize the script language. Double-clicking a script file with a wrong extension (.vb, for example) will open the Open With dialog box because no application is registered for this file type.

After you store the script, there should be a file named Hello.vbs on your hard disk containing the source code in Listing 1-1.

```
'*************************************************
' File:    Hello.vbs (WSH sample in VBScript)
' Author:  (c) G. Born
'
' Showing a simple dialog box
'*************************************************

WScript.Echo "Hello, world"

'*** End
```

Listing 1-1 *Hello.vbs*

You might wonder why I used eight lines even though I said that you needed just one command to invoke the dialog box. You can create a simple script file with just one line, but I encourage you to add comments with some additional information, such as your name (as the author of the file) and the purpose of the file. These comments can be helpful to other people and also to you. (Or do you always remember the purpose and contents of a script file after a few weeks? I don't!) The script engine ignores the comments.

Now let's go back to the code. Because we're using VBScript as the programming language, all statements must follow VBScript syntax. In VBScript, comments are marked with a leading single quote, as shown here:

```
' This is a comment.
```

The VBScript language engine used in WSH ignores any part of a line that follows a single quote. This means that you can comment an entire line or only the tail end of a line. For example, the following statement shows a dialog box with the text *Hello, world.* The comment at the end of the line is ignored.

```
WScript.Echo "Hello, world"  ' Show a message.
```

> **TIP** The sample file Hello.vbs, along with all the other sample files used in this chapter, is in the folder \WSHDevGuide\Chapter01 on the book's companion CD. You'll also find the template files VBScript.vbs and JScript.js in that folder. You can use these files as templates to create a new script file. Simply load the template into your editor (by right-clicking on the file's icon and choosing Edit from the shortcut menu), add the new commands, and save the contents to a new file.

Creating the Same Script in JScript

If you prefer JScript for your script programs, you can use the same steps we just discussed. However, you must enter all statements in JScript syntax. Listing 1-2 shows what the program from Listing 1-1 looks like in JScript.

```
//*************************************************
// File:    Hello.js (WSH sample in JScript)
// Author:  (c) G. Born
//
// Showing a simple dialog box
//*************************************************

WScript.Echo("Hello, world");

//*** End
```

Listing 1-2 *Hello.js*

In JScript, single-line comments are marked with two leading slashes (//) and the beginning and end of multiline comments are marked as follows: /* ... */. Listing 1-2 contains a comment header and a trailer. I also used the *Echo* method from the *WScript* object to show the message box. (You'll find out about objects and methods in Chapter 3.)

The statement that creates a simple dialog box containing the text *Hello, world* and the OK button looks different in JScript:

```
WScript.Echo("Hello, world");
```

Do you see the difference? In JScript, it's a good programming practice to terminate all statements (with a few exceptions) with semicolons, and the *Echo* method requires parentheses around the string *"Hello, world"*.

Executing WSH Scripts

If you have WSH scripts stored in .vbs or .js files, you can execute them in Windows by double-clicking on the script file's icon or by means of the Run dialog box, or you can execute them from the Command Prompt window.

Executing a script in Windows

You can execute a script in Windows by simply double-clicking on the script file's icon. Windows executes the script using the WScript.exe host by default (because the file types are registered for WSH during WSH installation).

> **NOTE**   Two files are used to implement WSH. WScript.exe is a Windows-based host for scripts, designed to interact with the user by means of dialog boxes. CScript.exe is a Windows console application. (It runs in a Command Prompt window and sends output to STDOUT like native MS-DOS and Windows NT commands do.) CScript.exe is intended primarily for noninteractive tasks. In Windows 98, WScript.exe is in the \Windows folder and CScript.exe is in the \Windows\Command folder. In Windows 2000, both hosts are in the \WINNT\System32 folder.

Let's give this a try. Find the file Hello.vbs in the folder \WSHDevGuide\ Chapter01, and then double-click on Hello.vbs to start the sample. The result of the script is the dialog box shown back in Figure 1-2. If you double-click Hello.js, the resulting dialog box is identical to the one shown in Figure 1-2. You can close the dialog box from either sample by clicking the OK button.

You can also use the Run dialog box to execute a script in WScript.exe or CScript.exe. (This method comes in handy if you need to submit arguments to a script.) Simply follow these steps:

1. Choose Run from the Start menu.

2. Type the executable command (such as WScript.exe C:\Test\Hello.vbs) in the Open text box.

3. Click OK to close the dialog box and execute the script.

Executing a script using the Command Prompt window

You can also use the Command Prompt window to execute a script. Both CScript.exe and WScript.exe support this approach.

To execute a script, you must enter the following command in the Command Prompt window:

```
CScript.exe path\script name [Host options] [Script arguments]
WScript.exe path\script name [Host options] [Script arguments]
```

The *script name* part is the placeholder for the script name, including the drive and the path to the script file. You can append additional options for the host and/or arguments for the script on the command line.

The host options, which enable or disable WSH functions, are always preceded by two forward slashes. Table 1-1 describes all the host options.

Table 1-1 **CSCRIPT.EXE AND WSCRIPT.EXE HOST OPTIONS**

Option	*Supported by WSH 1*	*Supported by WSH 2*	*Description*
//I	✔	✔	Enables interactive mode—allows display of user prompts and script errors. (This is the default; *//B* is the opposite.)
//B	✔	✔	Enables batch mode—suppresses the command-line display of user prompts and script errors. If a script uses the *Echo* method, all user prompts are disabled. In WSH 2, this option is also available for WScript.exe to disable echo mode.
//T:nn	✔	✔	Sets a time-out value (the maximum time in seconds that a script can run).
//logo	✔	✔	Displays a banner (the text shown in the Command Prompt window after execution of a script; see the upper lines in Figure 1-4). This is the default option; *//nologo* is the opposite.

(continued)

Table 1-1 *continued*

Option	Supported by WSH 1	Supported by WSH 2	Description
//nologo	✔	✔	Prevents the display of an execution banner.
//H:CScript *//H:WScript*	✔	✔	Registers CScript.exe or WScript.exe as the default application for running scripts (*//H:CScript* or *//H:WScript*, respectively). WScript.exe is set to be the default scripting host after installation.
//S	✔	✔	Saves the current command-line options for this user.
//?	✔	✔	Displays a help page with the host options.
//D		✔	Enables Active Debugging for .js and .vbs script files. (See Chapter 2.)
//E:engine		✔	Sets the script engine for script execution.
//Job:xxx		✔	Executes the job with the ID number *xxx* in a .wsf file.
//X		✔	Executes the script in the debugger.

Figure 1-4 shows a Command Prompt window with sample command lines calling the script Hello.vbs with several options.

Figure 1-4 *Command lines to call CScript.exe and WScript.exe*

You can see a list of all the host options by invoking the host using the command *CScript.exe //?*. The dialog box in Figure 1-5 shows the WScript.exe options. (Choose Run from the Start menu, type *WScript.exe //?*, and click OK to close the dialog box.)

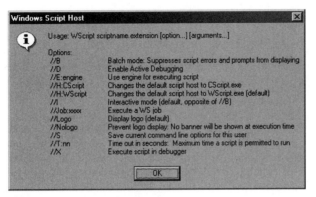

Figure 1-5 *WScript.exe host options*

Setting the script properties

As I mentioned earlier, you can set several host options for executing a script within WScript.exe or CScript.exe. In a Command Prompt window, you can type the options on the command line. If you prefer to execute a script in Windows, you can use the Run dialog box to set host options for a script.

Users generally prefer to start scripts with a double-click (on the script file itself or on a shortcut file). In such cases, you can define additional properties in Windows by right-clicking on the script file, choosing Properties from the shortcut menu, and selecting the options you want on the Script property page (shown in Figure 1-6).

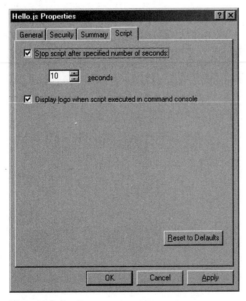

Figure 1-6 *The Script property page*

You can select the Stop Script After Specified Number Of Seconds check box and use the associated Seconds control to set a time-out value. If a script is still executing when the time-out is reached, Windows terminates the script. The Display Logo When Script Executed In Command Console check box forces CScript.exe to display the "Microsoft (R) Windows Script Host…" message in the Command Prompt window.

When you close the property page by clicking OK, Windows creates a new file with the name of the script file and a .wsh extension. Double-clicking on this file forces Windows to execute the script with the options set on the Script property page. Files with the extension .wsh are simple text files that are similar to .ini files. You can open a .wsh file with any text editor (such as Notepad). The contents of a .wsh file are as follows:

```
[ScriptFile]
Path=C:\WSHDevGuide\Chapter01\Hello.js
[Options]
Timeout=10
DisplayLogo=1
```

The *Path* statement in the *[ScriptFile]* section identifies the script file to be executed. The keywords in the *[Options]* section determine the run-time properties. *Timeout* is set to the time the user specified on the Script property page. *DisplayLogo=1* forces the display of the logo in the Command Prompt window. (See the *//logo* and *//nologo* entries in Table 1-1.)

> **NOTE**   You can edit the *Path* statement in a .wsh file so that it uses a relative or Universal Naming Convention (UNC) path. Using a relative or UNC path makes your .wsh files and their targets more portable because it frees them from a dependence on an absolute path. For example, the sample file Args.wsh uses the statement *Path=.\Args.vbs*, which references the Args.vbs file in the current directory. You can move Args.wsh and Args.vbs to a new drive and Args.wsh will be able to find Args.vbs as long as both files are in the same directory.

Submitting Arguments to a Script

The preceding samples don't require any arguments. In some cases, however, the user will submit one or more arguments, such as the name of a file, to the script. The VBScript in Listing 1-3 displays all arguments submitted to the script.

```
'********************************************************
' File:      Args.vbs (WSH sample in VBScript)
' Author:   (c) G. Born
'
```

Listing 1-3 *Args.vbs*

```
' Showing all arguments submitted to the script
' in a dialog box
'************************************************

text = "Arguments" & vbCrLf & vbCrLf

Set objArgs = WScript.Arguments          ' Create object.
For i = 0 to objArgs.Count - 1           ' Loop through all arguments.
    text = text & objArgs(i) & vbCrLf ' Get argument.
Next

WScript.Echo text ' Show arguments using Echo.

'*** End
```

POTENTIAL PROBLEMS WITH ARGUMENT PASSING

Before we go any further, I'd like to point out a few problems with submitting arguments. Let's say that you want to pass the argument *Hello, world* to your script. You can't use the following command because WSH interprets *Hello,* and *world* as separate arguments:

```
WScript.exe C:\WSHDevGuide\Chapter01\Args.vbs Hello, world
```

To submit a string that contains blanks as one argument, you must enclose the string in double quotes, as shown here:

```
WScript.exe C:\WSHDevGuide\Chapter01\Args.vbs "Hello, world"
```

Another problem can occur when you submit arguments to a script. If you use long filenames for your script files, you must enclose the entire pathname in double quotes. For example, if you use the following command to execute the script Args Test.vbs, mysterious things will happen:

```
WScript.exe C:\WSHDevGuide\Chapter01\Args Test.vbs "Hello, world"
```

In Windows 2000, you get a message about a wrong filename extension in Args. In Windows 95 and Windows 98, the script is executed but wrong arguments are reported. This behavior results from how Windows processes command lines. You can avoid this result by enclosing long filenames containing blanks within double quotes. The command line must be written as follows:

```
WScript.exe "C:\WSHDevGuide\Chapter01\Args Test.vbs" "Hello, world"
```

You can also use the command lines shown here with the host CScript.exe.

The script in Listing 1-3 obtains the *Arguments* collection of the *WScript* object and shows all arguments contained in this collection in a dialog box, as shown in Figure 1-7.

Figure 1-7 *Displaying submitted arguments*

Let's assume that you have an existing script file and want to submit some arguments to this script. A double-click on the script file isn't sufficient because it simply executes the script. To submit arguments to a script, choose Run from the Start menu to display the Run dialog box (shown in Figure 1-8). You enter the host name (CScript.exe or WScript.exe), the drive, the pathname, and the filename of the script file in the Open text box. The arguments are appended to the command line; they must be separated with blanks.

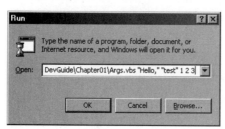

Figure 1-8 *Submitting arguments to a script using the Run dialog box*

If you feel uncomfortable submitting arguments using the Run dialog box, you can create a shortcut to your script file and set the arguments as properties of the shortcut (as long as the arguments won't change). Simply follow these steps:

1. Right-click on the script's file icon and choose Create Shortcut from the shortcut menu.

2. Right-click on the shortcut file and choose Properties from the shortcut menu.

3. Specify the command and the required arguments in the Target text box on the Shortcut property page (as shown in Figure 1-9).

Figure 1-9 *Shortcut properties for a script file*

When you close the property sheet using the OK button, Windows saves the arguments. These arguments are submitted automatically to the script when the user double-clicks on the shortcut file.

Passing arguments in the Command Prompt window

Does your script request arguments (such as a filename)? Do you use the Command Prompt window to execute your script (in CScript.exe or WScript.exe)? Besides specifying host options, which are preceded by two forward slashes, you can submit certain arguments as additional script options to the script. You simply place the script arguments at the end of the command line, separated by spaces.

You can thus call our Args.vbs sample in the Command Prompt window as follows:

```
CScript.exe C:\WSHDevGuide\Chapter01\Args.vbs //S "Hello, world" 1 2 3
WScript.exe C:\WSHDevGuide\Chapter01\Args.vbs //S "Hello, world" 1 2 3
```

Figure 1-10 shows some commands executed in a Command Prompt window using CScript.exe.

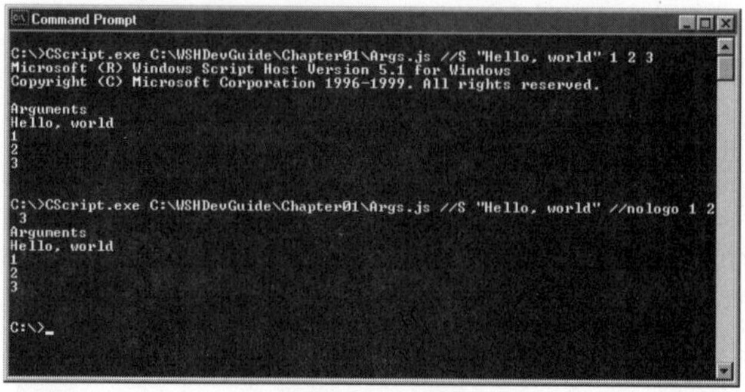

Figure 1-10 *Executing a script and passing arguments in the Command Prompt window*

NOTE   Because the individual arguments are optional, you must specify at least the name of the script file on the command line. You don't have to mark an argument with a forward slash, which is suggested in the WSH documentation. Also, you can mix the // options with the arguments to be passed to the script, as shown in the second command line in Figure 1-10.

In Figure 1-10, I used the JScript sample shown in Listing 1-4. This script uses the *Echo* method to show the submitted arguments. If you use CScript.exe as a host, the *Echo* method sends all output to the Command Prompt window (which is standard behavior for a Windows console program).

TIP   You can use this method with I/O redirection to send your script output to a file. The command *CScript.exe D:\Test.vbs "Hello" 1 > D:\Test.tmp* creates the file *D:\Test.tmp* and directs all script output to this file.

```
//**************************************************
// File:    Args.js (WSH sample in JScript)
// Author:  (c) G. Born
//
// Displaying the script arguments in a dialog box
//**************************************************

var objArgs;
var text = "Arguments \n\n";

var objArgs = WScript.Arguments;        // Create object.

for (var i = 0; i < objArgs.length; i++) // Loop for all arguments.
    text = text + objArgs(i) + '\n';     // Get argument.

WScript.Echo(text);  // Show arguments using Echo method.

//*** End
```

Listing 1-4 *Args.js*

The New .wsf File Format

Although you can use .vbs and .js script files in WSH 2, Microsoft has defined a new file format with the extension .wsf (for "Windows script file"). A .wsf file is a text document, as .js and .vbs files are, but it contains Extensible Markup Language (XML) code. A minimal .wsf file has the following structure:

```
<job id="T1">
    <script language="VBScript">
        WScript.Echo "Hello, world"
    </script>
</job>
```

The tags describe XML elements, and the *<script> ... </script>* element contains the ordinary script code.

> **NOTE**   Because .wsf files are XML documents, you can use any editor that supports XML to edit them. If you don't have such an editor, you can use any other text editor (such as Notepad).

Some XML extensions to .wsf files

The preceding sample code contains only the minimal XML elements required to create an executable .wsf file. For compatibility reasons with XML document specifications, I recommend using an extended structure within your .wsf files, as shown here:

```
<?xml version="1.0" encoding="ISO-8859-1"?>

<job id="T1">
    <script language="VBScript">
    <![CDATA[
        text = "world"
        WScript.Echo "Hello, " & text
    ]]>
    </script>
</job>
```

The content of the *<script>* element is encapsulated in the instruction

```
<![CDATA[ ... ]]>
```

which tells an XML document reader that the content (here the script code) should not be analyzed for XML features. The *encoding="ISO-8859-1"* attribute allows your scripts to contain special characters of Western European alphabets, such as the German umlauts (for example, Ä and ö) and the French accents (for example, é and à).

> **NOTE** The .wsf samples shown in the help files don't use the *<?xml...?>* element. But I recommend that you use the instructions in this section so that your .wsf files are compatible with XML tools and future versions of WSH.

Including External Files

If you have .js and .vbs files from previous WSH projects, you can use the .wsf file structure to include the files in a new WSH script. You can make the reference to the external .vbs or .js file within the *<script>* start tag using the *src* attribute. The following example includes the file Hello.js in the new WSH script Test.wsf:

```
<?xml version="1.0" encoding="ISO-8859-1"?>

<job id="T1">
    <script language="JScript" src="Hello.js"/>

    <script language="VBScript">
<![CDATA[
        WScript.Echo "Hello, world number 2"
]]>
    </script>
</job>
```

Executing the script file causes WSH to load and process the file Hello.js first. After control is passed back to the .wsf file, the second *<script>* element, which contains the *WScript.Echo* statement, is executed. You can also use the *src* attribute to define a reference to a script file containing only a function. Then you can call this function from within a script contained in the .wsf file.

> **NOTE** As you can see in the preceding sample, .wsf files enable you to combine scripts from different languages.

Using Type Libraries

The *<reference>* element in a .wsf file enables you to use constants defined in a type library in scripts. The following *<reference>* element retrieves a reference from the type library of the FileSystemObject object:

```
<reference guid='{420B2830-E718-11CF-893D-00A0C9054228}'/>
```

After defining such a reference, a script can use named constants exported from the type library. The following .wsf file sample shows the constants for drive types defined in the FileSystemObject object:

```
<?xml version="1.0" encoding="ISO-8859-1"?>

<job id="TypeLibExample">
    <reference guid='{420B2830-E718-11CF-893D-00A0C9054228}'/>
```

```
<script language="VBScript">
<![CDATA[
    WScript.Echo "CDRom = " & CDRom & vbCrLf & _
                 "Fixed = " & Fixed & vbCrLf & _
                 "RamDisk = " & RamDisk & vbCrLf & _
                 "Remote = " & Remote & vbCrLf & _
                 "Unknown = " & Unknown & vbCrLf & _
                 "Removable = " & Removable
]]>
</script>
</job>
```

I'll come back to the issue of using type libraries in Chapter 12, when we start dealing with drives, files, and folders. You can find a more in-depth discussion of the *<reference>* element, including techniques for finding the GUID value of type libraries, in *Advanced Development with Microsoft Windows Script Host 2.0* (Microsoft Press, forthcoming).

Debugging Features

You can use simple statements such as *stop* and *debugger* in your .vbs and .js script files (in WSH 1) to invoke the debugger (one that's already installed) automatically. To debug scripts in a WSH 2 environment, you must invoke your script using either the *//D* or the *//X* switch on the command line.

To debug a .wsf file by double-clicking it, use the *<?job debug="true"?>* processing instruction within your *<job>* elements. This instruction forces WSH to launch the script debugger if a *stop* or *debugger* instruction is found within a script. A *<?job debug="false"?>* statement within the *<job>* element disables the script debugger. The following code (sample file Test1.wsf) sets the *<?job ... ?>* processing instruction in a .wsf file:

```
<?xml version="1.0" encoding="ISO-8859-1"?>

<job id="T1">
    <?job debug="true"?>

    <script language="VBScript">
        stop
        WScript.Echo "Hello"
    </script>

    <script language="JScript">
        debugger
        WScript.Echo("Hello1");
    </script>
</job>
```

IF THE SCRIPT DEBUGGER WON'T WORK IN WSH 2

Some users have found that after they install WSH 2, the debugger won't work with .wsf files. This is a bug in WSH 2.0 and will be fixed in the next version. Fortunately, you can use a simple workaround to overcome this problem.

In the Registry, the following key contains the *DWORD* value *JITDebug*:

```
HKEY_CURRENT_USER\Software\Microsoft\Windows Script\Settings
```

If the value is set to 0, debugging is disabled. Set *JITDebug* to 1 to enable debugging. After you change the setting, debugging will work in WSH 2.

If you don't want to hack your Registry, use the sample file DebugOn.reg. Double-click on the file, and your Registry will be updated automatically.

Chapter 2

Development Tools
and Techniques

This chapter covers some tools and techniques that simplify script development. I'll introduce some script editors, explain how to install and uninstall ActiveX controls, and introduce some debugging tools.

CREATING SCRIPTS

You can prepare a script from scratch using Notepad, the editor in Microsoft Windows, simply by launching Notepad and entering statements using the syntax of the selected script language (as discussed in Chapter 1). Then you store the script program in a script file, as shown in Figure 2-1. For VBScript you use the extension .vbs, for JScript you use the extension .js, and for Microsoft Windows Script Host (WSH) 2 you use the extension .wsf. (For more information about .wsf files, refer to the section "The New .wsf File Format" in Chapter 1.)

> **TIP** In the Save As dialog box, select All Files in the Save As Type drop-down list to see all the script files in the selected folder.

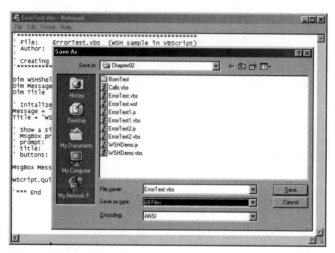

Figure 2-1 *Saving a script file in Notepad*

Using Script Templates

Building a script from scratch isn't the best approach, however. For example, if you use the header comments that I recommended in Chapter 1, you must add them explicitly each time you create a new script. Instead, you can use the template files VBScript.vbs and JScript.js to build script files and use the template file WSHfile.wsf for .wsf files. You simply configure Windows so that it recognizes script templates:

1. Open the folder \WSHDevGuide\Chapter01 on the companion CD, and copy the files VBScript.vbs, JScript.js, and WSHfile.wsf to a local folder on your hard drive.

2. In Control Panel, double-click the Tweak UI icon and then click the New tab in the Tweak UI dialog box.

3. Drag each template file from the folder window and drop it on the New tab to create a new entry for the template, as illustrated in Figure 2-2.

4. Click OK to close the Tweak UI dialog box. Tweak UI copies the files to the Windows folder \ShellNew (in Windows 98) or to the folder \Documents and Settings\<user name>\Templates (Windows 2000) and registers the new templates.

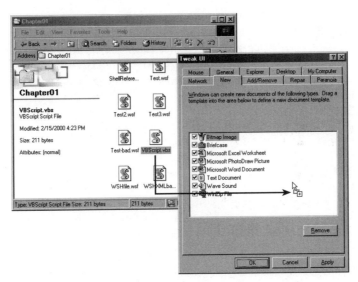

Figure 2-2 *Registering a script template using Tweak UI*

You'll find three new commands—JScript Script File, VBScript Script File, and Windows Script File—on the New shortcut menu, as shown in Figure 2-3. You can use these commands to create a new script file in any folder.

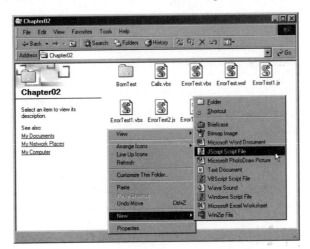

Figure 2-3 *Creating a new script file using the shortcut menu*

> **NOTE**   Tweak UI is a Windows tool for customizing the operating system, and you must install it explicitly. Windows 98 users can find this module on the Windows 98 CD in the \tools\reskit\powertoy folder. Windows 95, Windows NT 4, and Windows 2000 users can download a version of Tweak UI from several Internet sites. (Search *http://www.microsoft.com* for the most recent version.) To install the tool, browse the directory to find the folder with the Tweak UI installation files. Right-click on the file TweakUI.inf, and choose Install from the shortcut menu. After you install the tool, the Tweak UI icon will appear in the Control Panel folder.

EDITING SCRIPTS

You can use Notepad to create and edit script files. To load an existing script file into Notepad, right-click on the file and choose Edit from the shortcut menu. (The Edit command is added automatically when you install WSH.)

Unfortunately, Notepad provides only rudimentary features for editing text files. The real problem occurs during script debugging: WSH parses the source code, and if it finds a faulty statement or if a run-time error occurs, an error dialog box appears, indicating the error code and a line number, as shown in Figure 2-4.

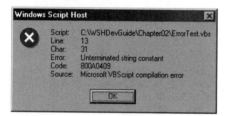

Figure 2-4 *An error dialog box that appears during script execution (in WSH 2)*

In this situation, you must edit the script file. Unfortunately, it can be difficult to locate the faulty statement using Notepad because you have to count the source code lines manually. This isn't feasible with lengthy scripts. You can use any of the script editors described a little later in this chapter, all of which support line numbering, to handle this chore for you.

> **NOTE**   Only the version of Notepad in Windows 2000 includes the Go To command, which allows you to jump to a specific line within a text file.

Invoking Script Editors

If you want to use your own script editor instead of the default (Notepad), you must launch it and load the script file. It's handy to have a custom command on the file's shortcut menu to invoke your script editor. Figure 2-5 shows the EditPlus custom shortcut command, which opens a .vbs or .js file in the EditPlus program.

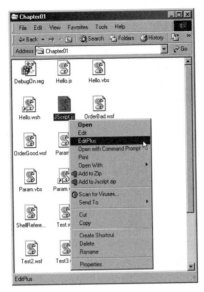

Figure 2-5 *Shortcut menu with a custom command that invokes a script editor*

To add a custom shortcut menu command, take the following steps:

1. Open a folder window. Choose Folder Options from the View menu (in Windows 95 or Windows 98) or from the Tools menu (in Windows 2000) to open the Folder Options dialog box.

2. On the File Types tab (shown in Figure 2-6), select your script file in the Registered File Types list, and then click Edit (in Windows 95, Windows 98, or Windows NT 4) or Advanced (in Windows 2000).

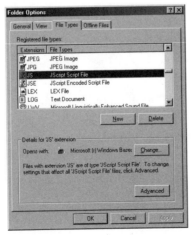

Figure 2-6 *The Folder Options dialog box*

3. In the Edit File Type dialog box that appears (Figure 2-7), click New to open the New Action dialog box (Figure 2-8).

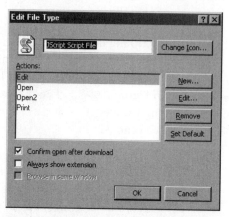

Figure 2-7 *The Edit File Type dialog box*

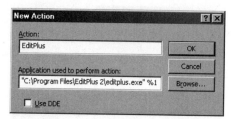

Figure 2-8 *The New Action dialog box*

4. Type the name of the new shortcut command in the Action text box, and type the command (the path and the EXE filename to invoke the application) in the Application Used To Perform Action text box. Characters such as *%1* are placeholders for the current file (which will be expanded during command execution). You can use the Browse button to select the program file in a folder window.

5. Close all the dialog boxes to register the new command.

   NOTE   Be sure to register file types (.vbs, .js, and perhaps .wsf) for scripts. For more information on registering file types and commands, see my book *Inside the Microsoft Windows 98 Registry* (Microsoft Press, 1998).

   Some of the available script editors are described next. A number of them are available free.

PrimalSCRIPT

PrimalSCRIPT is a powerful script editor for Windows developed by SAPIEN Technologies, Inc. If you're developing WSH scripts or scripts for different languages, PrimalSCRIPT might be your first choice. It provides a consistent user interface and development environment for several scripting languages. Version 1 was designed to support simple script editing. It allows you to insert code snippets (*For...To*, *If...Then...Else*, and so on) into the source code for all supported languages.

PrimalSCRIPT version 2, shown in Figure 2-9, is perfectly suited to WSH script development. It supports line numbering (to identify a line in an error dialog box), a type library viewer, and much more. You can edit .wsf files that contain several jobs or script elements. When you select a script element, the editor will show only the element's code—the element definition and attributes are treated as properties. PrimalSCRIPT 2 also handles well-formed Extensible Markup Language (XML) documents. Debugging is also simplified in PrimalSCRIPT 2. The program supports in-place debugging for WSH script files, so you can execute .js, .vbs, and .wsf files from the editor window or pass control to the script debugger.

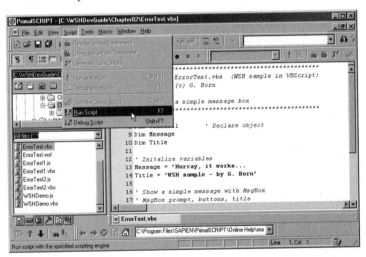

Figure 2-9 *PrimalSCRIPT 2*

NOTE To learn more about advanced XML topics such as well-formed documents, see my book *Advanced Development with Microsoft Windows Script Host 2.0*.

Because PrimalSCRIPT 2 supports type libraries, it can incorporate sophisticated editing features. For example, when you enter an object keyword, a ToolTip window shows you the definitions of the object's methods or properties (similar to Microsoft development environments such as Visual Basic for Applications [VBA]).

You can download a 30-day evaluation copy of PrimalSCRIPT 2 from *http:// www.sapien.com*. This site also contains a "Script Exchange" section from which you can get new sample scripts.

NOTE   PrimalSCRIPT is my favorite script editor, and not just because it's simple to use and has features for creating and debugging scripts. When you create .wsf files, PrimalSCRIPT splits the content of *<script>* elements into separate "units" and hides all XML definitions surrounding the pure code. When you save the file, PrimalSCRIPT automatically adds the XML structures.

Microsoft Script Editor

You can also use Microsoft Script Editor, which ships with Microsoft Office 2000, to edit script files. To install Script Editor, you need to use the Office 2000 installer. Just follow these steps:

1. From Control Panel, double-click Add/Remove Programs.

2. Click the Change Or Remove Programs button in the Add/Remove Programs dialog box.

3. Search for Microsoft Office, and then click the Change button. In the Microsoft Office 2000 Maintenance Mode dialog box, click Add Or Remove Feature.

4. Select Microsoft Office/Office Tools/HTML Source Editing/Web Scripting, and set the option to Run From My Computer.

5. Click the Update Now button.

Windows will install Script Editor from the Office CD.

After installing Script Editor, but before launching it, you need to enable script file support (for example, syntax color highlighting). To enable file support for script files (.vbs, .js, and .wsf), you need to update the Registry.

1. Launch Registry Editor (Regedit.exe), and search for the Registry key HKEY_LOCAL_MACHINE\Software\Microsoft\MSE\9.0\Editors\{C76D83F8-A489-11D0-8195-00A0C91BBEE3}\Extensions. This key contains the settings for the files already supported.

2. Add the DWORD value *vbs*, and set its value to 28 hexadecimal. (See Figure 2-10.)

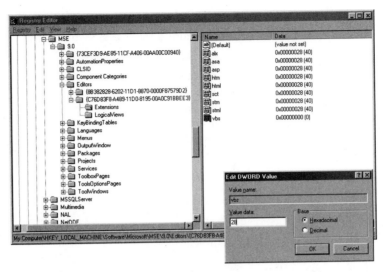

Figure 2-10 *Registry entries for Script Editor*

3. Repeat step 2, and add DWORD values for *js* and *wsh*.

    After closing Registry Editor, you can try to use Script Editor. There are two ways to launch Script Editor (also called the Microsoft Development Environment):

-   Launch it from an Office application. For example, launch Microsoft Word and from the Tools menu, select Macro and then Microsoft Script Editor.

-   Launch MSE.EXE directly or from a shortcut. The file MSE.EXE is located in the folder Program Files\Microsoft Visual Studio\Common\IDE\IDE98. (Keep in mind that the folder names can vary depending on which localized version of Windows is running.)

After launching Script Editor, you're ready to load and edit script files.

You can use the Define Window Layout command on the View menu to choose one of the predefined editor layouts. Figure 2-11 shows the Design mode with the Project Explorer window in the left pane and the code windows in the right pane.

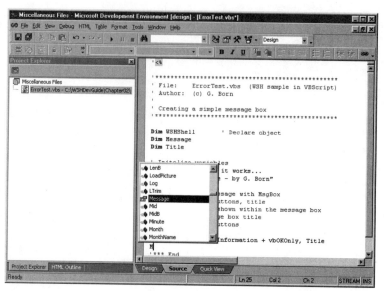

Figure 2-11 *Script Editor with script code*

To load and view a script file, simply drag it to the Project Explorer window (or use the Open File command on the File menu). The names of files already loaded are listed in the Project Explorer window (Figure 2-11, left pane).

You can reload a file by double-clicking its entry in the Project Explorer. To use Script Editor effectively for script development, you need to know a few tricks:

- You need to select the Source tab in the code window to show the document in Source View. If your code window is still empty after loading a .wsf file, or if the editor concatenates several lines of code after loading a .js or .vbs file, Design View is still selected.

- The content of a .wsf file will be shown with color coding for script elements. To apply color coding to a .js file, just insert a line //<% in the header. In a .vbs file, you need to insert the line '<% into the header (as in Figure 2-11). Both lines are comments, but Script Editor recognizes that you intend to use color coding. (If you add the '<% and //<% lines to your .vbs and .js templates, color coding and syntax highlighting will be enabled automatically for new script files.) After color coding is switched on, you can use the language features Script Editor provides. After you type the first characters of a keyword (such as Msg), just press Ctrl+Space. The editor uses the auto complete function to insert the keyword (such as MsgBox). If more than one keyword begins with the characters you've typed, a QuickInfo list with additional hints is also shown. (See Figure 2-11.)

■ To save a new file, click the Save button in the toolbar. In the Save As dialog box, select the file type HTML Files but enter the filename including the extension (.vbs, .js, or .wsf). If the filename includes an extension other than htm or html, the editor saves the code window without adding an HTML tag structure.

You can identify the line number you're on by clicking on the line. The line number is shown in the status bar. To create a new file, you can use the New File command on the File menu or press Ctrl+Shift+N to invoke the New File dialog box. (This dialog box also allows you to load existing and recent files.) In Chapter 1, I mentioned that you can create your own template files for .js, .vbs, and .wsf files. Just copy these template files into the Program Files\Microsoft Visual Studio\ Common\IDE\IDE98\NewFileItems folder. Then, on the New tab of the New File dialog box, you can select one of those templates to create a new VBScript, JScript, or Windows Script file.

Other editors

EditPlus is a 32-bit text editor for Windows 95, Windows 98, Windows NT 4, and Windows 2000 that is distributed as shareware. EditPlus is simple to use and provides a syntax-highlighting feature for HTML, C/C++, Perl, and Java that you extend to support other languages. The best feature of EditPlus is a toolbar button that enables line numbering in the loaded text file. You can download a 30-day evaluation copy of EditPlus from *http://www.editplus.com*.

EditPad is a small replacement for Notepad that you can use to edit text files in different formats. EditPad doesn't support line numbering, but it has a Go To Line command that allows you to enter the line number and can be a useful addition to Windows 95, Windows 98, and Windows NT 4. (The Windows 2000 version of Notepad already has a Go To command, so EditPad doesn't offer any advantages to Windows 2000 users.) You can download EditPad at no charge from *http://www.jgsoft.com*.

UltraEdit-32 is a powerful editor for Windows 95, Windows 98, Windows NT, and Windows 2000 that is available as shareware. The program supports the editing of text files with different filename extensions (.bat, .ini, .html, and more) and offers several features for script editing, such as color highlighting of keywords. In the code window, you can activate line numbering. You can download a 45-day evaluation copy of UltraEdit-32 from *http://www.ultraedit.com*. The site provides links for downloading several versions of UltraEdit.

Other editors that you can use for script editing (but which I haven't tried) include CodeMagic, TextPad, and NoteTab. CodeMagic is a scripting integrated development environment (IDE) that is free (in its first version) and fairly customizable. You can download it from *http://www.petes-place.com/codemagic.html*. TextPad and

NoteTab are shareware editors. NoteTab also comes in a Light version that's freeware. Neither editor supports text color highlighting. You can download TextPad from *http://www.textpad.com* and NoteTab from *http://www.notetab.com*.

> **TIP**   You can use the Print shortcut command to print the source code of your script files. If you use one of the script editors described in this chapter, you can also print the source code with line numbers, which can be helpful during the debugging process.

INSTALLING AND UNINSTALLING ACTIVEX CONTROLS

In addition to using objects provided by applications such as Microsoft Word and Microsoft Excel and objects that are exposed by WSH itself or by Windows, you can use many objects provided by ActiveX controls. In some cases, these controls come with a setup program that allows you to install and uninstall the components.

If you develop an ActiveX control using a development environment such as Visual Basic or Visual Basic 5 Control Creation Edition (CCE), the component is registered automatically on the development machine and the control is stored in an OCX file.

Registering a Control

Before you can use an ActiveX control (OCX file) in a script, you must register the control. If the developer of the OCX file didn't provide an installation program that registers the object, you must use the program RegSvr32.exe, which ships with several Microsoft applications and operating systems (including Windows 98 and Windows 2000). To register an OCX file as an ActiveX control, you invoke the RegSvr32.exe program by using a command such as the following:

```
RegSvr32.exe C:\TestControl.ocx
```

The program locates the file, analyzes its content, and adds all requested information to the Registry. You can then use the ActiveX control in a WSH script.

In Windows 98 and Windows 2000, you'll find RegSvr32.exe in the System or System32 folder. When you invoke this program without specifying an object's file, a dialog box with all the program's options appears, as shown in Figure 2-12.

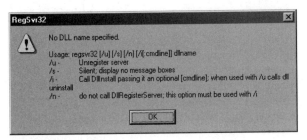

Figure 2-12 *Options for RegSvr32.exe*

TIP You can double-click on the sample file \WSHDevGuide\Chapter02\ OCXReg.reg to add two commands, Register OCX and Unregister OCX, to the shortcut menu of your OCX files. These commands register and unregister, respectively, the ActiveX control in the OCX file.

LICENSING ACTIVEX CONTROLS

While developing the samples for this book, I ran into a major problem—the licensing of ActiveX controls. When I installed several OCX files from Web sites, I couldn't use the objects in these ActiveX controls. Even though the controls were registered correctly, whenever I tried to execute the *CreateObject* method, I received the run-time error *Win32-Error 0x80040112*. This error isn't well documented in WSH 1, so it took me a while to figure out that it indicates a missing license for the control. If you receive a similar error, you need to license the control from your vendor. I go into more detail about licensing issues in my book *Advanced Development with Microsoft Windows Script Host 2.0*.

Uninstalling a Control

After installing ActiveX controls using RegSvr32.exe or after using a development environment such as Visual Basic or Visual Basic 5 CCE to create your own controls, your system (and your Registry) can become cluttered with installed ActiveX components. So how do you remove unneeded ActiveX controls? It's not sufficient just to delete the OCX file. You must uninstall the entire component, which means removing the Registry entries. To remove all the component's Registry entries, you should invoke RegSvr32.exe as follows:

```
RegSvr32.exe /u C:TestControl.ocx
```

The program locates the OCX file, and the */u* switch forces the program to remove all entries for this ActiveX component from the Registry. You can then safely delete the OCX file without the risk that unused entries will remain in your system.

> **TIP** If you imported the OCXReg.reg file, as described in the preceding Tip, you can right-click on the OCX file and use the shortcut command Unregister OCX to unregister the OCX file.

You can find more detailed information about installing and uninstalling ActiveX controls in my book *Advanced Development with Microsoft Windows Script Host 2.0.*

DEBUGGING SCRIPTS

A syntax error or a run-time error causes WSH to terminate script execution with the error message shown in Figure 2-13. The message includes the path and the filename of the script as well as the error category and an error description. It usually also shows the line number and the column in which the error occurred.

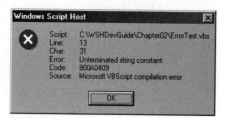

Figure 2-13 *The error message that terminates a script's execution in WSH 2*

You can also use one of the editors mentioned earlier in the chapter to identify the line that caused the error. After amending the source code, you can run the next test. If the script doesn't contain any more syntax errors, you can begin debugging.

> **NOTE** For testing purposes, you can use the file ErrorTest.vbs in the \WSHDevGuide\Chapter02 folder. The VBScript program contains a syntax error that brings up the error message shown in Figure 2-13. To execute the script correctly, you must edit the source code so that the string constant in line 13 is closed with a double quote (").

Tracing Your Programs

After removing all syntax errors from a WSH script, you can start functional tests. In most cases—except in trivial script programs—the script probably won't deliver the expected result. Sometimes it's helpful to place statements in the source code to display a message box with interim results. Each time such a statement is executed, a message box is displayed. In the message box, you can show script interim values and messages. This approach is shown in Listing 2-1.

```vbscript
'*************************************************
' File:   WSHDemo.vbs (WSH sample in VBScript)
' Author: (c) G. Born
'
' Showing interim results in a message box
'*************************************************
' The following lines deactivate and activate
' the trace messages. You must uncomment the
' appropriate line.

' DebugFlag = False    ' Trace output off
DebugFlag = True       ' Trace output on

j = 0
debug "Start:", 0, 0

For i = 1 To 10    ' Loop 10 times.
    debug "Step:", i, j
    j = j + i       ' Add all numbers.
Next

debug "End:", i, j

WScript.Echo "Result:", j

Sub debug(text, count, val)
    If DebugFlag Then    ' Debug mode active?
        WScript.Echo text, count, " Interim result:", val
    End If
End Sub

'*** End
```

Listing 2-1 *WSHDemo.vbs*

The program in Listing 2-1 is very simple. It uses a loop to calculate the sum of the numbers from 1 to 10, and it displays the results using the *Echo* method. For testing purposes, however, it's helpful to know when the program enters the loop and how many steps are executed within the loop. To trace these steps, you can call the *Echo* method within the loop or at an appropriate place. To keep the code as simple as possible, all trace messages are evaluated in their own procedure with the name *debug*. Thus, the program needs only the following statement to show the values used in the loop:

```
debug "Step:", i, j
```

The first parameter defines the text shown in the message box. The other parameters can contain numbers, which are also shown in the message box. In Listing 2-1, the *debug* procedure is called in several places. Within the loop, the *debug* call shows the index value and the calculated interim value, as shown in Figure 2-14.

Figure 2-14 *A message box with trace values*

When you test the program, the trace values should appear as shown in Figure 2-14. Once the script runs flawlessly, these trace messages are no longer needed, so you can remove them from the source code. But if you change something later in the program, you'll need the trace statements again. Removing and replacing trace statements is unnecessary in the WSHDemo.vbs, however, because you can control the trace output using an option in the *debug* procedure. This procedure contains the following condition:

```
If DebugFlag Then    ' Debug mode active?
```

Only if the value of the global variable *DebugFlag* is set to *True* is the *Echo* method called and the message box displayed. The variable *DebugFlag* is set in the script's header to the value *True*, as shown here:

```
' DebugFlag = False    ' Trace output off
DebugFlag = True        ' Trace output on
```

At any given time, one of the statements is active and the other is commented out, so you can toggle the value of *DebugFlag* between *True* and *False* by moving the comment sign from one line to the other. The trace output is shown or suppressed based on the value of *DebugFlag*.

> **NOTE** The script file WSHDemo.vbs (along with WSHDemo.js) is in the \WSHDevGuide\Chapter02 folder.

Using the Microsoft Script Debugger

You can use the technique shown in the preceding section only for simple scripts. If a script causes run-time errors or unexpected results, you must use a debugger to trace the program and its values. The Microsoft Script Debugger, which you can download free from *http://msdn.microsoft.com/scripting*, tests scripts in HTML documents or Active Server Pages (ASP) files. You can also use the debugger to test WSH scripts.

> **NOTE** When you download the Microsoft Script Debugger, it is installed in the \Program Files\Microsoft Script Debugger folder. The debugger comes in different versions for Windows 95, Windows 98, and Windows NT. Windows 2000 already includes the Microsoft Script Debugger. It's also possible to use the debugger that comes with Microsoft Script Editor, which ships with Microsoft Office 2000.

So how do you execute a script under the control of the debugger? WSH supports commands to launch the script debugger and execute the script under the control of the debugger. However, you need to know about some differences between WSH 1 and WSH 2, and you also can use a special command to debug .wsf files.

In WSH 1, you can insert the *Stop* statement in VBScript and the *debugger* statement in JScript; these statements invoke the debugger automatically when executed.

If you insert the *Stop* statement in VBScript files and the *debugger* statement in JScript files, as you do in WSH 1, nothing happens with the debugger in WSH 2.

To use the debugger in WSH 2, you must invoke the script using the *//D* switch. The following command forces WSH to enable script debugging:

```
WScript.exe //D C:\WSHDevGuide\Chapter02\ErrorTest2.vbs
```

After executing the first *Stop* statement (in VBScript) or *debugger* statement (in JScript), the debugger is launched and control is passed to the program, as shown in Figure 2-15. Then you can execute the script step by step in the debugger. (See also the section "Debugging Features" in Chapter 1.)

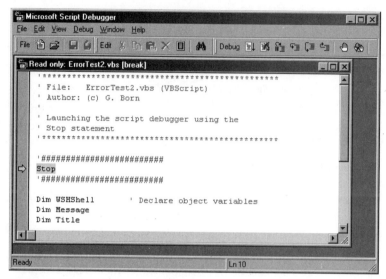

Figure 2-15 *Enabling script debugging statements*

If you don't want to insert *Stop* and *debugger* statements in your script code, you can use the *//X* flag to invoke the debugger, as shown here:

```
WScript.exe //X C:\WSHDevGuide\Chapter02\WSHDemo.vbs
```

WSH 2 launches the debugger and passes control to this program. The debugger stops script execution when it encounters the first executable command (as shown in Figure 2-16).

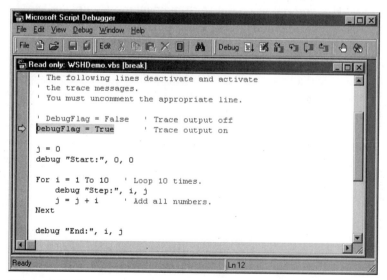

Figure 2-16 *Executing scripts under debugger control*

NOTE The sample files ErrorTest1.vbs and ErrorTest1.js in the \WSHDevGuide\Chapter02 folder contain a statement that shows a message box. The sample files ErrorTest2.js and ErrorTest2.vbs in the same folder contain the *Stop* and *debugger* statements.

Debugging .wsf files

One way to debug .wsf files is to add a *<?job ...?>* processing instruction with the *debug* attribute set to *true* (as mentioned in Chapter 1). Listing 2-2 contains such an instruction.

```
<?xml version="1.0"?>
<!--
    File:   ErrorTest.wsf (for WSH 2.0)
    Author: (c) G. Born
-->

<job id="T1">
    <?job debug="true"?>
    <script language="VBScript">
    <![CDATA[
        Stop
        WScript.Echo "Hello, VBScript"
    ]]>
    </script>

    <script language="JScript">
    <![CDATA[
        debugger
        WScript.Echo ("Hello, JScript");
    ]]>
    </script>
</job>
```

Listing 2-2 *ErrorTest.wsf*

This file can be executed with or without the *//X* or *//D* option; a double-click on the .wsf file invokes the debugger automatically if a *Stop* or *debugger* statement is executed. The following processing instruction in the .wsf file disables debugging in WSH 2. (It is independent of the *//X* or *//D* setting in the script's command line.)

```
<?job debug="false"?>
```

This statement comes in handy if you want to suppress debugging in .wsf files that contain *Stop* or *debugger* commands.

Once the Microsoft Script Debugger takes control of script execution, the source code appears in the debugger window (as shown earlier in Figure 2-15). You can step through the source code, but you can't edit it in the debugger window. To edit the source code, you must load it into a separate window.

Microsoft Script Debugger commands

The Microsoft Script Debugger contains several toolbars and menu commands for testing the script, as shown in Figure 2-17 and described in the following list. (Some commands can also be invoked using keystrokes.)

- **Run**   Executes the script statements until a breakpoint is encountered or until the script terminates.

- **Stop Debugging**   Aborts script execution and terminates debugging.

- **Break At Next Statement**   Ensures that the script isn't executed straight through to the end. You need this command if you invoke the debugger and take control of script execution manually using the Running Documents window. If the script is paused at a message box, the Break At Next Statement command stops script execution at the next statement when the user closes the message box.

- **Step Into (F8)**   Executes the next script statement.

- **Step Over (Shift+F8)**   Causes the debugger to execute an entire procedure or function until program control returns to the calling module. If the current statement isn't a call to a procedure or a function, the debugger uses Step Into mode.

- **Step Out (Ctrl+Shift+F8)**   Executes all statements in a procedure or a function until the command that transfers the control to the caller is reached.

- **Toggle Breakpoint (F9)**   Selects an executable statement in the debugger window and sets or clears a breakpoint on that line. Lines with breakpoints are marked with a dot on the left border of the debugger window. If a breakpoint is reached during script execution, the debugger stops.

- **Clear All Breakpoints**   Clears all breakpoints set in the script.

The Command Window button opens a window in which you can enter and execute program statements directly. The Call Stack button opens a window that shows the names of all active procedures on the stack. The stack is empty if your script uses only a linear program structure (one without calling procedures or functions).

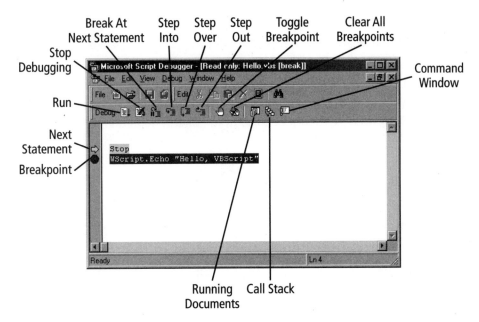

Figure 2-17 *Toolbar buttons in the debugger window*

Executing a script step by step

During debugging, Step Into (single-step) mode can be helpful. You click the Step Into button or press F8 to execute the next statement in a script. The next executable statement is marked on the left border of the debugger window with an arrow (as shown in Figure 2-17).

Using Step Over and Step Out modes

If your script contains already tested procedures and functions, single-step mode doesn't makes sense for executing the statements in these procedures or functions. Instead, you can use the Step Over button or press Shift+F8. If the next executable statement contains a procedure or function call, the entire procedure or function is executed without any disruption. Execution stops after control returns to the caller. If you use this command to execute other statements that don't call a procedure or function, it works like Step Into mode.

If the debugger hits a breakpoint within a procedure or a function, you can use the Step Out button or press Ctrl+Shift+F8 to finish executing all the statements in the procedure or function. The debugger then breaks at the first statement following the call to the procedure or function.

Using breakpoints

To interrupt script execution on a certain statement, you can use breakpoints. Select the statement in the debugger window and then set the breakpoint by using the Toggle

Breakpoint button or by pressing F9. If you resume program execution, the debugger stops execution if the line with the breakpoint is reached.

Showing the call stack

You can use the Call Stack command on the View menu or the Call Stack button on the toolbar to open the Call Stack window (shown in Figure 2-18), which lists all active procedures and functions. In the figure, the *Message* procedure from Calls.vbs is being executed.

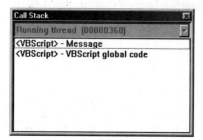

Figure 2-18 *The Call Stack window*

Showing interim values using the Command window

If a program is interrupted, you can inspect the current value of a variable (or a property) in the Command window. In VBScript, you type a question mark followed by a variable name (for example, *? color*) to show the associated value (as shown in Figure 2-19).

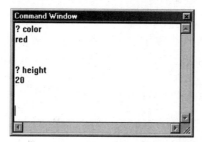

Figure 2-19 *Showing variable values in the Command window*

In JScript, you must use a statement such as *WScript.Echo(color)*; to show a variable value using the Command window. The debugger executes the statement and displays a message box with the value of the variable *color*.

To set the value of a variable, you enter the statement to associate a value with a variable into the command window, as shown here:

```
Message = "Hello, world"
```

The preceding techniques allow you to easily debug a WSH script written in VBScript or in JScript.

Chapter 3

Introduction to Programming with Objects

This chapter briefly introduces the basic concepts of programming with objects (also referred to as component-based programming), including collections, methods, and properties. You'll need to know this information for script programming.

OBJECTS

In the real world, a car, a house, a book, and a table are examples of objects. Each of these objects has properties that describe it. For example, a car has a color, a height, a weight, and so on. Another aspect of real-world objects is that you can perform actions with them: you can drive a car, clean a house, read a book, and so forth.

In the world of software development, programs can also take an object-oriented approach by defining software entities that have properties and perform actions. For example, a business application might define a customer software object that represents an individual customer. The customer object would contain data that corresponds to real-world customer properties, such as name, address, credit card number, and so on. The customer object would also define actions that are specific to it, such as placing an order or adding itself to the customer database. One advantage of using an object-oriented approach to software development, then, is that it allows developers to write code that closely models real-world problems.

A Simple Object

Let's look at a simple object, a message dialog box (Figure 3-1). A dialog box can be considered an object because it owns data (which it displays) and performs an action (shows information). The object also has several properties that can be manipulated. It has a position and a size, for example. It also has title text, text within the box itself, a background color, and so on.

Figure 3-1 *A dialog box, which is an object*

The number of properties depends on the object. Also, properties can be visible (exposed to the programmer) or invisible. Many properties of an object are exposed and can be read or set from a script.

The Object Model

An object can contain other objects. For example, the dialog box shown in Figure 3-1 contains two buttons (OK and Cancel) and a question mark icon. These items are subobjects of the dialog box object.

Now let's look at an entire application—Microsoft Word—to understand how it can also be an object, according to the definition of an object as an entity that owns data and performs an action. Word is an object because it has data (documents, words, numbers, formulas, and so forth) and because actions can be performed on the data (opening and closing documents, inserting and deleting text, and so forth).

You can use a hierarchical approach to define a structure for the objects in an entire application, as shown in Figure 3-2. If you intend to use the first word in the first chapter of a document, you can clearly define its position. The *Word* object is a subobject of the *Sentence* object, which is a subobject of the *Paragraph* object, which is a subobject of the *Document* object, which is loaded in the *Application* object.

You can refer to this hierarchy in code like this:

```
Application.Document.Paragraph.Sentence.Word
```

In this chain of subobjects, the object names are separated with dots. The leftmost object is the *Application* object, which is a parent of the *Document* object, and so on. If you know the object hierarchy, you can access any object by defining its exact position within the object hierarchy, which is known as the *object model*.

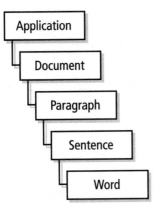

Figure 3-2 *An object model*

Collections

The chain of subobjects shown in the preceding line of code is misleading, however. An application such as Word can load more than one document at a time, and a document typically consists of more than one paragraph. A paragraph generally has more than one sentence, and a sentence contains more than one word.

To be more precise, we can say that a *Document* object consists of a collection of *Paragraph* objects, a *Paragraph* object can consist of a collection of *Sentence* objects, and so on. Figure 3-3 shows an object model with collections.

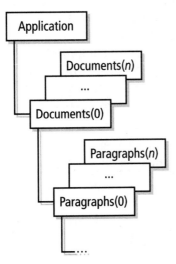

Figure 3-3 *An object model with collections*

A *collection* includes more than one subobject of the same type. To access a word in a document, you first have to identify a paragraph in the *Paragraphs* collection, a sentence in the *Sentences* collection, and so forth.

If we assume that objects in a collection are counted from 0, we can identify the first word in a document (which is the first word in the first sentence in the first paragraph) as follows:

```
Application.Documents(0).Paragraphs(0).Sentences(0).Words(0)
```

Notice that the object names are plural. The *Documents* object is a collection of *Document* objects. You use *Documents(0)* to indicate that you want the first member (the first *Document* object) of the *Documents* collection. The first *Document* object might consist of several paragraphs, so you use a *Paragraphs* object, which is a collection of all *Paragraph* objects in the document. You use *Paragraphs(0)* to indicate that you need the first *Paragraph* object in the *Paragraphs* collection.

> **TIP** In some Microsoft object models (such as Microsoft Word), object names ending with *s* identify collections and object names without an *s* ending identify simple objects. You access objects from a root object, which in most cases is the *Application* object.

Methods

Earlier in the chapter, I introduced a dialog box object. A *form* is a similar object, and it has properties, such as its *x,y* position. In principle, you can manipulate an object by using its properties. If you change the *x,y* property, the form window is moved on the desktop. However, you have to know that changing the *x,y* property of the object changes its position. A much better way to execute a specific operation on an object is to use a method, which frees you from having to know how the object implements its actions.

For example, you use the *Move* method to move the form's window to a new position. You can use the *Show* method to create the form window and set the caption, the background color, the position, and the size. Other methods are available for changing an object or its behavior in many other ways. Whether a certain method is supported depends on the object.

> **NOTE** A *method* is simply a function or a procedure call that is associated with a specific object. Also, *properties* are just variables that belong to the object.

The advantage of using objects is that you don't need to know how they work internally. All you need to know is an object's name and which properties and methods the object exposes. For example, to show a form containing two buttons, an icon, title text, and text within the box itself, you can simply use a (predefined) form object and set the properties for the title text, the inside text, the buttons, and the icon; the object handles the myriad other details needed to create and display the form.

A Practical Example

Let's turn now to Microsoft Windows Script Host (WSH). WSH itself offers a few objects. When a script is executed, WSH exposes the *WScript* object by default. This object represents the running script, and it supports a number of methods and properties. For example, the *WScript* object provides the *Echo* method for displaying dialog boxes within a script. In VBScript, you can write a statement like this to show a simple dialog box:

```
WScript.Echo "Hello, world"
```

This statement uses the object name *WScript*, a dot, and the *Echo* method. The parameter *"Hello, world"* contains the message for the dialog box. (In Chapter 6, I'll cover other ways of displaying dialog boxes from scripts.)

> **NOTE** The *Echo* method in the preceding line of code is really nothing more than a simple procedure call in VBScript. (It differs from a conventional procedure call only in that it includes an object name.) Therefore, the syntax of the method call is the same as that for a procedure call.

AVAILABLE OBJECTS

When you write scripts, you can use any of the Component Object Model (COM) objects installed on the target machine. This is a huge collection of objects exposed from WSH, Microsoft Windows, Microsoft Office, Microsoft ActiveX controls, and so on. These objects must be registered on the local system. WSH uses the programmatic identifier (ProgID) of an object in the script to create the object reference.

If you need additional objects, you can create them yourself. The easiest approach is to use Microsoft Windows Script Components (WSC). Or you can use Microsoft Visual Basic 5 Control Creation Edition (CCE), for example, to create your own ActiveX objects to extend WSH. A discussion of this technique is beyond the scope of this book, but you'll find that I cover WSC and the Visual Basic CCE in *Advanced Development with Microsoft Windows Script Host 2.0.* You can also use C++, Active Template Library (ATL), Visual Basic, and other languages and tools.

Getting Information About Objects, Methods, and Properties

One problem with using objects in WSH scripts is that some programmers don't supply documentation with their objects. To get information about the COM objects or ActiveX controls registered on your system, you can use the Microsoft OLE/COM Object Viewer. In addition, the Object Browser supplied with Microsoft's development environments shows the methods and properties exposed by objects. You can find out more about the OLE/COM Object Viewer and the Object Browser in *Advanced Development with Microsoft Windows Script Host 2.0.*

> **NOTE**   In later chapters, I'll go into more detail about several objects and show samples that use objects and their properties.

Chapter 4

Introduction to VBScript

This chapter offers a brief introduction to Microsoft Visual Basic, Scripting Edition (VBScript) for those of you who have never used the language or who would like information on special language constructs (such as *If* statements) in VBScript.

> **TIP** Microsoft offers the VBScript Language Reference and the VBScript Tutorial, which provide detailed information about VBScript. This book's companion CD includes the VBScript Language Reference and VBScript Tutorial in the \Docs\VBScript folder, but I recommend that you download the latest documentation from Microsoft's Web site (*http://msdn.microsoft.com/scripting*).

BASIC FEATURES

In the sections that follow, I'll introduce the basic features of VBScript. Later in the chapter, I'll introduce more advanced features (including some of those provided in the new version 5 scripting engines).

Statements, Continued Lines, and Comments

VBScript is a subset of Microsoft Visual Basic for Applications (VBA), the language provided with Microsoft Office and Visual Basic. Microsoft used several language constructs from VBA to define the VBScript syntax. If you've programmed in Visual Basic or Office, VBScript programming shouldn't be difficult for you.

Statements

You must enter statements using the syntax rules defined for VBScript. The following lines contain valid VBScript statements:

```
Value1 = 10
Value1 = Value1 + 10
If Value1 > 100 Then Value1 = 100
Tax = 0.1 : Price = Net * Tax
```

You can enter several statements on one line if you separate them with a colon (:), as in the last line of the preceding code. However, you should use this syntax sparingly to keep your programs more readable.

NOTE VBScript statements and keywords are not case sensitive, as they are in JScript.

Continued lines

Very long statements make your scripts less readable. The following statement, which shows a message box, is longer than the current page width:

```
WScript.Echo "You have entered a wrong name in the text box on the
previous form. Please reenter the value in the text box."
```

If a program contains many long lines, you waste time scrolling horizontally to edit the lines. A better approach is to append a blank and an underscore (_) at the end of a line and continue the statement on the next line, as shown here:

```
WScript.Echo "You have entered a wrong name in the text box " & _
    "on the previous form. Please reenter the value in the " & _
    "text box."
```

When the language engine detects a line that ends with an underscore, it assumes a continued line and treats the next line as part of the current statement.

NOTE The last line of a continued statement can't have an appended underscore. Also, you can't append comments to a line that contains an underscore. If you want to use a long string in continued lines, split the string into several substrings and terminate each substring with a double quote ("). Then you can insert an underscore to divide the statement into several lines. You can concatenate (join together) the substrings using the & operator or the + operator. I used this structure in the preceding statement.

Comments

As I mentioned in Chapter 1, if you want to tell VBScript not to interpret a line or a part of a statement, you can simply write the statement as a comment. In VBScript, you use a single quote (') or the *REM* statement to mark a comment. If the VBScript interpreter detects this character in a statement, it ignores the rest of the line. Both of the following lines contain comments:

```
' This is a whole line containing a comment.
Value1 = Net * Factor          ' Comment at line end
```

The second line has a comment after the statement. VBScript executes the statement and ignores the trailing comment.

VBScript program structure

A VBScript program can consist of comments and statements. The script files used in this book follow the structure of Listing 4-1. (This file and the other samples used in this chapter are in the \WSHDevGuide\Chapter04 folder on the companion CD.)

```
'************************************************
' File:   WSHDemo.vbs (WSH sample in VBScript)
' Author: (c) G. Born
'
' Using WSH to show a simple dialog box
'************************************************
Option Explicit

Dim Message

' Initialize variable.
Message = "Hurray, it works!"

WScript.Echo Message

'*** End
```

Listing 4-1 *WSHDemo.vbs*

As I mentioned in the previous chapters, it's good practice to add comments to your scripts. If you receive a script from another programmer, you'll definitely be grateful if the author noted the purpose of the script and other information in the program's header.

> **NOTE** You can also use VBScript programs within HTML documents and execute them in Microsoft Internet Explorer. Although Internet Explorer and Microsoft Windows Script Host (WSH) use the same language engine, they don't expose the same objects (or more precisely, the same object model). For example, the event handling provided with Internet Explorer is useless in the WSH environment. Therefore, it's helpful to have information in the header about the language, its version, and the environment the script is designed for.

Constants and Variables

In VBScript, you can use constants and variables to store values. The following sections discuss how to define constants and variables.

Constants

You'll definitely use constants in your scripts. You can use them directly in VBScript statements. The following code defines a constant:

```
result = price + 100.0
```

The formula takes the value of the variable *price*, adds 100.0, and assigns the result to a variable, *result*. The value 100.0 is a constant. This technique is common, and it's easy to read. However, it has a big disadvantage. Let's say that your script contains several hundred lines, and the value 100.0 appears on many lines. What happens if you have to change 100.0 to 110.0? You have to edit every line in the source code that contains the constant. You can use the editor's search-and-replace function, but this can be time consuming and can lead to errors because the value 100.0 might be used for different purposes.

To avoid this problem, you can set a constant or an identifier in the VBScript program header. This constant is a meaningful name that takes the place of a number or a string and never changes. You must declare a constant explicitly. In the following line of code, the keyword *Const* invokes the constant declaration. It is followed by the constant's name and its value:

```
Const profit = 100.0
```

You can use a named constant in any other statement in the VBScript program, as in this example:

```
Price = NetPrice * Amount + profit
```

The advantage of named constants is that you can change the value of a constant within the declaration instead of changing the value on lines spread throughout the source code. You can also assign a meaningful name to a value, which simplifies code maintenance.

> **NOTE**   At first glance, it might seem that you can use a named constant like you use a variable. But the constant's value is protected from being changed by executing code. Therefore, you can use its name only on the right side of an assignment statement.

You can also define several constants on a single line:

```
Const VAT = 0.16, Profit = 10
```

Unlike Visual Basic and VBA, VBScript supports only the *Variant* data type. Named constants are declared as public by default. This means that a constant declared in the script's header is available within the entire script. If you declare a constant within a procedure, the scope is valid only within the procedure. You can overwrite this default scope using the *Public* and *Private* keywords (as described later in this chapter).

> **TIP** Numeric constants are usually written in base 10 (decimal). However, you can also use constants in the hexadecimal system using the format *&Hxxxx*, where *xxxx* stands for a hexadecimal number. For example, the value *&H0C* corresponds to the decimal number 12. Literal constants containing text must be enclosed in double quotes (as in "Hello, world"). Time and date constants must be enclosed in number signs (as in #6/1/2000#).

Intrinsic constants

VBScript contains several predefined constants (also known as built-in or intrinsic constants) such as *vbOKOnly*. Take a look at this statement:

```
MsgBox "Hello", 0 + 64, "Test"
```

If you use named constants, the statement is much less cryptic:

```
MsgBox "Hello", vbOKOnly + vbInformation, "Test"
```

The only catch is that you must know the exact name of the intrinsic constant.

> **NOTE** All intrinsic constants are listed in the VBScript Language Reference.

Variables

Variables are placeholders that refer to a location in memory where a program can store values. Unlike constants, variables can change their value during program operation. You can use a variable directly in a program, as shown here:

```
Price = 45        ' Set the price.
Discount = 17
```

The first time a variable appears in the program, VBScript creates the variable in memory and assigns an initial value. VBScript supports only the Variant data type for a variable. This means that you can store different values, such as numbers and text, in a variable.

Variant subtypes

As I just mentioned, VBScript supports only the *Variant* data type, a special data type that can contain different kinds of information—strings, date values, logical values (*True* or *False*), integers, floating-point numbers, and so on. The format of a value stored in a *Variant* depends on the value. If you assign a number to a variable, it is stored in numeric format. A date value is stored in date format, text is stored in string format, and so on. The format of a value stored in a *Variant* is called its *subtype*.

Most operators in VBScript require values of a specific subtype and return a value of a specific subtype. For example, if you add the content of two variables that have numeric values, the result is also numeric. The following statement stores a numeric result in the variable *Sum1*:

```
Sum1 = Price + 15.0
```

Using the + operator, you can also concatenate two strings:

```
Message = "Thing1 and " + "Thing2"
```

But the following statement causes a problem:

```
Result = "Value " + Sum1
```

The first part of the expression on the right side of the assignment is a string, and the variable *Sum1* contains a numeric value. The VBScript interpreter can't add a string and a number, so it generates an error message (as shown in Figure 4-1).

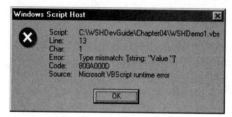

Figure 4-1 *An error message resulting from a type mismatch*

In this situation, you can convert the numeric subtype by using the following statement:

```
Result = "Value " + CStr(Sum1)
```

The VBScript function *CStr* converts the numeric value in the variable *Sum1* to a *Variant* data type with the string format. This result can be concatenated with the second string, *"Value "*, and the result can be assigned to the variable *Result*.

> **NOTE** Concatenating strings using the + operator isn't good programming practice (although I sometimes use it). The + operator adds two operands—when the operands are strings, the result is a concatenation operation. A better approach is to use the & operator for string concatenation (as in "Hello, " & "world"). When using the & operator to combine values that have different data formats, VBScript does the type conversion automatically, without using *CStr*.

You can also treat numbers as strings if they're defined as constants. You must enclose the constants in quotation marks. Look at the following statement:

```
Text = "15" + "30"
```

This statement doesn't produce the value 45. Instead, the variable *Text* contains the value "1530" after the statement is executed! According to my explanation given on the preceding page, it is much more readable if you write the statement as

```
Text = "15" & "30"
```

This statement makes it clear what you intend (a string concatenation). You can use conversion functions to convert data from one subtype to another *Variant* subtype.

> **NOTE** Unlike Visual Basic or VBA, VBScript doesn't allow you to predefine a subtype for a variable. VBScript assigns the subtypes automatically. But you can use conversion functions such as *Asc, CBool, CByte, CCur, CDate, CDbl, Chr, CInt, CLng, CSng, CStr, Hex,* and *Oct* to convert the data types. You can also use the *VarType* function to query the subtype. For a list of all *Variant* subtypes, see the VBScript Tutorial.

The *Option Explicit* statement

By default, VBScript allows implicit variable declarations, whereby a variable is created and used without first declaring it with a *Dim, Private, Public,* or *ReDim* statement. If you allow implicit variable declarations in your scripts, however, you run the risk of creating subtle programming errors. If you mistype a variable name, for example, the VBScript interpreter assumes that you're using an implicit declaration and creates a new variable. Let's say that you type *Pris* instead of *Price* in your source code, as in the following code snippet:

```
VAT = 16.0
Price = 0
Net = 115.00
Pris = Net * (1.0 + VAT/100)
MsgBox Price, vbOKOnly, "Price"
```

This sequence won't work the way you intended. The typo in the assignment statement causes the calculated price to be stored in the (new) variable *Pris* instead of the variable *Price*. The message box will show the result 0 instead of 133.4.

To detect mistyped variable names, you can use the *Option Explicit* statement in the first line of your program. The *Option Explicit* statement tells the interpreter to allow only variables that are declared explicitly within your script using a *Dim, Private, Public,* or *ReDim* statement. If you forget to declare your variables explicitly, WSH reports each implicitly declared variable in an error dialog box. This WSH feature also uncovers mistyped variable names. Listing 4-2 contains such a mistyped variable name.

```
'****************************************************
' File:     ErrorTest2.vbs (WSH sample in VBScript)
' Author:   (c) G. Born
'
' Using an undeclared (mistyped) variable to
' demonstrate the Option Explicit statement
'****************************************************
Option Explicit

' Declare variables.
Dim Message
Dim Title

' Initialize variables.
Message = "Hello, world"
Titel = "WSH sample "      ' This name isn't declared!!

' Show a message.
MsgBox Message, vbInformation + vbOKOnly, Title

'*** End
```

Listing 4-2 *ErrorTest2.vbs*

The script in Listing 4-2 contains a mistyped variable, *Titel*. If the interpreter reaches the line with the string assignment to the variable *Titel*, an error message appears (as shown in Figure 4-2).

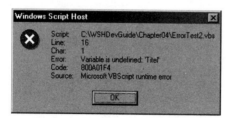

Figure 4-2 *An error message indicating an undefined variable*

WARNING If you use the *On Error Resume Next* statement within a script, undeclared variable names are no longer reported, even if the script contains an *Option Explicit* statement.

OPTION EXPLICIT IN .WSF FILES

If you use .wsf files, be sure that the *Option Explicit* statement is in every *<script ...> ... </script>* element. Otherwise, only scripts that contain the *Option Explicit* statement will be checked for undeclared variables. This code sample (the WSHDemo2.wsf sample file) shows this trap:

```
<?xml version="1.0"?>
<!--
    File:    WSHDemo2.wsf (for WSH 2.0)
    Author: (c) G. Born
-->

<job id="T1">
    <script language="VBScript">
    <![CDATA[
        Option Explicit
        Dim name
        name = "Microsoft"
        WScript.Echo name
    ]]>
    </script>

    <script language="VBScript">
    <![CDATA[
        Text = "Hello, world"
        WScript.Echo Text
    ]]>
    </script>
</job>
```

The first script contains the *Option Explicit* statement. Therefore, the variable *name* must be declared explicitly. The second script element doesn't include the *Option Explicit* statement. Executing this script should cause an error because the variable *Text* isn't declared, but if you execute this file, no error occurs because *Option Explicit* is defined only for the first *<script>* element. This behavior allows you to use *Option Explicit* selectively in your .wsf files, but you can get into trouble if you omit *Option Explicit* from subsequent *<script>* elements.

The *Dim* statement

You can use the keyword *Dim* to explicitly define a variable at the procedure, function, or script level or to define an array variable. If you use the *Option Explicit* statement, you must declare all variables by using the *Dim* keyword (in the script header or in a procedure or function), as shown here:

```
Dim text
Dim x
Dim Price, Vat
```

> **NOTE** When you declare a variable, its value is automatically initialized. Numeric variables receive the value 0, and strings are set to an empty string ("").

The *Public* and *Private* keywords

In addition to the *Dim* statement, VBScript has two other keywords that allow you to declare variables at the script level: *Public* and *Private*. You use *Public* to extend and *Private* to limit the scope of script-level variables.

```
Public Test
Private Price, Vat
```

The *Private* keyword restricts the scope of a declared variable to the script. If you use the *Public* keyword, the variable is visible to all scripts and procedures within the current file.

In a .vbs file, *Private* and *Public* have exactly the same effect as the *Dim* statement, so you might wonder why you'd ever use them. The answer is that *Private* and *Public* do matter in .wsf and .htm files. VBScript was originally developed for HTML documents, which can contain several scripts within <script> tags in the HTML code. Using the keyword *Public*, you can declare a variable that is also valid outside the local script (in other scripts in the same document).

> **NOTE** The *Public* and *Private* keywords are illegal inside procedures and functions and cause a syntax error. However, you can use *Public* and *Private* as part of a procedure or function declaration to set the scope of the procedure or function explicitly. (For more information on procedure and function declarations, see the "Functions and Procedures" section later in this chapter.)

Declaring arrays with *Dim*

VBScript supports arrays, which you must declare and access in the following order:

```
Dim value(10)
value(0) = 11
```

The first line of code defines an array with 11 items. (The index always starts with 0.) You can access the first array element using *value(0)*. The second line of code assigns the value 11 to the first array element.

VARIABLE SCOPE IN .WSF FILES

The variable scope previously described applies to several scripts in a single .wsf file. The following code sample (WSHDemo3.wsf) contains one job with two scripts:

```
<?xml version="1.0"?>
<!--
    File:   WSHDemo3.wsf (for WSH 2.0)
    Author: (c) G. Born
-->

<job id="T1">
    <script language="VBScript">
    <![CDATA[
        Option Explicit
        Dim name
        name = "Microsoft"
        WScript.Echo name
    ]]>
    </script>

    <script language="VBScript">
    <![CDATA[
        Option Explicit
        Dim text
        text = "Hello, "
        WScript.Echo text & name
    ]]>
    </script>
</job>
```

Both scripts contain the *Option Explicit* declaration, but the variable *name* is declared in the first script. The value of this variable is used in the second script. Therefore, the scope of the variable *name* is global to all *<script>* elements in the .wsf file.

The *Dim* statement also allows you to declare multidimensional arrays. The following statement declares a two-dimensional array:

```
Dim value(10, 10)
```

Value(0, 0) is the first element in row 0 and column 0. VBScript allows up to 60 dimensions for arrays. The lower bound for arrays is always set to 0; you can set only the upper bound of an array in the *Dim* declaration.

> **NOTE** You must use the *Dim* statement with empty parentheses—as in *Dim value()*—to define dynamic arrays. You can redefine the dimension of a dynamic array using the *ReDim* statement.

Variable names

A variable name can have up to 255 characters. You can choose any variable name as long as it follows these rules:

- It must begin with a letter. (*Test* is a valid name; *123* is not.)

- It can't include blanks, dots, commas, or certain other special characters (such as !, −, and +).

- You can't use keywords such as *Sub, If, End,* and *Dim* as variable names.

Assigning object references using the *Set* statement

The *Set* statement has a special meaning in VBScript. To access an object, you must assign a reference to it using *Set*, as in the following statement:

```
Set objAdr = WScript.Arguments
```

This statement assigns an object reference to the variable *objAdr*, which points to the *Arguments* property of the *WScript* object. The variable uses the *Variant* data type, but the subtype is set to *Object*. After assigning an object variable, you can use the reference in a statement, as shown here:

```
MsgBox objAdr.Item(0)
```

This statement shows the first argument passed to the script in a message box.

> **NOTE** Generally, when you use *Set* to assign an object to a variable, no copy of the object is created for that variable. Instead, a reference to the object is created. More than one object variable can refer to the same object. Because these variables are references to (rather than copies of) the object, any change in the object is reflected in all variables that refer to it.

> **NOTE** The names of objects, methods, and properties in a statement are separated by a dot—as in *objAdr.Item*, where *objAdr* is the object reference and *Item* is a property. (See Chapter 3 for more information about programming with objects.)

Operators

VBScript supports several types of operators: arithmetic operators, logical operators, comparison operators, and operators for concatenation.

Arithmetic operators

Table 4-1 describes the arithmetic operators available in VBScript.

Table 4-1 ARITHMETIC OPERATORS

Operator	Description	Example
∧	Exponentiation	x = y^Exponent
+	Addition	x = a + b
−	Subtraction or negative sign	x = −10 or x = a − 100
*	Multiplication	x = b * 30
/	Division	x = a / b
\	Integer-Division	x = a \ b
Mod	Modulo	x = a Mod b

NOTE If you use the + operator for concatenation and one of the operands contains the value *Null*, the result is also *Null*. For more information, see the VBScript Language Reference.

Logical operators

VBScript supports a few logical operators to evaluate expressions. Table 4-2 describes them.

Table 4-2 LOGICAL OPERATORS

Operator	Description	Example
Not	Negation	x = Not y
And	And	x = a And b
Or	Or	x = a Or b
Xor	Exclusive Or	x = a Xor b
Eqv	Equivalence	x = a Eqv b
Imp	Implication	x = a Imp b

Logical operators are often used in branches. The following statement tests two conditions:

```
If a > 100 And a < 1000 Then
```

Both conditions (*a > 100* and *a < 1000*) deliver a logical value of *True* or *False*, and the values are compared using *And*. If both conditions are *True*, the *If* branch is executed.

You can use the operators *Not*, *And*, *Or*, and *Xor* for logical expressions and also for bit operations on byte and integer values. Table 4-3 is the truth table for the logical *Not* operator.

Table 4-3   THE LOGICAL *NOT* OPERATOR

Expression A	Not A
True	False
False	True

As you can see from Table 4-3, the logical *Not* operator returns the opposite of a *True* or *False* expression. The bitwise *Not* operator uses the truth table in Table 4-4.

Table 4-4   THE BITWISE *NOT* OPERATOR

Bit	Not
1	0
0	1

The bitwise *Not* operator reads the bit and inverts its value. A 0 is converted to a 1, and vice versa. Such operations are best demonstrated in the binary or hexadecimal system. A decimal number 3 can be written in the binary system as 0011 (if you're using four digits for the representation). Using the bitwise *Not* operator yields a result of 1100. This binary number is equivalent to the hexadecimal value 0CH or decimal 12.

The logical *And* operator compares two expressions and returns a value of *True* only if both expressions are *True*. Table 4-5 summarizes the effect of the logical *And* operator.

Table 4-5   THE LOGICAL *AND* OPERATOR

Expression A	Expression B	A And B
True	True	True
True	False	False
False	True	False
False	False	False

The bitwise *And* operator compares two bits. If both bits are 1, the result is also 1, as shown in Table 4-6. The input values are in the Bit columns and the result is in the *And* column.

Table 4-6 THE BITWISE *AND* OPERATOR

Bit	*Bit*	And
1	1	1
1	0	0
0	1	0
0	0	0

The following statement uses the bitwise *And* operator:

```
MsgBox (3 And 7)
```

The result, 3, is shown in a message box. The statement in parentheses does a bitwise operation using *And*. (For novices: a decimal 3 can be represented as the binary value 0011, and decimal 7 is equivalent to the binary value 0111, so the result of the *And* operator is 0011, which is equivalent to decimal 3.)

The logical *Or* operator compares two expressions and returns *True* if either expression is *True*. Table 4-7 enumerates the possible inputs and the results of combining them with the logical *Or* operator.

Table 4-7 THE LOGICAL *OR* OPERATOR

Expression A	*Expression B*	A Or B
True	True	True
True	False	True
False	True	True
False	False	False

The bitwise *Or* operator compares two bits. If one bit is 1, the result is also 1. Table 4-8 shows the possible results of the bitwise *Or* operator.

Table 4-8 THE BITWISE *OR* OPERATOR

Bit	*Bit*	Or
1	1	1
1	0	1
0	1	1
0	0	0

The result of the following bitwise *Or* operation appears in a message box:

```
MsgBox (3 Or 7)
```

The decimal value 3 is equivalent to 0011 decimal, and 7 decimal is 0111 binary. The result of the *Or* operator is 0111 binary, which is 7 decimal.

The logical *Xor* (exclusive *Or*) operator compares two expressions and returns *True* if the expressions are different but returns *False* if both expressions are the same. The results of the logical *Xor* operator are shown in Table 4-9.

Table 4-9 THE LOGICAL *XOR* OPERATOR

Expression A	Expression B	A Xor B
True	True	False
True	False	True
False	True	True
False	False	False

The bitwise *Xor* operator yields a result of 1 if the two input values are different, as shown in Table 4-10.

Table 4-10 THE BITWISE *XOR* OPERATOR

Bit	Bit	Xor
1	1	0
1	0	1
0	1	1
0	0	0

Comparison operators

You can use comparison operators to compare expressions (which can contain numbers, strings, and so on). Table 4-11 describes the comparison operators in VBScript.

Table 4-11 COMPARISON OPERATORS

Operator	Description	Example
<	Less than	a < b
>	Greater than	a > b
=	Equal to	a = b
<=	Less than or equal to	a <= b
>=	Greater than or equal to	a >= b
<>	Not equal to	a <> b

Comparison operators are used in branches and loops, as shown here:

```
Do While a < 10
   ...
Loop
If a > 100 Then
   ...
End If
```

> **NOTE** When you use comparison operators, keep in mind that VBScript recognizes only *Variant* variables. If the two subtypes are of different data types, VBScript converts the data types automatically. As a result of this conversion, values that are not equal might be interpreted as equal.

Operator precedence

The VBScript parser uses implicit operator precedence to evaluate expressions that use more than one operator. For example, to evaluate the expression

```
1 + 2 * 3 + 4
```

the parser first evaluates *2 * 3* because multiplication has a higher precedence than addition. Here's the order of precedence for arithmetic operators: exponentiation has the highest precedence, followed by negation, multiplication/division, integer division, modulo, addition/subtraction, and then concatenation. Comparison operators have equal precedence and are evaluated in left-to-right order. For logical operators, the *Not* operator has the highest precedence, followed by *And, Or, Xor, Eqv,* and *Imp.* If an expression combines different categories of operators, the arithmetic operators are evaluated first, comparison operators second, and logical operators third.

> **NOTE** Parentheses can be used to override operator precedence; any part of an expression contained within parentheses is evaluated first.

Control Structures

VBScript supports the following control structures for controlling loops and branches.

If...Then

You can use *If...Then* to implement a branch using a compare operation. The following statement resets the variable *a* to 100 if its value is greater than 100:

```
If a > 100 Then a = 100
```

This sequence also compares the variable *a* with 100:

```
If a > 100 Then
    a = 100
    b = 20
End If
```

If the value is greater than 100, the statements between *If...Then* and *End If* are executed. If the value is less than or equal to 100, the program continues with the statement following the *End If* line.

If...Then...Else

You can use the *If...Then...Else* statement to create two branches. The following sequence tests the variable *a*:

```
If a > 100 Then
    a = 100
    b = 20
Else
    a = a + 10
    b = a \ 10
End If
```

If the value is greater than 100, the statements between *If...Then* and *Else* are executed. Otherwise, the statements between *Else* and *End If* are used.

If...Then...ElseIf

If...Then...ElseIf allows nesting of several *If* blocks. The following sequence tests the variable *a* for different values:

```
If a = 1 Then
    b = 100
    c = 20
ElseIf a = 2 Then
    b = 200
    c = 40
ElseIf a = 3 Then
    b = 300
    c = 60
End If
```

If a compare operation yields the result *True*, the statements between the compare operation and the next *ElseIf* or *End If* keyword are executed.

Select Case

You can use the *Select Case* keyword to test a variable for several conditions. Depending on the variable's value, you can execute one of several blocks of code. The following sequence tests the variable *a*:

```
Select Case a
    Case 1
        b = 100
        c = 20
    Case 2
        b = 200
        c = 40
```

```
    Case 3
        b = 300
        c = 60
    Case Else
        b = 0
        c = 0
        a = 1
End Select
```

The *Case* statements contain the value to be tested against the variable. If a condition is *True*, the statements within the *Case* block are executed. If none of the *Case* conditions is *True*, the (optional) *Case Else* block is used.

Loops

Loops are used to repeat a block of statements. The loop constructs available in VBScript are described as follows.

Do While

A *Do While* sequence creates a loop. The header of this loop contains a condition that must be *True* to execute the statements within the loop. If the condition is *False*, the interpreter continues execution with the first statement following the *Loop* keyword. The following code sequence uses a *Do While* loop:

```
a = 1
Do While a < 10
    a = a + 1
Loop
```

The condition *a < 10* is tested before the loop is entered. If the condition is *True*, the interpreter executes the statements until the *Loop* keyword is reached. The condition in the loop's header is tested repeatedly until the condition becomes *False*. Then the interpreter continues with the statement following the *Loop* keyword. Thus, the condition in the loop's header must yield the value *True* or *False* to execute or terminate the loop.

Do Until

The *Do Until* statement creates a loop that is tested at the entrance of the loop. If the condition is *False*, the loop is executed. The loop terminates once the condition becomes *True*. The following sequence uses the *Do Until* statement:

```
a = 1
Do Until a > 10
    a = a + 1
Loop
```

Within the loop, the condition *a > 10* is tested. If the condition isn't *True*, the statements within the loop are executed. Once the condition within the loop's header becomes *True*, the program continues with the statement following the *Loop* keyword.

Do...Loop While

You can use the *Do...Loop While* statement to create a loop containing the condition test at the end of the loop. If the condition at the end of the loop is *True*, the loop is executed repeatedly. The loop terminates if the condition becomes *False*. The following code uses *Do...Loop While*:

```
a = 1
Do
     a = a + 1
Loop While a < 10
```

This loop tests the condition *a < 10* at the end of the block. If the condition is *True*, the statements between *Do* and *Loop While* are processed again. If the condition becomes *False*, the statement following the loop is executed.

Do...Loop Until

You can use *Do...Loop Until* to create a loop that is tested at the end of the block. If the condition is *False*, the loop statements are processed again. If the condition becomes *True*, the loop terminates and the statement following the loop is executed, as shown here:

```
a = 1
Do
     a = a + 1
Loop Until a > 10
```

This code tests the condition *a > 10* at the loop's end. The loop is processed until the condition becomes *True*.

Exit Do

You can use the *Exit Do* statement within *Do* loops to terminate the loop. If the interpreter encounters this statement, the loop is terminated and execution resumes with the statement following the loop.

For...Next

You can use a *For* loop to process a predefined number of steps. All statements within the *For...Next* block are processed during each step. The following sequence uses a *For* statement in VBScript:

```
For i = 1 To 10
     a = a + 1
Next
```

The loop is repeated 10 times. The value *i* contains the loop index. The step width of a *For* loop determines how much the loop index is incremented each time through the loop and is set to 1 by default. However, you can use the *For i = start To end Step x* construction to set the step width to the value *x*.

For Each...Next

Another important construction is the *For Each* sequence, which you can use to create a loop to process all elements in a collection or an array. The loop is repeated for each item in the collection or array. The following lines use such a loop:

```
For Each x In Worksheets
    ...
Next
```

Exit For

You can use the *Exit For* statement to terminate a *For* loop. If the interpreter encounters this statement, the execution continues with the line following the loop.

While...Wend

You can use a *While...Wend* loop to process a code sequence several times. The loop terminates if the condition in the line containing the *While* statement becomes *False*. The following code uses this kind of loop:

```
Dim value
value = 1
While value < 10
    value = value + 1
Wend
```

The loop is repeated until *value* becomes 10.

> **NOTE** *While...Wend* pretty much has been superseded by *Do...Loop*, which is a much more structured and flexible looping construct.

Functions and Procedures

In VBScript, you can use built-in functions and procedures or define your own. The following sections explain the basics of creating and calling user-defined functions and procedures in VBScript.

Functions

You use a function when only one result (which can be a variable or an array) is returned to the calling program. You declare a function using the following statements:

```
Function Name(Parameters)
    ...
    Name = result
End Function
```

The return value must be assigned to the function name within the function body. In the preceding sequence, the *Name = result* statement is used. VBScript always uses a *Variant* data type for the return value. The first line defining a function must contain the keyword *Function*, followed by the function name (*GetValue*, for instance), followed by parentheses. Within the parentheses, you can declare parameters that are required for the function call. Listing 4-3 uses a function in VBScript.

```
'*************************************************
' File:    Function.vbs (WSH sample in VBScript)
' Author:  (c) G. Born
'
' Using a function
'*************************************************
Option Explicit

Dim i, j

j = 0

For i = 1 to 10    ' Loop 10 times.
    j = addx(i, j) ' Add values using function addx.
Next

WScript.Echo "Result: ", j

Function addx(val1, val2)
    addx = val1 + val2
End Function

'*** End
```

Listing 4-3 *Function.vbs*

This sample uses the function *addx* with two parameters, *val1* and *val2*, to add these two values. The result is returned as a function value in the following statement:

```
addx = val1 + val2
```

The function name *addx* is built into the function header. The result, *val1 + val2*, is assigned to this function name. The function block ends with the statement *End Function,* which terminates the function and returns control to the calling program.

NOTE VBScript also supports the optional *Exit Function* statement. If this statement is executed within a function, the function terminates and control is returned to the calling module.

You can use a user-defined function in the same way that you use a built-in VBScript function: insert the function name and the requested parameters (in parentheses) on the right side of an assignment statement. In Listing 4-3, the function is called using the statement

```
j = addx(i, j)
```

You can also use user-defined functions to extend VBScript. Let's say you need to calculate the sales price of several products, which will include a value-added tax (VAT). You can define a function named *GetPrice* using the following code:

```
Function GetPrice(Net, VAT) ' Get the price, including tax.
    GetPrice = Net * (1.0 + VAT/100.0)
End Function
```

The VAT value can be passed (as a percentage value) to the function. Using this function in a script requires only the function name and the parameters, as shown here:

```
Net = 10.0
Vat = 16.0
Price = GetPrice(Net, Vat)
Price1 = GetPrice(100.0, 16.0)
```

These statements show that you can use variables or constants as function parameters.

NOTE You can't define a function inside another function or procedure. The code of a function must be declared at the script level. Also, local variables declared in the function body are valid only during the function call.

Built-in functions

VBScript provides a collection of built-in (intrinsic) functions, which you can use in the same way that you use user-defined functions. The following statement assigns the ANSI code of the character *A* to the variable *i*:

```
i = Asc("A")
```

The conversion is done using the intrinsic function *Asc*, which takes the character as a parameter.

NOTE For more information on user-defined functions and built-in functions, see the VBScript Language Reference.

Procedures

You declare a procedure using this syntax:

```
Sub Name(Parameter)
   ...
End Sub
```

Unlike a function, a procedure delivers no return value. To pass a variable to a procedure, you can use one of these approaches:

- Declare a global variable at the script level. The scope of a global variable is also valid within a procedure.

- Pass a variable as a parameter to a procedure. You can change parameter values within the procedure to return the results to the calling module. (See the following section, "Passing parameters using *ByVal* and *ByRef*," for more on this approach.)

Listing 4-4 uses a procedure to calculate a price (including the VAT).

```
'***************************************************
' File:     Procedure.vbs (WSH sample in VBScript)
' Author:   (c) G. Born
'
' Using a procedure
'***************************************************
Option Explicit

Dim Price, Net, Tax

Tax = 16.0
Net = 100.0

GetPrice Net, Tax    ' Calculate value.
WScript.Echo "Result: ", Price

Sub GetPrice(net1, tax1)
    Price = net1 * (1.0 + (tax1/100.0))
End Sub

'*** End
```

Listing 4-4 *Procedure.vbs*

The sample in Listing 4-4 uses several techniques to exchange information with a procedure. On the script level, I defined several global variables. The variable *Price* is global and can be accessed within the procedure. The code uses this global variable to return the result to the calling program. The procedure itself requires two parameters during the call. Notice the syntax of the procedure call. You must specify the procedure name followed by the parameters. The parameters are separated with commas.

> **NOTE** The *Call* keyword isn't required in a procedure call. If you use it, however, you must enclose the parameters in parentheses. For example, the statement *Call GetPrice(100.0, 0.16)* is equivalent to *GetPrice 100.0, 0.16*.

Passing parameters using *ByVal* and *ByRef*

In a function or procedure declaration, you can place the *ByVal* or *ByRef* keyword in front of a parameter to denote that the parameter is passed to the routine using *call by value* or *call by reference*, respectively. In call by value, a copy of the parameter (the value of a constant or variable) is passed to the routine. The routine can change the value of the copy without affecting the original constant or variable. In call by reference, the address of the parameter's value (the address of a constant or a variable) is passed to the routine. Passing a parameter by reference allows the called function or procedure to change the value of a parameter. If you don't specify either *ByVal* or *ByRef* for a parameter, VBScript defaults to *ByRef*.

The Procedure1.vbs sample in Listing 4-4 declares a variable *Price* at the script level to allow a procedure to return the result. Writing a procedure that returns values in global variables isn't good programming style, however, because such procedures can't be used without restrictions. You have to know the name of the global variable that is changed within the procedure. If you mistype the variable name, the script won't work. It's better to pass the values as parameters to the procedure and use call by reference to get the results back through parameters. The modified code in Listing 4-5 shows that you don't need to use global variables to return a result from a procedure.

```
'*****************************************************
' File:    Procedure1.vbs (WSH sample in VBScript)
' Author:  (c) G. Born
'
' Using a procedure
'*****************************************************
Option Explicit

Dim Price, Net, Tax

Tax = 16.0
Net = 100.0
```

Listing 4-5 *Procedure1.vbs*

(continued)

Listing 4-5 *continued*

```
Call GetPrice(Price, Net, Tax)  ' Calculate value.
WScript.Echo "Result: ", Price

Sub GetPrice(pris, net, tax)
    pris = net * (1.0 + (tax/100.0))
End Sub

'*** End
```

Notice in Listing 4-5 that the new procedure call requires a third parameter, *Price*, which is used to return the result from the procedure. This parameter is declared as *pris* in the *GetPrice* procedure declaration and is *ByRef* by default. If the value of *pris* changes in the *GetPrice* procedure, this change is also reflected in the variable *Price*, so your program can use the result calculated in the procedure without using a global variable to exchange values. (Just for demonstration purposes, I used the *Call* statement in this sample to call the *GetPrice* procedure. The *Call* statement doesn't affect how the procedure works.)

In certain cases, a procedure can't change the values in the calling program. For example, consider a program that defines a variable named *tax*, which is set once to *16.0* and is used in several procedure calls. If a procedure changes this value accidentally, this action could be deadly because the calling program still needs the original value for further processing. The variables *Net* and *Tax* in Listing 4-5 must remain unchanged after the procedure call. To prevent modification of parameters within the procedure from changing variables in the calling program, you can declare that a parameter must be passed using call by value, as shown in Listing 4-6.

```
'*****************************************************
' File:    Procedure2.vbs (WSH sample in VBScript)
' Author:  (c) G. Born
'
' Using the call by value feature
'*****************************************************
Option Explicit

Dim Price, Net, VAT

VAT = 16.0
Net = 100.0
```

Listing 4-6 *Procedure2.vbs*

```
    Call GetPrice(Price, Net, VAT)   ' Calculate value.
    WScript.Echo "Result: ", Price, " VAT: ", VAT

    Sub GetPrice(ByRef pris, ByVal net, ByVal tax)
        pris = net * (1.0 + (tax/100.0))
        tax = 17.0
    End Sub

    '*** End
```

The procedure declaration indicates whether each parameter should be passed *ByVal* or *ByRef*. *Pris* is passed by reference (because we must return the result to the calling module), and *net* and *tax* are passed by value. If the parameter *net* or *tax* is changed in the procedure, the change has no effect on the value of *Net* or *VAT* in the script.

A PITFALL OF PROCEDURE CALLS IN VBSCRIPT

At this point, I'd like to mention a problem with procedure calls in VBScript. The following code contains three calls of a procedure named *Test*.

```
'**************************************************
' File:    WSHDemo4.vbs (WSH sample in VBScript)
' Author:  (c) G. Born
'
' Using procedures in VBScript
'**************************************************
Option Explicit

Dim x, y

Sub Test(x, y)
    x = x + y
End Sub

x = 10
y = 20

' Call the procedure Test.
Test(x, y)       ' Illegal call
WScript.Echo "x = " & x

Test x, y        ' Call OK
WScript.Echo "x = " & x
```

(continued)

```
Call Test(x, y) ' Valid call
WScript.Echo "x = " & x

'*** End
```

Test is defined as a procedure with two parameters. The parameters are added to the procedure, and the result is passed back in the first parameter. This works because both parameters are passed by reference.

In VBScript, the parameters passed to a procedure usually can't be enclosed in parentheses (as they are in JScript). A valid procedure call must take this form:

```
Test x, y
```

If you accidentally put parentheses around the parameters, as shown below, the VBScript engine reports an illegal statement when it parses the source code and you get the error message shown in Figure 4-3.

```
Test(x, y)
```

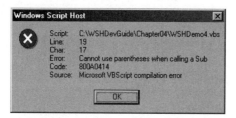

Figure 4-3 *An error message resulting from using parentheses around the parameters to a procedure call*

If you want to use parentheses in a procedure call, you must use the *Call* statement as follows:

```
Call Test(x, y)
```

So far, so good. Unfortunately, the language engine doesn't report all cases in which parentheses are used to call a procedure. Take a look at the following code.

```
'*************************************************
' File:    WSHDemo5.vbs (WSH sample in VBScript)
' Author:  (c) G. Born
'
' Using procedures in VBScript
'*************************************************
Option Explicit
```

```
Dim x

Sub Test(x)
    x = x + 1
End Sub

x = 10

' Call the procedure Test.
Test(x)          ' Illegal call; causes wrong result
WScript.Echo "x = " & x

Test x           ' Call OK, result OK
WScript.Echo "x = " & x

'*** End
```

This program uses a simple procedure named *Test* that uses one parameter, *x*. The value passed in the parameter is incremented by 1. If *x* is set to 10, for example, the following simple call returns *x=11*:

```
Test x
```

But the following call yields a mysterious result:

```
Test(x)
```

The call doesn't cause a syntax error. Instead, the result is 10 (not 11). The first time I found this behavior in my scripts, I expected an error in VBScript. However, it turns out the interpreter is doing its job correctly—it just can't read minds. The problem is that there's no way for the interpreter to distinguish the parameter list *(x)* from the expression *(x)*. When the interpreter encounters the *(x)* characters, it assumes the programmer wants everything inside the parentheses to be evaluated as an expression and passes the value of that expression instead of the address of the variable *x*. So, instead of executing the statement

```
Test x
```

the interpreter executes the statement equivalent to

```
Test 10
```

As a result, the value *x* isn't changed, and the wrong result, 10, occurs. To avoid this problem, you should omit the parentheses around procedure parameters.

ADVANCED FEATURES

The following sections describe some of the advanced features in VBScript. Some are supported only in the version 5 scripting engines (which ship with WSH 2).

Error Handling

Any run-time error that occurs in a script is fatal; that is, an error message is displayed and script execution terminates. However, you can change this behavior in all VBScript versions using this statement:

```
On Error Resume Next
```

This statement tells the script engine to suppress the error message, recover from a run-time error, and resume with the statement following the statement that caused the error.

RUN-TIME ERROR HANDLING AT THE PROCEDURE LEVEL

Run-time error handling is sensitive to procedure level. Let's say that a script calls a procedure and that this procedure calls a subprocedure. If a run-time error occurs in the subprocedure, the script engine checks whether inline error handling is activated (with an *On Error Resume Next* statement executed at the procedure level). If inline error handling isn't activated, the interpreter falls back to the calling procedure and repeats this check. If the calling procedure also doesn't have inline error handling, execution falls back to the script level. If no inline error handling is activated at the script level (no *On Error Resume Next* statement is already executed), the language engine activates the built-in error handler, which displays an error message with the erroneous line. After you close the error dialog box, the error handler terminates the script.

You should add the *On Error Resume Next* statement in each called procedure if you intend to use inline error handling. (If another procedure is called, the statement becomes inactive at the subprocedure level.)

To disable inline error handling, you can insert this statement in your script code:

```
On Error GoTo 0
```

You need to disable inline error handling as early as possible to avoid unexpected results (as you can see in Listing 4-7). During inline error handling, your script must catch and explicitly report run-time errors. Listing 4-7 establishes run-time error handling in a VBScript script.

```vbscript
'*******************************************************
' File:    RunTimeError.vbs (WSH sample in VBScript)
' Author:  (c) G. Born
'
' Simulating a run-time error to demonstrate
' run-time error handling and a pitfall
'*******************************************************
Option Explicit

Sub Test1()
    Err.Raise 6  ' Raise an overflow error.
    WScript.Echo "Test1 executed"
End Sub

Sub Test2()
    ' Here we have no run-time error handling.
    On Error Resume Next

    Err.Raise 6  ' Raise an overflow error.
    WScript.Echo "Level: Test2" & vbCrLf & "Errorcode: " & _
                 Err.Number & "=" & Err.Description
    Err.Clear    ' Clear error code.
End Sub


' The main part
WScript.Echo "Testing in progress"
On Error Resume Next


Test1
WScript.Echo "Level: Main (back from Test1)" & vbCrLf & _
             "Errorcode: " & Err.Number & "=" & Err.Description
Test2
WScript.Echo "Level: Main (back from Test2)" & vbCrLf & _
             "Errorcode: " & Err.Number & "=" & Err.Description


' Here's the pitfall: the next statement contains an
' undeclared variable but doesn't cause a run-time
' error because of On Error Resume Next.
WScript.Echo "Hello" & world  ' Dialog box is never shown!

On Error Goto 0 ' Disable run-time error handling at script level.

Test2           ' Inline error handling is done in the procedure.
Test1           ' A run-time error terminates the script.
WScript.Echo "Ready"


'*** End
```

Listing 4-7 *RunTimeError.vbs*

The script calls two procedures, *Test1* and *Test2*. No run-time error handling is activated in *Test1*, so the script engine falls back to the caller if a run-time error occurs. The run-time error is simulated using this statement:

```
Err.Raise 6   ' Raise an overflow error.
```

The *Raise* method of the *Err* object raises the run-time error of the number submitted to the method. This example uses code 6, which simulates an overflow error. Because *Test1* doesn't contain run-time error handling, the following statement is never reached and execution falls back to the script level, where run-time error handling is activated.

```
WScript.Echo "Test1 executed"
```

The following statement displays the current error in a dialog box:

```
WScript.Echo "Level: Main (back from Test1)" & vbCrLf & _
        "Errorcode: " & Err.Number & "=" & Err.Description
```

The error code is obtained from the *Number* property of the *Err* object, and the description is retrieved from *Err.Description*.

After the user closes the dialog box, the script calls *Test2*, which also simulates a run-time error using the *Err.Raise* method. Because run-time error handling is activated in this procedure, the execution continues in the procedure and a dialog box is displayed, showing the current error. Execution of the procedure resumes after the user closes the dialog box.

The following statement clears the error code:

```
Err.Clear
```

As a result, the next message box invoked on the script level doesn't show an error code. After calling both procedures with active error handling, the script disables run-time error handling on the script level. *Test2* results in a run-time error, but this error is handled within the procedure, so the script continues after the user closes the dialog box. The script then calls *Test1* again. Because inline run-time error handling is disabled, the execution falls back from *Test1* to the script level and then back to the built-in error handling routine. As a result, the default error dialog box is shown and the script terminates.

Regular Expressions (in VBScript 5.0 and Later)

In versions 5.0 and later, VBScript supports regular expressions, which you can use to find patterns in strings or replace one pattern with another in a string. You create a regular expression object in the script by using the following statement:

```
Set regEx = New RegExp
```

After this statement is executed, the object variable *regEx* contains a reference to the regular expression object. You can then use the methods of this object to force pattern matching, replacement operations, and so on.

Let's look at a simple example that detects all occurrences of the letter *b* in a given text. In this case, the pattern is defined as the letter *b*. To tell the object this fact, you use the *Pattern* property as follows:

```
regEx.Pattern = "b"
```

The name of the object variable is used with the name of the property. The property is set to the pattern value, *b*.

You must be careful about case sensitivity. The character *B* is different from *b*. Fortunately, you can set the *IgnoreCase* property to *True* or *False*. The following statement forces the pattern matching process to be case insensitive:

```
regEx.IgnoreCase = True
```

You can use the *Global* property to define whether the pattern should match all occurrences in an entire search string or just the first one. To retrieve all occurrences, you set the property to *True*:

```
regEx.Global = True
```

After defining the regular expression object, the search pattern, and the *Global* property, you can invoke the following methods:

■ **Test** Executes a regular expression search against a specified string and returns a Boolean (*True* or *False*) value that indicates whether a pattern match was found. The method uses the syntax *object.Test(string)*, where *string* is the string on which the regular expression is executed.

■ **Execute** Executes a regular expression search against a specified string. The method uses the syntax *object.Execute(string)*, where *string* is the string on which the regular expression is executed.

■ **Replace** Replaces text found in a regular expression search. The method uses the syntax *object.Replace(string1, string2)*, where *string1* is the text string in which the text replacement is to occur and *string2* is the replacement text.

You can find details about these methods and properties in the VBScript Language Reference. Listing 4-8 illustrates the use of the *RegExp* object.

```vbscript
'*************************************************************
' File:    RegExpression.vbs  (WSH sample in VBScript)
' Author:  (c) G. Born
'
' Finding a pattern in a string using the RegExp object
'*************************************************************
Option Explicit

Const Test = "The quick brown fox jumps over the lazy dog..."

Function RegExpTest(patrn, strng)
    Dim regEx, Match, Matches    ' Create variable.
    Dim retStr                   ' Result

    Set regEx = New RegExp       ' Create a regular expression.
    regEx.Pattern = patrn        ' Set pattern.
    regEx.IgnoreCase = True      ' Set case insensitivity.
    regEx.Global = True          ' Set global applicability.
    Set Matches = regEx.Execute(strng)    ' Execute search.
    For Each Match in Matches    ' Iterate Matches collection.
        RetStr = RetStr & "Match found at position "
        RetStr = RetStr & Match.FirstIndex & ". Match Value is '"
        RetStr = RetStr & Match.Value & "'." & vbCrLf
    Next
    RegExpTest = RetStr          ' Return result.
End Function

WScript.Echo RegExpTest("b.", Test)

'*** End
```

Listing 4-8 *RegExpression.vbs*

The function *RegExpTest,* obtained from the VBScript Language Reference, creates a regular expression object; sets the *Pattern, IgnoreCase,* and *Global* properties; and applies the *Execute* method to the string. This method returns a collection of matches to an object variable. You can separate the items of the collection in a *For Each* loop, as follows:

```vbscript
For Each Match In Matches
    ...
Next
```

This loop is executed until all members of the *Matches* collection are processed. The results are collected in a text variable, which is returned as the function value. The function is called within the main script, and the results are shown in a simple dialog box.

Classes (in VBScript 5.0)

You can use classes to create objects internally to implement some new features in VBScript 5.0. You're probably familiar with structured, user-defined variable types in other languages. For example, in Visual Basic you define structured variables as follows:

```
Private Type MyType
    MyName As String
    MyAge As String
End Type
```

Using this type definition, you can create a variable based on *MyType* by using the following statement. (The *customer* variable has the members *customer.MyName* and *customer.MyAge*.)

```
Dim customer As MyType
```

In VBScript, you can't work with user-defined variable types in this way. But in VBScript 5.0, you can use the class feature to define your own structured variables. For example, the customer data might consist of a name, an address, a phone number, and so on. To capture this data in a script, you can use a group of variables to describe a customer:

```
Dim Name, Street, Zipcode, Phone
```

If you also have a supplier, you need a second set of variable names, as shown below. (The prefix *s* indicates that these variables are part of the supplier data.)

```
Dim sName, sStreet, sZipcode, sPhone
```

Wouldn't it be much better to have a user-defined data type that describes an item more globally? The following code snippet uses the new *Class* construction to define the data structure:

```
Class MyType
    Dim Name
    Dim Street
    Dim Zipcode
    Dim Phone
End Class
```

Within your script, you can create an instance of the class *MyType* and assign it to a new object variable by using this statement:

```
Set customer = New MyType
```

The object variable *customer* owns all members of the class (*Name*, *Street*, *Zipcode*, and *Phone*). To access the *Phone* item, you can write this:

```
customer.Phone = "(555) 803-7892"
```

This approach is particularly handy if you also need a variable for a different entity, such as a supplier, which has all the same type of information as a customer. You can use the following statement to create a new instance of the class *MyType*, which you can use to store the supplier data:

```
Set supplier = new MyType
```

This statement is used in Listing 4-9, which creates two instances of the class, assigns values to the class members, and shows them in a dialog box.

```
'***************************************************
' File:     ClassSample.vbs (WSH sample in VBScript)
' Author:   (c) G. Born
'
' Using the new class feature in VBScript 5 to
' create structured variables, which simulate user-
' defined types
'***************************************************
Option Explicit

Dim customer, supplier

' Here comes a class definition.
Class MyType
     Dim Name
     Dim Street
     Dim Zipcode
     Dim Phone
End Class

' Now create a new variable for customer.
Set customer = new MyType

' Assign values
customer.Name = "Jo Brown"
customer.Phone = "(555) 203-2466"
```

Listing 4-9 *ClassSample.vbs*

```
' Now create a new variable for supplier.
Set supplier = new MyType

' Assign values.
supplier.Name = "Northwind Traders"
supplier.Phone = "(555) 203-3457"

WScript.Echo "Customer: " & customer.Name & " " & _
             customer.Phone & vbCrLf & _
             "Supplier: " & supplier.Name & " " & _
             supplier.Phone


'*** End
```

Example: Extending a class

You can also use classes to define your own properties and methods. The technique in VBScript is the same as in Visual Basic: you use the *Public* and *Private* keywords and the *Property* keyword. Here's an example derived from a sample I found in a Microsoft document. The class defines an *address* object.

```
Class address
    Public FirstName, LastName
    Private strEmailName

    Property Get EmailName
        EmailName = strEmailName
    End Property
    Property Let EmailName(strName)
        StrEmailName = strName
    End Property

    Property Get FullName
        FullName = FirstName & " " & LastName
    End Property

    Sub Add(First, Last)
        FirstName = First
        LastName = Last
    End Sub
End Class
```

The class has two public properties, *FirstName* and *LastName*, which are read/write. Neither property uses any code for the read/write process. The class also provides a read/write property named *EmailName*, which has code associated with it. The *FullName* property is read-only because it has only a *Property Get* statement. The class also defines the *Add* method, which adds a name to the object. All functions and subroutines in a class are public unless they are declared private by using the *Private* keyword.

After defining the class, you can create an object instance using the following statement:

```
Set customer = New address
```

You can add the values to the object instance using the *Add* method:

```
customer.Add "Frank", "Miller"
```

Listing 4-10 creates and uses this class.

```
'*****************************************************
' File:     ClassSample1.vbs (WSH sample in VBScript)
' Author:   (c) G. Born
'
' Using the new class feature in VBScript 5
' (Code derived from a sample by Andrew Clinick
' of Microsoft)
'*****************************************************
Option Explicit

Dim customer

' Here comes a class definition.
Class address
    Public FirstName, LastName
    Private strEmailName

    Property Get EmailName
        EmailName = strEmailName
    End Property
    Property Let EmailName(strName)
        StrEmailName = strName
    End Property

    Property Get FullName
        FullName = FirstName & " " & LastName
    End Property

    Sub Add(First, Last)
        FirstName = First
        LastName = Last
    End Sub
End Class
```

Listing 4-10 *ClassSample1.vbs*

```
' Now create a new variable for customer.
Set customer = New address

' Add a new customer.
customer.Add "Douglas", "Groncki"

' Set e-mail address.
customer.EmailName = "dgroncki@microsoft.com"

' Display the customer's data.
WScript.Echo customer.FullName & " " & customer.EmailName

'*** End
```

Using the *With* Statement (in VBScript 5.0)

The normal syntax for accessing properties or methods of an object is *object.property* or *object.method*. This syntax requires you to name the object explicitly in each statement. The following code (from the RegExpression.vbs sample file) demonstrates this behavior:

```
Set regEx = New RegExp       ' Create a regular expression.
regEx.Pattern = patrn        ' Set pattern.
regEx.IgnoreCase = True      ' Set case insensitivity.
regEx.Global = True          ' Set global applicability.
```

After you create the object instance, you assign it to the object variable *regEx*. In subsequent statements, you can use the *RegExp* object, but you have to type *regEx* repeatedly and the VBScript interpreter has to parse the name again and again, which is inefficient. Instead, you can use the *With* statement to qualify an object once for a series of statements. You can rewrite the preceding code snippet as follows:

```
Set regEx = New RegExp       ' Create a regular expression.
With regEx
    .Pattern = patrn         ' Set pattern.
    .IgnoreCase = True       ' Set case insensitivity.
    .Global = True           ' Set global applicability.
End With
```

Inside the *With* block, the VBScript engine knows that all unqualified references to properties and methods belong to *regEx*. By using the *With* statement, the VBScript engine can optimize calls to an object, and your code will be much shorter and more manageable.

NOTE   The *With* statement isn't supported in versions of VBScript before version 5.0, so most of the samples in this book don't use the statement (in order to be compatible with WSH 1).

VBScript 5.0 comes with several other new features, including function pointers to bind a procedure to an event, the ability to call objects on other workstations, and the ability to execute statements to evaluate a string expression. We'll use some of these features later in this book. For detailed information about VBScript's advanced features, see the VBScript Language Reference and VBScript Tutorial.

Chapter 5

Introduction to JScript

This chapter offers a short introduction to Microsoft JScript. If you've used JavaScript or Java, programming in JScript shouldn't be difficult for you. In this chapter, you'll find out how a JScript program is structured and how to use constants, variables, functions, and other program constructs in JScript.

> **NOTE** For more detailed information on JScript, see the JScript Language Reference and JScript Tutorial. You'll find a version of them in the \Docs\JScript folder on the book's companion CD. You can download the latest version from Microsoft's Web site at *http://msdn.microsoft.com/scripting*.

WHAT IS JSCRIPT?

JScript is Microsoft's implementation of the ECMA-262 specification. ECMA (European Computer Manufacturers Association) is a European group that develops standards for technologies ranging from electronics to script languages. ECMAScript is the language standardized in the ECMA-262 specification, which was originally based on Netscape JavaScript1.1 and JScript 2.0. JavaScript 1.5 is also compliant with the ECMA-262 specification. JScript is a complete implementation of the ECMA-262 standard with a few additional features to support Microsoft Windows more fully, such as the capability to call COM objects.

NOTE   Like VBScript, JScript is an interpreted language—you need only the source code in a .js file to execute a script in WSH. Like C++, JScript is object-oriented.

THE STRUCTURE OF A JSCRIPT PROGRAM

If you've used JScript or JavaScript in HTML documents, you'll notice that JScript programs for WSH are different. First, JScript programs for WSH contain no HTML tags. The entire script is stored in a .js file. Listing 5-1 is a typical JScript program. (This file, like the other code samples shown in this chapter, is in the \WSHDevGuide\ Chapter05 folder on the book's companion CD.)

```
//************************************************
// File:   OKCancel.js   (WSH Sample in JScript)
// Author: (c) G. Born
// WSH script creating an OK/Cancel dialog box
//************************************************

var mbOKCancel = 1;        // Declare variable.
var mbInformation = 64;
var mbCancel = 2;

var Text  = "Test sample";
var Title = "Born's Windows Script Host sample";

var WshShell = WScript.CreateObject("WScript.Shell");
var intDoIt =  WshShell.Popup(Text,
                              0,
                              Title,
                              mbOKCancel + mbInformation);
if (intDoIt == mbCancel)
{
    WScript.Quit();
}

WScript.Echo("Sample executed");

//*** End
```

Listing 5-1 *OKCancel.js*

Unlike a JScript program in an HTML document, a WSH script needs no event handling.

Comments

If you want the interpreter not to interpret a line or part of a line in your code, you can mark it as a comment. Comments in JScript begin with two forward slashes, as shown here:

```
// This is a comment.
WScript.Quit();    // Terminate script.
```

The comment can appear on its own line or can be appended to an executable statement (as shown in the second line above). When the interpreter finds a comment, it ignores the rest of the line.

> **NOTE** JScript also supports multiple-line comments in the format /* ... */. I don't use that format in this book, however.

Statements

You must enter JScript statements according to the JScript syntax rules, which differ in a few significant ways from the syntax rules of VBScript and other languages.

> **IMPORTANT** Keywords, function names, and variable names in JScript are case sensitive, so you must be careful how you write a statement. For example, *res = Test();* and *res = test();* are different. Beginners often overlook case sensitivity and create syntax errors.

It's a good programming practice to close statements with a semicolon (except statements in front of the closing brace of a code block or control statements such as *if* and *do*). To simplify the code, you can terminate every statement with a semicolon. The following lines are valid JScript statements:

```
value = 10;
value = value + 10;
Tax = 0.1;
```

Continued lines

Unlike VBScript, JScript doesn't have a special character for marking statements that span several lines because the semicolon identifies the end of a valid statement, as shown here:

```
WScript.Echo("Hello",
             "I was here");
```

If a statement contains a string, the line break must not be within the string. You can break the string into several substrings and concatenate the substrings by using the + sign.

Using several statements per line

As you learned in Chapter 4, you use a colon to separate several statements on a line in VBScript. In JScript, you use a comma or a semicolon, as shown in the following code sequence, which creates a message box showing the value *35*:

```
var x = 15, y = 20;
WScript.Echo(x + y); WScript.Echo("Done");
```

To keep your code transparent and more readable, however, I recommend that you avoid this construction. Or can you immediately understand the following line?

```
for (var i = 0; i <= 10; i++, j++)
```

In this code, I used a comma within the loop to increment the variable *j* for each pass. It's easy to move the statement to increment the variable *j* in the body of the loop.

Constants

Constants are numbers or strings in a JScript statement. You can define constants in the following ways in JScript:

```
Result = 15 + 10;
Name = "Born";
Pi = 3.14;
```

The first line contains the constants *15* and *10*, which are added. The result is assigned to the variable *Result*. The second line assigns a string constant *"Born"* to a variable. The last line contains a constant with the value *3.14*.

JScript doesn't use predefined constants, as VBScript does. If you want to use symbolic constants (such as *vbOKOnly*) in your scripts, you must declare them as variables. I'll use this technique in upcoming samples to improve the readability of the source code.

Variables

In JScript, you can use variables to store values in memory and identify them with a name. You must declare a variable before it is used for the first time. The declaration can be implicit, using an assignment statement, or it can be explicit, using the *var* statement. The following code declares a variable implicitly:

```
Price = 17;
Tax = 16;
```

It's better programming practice to declare a variable explicitly, using the *var* statement, as shown here:

```
var text;    // Declare a variable without assigning a value.
var x = 19;  // Declare a variable and set its value.
```

```
var Price = 19;
var y = Math.sin(x);
var text2 = "Value ";
```

The first statement declares a variable. (Its value is undefined, however.) The other lines contain variable declarations with assignment statements that define each variable's value and type.

Variable scope

Why should you declare a variable using the *var* statement if it's sufficient to use the variable name in an assignment statement? Because the type of declaration influences the scope of a variable, and the scope determines where you can access the variable. The rules are as follows:

■ A variable declared within a function using *var* (*var sumx = 0;*, for example) is valid only within that function.

■ A variable declared implicitly within a function (such as *Vat = 16;*) has global scope, so you can use the variable in the entire script.

■ A variable declared at the script level has global scope, regardless of whether the declaration uses *var*.

I recommend using the *var* statement to declare a variable within a function because the variable's scope is restricted to the function level. If you need a global variable or pseudoconstant, you can declare it using a *var* statement in the script's header. This improves readability and makes your script programs easier to maintain.

Variable names

You should follow these rules and guidelines when choosing variable names in JScript:

■ JScript is a case-sensitive language. For example, the variable *Test* is not equivalent to *test*.

■ The first character of a variable name must be a letter, an underscore (_), or a dollar sign ($). For example, *Test12* is valid, but *12Test* isn't.

■ The other characters in a variable name can be letters, numerals, the underscore character, or the dollar sign. Blanks and certain other special characters (such as characters with umlauts or other diacritical marks, +, –, and *) are not allowed. For example, *My name* isn't valid because it contains a blank. You can write the variable name as *My_name* instead.

■ A variable name can contain an unlimited number of characters. Still, you should try to keep names to between 8 and 15 characters to minimize typing and reduce the chance of misspellings.

- You should make variable names easily understandable. Do you remember half a year later what the variable name *x1* represents? A name such as *temperature* is much more obvious.

- Variable names can't be identical to reserved JScript keywords. The following is a list of reserved keywords in JScript and a few additional keywords from JavaScript (which you should also avoid):

abstract	*else*	*instanceof*	*switch*
boolean	*enum*	*int*	*synchronize*
break	*export*	*interface*	*this*
byte	*extends*	*long*	*throw*
case	*false*	*native*	*throws*
catch	*final*	*new*	*transient*
char	*finally*	*null*	*true*
class	*float*	*package*	*try*
const	*for*	*private*	*typeof*
continue	*function*	*protected*	*var*
debugger	*goto*	*public*	*void*
default	*if*	*return*	*while*
delete	*implements*	*short*	*with*
do	*import*	*static*	
double	*in*	*super*	

If you declare a variable without assigning a value, the interpreter creates the variable in memory but the value is set to *undefined*. Using such an uninitialized variable on the right side of an assignment statement, as shown here, causes trouble:

```
var factor;              // Value still undefined.
var Price = 100 * factor;    // Price is set to "NaN."
```

The value of the first variable, *factor*, is still undefined, so the interpreter assigns the value *NaN* to the variable *Price*. (*NaN* stands for "Not a Number.") The result, *Price*, in the second statement is also undefined.

When you declare a variable, you can assign the value *null* or any other value:

```
var fact1 = null;         // Assign a special value null.
var note = 3 * fact1;     // Value is set to 0.
```

Initializing your variables before you use them is good programming practice. If you don't, you run the risk of introducing undefined values into your calculations, as in the following code sequence:

```
var first_name = "Born";        // Initialized variable
var last_name;                  // Uninitialized variable
var aMess = first_name + " " + last_name;

WScript.Echo(aMess);            // Displays "Born undefined"
```

You also risk causing run-time errors, as in the following code sequence:

```
last_name = "";                          // Implicit variable declaration
var aMess = last_name + first_name;  // first_name still undefined
```

The second line causes a run-time error because the variable, *first_name*, is still undefined.

Data types

JScript variables don't have a fixed data type. The language uses a *Variant* data type, so you can't define an explicit data type when you declare a variable. The *Variant* data type keeps variable values in the required format (numbers, strings, dates, and so on). The JScript interpreter uses an implicit type conversion when performing operations on values that have different types. For example, to embed a number in a string, you could use an expression such as *"Text" + 99*; JScript implicitly converts the number *99* to the string *"99"* and then concatenates the two strings to form *"Text99"*. If you want to assign a string such as *"99"* to a numeric value, you must use the type conversion functions *parseInt* and *parseFloat*.

The following code uses implicit type conversion to assign a numeric variable to a string:

```
var from = 1;
var to = 10;
var action = "Count from ";
action += from + " to " + to + ".";
```

This code sets the variable *action* to the string *"Count from 1 to 10."* The numeric values are converted to strings.

The following code sequence (which is taken from the JScript Language Reference) assigns the value *0110* to the variable *x*:

```
var x = 0;
x += 1 + "10";
```

This code is really tricky—too tricky to use in your programs if you want your code to be readable. The expression *1 + "10"* on the right side of the assignment statement concatenates a numeric value with a string. The JScript interpreter converts the numeric value *1* to the string *"1"* and returns the string *"110"*. The string is then assigned to the variable *x*. The assignment operator is preceded by a + character, which forces the new value to be added to the value contained in the variable *x*.

The variable *x* contains the numeric value *0* set in the first line. To add the string evaluated on the right side of the assignment, the current value of *x* is converted to the string *"0"*. Then the value *"0"* is concatenated with *"110"* using the += operator. The result is *"0110"*.

Data subtypes

JScript uses only a few subtypes for variables and constants:

- **Numeric**   You can use this type to insert constants such as *423* or *3.14159* directly into your source code. JScript supports both integer and floating-point numbers. You can write constants using different radix. If a number begins with the characters *0x* or *0X* (a zero followed by the letter *x*), it is a hexadecimal number (which can contain the characters 0 through 9 and the letters A, B, C, D, E, and F). A number beginning with *0* (zero without the *x*) is an octal value (which can contain only numerals from 0 to 7). Decimal numbers are represented with numerals between 0 and 9. Floating-point numbers contain either a decimal point or an optional *e* or *E*, which represents the exponent (as in *12.30*, *10.0E20*, and *20E-10*). You can also use the + or − symbol to represent positive and negative values, respectively.

- **Boolean**   Variables of this type contain the constant *true* or *false*. The result of a compare operation can also be a Boolean value.

- **Strings**   These variables are defined with an assignment of string constants, as in *"This is a test"* or *'1234'*. Strings are enclosed in single or double quotes.

- **Null**   This is a special value belonging to an uninitialized variable.

For a more detailed discussion of data types, see the JScript Tutorial.

Escape Sequences in Strings

Some characters on the keyboard, such as Backspace and Enter, are impossible to type directly into a string. Other characters, such as the single and double quotes, won't work in a string because single and double quotes already are reserved to indicate the beginning or end of a string. Fortunately, JScript allows you to embed these characters in a string by using a special combination of characters called an *escape sequence*. Table 5-1 lists the escape sequences for JScript strings.

Table 5-1 ESCAPE SEQUENCES

Escape Sequence	Meaning
\b	Backspace
\f	Form feed
\n	New line
\r	Carriage return
\t	Tab
\'	Single quote
\"	Double quote
\\	Backslash

The backslash character is used as an escape character; the character follow-ing it is inserted into the string. Therefore, to insert a backslash into a string, you must use a double backslash. (The double backslash is important, for example, if a string contains a path definition.) The string *"C:\name"* won't result in a valid pathname in JScript because \n is interpreted as "new line." You must write *"C:\\name"* instead. You can use \n\r (the equivalent of *vbCrLf* in VBScript) in a string to format the output to a message box. To insert a single quote or double quotes into a string, you must write \' or \".

The following statement causes a run-time error:

```
Text = "He says: "WSH is cool!""
```

The interpreter recognizes two strings and a constant that can't be resolved. To insert a double quote into the string, you must write the statement as follows:

```
Text = "He says: \"WSH is cool!\""
```

The interpreter detects the \" sequence and inserts the double quote.

OPERATORS

In JScript, a simple expression is any part of a program statement that can be inter-preted as a single value. JScript allows you to create complex expressions by com-bining simple expressions using one or more operators. JScript also supports several types of operators: the assignment operators, comparison operators, calculation operators, increment and decrement operators, and logical operators. In this section, you'll find out how to use these operators effectively in your scripts.

Assignment Operator

Earlier, we used the assignment operator (=) in a variable definition. The following statement declares a variable and assigns the value *17*:

```
var tax = 17;
```

In the upcoming section "Increment and Decrement Operators," you'll find out how to combine the assignment operator with other operators (as in +=).

Comparison Operators

The *if* statement uses comparison operators (for example, to check two values), which return a Boolean value (*true* or *false*). The JScript comparison operators are listed in Table 5-2.

Table 5-2   **COMPARISON OPERATORS**

Operator	Description
==	Equal to
!=	Not equal to
>=	Greater than or equal to
<=	Less than or equal to
<	Less than
>	Greater than

The following statement uses a comparison operator:

```
if (tax == 17) flag = 1;
```

If the variable *tax* is equal to *17*, the variable *flag* is set to *1*.

> **NOTE** The operators = = and != sometimes cause an automatic type conversion. If you want to suppress automatic type conversion, you must write the operators as = = = and ! = =.

Calculation Operators

The simplest calculation operator is the + operator (which we used earlier). The following statements use the calculation operators +, −, *, and /:

```
var price = 10 + 1;
end_price = net * (1.0 + tax);
net = price - discount;
var res = 100 / 25;
```

JScript follows the commonly used rules for evaluating expressions with several operators. (The operators * and / have higher priority than + and −.) But you can use parentheses to group subexpressions, which are evaluated first. The JScript calculation operators are listed in Table 5-3.

Table 5-3 CALCULATION OPERATORS

Operator	Description	Example
+	Addition	a = a + b
−	Subtraction	a = a − b
*	Multiplication	a = a * b
/	Division	a = a / b
%	Modulo division	a = a % b

You can combine these operators with the assignment operator = (as you can in the C programming language). It is valid, for example, to write += (as you'll see in upcoming samples).

NOTE You must use the + operator for string concatenation in JScript (as in *var name = "Günter" + " Born";*). This requirement is different from VBScript, in which it's better to use the & operator for concatenation (even though the + operator works). JScript doesn't have a built-in exponentiation operator, such as the VBScript ^ operator. Instead, JScript provides this functionality through the *Math.pow(base, exponent)* method.

Increment and Decrement Operators

To add or subtract 1 from a variable, you can use the increment operator (++) or the decrement operator (−−), respectively; Table 5-4 lists these and other JScript incrementation operators.

Table 5-4 INCREMENT AND DECREMENT OPERATORS

Operator	Description
++i, i++	Increments i by 1
−−i, i−−	Decrements i by 1
+=	Addition incrementation
−=	Subtraction incrementation
*=	Multiplication incrementation
/=	Division incrementation
%=	Modulo division incrementation

The operators in Table 5-4 are unfamiliar to many Pascal and Basic programmers but are much loved by C programmers because they save you time when you write code. I recommend, however, that you use the more familiar operators to assign and add a value (as in $i = i + 1$). The following two columns contain equivalent code; the statement in the left column uses the increment or decrement operator, and the statement or statements in the right column use the standard calculation operators:

```
a += b;     a = a + b;
a -= b;     a = a - b;
a *= b;     a = a * b;
a /= b;     a = a / b;
a %= b;     a = a % b;
a = ++i;    i = i + 1; a = i;
a = i++     a = i; i = i + 1;
a = --i     i = i - 1; a = i;
a = i--     a = i; i = i - 1;
```

The increment and decrement operators also come in handy within loops.

NOTE The position of the ++ or -- operator determines when the value is incremented or decremented. In the statement $a = ++b;$, the ++ operator precedes a variable, which means that the variable is incremented before the rest of the expression is evaluated. In this case, *b* is incremented and then its value is assigned to the variable *a*. In the statement $a = b++;$, the increment operator follows the variable, which means that the expression is evaluated before the increment operator is applied. In the second example, the value of *b* is assigned to *a*, and then the value of *b* is incremented.

Logical Operators

Sometimes you need logical operators (in bit operations, for example). Table 5-5 lists the logical operators that JScript supports.

Table 5-5 LOGICAL OPERATORS

Operator	Description
&&	Logical *And*
||	Logical *Or*
!	Logical *Not*
>>	Bits shift right
<<	Bits shift left
>>>	Unsigned bits shift right

Operator	Description
&	Bitwise *And*
|	Bitwise *Or*
~	Bitwise *Not*
^	Bitwise exclusive *Or* (*Xor*)

NOTE See Chapter 4 for a discussion of how the bit operators *And*, *Or*, and *Xor* work in VBScript.

Operator Precedence

If a statement contains several operators that aren't set in parentheses, JScript follows a predefined precedence list. The operator precedences are shown in Table 5-6, listed in ascending order.

Table 5-6 OPERATOR PRECEDENCE IN JSCRIPT

Operator	Symbols
Comma	,
Assignment	= += −= *= /= %= <<= >>= >>>= &= ^= |=
Conditional	? :
Logical *Or*	||
Logical *And*	&&
Bitwise *Or*	|
Bitwise *Xor*	^
Bitwise *And*	&
Equal to, not equal to	== != === !==
Relational	< <= > >=
Bitwise shift	<< >> >>>
Addition, subtraction, string concatenation	+ − +
Multiplication, division	* / %
Negation, increment	! ~ − ++ −−
Call, member	( ) [ ] .

CONTROL STRUCTURES

Rarely will your scripts be linear. They will generally contain branches, along with control structures that determine which branch should be executed.

if Statement

You can use the *if* statement in different ways. The following code tests a condition:

```
if (condition)
{
    statements, if condition is true
}
```

The condition must be set in parentheses and can contain the comparison operators mentioned earlier. If the condition is *true*, the statements in the *if* block are executed. If the block contains only one statement, this statement can follow on the next line, without the braces. Blocks containing several statements must be enclosed in braces, as shown in the following code snippet:

```
if (value <= 16.0)
{
    WScript.Echo("Sorry, you lose the game");
    value = 0
}
```

The variable *value* is set to *0* if the current value is less than or equal to *16*. The braces enclose a block of statements. By the way, the semicolon in the last statement in a block is optional because the closing brace marks the statement's end.

If you need a condition that executes one of two branches, you use the *if…else* structure:

```
if (condition)
{
    statements, if condition is true
}
else
{
    statements, if condition is false
}
```

The *if* statement tests the condition. If the result is *true*, the statements in the block following the *if* statement are executed. If the condition is *false*, the statements in the *else* block are executed, as shown here:

```
if (value <= 16.0)
{
    WScript.Echo("Sorry, you lose the game");
    value = 0
}
else
{
    WScript.Echo("Congratulations, you won");
}
```

> **TIP** You can omit the braces if a single statement follows *if* or *else*.

Conditional Operator

JScript supports a conditional operator that assigns a value based on a condition. The operator uses the following syntax:

```
(condition) ? value1 : value2
```

The condition, which is set in parentheses, is followed by a question mark. If the condition is *true*, the value in front of the colon (*value1*) is used. Otherwise, the second value is used.

In the following line, if *age* is equal to or greater than *18*, *status* is set to *"Adult"*. Otherwise, *status* is set to *"Child"*.

```
status = (age >=18) ? "Adult" : "Child";
```

for Loop

You can use a *for* loop to repeat a block of statements in a defined manner. A counter defines the number of repetitions. The *for* loop uses the following syntax:

```
for (initialization; condition; increment statement)
{
    statements
}
```

Here's an example of a *for* loop:

```
for (var count = 1; count <= 100; count++)
{
    statement1;
    statement2;
    :
    statementn;
}
```

The variable *count* in the header of a loop is set to the start value when the program enters the loop. The optional keyword *var* declares a local variable for the counter used in the body of the loop. During each pass, the value of *count* is incremented (using *count++*) or decremented (using *count−−*) in the third argument. Because ++ follows the variable name, the variable value is incremented at the end of each iteration of the loop. The end condition for the loop is defined in the second argument (*count <= 100*).

Listing 5-2 uses a loop in a WSH script. (Don't be surprised if this code looks familiar: you saw the VBScript version as Listing 2-1.)

```
//***************************************************
// File:     WSHDemo.js (WSH sample in JScript)
// Author:   (c) G. Born
//
// Showing interim results in a message box
//***************************************************
// The following statements deactivate and activate
// the trace messages. You must uncomment the
// appropriate line.

// var DebugFlag = false;    // Trace output off
var DebugFlag = true;        // Trace output on

var j = 0;
debug("Start:", 0, 0);

for (var i = 1; i <= 10; i++)    // Loop 10 times.
{
    debug("Step: ", i, j);
    j = j + i;                   // Add all numbers.
}

debug("End:", i, j);

WScript.Echo("Result: ", j);

function debug(text, count, val)
{
    if (DebugFlag)          // Debug mode active?
        WScript.Echo(text, count, "Interim result: ", val);
}

//*** End
```

Listing 5-2 *WSHDemo.js*

for...in Loop

You can use a *for...in* loop to access elements (properties of an object or items in an array). This loop uses the following syntax:

```
for (variable in [object | array])
{
    statements
}
```

The keyword *in* is followed by the name of a JScript collection object or of an array. The *for* loop assigns a reference to each item in the collection or array to the variable *variable*. The loop terminates after all elements are processed.

ACCESSING ENUMERATION ITEMS

In Microsoft Visual Basic, you can use the *For Each item In collection* construction to access the members of a collection. Although JScript has a *for (xxx in yyy)* structure, you can't use this structure to access the members of a collection. Instead, you must use the *Enumerator* object, as shown in this code snippet:

```
var fso = WScript.CreateObject("Scripting.FileSystemObject");

// Get Folders collection.
var oFolder = fso.GetFolder("Test");
for (var oFiles = new Enumerator(oFolder.Files);
     !oFiles.atEnd(); oFiles.moveNext())    // All files
{
    ⋮
}
```

An object instance of the *Enumerator* object is assigned to the object variable *oFiles*. The *atEnd* method is used to test whether the end of the collection has been reached. The *moveNext* method moves the pointer to the next member of the collection.

---

while Loop

A *while* loop is executed until a loop condition becomes *false*. A *while* loop uses the following syntax:

```
while (condition)
{
    statements
}
```

The condition is tested during each pass. If the condition is *true*, the statements within the { } block are executed. (As in the *for* loop, you can omit the braces if the loop contains only one statement.) The following sample uses a *while* loop:

```
var i = 0;

while (i <= 10)    // Try 10 passes.
{
    WScript.Echo ("Step: ", i);
    i++;                        // Increment index.
}
```

The program loops until the index is set to 11. Each pass shows the current index in a message box.

do...while Loop

A *do...while* loop is similar to a *while* loop. You can use a *do...while* loop to process a block of statements several times, until the condition becomes *false*. The following syntax is used:

```
do
{
    statements
}
while (condition);
```

The condition in a *do...while* loop is tested at the loop's end. This means that the loop is executed at least once (even if the condition is *false*). If the condition is *true*, the statements within the { } block are executed again. (If the loop contains only one statement, you can omit the braces.)

The following code snippet (derived from the JScript Tutorial) uses this loop to process all drives of a *Drives* collection:

```
function GetDriveList()
{
    // Declare local variables.
    var fso, s, sharename, objDrives, drive;

    // Use FileSystemObject.
    fso = new ActiveXObject("Scripting.FileSystemObject");

    // Get Drives collection.
    objDrives = new Enumerator(fso.Drives);
```

```
    s = "";                         // Initialize result variable.
    do                              // The loop
    {
        drive = objDrives.item();       // Get item.
        s = s + drive.DriveLetter;      // Store drive letter
                                        // in result.

        s += " - ";
        if (drive.DriveType == 3)       // Shared drive?
            sharename = drive.ShareName;    // Use share name.
        else if (drive.IsReady)         // Local fixed drive?
            sharename = drive.VolumeName;   // Yes, use volume name.
        else
            sharename = "[Drive not ready]"; // Removable drive
        s +=  sharename + "\n";         // Add new line.
        objDrives.moveNext();           // Skip to next item.
    }
    while (!objDrives.atEnd());          // Test end condition.

    return(s);                      // Terminate and return result.
}
```

switch Statement

You can use the *switch* statement to execute several blocks of statements based on the value of an expression. The statement has the following syntax:

```
switch (expression)
{
    case label :
        statements
    case label :
        statements
    ⋮
    default :
        statements
}
```

The expression is placed at the beginning of the construction. The first *case* branch that matches the expression is selected and the statements within the corresponding block are executed. (The *label* identifier is a placeholder for the value of the expression.) If no block matches the expression, the statements in the *default* branch are executed.

The following sequence uses the *switch* statement:

```
function Test(x)
{
    switch (x)
    {
        case 1:
            ⋮
        case 2:
            ⋮
        case 3:
            ⋮
        default:
            ⋮
    }
}
```

This code uses a variable *x* for the expression. If *x = 1*, the first branch, *case 1:*, is executed. If *x = 2*, the next branch is processed, and so on. Keep in mind that you must use a *break* statement (as you do in C) to prevent execution from falling through to the next branch.

break and *continue* Keywords

In JScript, you can use the optional *break* keyword to terminate a loop unconditionally. (The *break* keyword is similar to the *Exit* statement in VBScript.) If the interpreter detects this keyword, the current loop terminates and the code following the loop is executed.

The *continue* keyword has the opposite effect in a loop. If the interpreter detects this keyword, program control is immediately transferred to the beginning of the loop. The loop index is incremented or decremented, and the loop is executed again.

FUNCTIONS AND OBJECTS

JScript supports a few built-in functions and objects. In addition, JScript allows you to create your own functions.

User-Defined Functions

Functions combine several operations under one name. If the function terminates correctly, it can return a result. JScript supports both user-defined and built-in functions. User-defined functions have the following syntax:

```
function test(parameters)
{
    body with statements
    return [return value];
}
```

You declare a function using the keyword *function* followed by a function name and a parameter list set in parentheses. The statements in the function body must be enclosed in braces. The *return* statement terminates a function and, optionally, returns a value.

To call a function in a script, you insert the function name and the parameters (set in parentheses). If you want to use the return value of a function, the function call must be on the right side of an assignment statement; if you want to ignore the return value, the function call can appear by itself on a line. The following statement calls the function *test* and assigns the return value to the variable *result*:

```
result = test();
```

If the function doesn't require parameters, you must use empty parentheses. You use commas to separate multiple parameters.

Built-In Functions

JScript has a few built-in functions to handle expressions and special characters and to convert strings and numeric values.

The *eval* function executes JScript code in a string, which is passed as a parameter, and returns the resulting value, as in *value = eval("14+15");*. The *parseFloat* function receives a string parameter and tries to convert it to a floating-point value. If the string parameter contains an illegal character (a character that isn't +, −, 0 to 9, ., or e), the string is converted only from the beginning to the illegal character. If the parameter doesn't contain a number, the *NaN* value is returned. The function *parseInt* requires a string as the first parameter. The second parameter must contain the code for the base (10 = decimal, 8 = octal, 16 = hexadecimal, and so on). An illegal string causes the result *NaN*. The *parseInt* function always returns an integer value.

NOTE For more details on built-in functions in JScript, see the JScript Language Reference.

Objects

JScript also supports a few built-in objects for processing strings, executing mathematical operations, and manipulating date and time values. You use the *String* object if a string is assigned to a variable or a property (as in *name = "Born";*). The object has several methods for manipulating strings. The *Math* object offers methods and properties for mathematical operators. For example, *value = Math.PI;* assigns the property *PI* to the variable *value*. The *Date* object handles date and time values. For example, *var Name = new Date(parameters);* creates a new date object and *today = new Date();* returns the current date.

In JScript, you can handle objects and arrays in the same way. You can also access objects and collections in a similar way. To access a method or property of an object, you use the object name followed by a dot and the name of the property or method. The following statement uses the *Echo* method of the *WScript* object to display text in a message box:

```
WScript.Echo("Hello");
```

> **NOTE** In JScript, you must submit parameters in parentheses (unlike in VBScript).

To access an object in a collection, you can use an index value. The following statements are equivalent:

```
Res = Object.width;
Res = Object[3];    // [3] should be equivalent to index "width".
Res = Object["width"];
```

The brackets are valid when you access the numeric index, but you must omit the dot if an index value is used. Thus, the following statement causes a syntax error:

```
Res = Object.3;
```

If an object contains another object as a property, the naming scheme must be extended as follows:

```
var x4 = toDoToday.shoppingList[3].substring(0, 1);
```

The object property is followed by a dot, which is followed by a subobject.

Arrays

Arrays are variables that contain a collection of values. When you create and handle arrays in JScript, you must use the *Array* object, as in the following statement:

```
var cities = new Array (10);
```

This statement creates the variable *cities*, which can contain 10 array items. The array items use the indexes from 0 to 9. You can access the items in this array using the array name and an index, as shown here:

```
cities[0] = "Rome";
cities[1] = "New York";
```

```
cities[2] = "Detroit";
cities[3] = "Manila";
  ⋮
```

The number in brackets is the index value, which indicates an array item. You can estimate the number of array items using the following code:

```
number = name.length;
```

To declare an array and initialize all array elements, you can use the following statement:

```
var cdays = new Array("Sunday", "Monday", "Tuesday",
                      "Wednesday", "Thursday", "Friday", "Saturday");
```

This statement creates a new array and assigns the data in parentheses to the array elements.

> **NOTE** I'll discuss additional JScript features in later chapters. Different JScript language engines are available. Microsoft Windows 98 and Internet Explorer 4 include version 3 of the JScript language engine. Internet Explorer 5 comes with version 5 of the JScript language engine. WSH 2 and Internet Explorer 5.1 use version 5.1.

Part II

Interactive Scripting

Chapter 6

Creating Simple Dialog Boxes in WSH

Most Microsoft Windows Script Host (WSH) scripts use dialog boxes to show results or collect user input. In this chapter, you'll learn a few techniques for using VBScript and JScript to create dialog boxes in WSH scripts.

USING THE *ECHO* METHOD

In previous chapters, I used the *Echo* method to create a dialog box in WSH. You can use the *Echo* method in either VBScript or JScript. This method has the following syntax:

```
WScript.Echo Parameters
```

WSH automatically exposes the *WScript* object to the running script, and the *WScript* object exposes the *Echo* method. You can use the *Echo* method in a statement such as the following:

```
WScript.Echo "Hello, world"
```

You can call the *Echo* method with one or more parameters. Use commas to separate multiple parameters, as shown here:

```
WScript.Echo "Hello,", "world"
```

These parameters pass the information displayed in the dialog box. The parameters can contain values of different data types. For example, the first parameter can contain a string value, the second parameter can contain a number, and so on. *Echo* parses the parameters, converts their values to strings, and shows the results in the dialog box. *Echo* automatically inserts blanks between the values in the dialog box.

> **NOTE** In Chapter 3, I mentioned that the *Echo* method is a procedure call—that is, it doesn't return a value. Therefore, in VBScript you must pass parameters to the *Echo* method without using parentheses, as in *WScript.Echo "Hello, world"*. In JScript, you always enclose parameters in parentheses, as in *WScript.Echo ("Hello, world");*.

Using *Echo* in VBScript

Listing 6-1 uses the *Echo* method of the *WScript* object to display a simple dialog box in VBScript. (This sample file, like most of the others used in this chapter, is in the \WSHDevGuide\Chapter06 folder on the book's companion CD.)

```
'*************************************************
' File:    Echo.vbs (WSH sample in VBScript)
' Author:  (c) G. Born
'
' Using the Echo method in VBScript
'*************************************************
Option Explicit

' Declare several variables.
Dim price, vat, net

vat = 16.0
net = 100.0

' Calculate price.
price = net * (1.0 + vat/100.0)

' Display results. Because the WScript (application) object is
' automatically available, no further steps are necessary.
WScript.Echo "Price: ", price, "US $ Tax: ", vat, _
             "% ", price - net, " US $"

'*** End
```

Listing 6-1 *Echo.vbs*

The program in Listing 6-1 uses a net price, applies a value-added tax (VAT) rate, and shows the results in a dialog box. The net price and the VAT are declared as the variables *net* and *vat* using the *Dim* statement in the program header. The values are then assigned to the variables. Next, a simple calculation is made to get the final price and store it in the variable *price*. The result is shown in a dialog box using the *Echo* method.

```
WScript.Echo "Price: ", price, "US $ Tax: ", vat, _
             "% ", price - net, " US $"
```

The parameters are separated with commas. The preceding lines also contain a continuation character (_) to split the command into two lines. The result of this statement is shown in Figure 6-1.

Figure 6-1 *A dialog box created using the* Echo *method*

NOTE Recall from Chapter 3 that the dot is used to separate the object name, *WScript*, from the method name, *Echo*. This notation is also used to separate the object name from a property name.

Using *Echo* in the Command Prompt Window

You can also launch a script in the Command Prompt window in Microsoft Windows. If you use CScript.exe as the host, the *Echo* method sends all output to the Command Prompt window, as shown in Figure 6-2. Because CScript.exe is a console-oriented application, it doesn't show a dialog box.

```
Command Prompt

C:\WSH Dev Guide\Chapter06>CScript.exe Echo.vbs
Microsoft (R) Windows Script Host Version 5.1 for Windows
Copyright (C) Microsoft Corporation 1996-1999. All rights reserved.

Price:  116 US $ Tax:  16 %  16  US $

C:\WSH Dev Guide\Chapter06>_
```

Figure 6-2 Echo *output in the Command Prompt window*

You can change where the output is sent if you need to write results obtained by a script into a file (for example, as a kind of logging). Console applications such as CScript.exe write to the *stdout* device, which sends all output to the Command Prompt window by default. However, you can use any of the *stdout* redirection operators (>, >>, and |) to send the output elsewhere. For example, you can redirect the *Echo* output to a text file by using the following command:

```
CScript.exe //NoLogo Echo.vbs > logfile.txt
```

This command does two things. The *//NoLogo* switch suppresses the two logo lines shown in the Command Prompt window after the scripting host starts. (See Chapter 1 for more detailed information about CScript.exe switches.) The redirection > *logfile.txt* causes *stdout* to write all program output created with *Echo* into the file logfile.txt instead of displaying it in the Command Prompt window. To append the output to an existing file, you must use the >> characters for redirection. Figure 6-3 shows the Command Prompt window with the command for redirecting the script output to a text file; the Notepad window in the foreground shows the content of the text file.

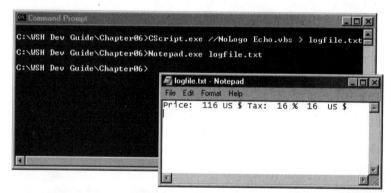

Figure 6-3 *Redirecting* Echo *output in the Command Prompt window and viewing the result in Notepad*

Using *Echo* in JScript

In JScript, using the *Echo* method is the only way to show a dialog box without creating additional objects (because WSH automatically exposes the *WScript* object). You saw the dialog box displayed by the *Echo* method in Figure 6-1. Listing 6-2 uses the

Echo method in JScript. (Remember that you must enclose the parameters in parentheses and that the statement must be terminated with a semicolon.)

```
//**************************************************
// File:    Echo.js (WSH sample in JScript)
// Author:  (c) G. Born
//
// Using the Echo method in JScript
//**************************************************
// Declare variables.
var price;
var vat = 16.0;
var net = 100.0;

// Calculate price.
price = net * (1.0 + vat/100.0);

// Show results. Because we're using the WScript object, we don't need
// to create the WScript object.
WScript.Echo("Price: ", price, "US $ Tax: ", vat,
             "% ", price - net, " US $");

//*** End
```

Listing 6-2 *Echo.js*

Listing 6-2 shows once again how you can use a method in a script. The *Echo* statement uses the *WScript* object. A dot separates the object name and the method name. The *Echo* method uses several parameters for the results to be displayed. All parameters are separated with commas. Numeric values in a parameter are converted automatically by the *Echo* method to strings. The title text of the dialog box and the button for closing the dialog box are created by the method itself. (Later you'll learn how to define your own title text.)

Using a Line Feed with *Echo*

I've been asked many times how you can force the *Echo* method (or other methods that I'll mention later) to wrap a string onto several lines. If you pass text to the *Echo* method, the run-time system does the formatting and line wrapping automatically. Parameters are separated with spaces within the dialog box window. A long piece of text is wrapped onto multiple lines, but short text is shown on one line.

Unfortunately, the *Echo* method (and the *MsgBox* function discussed in the next section) doesn't provide an explicit option to force a line feed during output. But as you can see in Figure 6-4, you can use a line feed in the dialog box. So how do you force the lines to break?

Figure 6-4 *Text on multiple lines in a dialog box*

The solution is rather simple: you insert the code for a new line into the text stream. The implementation is different in JScript and VBScript. JScript has several escape sequences for embedding special control codes into a string. You force a new line with the escape sequence "\n". If you need to direct the output of the *Echo* method onto several lines, you insert "\n" into the parameters. (See Table 5-1 on page 99 for a list of all the escape sequences for JScript strings.) The following statement uses this approach to divide the text into two lines:

```
WScript.Echo("Price: ", price, "US $ \nTax: ", vat,
        "% ", price - net, " US $");
```

Alternatively, you can set the escape string as a separate parameter:

```
WScript.Echo("Price: ", price, "US $", "\n", "Tax: ", vat,
        "% ", price - net, " US $");
```

VBScript doesn't recognize the "\n" escape sequence. Instead, it offers the predefined named constant *vbCrLf*, which contains the character codes to force a new line. In VBScript, the *Echo* method with a line feed can be written as follows:

```
WScript.Echo "Price: ", price, "US $" & vbCrLf & _
        "Tax: ", vat, "% ", price - net, " US $"
```

The & character concatenates the named constant *vbCrLf* with the other substrings. You can also insert *vbCrLf* as a separate parameter, like this:

```
WScript.Echo "Hello,", vbCrLf, "world"
```

USING THE *MSGBOX* FUNCTION IN VBSCRIPT

The *Echo* method offers a simple way to create dialog boxes in a script. You simply call the method and pass all values to be displayed as parameters. But *Echo* doesn't provide any options for influencing the layout of the dialog box. You might want to define particular text for the dialog box's title bar, for example, or you might want to insert buttons in addition to the OK button.

If you've worked with Microsoft Visual Basic or Visual Basic for Applications (VBA), you're probably familiar with the *MsgBox* function, which provides an easy way to show a message in a dialog box. (JScript doesn't support the *MsgBox* function.) This function also allows you to define the title text, the icon that appears in the dialog box, the number of buttons, and so on. Fortunately, the *MsgBox* function is implemented in VBScript, so you can use all its features in a VBScript program.

> **NOTE** You can use *MsgBox* as a procedure to display some results, or you can call *MsgBox* as a function to retrieve some values from the dialog box. I'll go into more detail shortly.

If you don't care about the value returned by the *MsgBox* function, you can call it using the following syntax:

```
MsgBox prompt, buttons, title
```

The parameters in this call are as follows:

- **prompt** A required parameter that defines the text that appears in the dialog box itself. You can insert the VBScript constant *vbCrLf* into the output string to force a new line in the text.

- **buttons** An optional parameter that defines the buttons and the icon shown in the dialog box. If you omit this parameter, VBScript uses only the OK button in the dialog box.

- **title** An optional parameter that defines the text of the dialog box's title bar. If you omit this parameter, Windows shows the application name in the title bar.

> **NOTE** *MsgBox* supports two additional optional parameters, *helpfile* and *context*, which allow you to include a Help button in the dialog box. Because creating help files is beyond the scope of this book, I don't explain how to use these parameters. (I don't think it makes much sense to use them without having a customized help file.)

As you can see, you can omit some parameters, but you must pass a value for the *prompt* parameter. Let's look at what happens if you omit optional parameters. Listing 6-3 is a minimal VBScript program. (MsgBox.vbs is in the \WSHDevGuide\ Chapter06 folder on the companion CD.)

```
'***************************************************
' File:    MsgBox.vbs (WSH sample in VBScript)
' Author:  (c) G. Born
'
' Using the MsgBox procedure to show a message
'***************************************************
Option Explicit

' Use all parameters in this call.
MsgBox "This is step 1", 0, "WSH sample by G. Born"

' Now omit the second parameter.
MsgBox "This is step 2", , "WSH sample by G. Born"

' Now omit the third parameter.
MsgBox "This is step 3", 0

'*** End
```

Listing 6-3 *MsgBox.vbs*

The program in Listing 6-3 creates three dialog boxes. The first *MsgBox* call, shown here, defines all parameters in the statement:

```
MsgBox "This is step 1", 0, "WSH sample by G. Born"
```

This statement creates a simple dialog box (the first dialog box in Figure 6-5). The first parameter, *"This is step 1"*, is the message shown in the dialog box. The second parameter is set to 0, so the only button is the OK button. The last parameter contains the string *"WSH sample by G. Born"*, which appears as the title bar text.

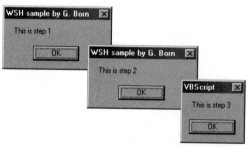

Figure 6-5 *Dialog boxes created with* MsgBox

In the second *MsgBox* call, the value of the *buttons* parameter is omitted by using two commas as follows:

```
MsgBox "This is step 2", , "WSH sample by G. Born"
```

This call creates the second dialog box shown in Figure 6-5. It is identical to the first dialog box (except for the message text) because omitting the *buttons* parameter is the same as setting the value to 0 (the default).

If you omit the third parameter, the one for the title text, you get the third dialog box in Figure 6-5.

```
MsgBox "This is step 3", 0
```

The title bar contains only the application's name. In WSH 2, the VBScript language engine shows the text *VBScript*.

> **NOTE** Omitting the second and third parameters in a *MsgBox* call is similar to using an *Echo* method call, which creates a dialog box with an OK button and the text passed in the first parameter. Only the title text parameter distinguishes *Echo* and *MsgBox*. *Echo* creates the *Windows Script Host* title bar text because this method is exposed from WSH. *MsgBox* creates the *VBScript* title text, which indicates that the language engine provides the procedure.

Defining the Icon and Buttons in a Dialog Box

You can use the second parameter of the *MsgBox* call to define the icon, the number of buttons, and their captions in the dialog box. The values for this parameter are predefined in Windows; VBScript provides named constants for their values. Table 6-1 describes the *MsgBox* constants for the icons.

Table 6-1 *MsgBox* Constants for Icons

Constant*	Icon	Description
0	none	No icon (default)
16 or *vbCritical*	❌	Stop
32 or *vbQuestion*	❓	Question mark
48 or *vbExclamation*	⚠️	Exclamation point
64 or *vbInformation*	ℹ️	Information

* This first column contains numeric as well as named VBScript constants. You can use either one, but named constants are much more readable.

The *buttons* parameter can also contain additional constants to define the buttons in the dialog box. Table 6-2 lists the predefined constants used for this purpose.

To show an icon and a button combination in the dialog box, you simply add the constants shown in Table 6-1 and Table 6-2.

Table 6-2   *MSGBOX* CONSTANTS FOR BUTTONS

Constant	Description
0 or *vbOKOnly*	OK button (default)
1 or *vbOKCancel*	OK and Cancel buttons
2 or *vbAbortRetryIgnore*	Abort, Retry, and Ignore buttons
3 or *vbYesNoCancel*	Yes, No, and Cancel buttons
4 or *vbYesNo*	Yes and No buttons
5 or *vbRetryCancel*	Retry and Cancel buttons

To show a dialog box containing a question mark icon and the OK button, you can write this statement:

```
MsgBox "Question", _
      vbOKOnly + vbQuestion, _
      "MsgBox demo"
```

You can see how useful named constants are. Using *vbOKOnly + vbQuestion* clearly indicates what you want; the equivalent constant 32 is a bit cryptic.

Example: Showing different buttons

Listing 6-4 creates a dialog box for each of the six available button combinations. (Figure 6-6 shows a three-button dialog box only.)

Figure 6-6 *A dialog box with three buttons created using* MsgBox

```
'*****************************************************
' File:    MsgBox1.vbs (WSH sample in VBScript)
' Author:  (c) G. Born
'
' Showing buttons in a dialog box
'*****************************************************
Option Explicit

Dim text
```

Listing 6-4 *MsgBox1.vbs*

```
text = "WSH sample by G. Born"

' Use three parameters in each call.
MsgBox "vbOKOnly " & vbOKOnly, vbOKOnly, text

MsgBox "vbOKCancel " & vbOKCancel, vbOKCancel, text

MsgBox "vbAbortRetryIgnore " & vbAbortRetryIgnore, _
       vbAbortRetryIgnore, text

MsgBox "vbYesNoCancel " & vbYesNoCancel, vbYesNoCancel, text

MsgBox "vbYesNo " & vbYesNo, vbYesNo, text

MsgBox "vbRetryCancel " & vbRetryCancel, vbRetryCancel, text

'*** End
```

NOTE The captions that appear on the buttons depend on the localized Windows version. Table 6-2 lists the button captions for the U.S. Windows version.

Setting the Focus on a Button

One button in the dialog box receives the focus for closing the dialog box. By default, the leftmost button gets the focus. If the user presses the Enter key, the button with the focus is used to close the dialog box.

You can set the focus on a button other than the default button. For example, in a dialog box that includes OK and Cancel buttons and that asks whether the user wants to delete a file, you probably want to set the focus on the Cancel button so that the user won't inadvertently delete the file by pressing Enter.

You set the focus by using a value passed in the *buttons* parameter. Table 6-3 lists the constants you can use to set the button that gets the focus. You must add the constant to the values for the icon and the button.

Table 6-3 MSGBOX CONSTANTS FOR SETTING THE BUTTON FOCUS

Constant*	Description
0 or *vbDefaultButton1*	Sets the focus to the first button (default)
256 or *vbDefaultButton2*	Sets the focus to the second button
512 or *vbDefaultButton3*	Sets the focus to the third button

* The value 768 (*vbDefaultButton4*) sets the focus to the fourth button. Because ordinary dialog boxes don't have four help buttons, I haven't added an entry to the table.

TIP *MsgBox* also supports the constant *vbSystemModal* (value 4096). Adding this constant to the *buttons* parameter (as in *MsgBox "Hello", vbOKOnly + vbSystemModal, "Foreground"*) forces Windows always to show the dialog box window in the foreground.

Determining Which Button Was Used to Close a Dialog Box

Sometimes you need to know which button the user clicked to close a dialog box. In the dialog box on the left in Figure 6-7, the user can click either OK or Cancel to close the dialog box. The dialog box on the right indicates which button was used.

In VBScript, you can use the return value of the *MsgBox* function to determine which button was clicked to close the dialog box. To retrieve its return value, you call the *MsgBox* function using the following syntax:

```
result = MsgBox(prompt, buttons, title)
```

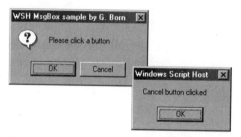

Figure 6-7 *A dialog box with two buttons and a dialog box showing which button was clicked*

You can create the dialog box on the left in Figure 6-7 using the following statement:

```
result = MsgBox("Please click a button", _
                vbQuestion + vbOKCancel, _
                "WSH MsgBox sample by G. Born")
```

You can assign the *MsgBox* return value to a variable and then test the value to determine which button was used to close the dialog box. Table 6-4 lists valid return values from the *MsgBox* function. The values returned depend on which buttons are in the dialog box.

Table 6-4   *MSGBOX* RETURN CODES

Constant	Button Clicked
1 or *vbOK*	OK
2 or *vbCancel*	Cancel
3 or *vbAbort*	Abort

Constant	Button Clicked
4 or *vbRetry*	Retry
5 or *vbIgnore*	Ignore
6 or *vbYes*	Yes
7 or *vbNo*	No

You can use either the numeric or the symbolic constant. Being able to check which button is clicked enables you to write code that allows the user to choose between options at run time.

The VBScript sample shown in Listing 6-5 checks which button was used to close the second dialog box. The result, with the button's name, is shown in a third dialog box.

```
'************************************************
' File:    MsgBox2.vbs (WSH sample in VBScript)
' Author:  (c) G. Born
'
' Checking the value returned by MsgBox
'************************************************
Option Explicit

Dim Text1, Text2, Text3, Text4
Dim Title, result

' Define texts.
Title = "WSH MsgBox sample by G. Born"
Text1 = "Just a note: Windows Script Host"
Text2 = "OK button clicked"
Text3 = "Cancel button clicked"
Text4 = "Please click a button"

' Call the MsgBox function.
' MsgBox prompt, buttons, and title
' prompt:   the text shown in the dialog box
' title:    the dialog box title
' buttons:  the buttons
MsgBox Text1, vbInformation + vbOKOnly, Title

' Check which button was clicked.
' result = MsgBox(prompt, buttons, title)
result = MsgBox(Text4, vbQuestion + vbOKCancel, Title)
```

Listing 6-5 *MsgBox2.vbs*   *(continued)*

Listing 6-5 *continued*

```
' Inspect the return value.
If result = vbOK Then
    WScript.Echo Text2    ' Show result using the Echo method.
Else
    WScript.Echo Text3
End If


'*** End
```

The variables *Text1*, *Text2*, and so on define the messages shown in the dialog boxes. During execution, the script shows three dialog boxes. The first dialog box has only an OK button, and the second one has two buttons that close the dialog box. Listing 6-5 uses the following statements to check the *MsgBox* return code:

```
' Inspect the return value.
If result = vbOK Then
    WScript.Echo Text2    ' Show result using the Echo method.
Else
    WScript.Echo Text3
End If
```

After the user closes the dialog box, the program checks the return value to see whether OK or Cancel was used. If the return value is *vbOK*, the *If* block is executed and the result is shown in a third dialog box (which is created using the *Echo* method).

```
WScript.Echo Text2
```

In this statement, *WScript.Echo* shows the content of the variable *Text2* in the dialog box. If the return value is *vbCancel*, however, the *Else* block is executed and *Text3* is displayed in the dialog box.

Example: A Welcome Login Message in VBScript

Let's look at another example that uses *MsgBox*. An administrator can define a custom welcome message for a machine running Microsoft Windows 95, Windows 98, Windows NT, or Windows 2000. By default, the user sees a static welcome message after logging in. We'll define a custom version of that dialog box that has a different message for each day of the week. Figure 6-8 shows the messages for Sunday and Monday.

Figure 6-8 *Welcome dialog boxes for Sunday and Monday*

You can implement this custom dialog box by using just a few script statements. Let's go over each step. You display a dialog box with a title bar using a *MsgBox* procedure call. If you don't know how to get the user's name, you can define a name as a constant:

```
Const title = "Hello, Jim!"     ' The user name
```

Then you define two variables, *text* and *cNotes*:

```
Dim text
Dim cNotes
```

The variable *text* collects the current date. The variable *cNotes* stores the messages for each day. Unfortunately, a simple variable can contain only one value (a text string, for example). To show a different message for each day of the week, you need several distinct strings, which can't be assigned to a simple variable.

Instead, you must use an array to hold the strings. An array is a variable that can contain several distinct values. In VBScript, you can define an array as follows:

```
Dim cNotes(10)
```

The array *cNotes* consists of 11 elements: *cNotes(0)*, *cNotes(1)*, and so on through *cNotes(10)*. You can assign a value to each array element by using the following code:

```
cNotes(0) = "Hey, it's Sunday. Please take a rest, my friend."
cNotes(1) = "It's Monday. Let's begin the week."
MsgBox cNotes(0) & vbCrLf & cNotes(1)
```

With this approach, you have to write down a lot of assignment statements to fill the array with its content. Because you need seven strings, one for each day of the week, it's better to use the VBScript *Array* function. The *Array* function lets you define all array items within one statement:

```
cNumber = Array(1, 2, 3, 4)
```

This statement assigns the numbers 1, 2, 3, and 4 to the array elements *cNumber(0)*, *cNumber(1)*, *cNumber(2)*, and *cNumber(3)*. You can thus use the following statement to fill a string array:

```
cNotes = Array( _
            "Hey, it's Sunday. Please take a rest, my friend.", _
            "It's Monday. Let's begin the week.", _
            "Oops, it's Tuesday. One day of the week is gone.", _
            "Don't worry, it's Wednesday.", _
            "Hurray, it's Thursday.", _
            "Thank goodness it's Friday.", _
            "Saturday! Why don't you relax this weekend?")
```

The variable *cNotes* is used as an array that contains messages for each day of the week. The following statement shows the message for Sunday:

```
MsgBox cNotes(0)
```

Now you need to determine the current day, derive the day of the week, and use the weekday value as an index into the *cNotes* array to retrieve the correct greeting. The VBScript function *Weekday* returns the weekday code of a given date. The code *Weekday(Now())* returns a value of 1 for Sunday, 2 for Monday, 3 for Tuesday, and so on. Note that the string for Sunday must be recalled using *cNotes(0)*. Thus, the statement *cNotes(Weekday(Now()) – 1)* retrieves the day's message stored in the *cNotes* array.

The dialog boxes shown earlier in Figure 6-8 also contain the current date, which you get using the *Now* function. Because this function delivers the date in a predefined format, you can use other VBScript functions to extract the day, the month, and the year from the current date:

```
text = WeekDayName(Weekday(Now()), False, 1) & _
       ", " & MonthName(Month(Now)) & " " & _
       Day(Now()) & ", " & _
       Year(Now())
```

You obtain the name of the day of the week using the *WeekDayName* function. The first parameter passed to this function is the code for the day of the week. The second parameter defines whether the return value is abbreviated. A value of *False* forces the function to return the full day-of-the-week name. The last parameter is optional and defines the code for the first day of the week. *WeekDayName (Weekday(Now()), False, 1)* returns a string such as *Sunday* or *Monday*.

MonthName(Month(Now)) works in a similar way. The VBScript function *Month* gets the current date from the function *Now* (which is passed as a parameter). *Month* extracts the month value from the date passed as a parameter, and *MonthName* returns the name of the month. By using these VBScript functions, you can format the date as needed. You can omit the year or the month, and you can sort the date based on your local time zone.

The full sample is shown in Listing 6-6. (For details about all the VBScript functions, see the VBScript Language Reference, which is available on the book's CD.)

```
'********************************************
' File:    Welcome.vbs (WSH sample in VBScript)
' Author:  (c) G. Born
'
' Using MsgBox to show a welcome message that
' changes daily
'********************************************
Option Explicit

' Define constant and variables.
Const title = "Hello, Jim!"    ' The user's name
Dim text
Dim cNotes

' Now we define an array with the daily messages.
cNotes = Array ( _
            "Hey, it's Sunday. Please take a rest, my friend.", _
            "It's Monday. Let's begin the week.", _
            "Oops, it's Tuesday. One day of the week is gone.", _
            "Don't worry, it's Wednesday.", _
            "Hurray, it's Thursday.", _
            "Thank goodness it's Friday.", _
            "Saturday! Why don't you relax this weekend?")

' Here we define the date within the welcome message.
text = WeekDayName(Weekday(Now()), False, 1) & _
       ", " & MonthName(Month(Now)) & " " & _
       Day(Now()) & ", " & _
       Year(Now())

' Now we append a custom message to the date.
text = text & vbCrLf & vbCrLf & cNotes(Weekday(Now()) - 1)

' Display the message.
MsgBox Text, vbOKOnly + vbInformation, title

'*** End
```

Listing 6-6 *Welcome.vbs*

> **NOTE** To display the welcome messages in Listing 6-6, copy the sample file Welcome.vbs to a local folder on your hard disk. Drag the file's icon to the Start button, to Programs, and then to Startup. Each time Windows starts, the content of the Startup folder is executed and the welcome message will appear.

USING THE *POPUP* METHOD

Unfortunately, JScript doesn't support the *MsgBox* function. Instead, you can use the *Popup* method provided by WSH. (You can also use the *Popup* method in VBScript instead of the *MsgBox* function.)

Because *Popup* is a method, it isn't part of the script language itself. It's part of the WSH object model and is exposed from the *WshShell* object, as you can see in Figure 6-9.

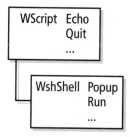

Figure 6-9 *The* WScript *and* WshShell *objects in the WSH object model*

To use the *Popup* method to create the same customized dialog boxes that we created earlier by using the *MsgBox* function, you can use the following statement:

```
object.Popup parameters
```

But how do you get the *object* in this statement? *WScript* doesn't provide the *Popup* method, and WSH doesn't expose a *WshShell* object automatically. You need an interim step to *instantiate* (create an instance of) the *WshShell* object and retrieve a reference to the object instance before you can use the *Popup* method.

You can instantiate an object in several ways. In WSH scripts, you can use the *CreateObject* method of the *WScript* object. *CreateObject* uses the ProgID of the requested object as a parameter. The *WshShell* object, which is a subobject of *WScript*, exposes the *Popup* method. The following statement creates a reference to the object in JScript:

```
var WshShell = WScript.CreateObject("WScript.Shell");
```

WScript is the object, and it supports the *CreateObject* method. This method requires one parameter containing the ProgID. For the *WshShell* object, this ProgID is defined as *WScript.Shell*. The *CreateObject* method searches the registry for the required object. If the object is already installed, an instance is loaded into memory and a reference to the instance is returned by the *CreateObject* method. This value is assigned to a variable (such as *WshShell* in the statement above).

The preceding statement creates a new object instance and stores a reference to it in the object variable. You can use this object variable to access the object's methods and properties. The following statements use the *Popup* method in JScript:

```
var WshShell = WScript.CreateObject("WScript.Shell");
var intDoIt;
intDoIt = WshShell.Popup(Message,
                         0,
                         Title,
                         vbOKCancel + vbInformation);
```

After creating the object variable *WshShell*, you can use *WshShell.Popup* to display the dialog box. The call to *WshShell.Popup* uses the following syntax:

```
res = WshShell.Popup(prompt, wait, title, buttons);
```

The *Popup* method has the following parameters:

- **prompt**   Contains the text that should be displayed in the dialog box. This parameter is similar to the *prompt* parameter used in a *MsgBox* call. You can concatenate constants, substrings, and variables in this parameter.

- **wait**   Defines a time-out value for the dialog box. If the user doesn't click a button within the time-out interval, the script closes the dialog box automatically. A value of 0 disables the time-out; the dialog box must be closed by a user.

- **title**   Defines the dialog box's title text.

- **buttons**   Defines the icon and buttons shown in the dialog box. The values used for this parameter are the same as for the VBScript *MsgBox* function. (See Tables 6-1 through Table 6-3 for the *MsgBox* constants for icons, buttons, and setting button focus.)

After the dialog box is closed, *Popup* returns the code of the button that the user clicked to close the dialog box.

NOTE The *CreateObject* method has an additional parameter, which I've skipped here, related to event handling. VBScript and JScript also have similar, built-in functions for creating objects. I'll go into more detail about *CreateObject* and the native object-creation functions in later chapters.

After creating the object variable *WshShell* using *CreateObject*, you can use *WshShell.Popup* to display the dialog box. But JScript doesn't use predefined symbolic constants (such as VBScript's *vbOKOnly*), so you have to combine the numbers given in Tables 6-1 through 6-4 to define the icon, buttons, and return value, as shown here:

```
var vbOKCancel = 1;
var vbOK = 1;
var vbInformation = 64;
var vbCancel = 2;
```

Using these variables as "pseudoconstants" improves the readability of your JScript script and simplifies porting between VBScript and JScript.

> NOTE The *Popup* method uses similar parameters and returns the same results as the *MsgBox* call. But the number of parameters and their order aren't the same.

Listing 6-7 is a JScript sample that uses the *Popup* method.

```
//*************************************************
// File:    Popup.js (WSH sample in JScript)
// Author:  (c) G. Born
//
// Using the Popup method to show a dialog box
//*************************************************

// Declare variables.
var vbOKCancel = 1;
var vbOK = 1;
var vbInformation = 64;
var vbCancel = 2;
var result;

var Message = "Click a button";
var Title = "WSH Popup sample";

// Create the WshShell object variable.
var WshShell = WScript.CreateObject("WScript.Shell");

result = WshShell.Popup(
          Message,
          0,
          Title,
          vbOKCancel + vbInformation); // Show dialog box.

if (result == vbOK) // Check and show results.
{
    WScript.Echo ("OK button clicked " +
              "(Code: " + result + ")");
}
else
{
    WScript.Echo ("Cancel button clicked " +
              "(Code: " + result + ")");
}

WScript.Echo("We are ready");

//*** End
```

Listing 6-7 *Popup.js*

The following statement uses the *Popup* method to create the dialog box:

```
result = WshShell.Popup(
        Message,
        0,
        Title,
        vbOKCancel + vbInformation); // Show dialog box.
```

The pseudoconstants *vbOKCancel* and *vbInformation* set the *buttons* value. After the dialog box is closed, the *Popup* method returns the code for the button that the user clicked.

This statement tests the value returned from *Popup*:

```
if (result == vbOK)
```

If the value stored in *result* equals *vbOK*, the *Echo* method displays a message saying that the OK button was clicked:

```
WScript.Echo("OK button clicked " + "(Code: " + result + ")");
```

If the value in *result* isn't equal to *vbOK*, the *else* block is executed and the *Echo* method displays a message saying that the Cancel button was clicked.

Using *Popup* in VBScript

Most Visual Basic programmers will probably use the *MsgBox* call in their VBScript code. But if you want to use the *Popup* method exposed by the *WshShell* object, you can take the approach shown in Listing 6-8. I kept the code simple to highlight the use of *Popup*.

```
'******************************************************
' File:    Popup.vbs (WSH sample in VBScript)
' Author:  (c) G. Born
'
' Creating a dialog box using the Popup method
'******************************************************
Option Explicit

Dim result
Dim WshShell

' We need the WshShell object.
Set WshShell = WScript.CreateObject("WScript.Shell")
```

Listing 6-8 *Popup.vbs*   *(continued)*

Listing 6-8 *continued*

```
' Use the Popup method.
result =  WshShell.Popup("Click a button", _
                         0, _
                         "WSH Popup sample", _
                         vbOKCancel + vbInformation)

WScript.Echo "Return value ", result

'*** End
```

Another JScript Example Using *Popup*

Let's look at another JScript example that uses the *Popup* method. We'll create a welcome dialog box (as shown in Figure 6-10) that shows a user name and the current date.

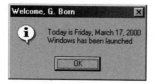

Figure 6-10 *A welcome dialog box containing the current date*

You can use *Popup* to create title text, and you can use the time-out value to close the dialog box after 10 seconds without any user interaction.

The following lines define two psuedoconstants containing the values for the *buttons* parameter in a *Popup* call:

```
var vbOKOnly = 0;              // OK button
var vbInformation = 64;        // Information icon
```

You can define an array in JScript using the following statement:

```
var cmonth = new Array("January", "February", "March",
           "April", "May", "June", "July", "August",
           "September", "October", "November", "December");
```

The variable *cmonth* is an object containing the array data. The *new Array* keyword creates an array and assigns the values in parentheses to the new object variable *cmonth*. Later, you can access the array values using an index:

```
WScript.Echo(cmonth[0]);
```

The following commands use JScript functions to retrieve the date and split the date value into day, month, and year:

```
var mydate = new Date();         // Create date variable.
var weekday = mydate.getDay();   // Retrieve day of the week.
var day = mydate.getDate();      // Day
var month = mydate.getMonth();   // Month (start with 0)
var year = mydate.getYear();     // Year
```

Because a date must be stored in an object variable, the first line uses the *new* operator to create an object variable. The *Date* method returns a reference to a *Date* object, which is assigned to the variable *mydate*. The following line creates the message shown in the dialog box:

```
var text = "Today is " + cday[weekday]  + ", "
       + cmonth[month] + " " + day + ", " + year + "\n"
       + "Windows has been launched";
```

You use the values of the variables *weekday* and *month* as index values for the arrays. As a result, the day of the week and the month name are concatenated into a string, which is assigned to the *text* variable.

The following statement creates the dialog box containing the message.

```
objAdr.Popup(text, 10, title, vbOKOnly + vbInformation);
```

If the user doesn't close the dialog box within 10 seconds, *Popup* closes it automatically. You can see the details in Listing 6-9. (For more information on all the JScript functions, see the JScript Language Reference, which is available on the book's companion CD.)

```
//***************************************************
// File:    Welcome.js (WSH sample in JScript)
// Author:  (c) G. Born
//
// Using Popup to create a welcome dialog box
// containing the current date
//***************************************************

// Define "constants" for Popup.
var vbOKOnly = 0;             // OK button
var vbInformation = 64;       // Information icon

// Create array variables for the message strings.
var cmonth = new Array("January", "February", "March",
         "April", "May", "June", "July", "August",
         "September", "October", "November", "December");
```

Listing 6-9 *Welcome.js*   *(continued)*

Listing 6-9 *continued*

```
var cday = new Array("Sunday", "Monday", "Tuesday",
          "Wednesday", "Thursday", "Friday", "Saturday");

var name = "Born";              // Set user name.
var firstname = "G.";

// Create a welcome message.
var title = "Welcome, " + firstname + " " + name;

// Create object to use the Popup method.
var objAdr = WScript.CreateObject("WScript.Shell");

var mydate = new Date();         // Create date variable.
var weekday = mydate.getDay();   // Retrieve day of the week.
var day = mydate.getDate();      // Day
var month = mydate.getMonth();   // Month (start with 0)
var year = mydate.getYear();     // Year

var text = "Today is " + cday[weekday] + ", "
        + cmonth[month] + " " + day + ", " + year + "\n"
        + "Windows has been launched";

// Create the dialog box using Popup; define 10-second time-out.
objAdr.Popup(text, 10, title, vbOKOnly + vbInformation);

//*** End
```

NOTE To show the welcome message in the Welcome.js sample, follow the directions given earlier for copying Welcome.vbs to your Startup folder.

Chapter 7

Working with WSH Objects

In Chapter 6, we covered the basics of script programming and examined some examples that use objects, methods, and properties. In this chapter, we'll discuss how to use Microsoft Windows Script Host (WSH) to automate certain tasks. You'll learn how to read the properties of the *WScript* object and display them in a dialog box so that you can retrieve important information from WSH and the current script or access environment variables in your operating system. You'll also learn how to access the arguments passed to a WSH script and use methods such as *CreateObject* and *GetObject* to create object instances. Finally, you'll find out how to launch an external application from a script by using the *Run* method.

USING THE *WSCRIPT* OBJECT

The *WScript* object is the WSH application object. It is exposed automatically when a script runs—you don't have to create a reference to it. The object exposes several methods and properties. In previous chapters, we used its *Echo* and *Quit* methods. In this chapter, we'll access the object's properties.

Retrieving WSH and Script Properties

In Chapter 6, I mentioned that certain attributes of WSH and the currently running script are available as read-only properties of the *WScript* object. If you execute a script in the Command Prompt window in Microsoft Windows using CScript.exe, the host program echoes the current version number on the command line. This version number is important because several different WSH versions are available. Properties such as the path to the host program and the host's name can also be useful. Table 7-1 describes some of the properties exposed by the *WScript* object.

Table 7-1 PROPERTIES OF THE *WSCRIPT* OBJECT

Property	*Description*
Application	Returns the *IDispatch* interface of the *WScript* object
Arguments	Returns a collection object containing the script arguments
FullName	Contains the full path to the host executable (CScript.exe or WScript.exe)
Name	The friendly name of *WScript* (This is the default property.)
Path	The name of the directory in which the host (WScript.exe or CScript.exe) resides
ScriptFullName	The full path to the script that is currently running in WSH
ScriptName	The filename of the script that is currently running in WSH
Version	A string containing the WSH version (not the language engine version)

NOTE For further details about the WScript properties, see the Windows Script Host Reference, which you can find on this book's companion CD (in the \Docs\WSH folder) or at *http://msdn.microsoft.com/scripting*.

Now let's write a script that retrieves the host and script properties and displays the results in a dialog box. (See Figure 7-1.)

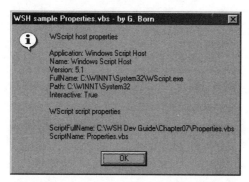

Figure 7-1 WScript *host and script properties*

It's easy to retrieve the properties of the *WScript* object. The *WScript* object is automatically exposed to the script from WSH during execution. The following statement reads the *Application* property of the *WScript* object and assigns this value to the variable *Name*:

```
Name = WScript.Application
```

If the script is executed in WSH, the variable contains the text *Windows Scripting Host* (for WSH 1) or *Windows Script Host* (for WSH 2). You can use this property to check whether the script is executed in a WSH environment (rather than in Microsoft Internet Explorer, for example, or as an external script of an Active Server Pages [ASP] file).

> **NOTE** The WSH properties can be helpful when you need the name of a script or the path of a script file. For additional information about *WScript* properties, see the Windows Script Host Reference.

Retrieving properties in VBScript

Listing 7-1 retrieves *WScript* properties by using VBScript. All you need is the object name *WScript* followed by a dot and then the property name. You use the following statement to retrieve the host name and assign it to a variable:

```
text = WScript.Name
```

This sample uses the *Message* variable to collect all properties in one string. The constant *vbCrLf* wraps the output onto several lines. The sample also uses the *ScriptName* property to show the script name in the dialog box title bar. (Like the other samples in this chapter, Properties.vbs is in the \WSHDevGuide\Chapter07 folder on the book's companion CD.)

```vbscript
'*****************************************************
' File:    Properties.vbs (WSH sample in VBScript)
' Author:  (c) G. Born
'
' Showing the properties of the WScript object
' in a dialog box
'*****************************************************
Option Explicit

Dim Message
Dim Title

' Show the properties of the WScript object.
' We start with the host properties.
Message = "WScript host properties" & vbCrLf & vbCrLf
Message = Message & "Application: " & WScript.Application & vbCrLf
```

Listing 7-1 *Properties.vbs*

(continued)

Listing 7-1 *continued*

```
Message = Message & "Name: " & WScript.Name & vbCrLf
Message = Message & "Version: " & WScript.Version & vbCrLf
Message = Message & "FullName: " & WScript.FullName & vbCrLf
Message = Message & "Path: " & WScript.Path & vbCrLf

' Get interactive status.
If (WScript.Interactive) Then
    Message = Message & "Interactive: True" & vbCrLf
Else
    Message = Message & "Interactive: False" & vbCrLf
End If

' Get script properties.
Message = Message & vbCrLf
Message = Message & "WScript script properties" & vbCrLf & vbCrLf
Message = Message & "ScriptFullName: " & WScript.ScriptFullName & vbCrLf
Message = Message & "ScriptName: " & WScript.ScriptName & vbCrLf

' Initialize title.
Title = "WSH sample " & WScript.ScriptName & " - by G. Born"

MsgBox Message, vbInformation + vbOKOnly, Title

'*** End
```

Retrieving properties in JScript

In JScript, you can also retrieve the *WScript* properties by using the *WScript* object followed by a dot and then the property name, as shown in Listing 7-2. The information is collected in the *Message* variable. New lines in the output text are generated with the "\n" escape sequence.

```
//**************************************************
// File:      Properties.js (WSH sample in JScript)
// Author:    (c) G. Born
//
// Showing the properties of the WScript object
// in a dialog box
//**************************************************

var Message, Title, tmp;
var vbInformation = 64;    // A couple of constants
var vbOKOnly = 0;
```

Listing 7-2 *Properties.js*

```
// Collect the properties of the WScript object.
// Read the host properties.
Message = "WScript host properties\n\n";
Message = Message + "Application: " + WScript.Application + "\n";
Message = Message + "Name: " + WScript.Name + "\n";
Message = Message + "Version: " + WScript.Version + "\n";
Message = Message + "FullName: " + WScript.FullName + "\n";
Message = Message + "Path: " + WScript.Path + "\n";

// Get interactive status.
if (WScript.Interactive)
    Message = Message + "Interactive: true" + "\n"
else
    Message = Message + "Interactive: false" + "\n";

// Get the script properties.
Message = Message + "\n";
Message = Message + "WScript script properties\n\n";
Message = Message + "ScriptFullName: " + WScript.ScriptFullName + "\n";
Message = Message + "ScriptName: " + WScript.ScriptName + "\n";

// Initialize title.
Title = "WSH sample  " + WScript.ScriptName + " - by G. Born";

var objAdr = WScript.CreateObject("WScript.Shell");

tmp = objAdr.Popup(Message, vbInformation + vbOKOnly, Title);

//*** End
```

Retrieving Language Engine Properties

Besides the host and script properties, you might need the properties of the language engine. For example, you might want to request the version number from the interpreter. Both VBScript and JScript provide functions for checking the version of a language engine:

■   *ScriptEngine*   Returns a string that identifies the script language supported by the engine

■   *ScriptEngineMajorVersion*   Returns the major version number of the language engine as a string

- ***ScriptEngineMinorVersion***   Returns the minor version number of the language engine as a string

- ***ScriptEngineBuildVersion***   Returns the build number of a script engine

Retrieving language engine properties in VBScript

Listing 7-3 uses VBScript to query the language engine properties and display the results in a dialog box (shown in Figure 7-2).

```
'*************************************************
' File:     Engine.vbs (WSH sample in VBScript)
' Author:  (c) G. Born
'
' Displaying the version of the language engine
'*************************************************
Option Explicit

Dim txt

' Get the version of the language engine.
txt = "Language Engine: " & ScriptEngine() & vbCrLf
txt = txt & "Version: " & ScriptEngineMajorVersion()
txt = txt & "." + CStr(ScriptEngineMinorVersion()) & vbCrLf
txt = txt & "Build: " + CStr(ScriptEngineBuildVersion())

WScript.Echo txt

'*** End
```

Listing 7-3 *Engine.vbs*

Figure 7-2 WScript *language engine properties*

Retrieving language engine properties in JScript

Listing 7-4 uses JScript to retrieve the properties of the language engine.

```
//*************************************************
// File:    Engine.js (WSH sample in JScript)
// Author:  (c) G. Born
//
// Displaying the version of the language engine
//*************************************************

var txt = "Language Engine: " + ScriptEngine() + "\n" +
          "Version: " + ScriptEngineMajorVersion() +
          "." + ScriptEngineMinorVersion() + "\n" +
          "Build: " + ScriptEngineBuildVersion();

WScript.Echo(txt);

//*** End
```

Listing 7-4 *Engine.js*

Accessing Script Arguments

In Chapter 1, I explained some techniques for submitting arguments such as filenames or switches to a script. (See the section "Submitting Arguments to a Script" on page 14.) You access these arguments within the script. Chapter 1 showed a script for displaying submitted arguments but didn't go into the details. Let's look at the details now.

You can use the *WshArguments* object in WSH to handle script arguments. Table 7-2 describes the properties associated with the *WshArguments* object.

Table 7-2 PROPERTIES OF THE *WSHARGUMENTS* OBJECT

Property	*Description*
Count	Returns the number of command line arguments
Item	Default property that defines the *n*th argument on the command line, which is used to call the script
Length	Returns the number of arguments and is used for JScript compatibility

How do you access these properties? Unfortunately, the *WshArguments* object is not exposed directly. You must use the *Arguments* property of the *WScript* object to access the script arguments. We'll look at the steps for VBScript.

The following statement assigns the *Arguments* property of the *WScript* object to the object variable *objArgs*:

```
Set objArgs = WScript.Arguments
```

The *Set* keyword is required because the property is a collection object, so *objArgs* must be an object variable. You can use *objArgs* to access the objects and their properties in this collection. You can access the first object of the collection by using the following statement:

```
Arg1 = objArgs(0)
```

In this case, the variable *Arg1* receives the content of the default property of the object *objArgs(0)*—the first item of the collection. By the way, until now we've always used an object name and a property name, separated by a dot, to read a property value (as in *WScript.Name*). The preceding statement doesn't follow this scheme because the argument strings are in the *Item* property of the *WshArguments* object, and the *Item* property is the default property. Therefore, the statement above is equivalent to this statement:

```
Arg1 = objArgs.Item(0)
```

Both statements return the script argument stored in the *Item* property as a string into the variable *Arg1*.

But how do you get the number of submitted arguments in a collection? If the script is executed without an argument, the collection in the *Arguments* property is empty. Any attempt to access the object variable *objArgs(0)* causes a run-time error. According to Table 7-2, the *WshArguments* object obtained from the *Arguments* property also exposes the *Count* property, which you can use to check the number of items in the collection, which corresponds to the number of script arguments. Therefore, you can use the following code to access the first script argument:

```
If objArgs.Count >= 1 Then ' Is there at least one argument?
    Arg1 = objArgs.Item(0)
End If
```

If you want to access more than two arguments, this approach can become laborious. To access all script arguments, you should use a loop instead. The following VBScript code gets all arguments into a text variable:

```
For i = 0 To objArgs.Count - 1       ' Loop through all arguments.
    text = text & objArgs(i) & vbCrLf ' Get argument.
Next
```

You can retrieve the number of items in the collection by using *objArgs.Count*. Then you can use a simple *For* loop to process all the items. You can access an item using *objArgs(i)* because *objArgs.Item(i)* is the default property.

Accessing arguments in VBScript: Solution 1

Listing 7-5 uses the approach just described. If arguments are submitted to the script, the arguments are shown in a dialog box that lists each argument on a separate line (as in Figure 7-3). This script retrieves the number of items in the *WshArguments* collection and then uses a simple *For* loop to access each entry in the collection.

Figure 7-3 *Displaying script arguments*

```
'***********************************************
' File:    Args.vbs (WSH sample in VBScript)
' Author:  (c) G. Born
'
' Showing script arguments in a dialog box
'***********************************************
Option Explicit


Dim text, objArgs, i

text = "Arguments" & vbCrLf & vbCrLf

Set objArgs = WScript.Arguments        ' Create object.
For i = 0 To objArgs.Count - 1         ' Loop through all arguments.
    text = text & objArgs(i) & vbCrLf  ' Get argument.
Next

WScript.Echo text ' Show arguments.

'*** End
```

Listing 7-5 *Args.vbs*

You can submit arguments to the script in a shortcut file, the Run dialog box, or the Command Prompt window (as explained in Chapter 1). In WSH 2, you can also drag one or more files to the script file's icon. The dragged objects are submitted as arguments to the script.

NOTE The shortcut file Args_vbs.lnk defines a command line for calling the script with predefined arguments. After copying Args.vbs and Args_vbs.lnk to a local folder, you must set the proper paths in the shortcut file.

Accessing arguments in VBScript: Solution 2

In VBScript, you can use a *For Each…In* loop to enumerate all elements in a collection (or an array); within the loop, you can evaluate each individual element:

```
For Each i In WScript.Arguments ' Loop through all arguments.
    text = text & i & vbCrLf     ' Get argument.
Next
```

The *For Each i In WScript.Arguments* statement processes each element in the collection. The loop index *i* contains the current element. Therefore, you can use the default value of the object *i* to read the script argument. The following code assigns the argument to the variable *Arg1*:

```
Arg1 = i
```

Listing 7-6 demonstrates the use of a *For Each…In* loop to access arguments in VBScript.

```
'**************************************************
' File:    Args1.vbs (WSH sample in VBScript)
' Author:  (c) G. Born
'
' Showing script arguments in a dialog box
'**************************************************
Option Explicit

Dim text, objArgs, i

text = "Arguments" & vbCrLf & vbCrLf

Set objArgs = WScript.Arguments    ' Create object.
For Each i In objArgs              ' Loop through all arguments.
    text = text & i & vbCrLf       ' Get argument.
Next

WScript.Echo text ' Show arguments.

'*** End
```

Listing 7-6 *Args1.vbs*

NOTE The shortcut file Args1_vbs.lnk calls the script with predefined arguments.

Accessing arguments in JScript

In JScript, you can also access arguments by using the *WScript.Arguments* property, but the code used is slightly different. You don't need the *Set* keyword to access the *Arguments* property. JScript automatically creates the data subtype for the requested value. You can thus use the following statement to get the *WshArguments* collection:

```
var objArgs = WScript.Arguments;        // Create object.
```

This statement creates a variable and assigns the object reference. You can then access the items by using the following code:

```
for (var i=0; i < objArgs.Length; i++) // Loop through all arguments.
    text = text + objArgs(i) + '\n';    // Get argument.
```

This code assigns the content of the *Item* property (the default property of the *WshArguments* object) of the current element to the variable *text*. Note that in JScript you must use the *Length* property (instead of *Count*) to determine the number of items in the collection. This property is provided for compatibility purposes because the *Count* property causes a run-time error in JScript.

Listing 7-7 shows the entire script. If you execute this script with arguments, the arguments are shown in a dialog box similar to that in Figure 7-3.

```
//************************************************
// File:    Args.js (WSH sample in JScript)
// Author:  (c) G. Born
//
// Showing script arguments in a dialog box
//************************************************

var objArgs;
var text = "Arguments\n\n";

var objArgs = WScript.Arguments;        // Create object.
for (var i=0; i < objArgs.Length; i++) // Loop through all arguments.
    text = text + objArgs(i) + '\n';    // Get argument.

WScript.Echo(text);  // Show arguments.

//*** End
```

Listing 7-7 *Args.js*

NOTE The shortcut file Args_js.lnk calls the script with predefined arguments.

ACCESSING ENVIRONMENT VARIABLES

Windows 95, Windows 98, Windows NT 4, and Windows 2000 store several kinds of information in environment variables. An environment variable contains a string value. You can display environment variables and their content in the Command Prompt window by using the *Set* command.

Figure 7-4 shows a Command Prompt window containing environment variables on a machine running Windows 2000. If you examine the environment variables on machines running Windows 95 or Windows 98, you'll notice that the variable names differ from those in Windows 2000. Windows 95 and Windows 98 inherited their environment variables from MS-DOS, so you'll find only a few variables, such as *PATH*, *PROMPT*, and *WINDIR*.

Figure 7-4 *Environment variables in Windows 2000*

Windows NT and Windows 2000 use many more environment variables than Windows 95 and Windows 98. In Windows NT and Windows 2000, you can retrieve the operating system name, the number of processors, the platform, and so on.

Accessing Environment Variables in a Script

One use for environment variables is to tell the script what platform (Intel or Alpha) the code is executed on. You can also determine which operating system (Windows 98 or Windows 2000) is being used. But you must be careful because, as just mentioned, Windows 2000 environment variables are different from environment variables in Windows 95 and Windows 98.

How do you access the environment variables in a script? To access environment variables on a particular system, you can use the *Environment* property of the *WshShell* object, which returns the *WshEnvironment* collection object. According to the Windows Script Host Reference, the *Environment* property has the following syntax:

```
object.Environment([strType])
```

The index *strType* specifies the category in which the environment variable resides. In Windows NT and Windows 2000, the operating system groups environment variables internally into the System, User, Volatile, and Process categories, so you can use the *"System"*, *"User"*, *"Volatile"*, or *"Process"* string as the index. In Windows 95 and Windows 98, the method supports only the *"Process"* entry. If you omit the index value, the method retrieves the environment variables from the System category in Windows NT or Windows 2000. In Windows 95 and Windows 98, the method retrieves the Process environment variables because Process is the only category supported.

Table 7-3 describes some of the environment variables the operating system sets. You can use the following statements to access the *Environment* property:

```
Set WshShell = CreateObject("WScript.Shell")
Set objEnv = WshShell.Enviroment("Process")
```

The first line creates a reference to the *WshShell* object and stores it in the object variable *WshShell*. The next statement uses this object variable to access the *Environment* property. The parameter specifies the category in which the environment variables reside. *Environment* returns a collection object, so you must assign the result to an object variable by using the *Set* statement. (The items in the collection are the values of the environment variables in the category.)

This next line retrieves the value of a specific environment variable:

```
Text = objEnv("PATH")
```

This statement requires that *objEnv* contain a collection obtained from the *Environment* property. The index for the *objEnv* object must contain the name of an environment variable. The preceding statement assigns the value of the environment variable *PATH* to the variable *Text*.

Table 7-3   **ENVIRONMENT VARIABLES SET BY THE OPERATING SYSTEM**

Name	Description	Windows NT or Windows 2000 System	Windows NT or Windows 2000 User	Windows NT or Windows 2000 Process	Windows 95 or Windows 98 Process
COMSPEC	Executable for Command Prompt (typically cmd.exe or command.com).	✓		✓	✓
HOMEDRIVE	The primary local drive (typically C:\).			✓	
HOMEPATH	The default directory for users (typically \users\default).			✓	
NUMBER_OF_PROCESSORS	The number of processors running on the machine.	✓		✓	
OS	Operating system on the user's machine.	✓		✓	
PATH	The path.	✓		✓	✓
PATHEXT	Extensions for executable files (typically .com, .exe, .bat, or .cmd).	✓		✓	
PROCESSOR_ARCHITECTURE	The processor type of the user's machine.	✓		✓	
PROCESSOR_IDENTIFIER	The processor ID of the user's machine.	✓		✓	
PROCESSOR_LEVEL	The processor level of the user's machine.	✓		✓	
PROCESSOR_REVISION	The processor version of the user's machine.	✓		✓	

Name	Description	Windows NT or Windows 2000 System	Windows NT or Windows 2000 User	Windows NT or Windows 2000 Process	Windows 95 or Windows 98 Process
PROMPT	Command prompt (typically PG) for MS-DOS.			✓	✓
SYSTEMDRIVE	The local drive on which the system directory resides (C:\, for example).			✓	✓
SYSTEMROOT	The system directory (such as C:\WINNT); the same as WINDIR.			✓	✓
TEMP	Directory for storing temporary files (C:\temp, for example). Available in all Windows versions. In Windows NT, contained in the categories User and Volatile.		✓	✓	✓
TMP	Directory for storing temporary files (C:\temp, for example). Available in all Windows versions. Categories: User and Volatile under Windows NT.		✓	✓	✓
WINDIR	System directory under Windows NT (such as C:\WINNT); same as SYSTEMROOT.	✓			✓

> **NOTE**   For a list of predefined environment variables and a description of their methods and properties, see the Windows Script Host Reference.

Accessing environment variables in VBScript

The program in Listing 7-8 reads system environment variables and a user-defined environment variable and displays their values in a dialog box. (The user-defined variable, *BLASTER*, stores hardware settings for certain sound cards.)

You can execute the script in Windows 95, Windows 98, Windows NT 4, or Windows 2000 (as long as WSH is installed). The environment variables shown will depend on the operating system platform. For example, Windows 98 doesn't recognize the environment variable *OS* (which indicates the operating system platform).

Figure 7-5 shows the dialog box displayed by the script in Windows 2000. Because several environment variables (*OS, BLASTER*) are not defined on this platform, some entries are empty. (Only the variable name is shown.) If you execute this script in Windows 95 or Windows 98, not all entries will contain values.

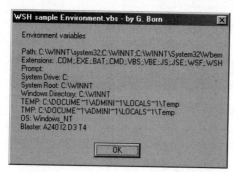

Figure 7-5 *Environment variables retrieved by Environment.vbs*

> **TIP**   You can use the environment variable *OS* to detect the operating system platform. If the environment variable is undefined (an empty string is returned), the script is running in Windows 95 or Windows 98. In Windows NT, you can also test for the platform (*x86* or *Alpha*).

Listing 7-8 accesses environment variables in VBScript.

```
'*****************************************************
' File:     Environment.vbs (WSH sample in VBScript)
' Author:   (c) G. Born
'
' Displaying environment variables by using the
' WshShell object
'*****************************************************
Option Explicit
```

Listing 7-8 *Environment.vbs*

```
Dim Message, Title
Dim WshShell, objEnv

' Get the WshShell object.
Set WshShell = CreateObject("WScript.Shell")

' Get collection by using the Environment property.
Set objEnv = WshShell.Environment("Process")

' Read environment variables.
Message = "Environment variables" & vbCrLf & vbCrLf
Message = Message & "Path: " & objEnv("PATH") & vbCrLf
Message = Message & "Extensions: " & objEnv("PATHEXT") & vbCrLf
Message = Message & "Prompt: " & objEnv("PROMPT") & vbCrLf

Message = Message & "System Drive: " & objEnv("SYSTEMDRIVE") & vbCrLf
Message = Message & "System Root: " & objEnv("SYSTEMROOT") & vbCrLf
Message = Message & "Windows Directory: " & objEnv("WINDIR") & vbCrLf

Message = Message & "TEMP: " & objEnv("TEMP") & vbCrLf
Message = Message & "TMP: " & objEnv("TMP") & vbCrLf

Message = Message & "OS: " & objEnv("OS") & vbCrLf

' Get user-defined environment variable.
Message = Message & "Blaster: " & objEnv("BLASTER") & vbCrLf

' Initialize title text.
Title = "WSH sample " & WScript.ScriptName & " - by G. Born"

MsgBox Message, vbInformation & vbOKOnly, Title

'*** End
```

Accessing environment variables in JScript

The sample in Listing 7-9 reads the same environment variables as the preceding VBScript sample and shows the results in a dialog box. Not all environment variables are defined on every platform.

```
//****************************************************
// File:     Environment.js (WSH sample in JScript)
// Author:   (c) G. Born
//
// Displaying environment variables by using the
// WshShell object
//****************************************************
```

Listing 7-9 *Environment.js*

(continued)

Listing 7-9 *continued*

```
var Message, Title;
var vbInformation = 64;
var vbOKOnly = 0;

// Get WshShell object.
var WshShell = WScript.CreateObject("WScript.Shell");

// Get collection by using the Environment property.
var objEnv = WshShell.Environment("Process");

// Read environment variables.
Message = "Environment variables\n\n";
Message = Message + "Path: " + objEnv("PATH") + "\n";
Message = Message + "Extensions: " + objEnv("PATHEXT") + "\n";
Message = Message + "Prompt: " + objEnv("PROMPT") + "\n";

Message = Message + "System Drive: " + objEnv("SYSTEMDRIVE") + "\n";
Message = Message + "System Root: " + objEnv("SYSTEMROOT") + "\n";
Message = Message + "Windows Directory: " + objEnv("WINDIR") + "\n";

Message = Message + "TEMP: " + objEnv("TEMP") + "\n";
Message = Message + "TMP: " + objEnv("TMP") + "\n";

Message = Message + "OS: " + objEnv("OS") + "\n";

// Get user-defined environment variable.
Message = Message + "Blaster: " + objEnv("BLASTER") + "\n";

// Initialize title text.
Title = "WSH sample " + WScript.ScriptName + " - by G. Born";

WshShell.Popup(Message, vbInformation + vbOKOnly, Title);

//*** End
```

Setting environment variables

In the Command Prompt window, you can set environment variables only for the current process. Environment variables created in the Command Prompt window are volatile—they're lost when you end the session. In Windows 95 and Windows 98, you can set a permanent environment variable by using the *Set* command in the

Autoexec.bat file. In Windows NT and Windows 2000, you must use the Environment Variables dialog box to set the environment variables. (In Control Panel, double-click on the System icon, select the Advanced property page, and click the Environment Variables button.) As a result, you can't create a permanent environment variable in a WSH script. All environment variables that you create are volatile because when you execute a script, Windows creates a copy of the master environment in the address space of the new process. Access to the environment means access to the local copy. If the process terminates, the associated address space is released and the variables are lost.

To demonstrate this temporary nature of environment variables, I've written a small VBScript program, Environment1.vbs, which starts with a dialog box that asks the user whether a new environment variable *BORN* should be created. If the user clicks Yes, the script creates the new environment variable, as shown here:

```
Set WshShell = CreateObject("WScript.Shell")
Set objEnv = WshShell.Environment("Process")
objEnv("BORN") = "Hello. WSH is super!"
```

The first statement creates a reference to the *WshShell* object. The second line accesses the *Environment* property, which contains the collection with all environment variables of the Process category. (Using the Process category assures that this script can also be executed with full results in Windows 95 and Windows 98.) The third statement creates the new environment variable, named *BORN*, and assigns a string to it. If the variable doesn't exist, a new entry is created in the local environment of the WSH process.

The code in Listing 7-10 lists all environment variables found after the new entry is created by rereading the *Environment* property and accessing all entries of the collection by using a *For Each...In* loop.

> **NOTE** If you want to analyze the lifetime of an environment variable, when the Environment1.vbs script asks whether you want to create the new variable and list all environment variables in the environment in a dialog box, click Yes and leave the new dialog box displayed. Start a second copy of the WSH script, and click No to prevent a new variable from being created. The second dialog box won't contain the entry *BORN*, which means that the environment variables created from the first process are local. If you terminate the script and restart it without creating a new environment variable, you'll see a dialog box without the entry *BORN*. This experiment indicates that the lifetime of a variable is coupled with the lifetime of the current process.

```
'*******************************************************
' File:     Environment1.vbs (WSH sample in VBScript)
' Author:   (c) G. Born
'
' Creating an environment variable, reading all
' the environment variables in the Process category,
' and displaying the results in a dialog box
'*******************************************************
Option Explicit

Dim Message, Title
Dim WshShell, objEnv
Dim i, tmp

' Get WshShell object.
Set WshShell = CreateObject("WScript.Shell")

' Get collection by using the Environment property.
Set objEnv = WshShell.Environment("Process")

' Create a (temporary) environment variable.
tmp = MsgBox("Create environment variable BORN?", _
        vbYesNo + vbQuestion, _
        "WSH sample - by G. Born")

If tmp = vbYes Then
    objEnv("BORN") = "Hello. WSH is super!"
End If

' Read environment variables.
Message = "Environment variables" & vbCrLf & vbCrLf

For Each i In objEnv
    Message = Message & i & vbCrLf
Next

' Initialize title text.
Title = "WSH sample " & WScript.ScriptName & " - by G. Born"

MsgBox Message, vbInformation + vbOKOnly, Title

'*** End
```

Listing 7-10 *Environment1.vbs*

NOTE If a script launches a second script using the *Run* method, the environment variables created from the child script can be accessed from the parent script.

Deleting environment variables

The *Environment* object supports a *Remove* method for deleting an environment variable. You can use this method as follows:

```
Set WshShell = WScript.CreateObject("WScript.Shell")
WshShell.Environment("Process").Remove("PATH")
```

This method accesses only the local environment variables of the current process. This means that the environment variable is deleted only within this copy of the environment. All global environment variable settings remain.

Listing 7-11 tests this behavior. In the first step, all environment variables (the original state) are shown in a dialog box. Then a new variable, *BORN*, is added to the environment. The content of all environment variables is shown a second time. In step 3, the script deletes the environment variables *BORN* and *PATH*. The result is shown in a third dialog box. If you start the script again, the environment variable *PATH* remains. A WSH script can't delete an environment variable permanently.

```
'*******************************************************
' File:     Environment2.vbs (WSH sample in VBScript)
' Author:   (c) G. Born
'
' Creating and deleting an environment variable
' in the Process category
'*******************************************************
Option Explicit

Dim Message, Title
Dim WshShell, objEnv
Dim i

' Get WshShell object.
Set WshShell = CreateObject("WScript.Shell")

' Get collection by using the Environment property.
Set objEnv = WshShell.Environment("Process")

' Initialize title text.
Title = "WSH sample " & WScript.ScriptName & " - by G. Born"

' Read environment variables.
Message = "Environment variables (original state)" & vbCrLf & vbCrLf
```

Listing 7-11 *Environment2.vbs*   *(continued)*

Listing 7-11 *continued*

```
For Each i In objEnv
    Message = Message & i & vbCrLf
Next

MsgBox Message, vbInformation + vbOKOnly, Title

' Create a (temporary) environment variable.
objEnv("BORN") = "Hello. WSH is super!"

' Read environment variables.
Message = "Environment variables (extended)" & vbCrLf & vbCrLf

For Each i In objEnv
    Message = Message & i & vbCrLf
Next

MsgBox Message, vbInformation + vbOKOnly, Title

' Delete the environment variables.
objEnv.Remove("BORN")
objEnv.Remove("PATH")

' Read the environment variables.
Message = "Environment variables (after deleting)" & vbCrLf & vbCrLf

For Each i In objEnv
    Message = Message & i & vbCrLf
Next

MsgBox Message, vbInformation & vbOKOnly, Title

'*** End
```

Expanding environment variables by using *ExpandEnvironmentStrings*

There's another technique you can use to retrieve the information stored in environment variables. If you've created MS-DOS batch programs, you probably know how to use the content of an environment variable in a batch command. For example, the following command uses the content of the environment variable *TEXT* to set the path to the editor:

```
%TEXT%\Edit.com %DOCUMENT%
```

The document, which will be loaded, is defined in the environment variable *DOCUMENT*. You can use a similar approach in the Registry in Windows NT or Windows

2000. For example, this Registry entry causes Windows to insert the path to the Windows folder into the placeholder *%WINDIR%*:

```
%WINDIR%\Notepad.exe %1
```

If Windows is installed in the folder C:\WINNT, the command is expanded as follows:

```
C:\WINNT\Notepad.exe %1
```

> **NOTE**   The characters *%1* are a placeholder for the file selected in the shell and have nothing to do with environment variables.

The advantage of using the *%WINDIR%* placeholder is that the command is valid no matter where the user installs the operating system.

As a script programmer, you probably prefer to use certain path definitions to build your commands. But you can't be sure that absolute paths defined in your script will remain valid for a long time and on different machines. For example, if you want to specify the folder in which the user has installed Windows, you can access the environment variable *WINDIR* (in Windows 95 or Windows 98), which is created at system startup and contains the current path to the Windows folder. By using the *WINDIR* environment variable instead of a hard-coded path, your script will always find the Windows directory, even if the path differs from machine to machine.

How can a script access this information about the Windows folder? And how can you use the content of another environment variable within an expression? One approach is to use the methods and properties already mentioned to read the content of the environment variables and then to insert the result into the expression. But before you try this, I'd like to show you a simpler solution.

In Chapter 6, we used the *WshShell* object to access the *Popup* method. This object also exposed other methods. Table 7-4 describes the methods of the *WshShell* object.

Table 7-4 METHODS OF THE *WSHSHELL* OBJECT

Method	Description
CreateShortcut	Creates a *WshShortcut* or *WshURLShortcut* object and returns it
ExpandEnvironmentStrings	Expands a Process environment variable and returns the result string
Popup	Shows a message box containing specified text
RegDelete	Deletes a specified key or value from the Registry
RegRead	Reads a Registry key or value
RegWrite	Sets a Registry key or value
Run	Creates a new process that executes a specified command with a specified window style

The *ExpandEnvironmentStrings* method of the *WshShell* object requests a string as a parameter. If this string contains the name of an environment variable enclosed in % characters, the method expands this name with the content of the variable and returns the expanded string. If you insert the name of an environment variable into a command, you can easily expand the command using this method.

The VBScript sample in Listing 7-12 uses this approach. The script contains the following command, which expands the environment variable *%WINDIR%*:

```
Command = "%WINDIR%\Explorer.exe"    ' Command to be expanded
```

The result is shown in a dialog box. (See Figure 7-6.)

Figure 7-6 *An expanded environment variable*

NOTE   The *Run* method automatically expands all environment variables in the format %...% in a command string.

```
'***********************************************************
' File:    Environment3.vbs (WSH sample in VBScript)
' Author:  (c) G. Born
'
' Using the ExpandEnvironmentStrings method of the
' WshShell object
'***********************************************************
Option Explicit

Dim Command
Dim WshShell

Command = "%WINDIR%\Explorer.exe"    ' Command to be expanded

' Get WshShell object.
Set WshShell = WScript.CreateObject("WScript.Shell")

' Now we can use the ExpandEnvironmentStrings method.
WScript.Echo "Command: " & Command & vbCrLf & _
             "Expanded: " & WshShell.ExpandEnvironmentStrings(Command)

'*** End
```

Listing 7-12 *Environment3.vbs*

In JScript, you can use a similar approach, but you use escape characters to define a command string with \ characters. Thus, the command *%WINDIR%\Explorer.exe* must be written as *%WINDIR%\\Explorer.exe*. After defining the command string, you retrieve a reference to *WshShell* and assign it to an object variable. Then you can use a string containing the environment variable name and pass it to the *Expand-EnvironmentStrings* method, as shown in Listing 7-13.

```
//***************************************************
// File:     Environment3.js (WSH sample in JScript)
// Author:   (c) G. Born
//
// Using the ExpandEnvironmentStrings method of the
// WshShell object
//***************************************************

var Command = "%WINDIR%\\Explorer.exe";   // Command to be expanded

// Get WshShell object.
var WshShell = WScript.CreateObject("WScript.Shell");

// Now we can use the ExpandEnvironmentStrings method.
WScript.Echo("Command:  " + Command,
        "\nExpanded: " + WshShell.ExpandEnvironmentStrings(Command));

//*** End
```

Listing 7-13 *Environment3.js*

CREATING AND RELEASING OBJECTS

If an object isn't exposed automatically from WSH (as is the case with *WScript*), you must "create" the object before using it—that is, you must load an instance of the object into memory and assign a reference to it to an object variable. The following statement uses the *CreateObject* method in VBScript to create an object:

```
Set Object_variable = WScript.CreateObject("ProgID")
```

JScript uses the following syntax:

```
var Object_variable = WScript.CreateObject("ProgID");
```

The only object variable that WSH exposes automatically is *WScript*. You must create all other objects explicitly. In VBScript, you create the object variable (which is used to keep the object) by using the *Set* keyword. You can use any valid name for the object variable (such as *objAdr* or *WshObj*).

To create the *WshShell* object, you can use the following statement in VBScript:

```
Set WshShell = WScript.CreateObject("WScript.Shell")
```

A JScript statement has the same syntax except that the keyword *Set* is replaced by *var* and the line terminates with a semicolon. Let's look again at the statements shown at the beginning of this section. *WScript.CreateObject* tells the language engine that you want to create an object and get a reference to it. You pass the ProgID within parentheses as a parameter to *CreateObject*. This ProgID identifies the object. In the statement above, the ProgID for the *WshShell* object is *"WScript.Shell"*.

> **NOTE**   The hardest part of this process is getting the ProgID for an object. The examples in this book include the requested ProgIDs. You have to get the ProgIDs of foreign objects from their program documentation. If the documentation is missing, you can use tools such as the OLE/COM Object Viewer to determine an object's ProgID. The Object Browser of the Microsoft Visual Basic 5 Control Creation Edition (CCE) and Microsoft Office also give you the ProgID of a component. My book *Advanced Development with Microsoft Windows Script Host 2.0* discusses these more advanced ways to obtain an object's ProgID.

The preceding statement contains the word *WScript* twice, which might confuse you. The term *WScript* in *WScript.CreateObject* is an object; the word *WScript* in the parameter *"WScript.Shell"* is the ProgID of the object library.

> **NOTE**   When you use the *CreateObject* method, you must be careful about the object hierarchy. In Chapter 6, I mentioned that objects can contain other objects. The dependencies are described within the object model. For example, an application such as Microsoft Word can contain a document. To access the document object, you use the *CreateObject* method on the application object and then on the document object. Keep in mind that using *CreateObject* is only one way to create an object. You'll learn about other ways later in this book.

THE *CREATEOBJECT* METHOD AND TYPE LIBRARIES

When you use the *CreateObject* method, you enlist the help of Microsoft's Component Object Model (COM) technology. The idea behind COM is that all functionality is provided by objects within the system in the form of *interfaces*, which are collections of related functions. Information about these objects and their interfaces is stored in type libraries. Type libraries are either stand-alone files (.tlb files) or part of the file that contains the executable code for the object.

To use the *CreateObject* method, you must describe precisely where the object and its interface description can be found. Theoretically, you'd have to specify a drive and a path to the library files as an argument for *CreateObject*. But any change in the path would cause an error in the *CreateObject* method. Microsoft chose a smarter solution: information about an object library is stored in the Registry. In Chapter 2, you learned how a user can register such a library by using RegSvr32.exe. During registration, the installation program deposits all information about the objects in the library into the Windows Registry. If you use the OLE/COM Object Viewer, for example, you'll get the ProgID (and the path to the object server).

To create an object, you can use the *CreateObject* method and pass its ProgID as a parameter. This ProgID has two parts, as shown here:

```
TypeLibName.ClassName
```

The name of the type library comes before the dot. In the previous samples, we used the *WScript* type library. Other type libraries are provided in Word (*Word*), Microsoft Excel (*Excel*), or ActiveX components. The type library contains the elements that you can use from external applications. These elements are registered under a name in classes or subclasses. The *WScript* type library, for example, contains the *Shell* class. To create an instance of the *Shell* class, therefore, the parameter for the *CreateObject* method must be *"WScript.Shell"*. To access Excel, you use *"Excel.Application"*. To access Internet Explorer, you set the parameter to *"InternetExplorer.Application"*.

When the interpreter executes the *CreateObject* method, the ProgID is used to get the path to the library files from the Registry entries. Then the object instance (as a part of a library) is loaded into memory (the working space of the process) and the outgoing interface of the object is linked to the script. These steps are executed behind the scenes and are invisible to the user. The programmer must know only that the *CreateObject* method creates an object and stores the reference to the given object into the object variable specified in the statement. You can use this object variable to access the methods and properties of the object. You can also use this object variable in subsequent *CreateObject* calls to access subobjects.

CreateObject vs. *GetObject*

The *WScript* object exposes two methods for creating a new object reference: *CreateObject* and *GetObject*. *CreateObject* creates an object and establishes its event handling, and *GetObject* retrieves an Automation object from a file. What, exactly, is the difference between these two methods?

The *CreateObject* method creates the object specified in the *strProgID* parameter. You already saw a simple version of a *CreateObject* call that uses only one parameter. The *CreateObject* method also has a second, optional parameter, as shown here:

```
Set objAdr = WScript.CreateObject(strProgID[, strPrefix])
```

The first parameter contains the object's ProgID ("*WScript.Shell*", for example). The optional parameter *strPrefix* can contain a prefix string. If this parameter is specified, the method connects the script to the outgoing interface of the object after creating this object. This connection allows you to use event handling using callback functions declared within the script. For example, if *strPrefix* is set to "*Test_*" and the object fires an event named *OnBegin*, WSH calls the function *Test_OnBegin* in the script. (Listing 7-14 uses this method.) I'll discuss this technique in detail in Chapter 9.

You can also access objects by using the *GetObject* method, which retrieves an Automation object from a file or an object specified by the *strProgID* parameter. You use the *GetObject* method when there's a current instance of the object or when you want to create the object from a file that's already loaded. If there's no current instance and you don't want the object started from a file that's already loaded, use the *CreateObject* method instead.

The *GetObject* method has this syntax (which is similar to that of *CreateObject*):

```
Set objAdr = WScript.GetObject(strPathname[, [strProgID][, strPrefix]])
```

The *strPathname* parameter specifies the path to the file containing the Automation object. The optional parameter *strProgID* contains a string with the object's ProgID so that the method can load the object using Registry entries. The third parameter connects the script to the object's outgoing interface. The second and third parameters have the same meaning as the corresponding parameters of the *CreateObject* method.

Using *DisconnectObject*

When you create an object using *GetObject* or *CreateObject*, the object is loaded into memory and remains connected to WSH until the script terminates. The script can use the second optional parameter in *CreateObject* to connect a script's event handler to the outgoing interface of this object. Then the object can raise an event that is handled from an event handler within the script. You can use the *DisconnectObject* method to disconnect the object from the event handling procedure during the script's lifetime:

```
WScript.DisconnectObject Object_name
```

Object_name is the name of an object variable. In VBScript, you can also reset the object variable:

```
Object_name = Nothing
```

NATIVE METHODS FOR CREATING OBJECTS

In addition to the *CreateObject* method provided by the *WScript* object, VBScript and JScript support native methods for creating objects. The following code uses the native VBScript method to connect an object to the script:

```
Dim oIE
Set oIE = CreateObject("InternetExplorer.Application")
```

The second line doesn't contain the *WScript* object name; it uses the native *CreateObject* method of VBScript. The statement creates a reference to the Internet Explorer *Application* object. (I'll talk about using Internet Explorer objects in detail later in this book.)

JScript also has a native method for creating an object reference:

```
var oIE = new ActiveXObject("InternetExplorer.Application");
```

The JScript *new* method is applied to the *ActiveXObject* object to create a new object instance and assign a reference to the object variable *oIE*.

You can use either the native method or the *WScript.CreateObject* method to assign the reference to the object variable. But keep in mind that the *CreateObject* method provided from the *WScript* object supports an additional parameter that allows you to establish event handling from your script—behavior that isn't available in the native methods.

Listing 7-14 uses this method. It launches Internet Explorer with an empty page and establishes event handling for Internet Explorer's *DownloadBegin* and *OnQuit* events. Because of the *DisconnectObject* call, the *IE_OnQuit* event handler procedure is never called. If you comment this line, the sample raises a dialog box after calling *oIE.Quit*.

```
'*****************************************************
' File:    Disconnect.vbs (WSH sample in VBScript)
' Author:  (c) G. Born
'
' Using the DisconnectObject method to disconnect
' from Internet Explorer event handling
'*****************************************************
Option Explicit

Dim oIE
```

Listing 7-14 *Disconnect.vbs*   *(continued)*

Listing 7-14 *continued*

```
' Launch Internet Explorer, and define event-handler prefix.
Set oIE = WScript.CreateObject( _
          "InternetExplorer.Application", "IE_")
oIE.navigate "about:blank"        ' Empty page
oIE.visible = 1                   ' Visible

' Pause script by displaying a message box.
WScript.Echo "Please click OK"

WScript.DisconnectObject oIE  ' Disconnect from Internet Explorer.

oIE.Quit                      ' Terminate Internet Explorer.

WScript.Echo "Disconnected"

' Script terminates here.

'*************************************************
' Here are the Internet Explorer event handlers.
'*************************************************

Sub IE_DownloadBegin()
    ' Raised from loading a document in Internet Explorer
    WScript.Echo "Event: Download begins"
End Sub

Sub IE_OnQuit()
    ' Raised from quitting Internet Explorer, but we're
    ' disconnecting from the object before calling
    ' the Quit method to terminate Internet Explorer, so
    ' the dialog box isn't shown.
    WScript.Echo "Event: Quit Internet Explorer"
End Sub

'*** End
```

LAUNCHING OTHER PROGRAMS FROM A SCRIPT

To launch another application from a WSH script, you must use the *Run* method provided by the *WshShell* object. The *Run* method creates a new process and executes the command contained in the *strCommand* parameter. You can use a second parameter, *intWindowStyle*, to specify the window style. The method has the following syntax:

```
WshShell.Run(strCommand[, [intWindowStyle][, bWaitOnReturn]])
```

The parameter *strCommand* is required because it contains the path and the name of the application or the command to be executed.

> **NOTE**   At this point, I should mention two things. First, remember that a path containing blanks must be enclosed in double quotes, such as "C:\Test Folder\MyApp.exe". Otherwise, the *Run* method raises a run-time error, "The system cannot find the file specified." I described this behavior in Chapter 1, and a little later in this chapter, you'll also see a VBScript sample that demonstrates how to enclose a path with double quotes. Second, keep in mind that the *Run* method automatically expands environment variable names contained in the parameter *strCommand*.

The following sequence causes the script to expand the environment variable *%WINDIR%* contained in *Command* and launches the Windows program Calc.exe:

```
Set WshShell = WScript.CreateObject("WScript.Shell")
Command = "%WINDIR%\Calc.exe"
WshShell.Run Command
```

> **NOTE**   Here I need to caution you about using the *%WINDIR%* environment variable: *%WINDIR%* returns the right path to the Windows folder, but not all applications are located in this folder. The preceding command works just fine for Windows 95 and Windows 98, but it fails in Windows NT and Windows 2000 because Calc.exe is located in the subfolder \System32. Therefore, it's better to omit the *%WINDIR%* environment variable in all commands launching Windows system applications (such as Calc) that locate the executable in either the Windows folder or the Windows system folder, depending on the Windows platform. In this case, Windows searches the Windows folder and the default system folder (which is \System for Windows 95 and Windows 98 and \System32 for Windows NT and Windows 2000).

The other two optional parameters control how the application window is displayed and whether the script should wait until the executed process terminates. The parameter *intWindowStyle* is an optional parameter that specifies the window style of the new process. The parameter can contain an integer between 0 and 10. If the parameter *intWindowStyle* is omitted, the window gets the focus and is shown in normal mode. Table 7-5 shows the values of *intWindowStyle*.

Table 7-5 VALUES OF THE *intWindowStyle* PARAMETER

Value	Visual Basic Constant	Description
0	*vbHide*	Hides the window. Another window is activated (is shown and gets the focus).
1	*vbNormalFocus*	Activates the window and shows it. If the process is already active and the window is minimized or maximized, the previous size and position are restored.
2	*vbMinimizedFocus*	Activates the window and minimizes it. The button on the taskbar receives the focus.
3	*vbMaximizedFocus*	Activates the window, maximizes it, and gives it the focus.
4	*vbNormalNoFocus*	Displays a window in its most recent size and position. The active window remains active.
5		Activates the window in its current size and position.
6	*vbMinimizedNoFocus*	Minimizes the window and activates the next top-level window in the z-order.
7		Displays the window as an icon (minimized). The active window remains active.
8		Displays the window in its current state. The active window remains active.
9		Activates and displays the window. If a window is minimized or maximized, Windows restores the original size and position. An application should specify this flag when restoring a minimized window. (This parameter can't be used with the *Run* method.)
10		Sets the show state based on the state of the program that started the application.

The values in Table 7-5 imply that you can use the *Run* method either to call up an instance of an application or to switch an already running application in the foreground. Unfortunately, the *Run* method always creates a new instance of the process. You can't reactivate a window of a running application or minimize or maximize it. Therefore, you can't use all the values shown in the table. I also found that the window styles work only with applications that support those styles. Notepad accepts the styles, but Calculator causes trouble because the window can't be maximized. Keep in mind that Table 7-5 shows the named constants defined by Visual Basic for the window styles. In WSH scripts, you must use the numeric constants because the named constants aren't defined in VBScript or JScript.

The optional *Run* parameter *bWaitOnReturn* is of subtype *Boolean*. (It can contain the values *True* and *False*.) The parameter controls whether the script waits for the termination of the executed process. If *bWaitOnReturn* is missing or is set to *False*, the *Run* method executes the command and returns immediately. If *bWaitOnReturn* is set to *True*, the *Run* method creates a new process, executes the command, and waits until the process terminates. In this case, the *Run* method returns the error code obtained from the terminated process. If *bWaitOnReturn* is missing or is set to *False*, *Run* returns the error code 0.

NOTE You can set the error code in a script by using the *Quit* method (as explained shortly).

Launching Notepad from VBScript

Let's create a few small scripts. Notepad supports the window styles listed in Table 7-5. The script in Listing 7-15 launches Notepad from VBScript. In a second step, the script launches Notepad again and minimizes Notepad's window (to a button on the taskbar). As part of the command, Notepad should load the source code of the currently executing script.

```
'*************************************************
' File:    Run.vbs (WSH sample in VBScript)
' Author:  (c) G. Born
'
' Launching Notepad using the Run method
'*************************************************
Option Explicit

Dim WshShell

Set WshShell = WScript.CreateObject("WScript.Shell")

WshShell.Run "Notepad.exe", 1

WScript.Echo "Load source code in a minimized window"

WshShell.Run "Notepad.exe " & WScript.ScriptFullName, 6

'*** End
```

Listing 7-15 *Run.vbs*

Launching Calculator from JScript

The JScript sample in Listing 7-16 launches the Calculator program. The script needs some named constants, which I've declared as variables in the program's header. But Calculator doesn't support all window styles, so the style to minimize the window is ignored. Note also that the location of Calc.exe depends on the operating system, so using the environment variable *%WINDIR%* isn't a good idea. If you port a VBScript sample to JScript, you must be careful about the different syntax—you must put the parameters for the *Run* method in parentheses, and you must use \\ within paths to separate folder names because JScript interprets \ as an escape sequence.

```
//*************************************************
// File:      Run.js (WSH sample in JScript)
// Author:    (c) G. Born
//
// Launching Calculator using Run.
// Attention: The Run method doesn't support
// all window styles!
//*************************************************

var SW_SHOWNORMAL = 1;
var SW_MINIMIZE = 6;

// Define command to invoke Calc.exe.
// Attention: Don't use %WINDIR%\\Calc.exe because Windows NT
// and Windows 2000 store Calc.exe in %WINDIR%\\System32,
// and Windows 95 and Windows 98 keep the program in the
// Windows folder.
var command = "Calc.exe"

var WshShell = WScript.CreateObject("WScript.Shell");

// First try
WshShell.Run(command, SW_SHOWNORMAL);

WScript.Echo("Launching Calculator minimized");

// Shouldn't work. Calculator is still maximized!
WshShell.Run(command, SW_MINIMIZE);

//*** End
```

Listing 7-16 *Run.js*

Paths Containing Blanks

Earlier in this chapter, I mentioned that the *Run* method fails to call an application located in a folder that has blanks in its path. If a path contains blanks, you need to enclose it in double quotes. Let's do a small experiment. Copy an existing script program (for example, Run.vbs from Listing 7-15) into a folder named C:\Test Folder, and rename the file to Test.vbs. Then try to execute the VBScript program in Listing 7-17. The program uses the *Run* method to launch a file with the name Test.vbs.

```
'*****************************************************
' File:    RunTest.vbs (WSH sample in VBScript)
' Author:  (c) G. Born
'
' Using the Run method with a path containing blanks
'*****************************************************
Option Explicit

' Define a path containing a blank.
Const command = "C:\Test Folder\Test.vbs"

Dim WshShell

' Create WshShell object.
Set WshShell = WScript.CreateObject("WScript.Shell")

' Enable run-time error handling in Script.
On Error Resume Next

' First try the test without double quotes.
WshShell.Run command, 1, True

' A run-time error occurs.
If Err <> 0 Then _
    If Err = -2147024894 Then _
        WScript.Echo "Calling '" & command, vbCrLf & _
                     "Error: The system cannot find the file specified"
On Error Goto 0     ' No more run-time error handling

' For the second test, enclose pathname in double quotes.
WshShell.Run """" & command & """", 1, True

WScript.Echo "Ready"

'*** End
```

Listing 7-17 *RunTest.vbs*

The parent script tries to execute Test.vbs twice. The first call fails, prompting a dialog box showing a message that the file couldn't be located (because the path isn't enclosed in double quotes). The second attempt to call the child script succeeds. The line demonstrates how to enclose a variable value in VBScript in double quotes. You need something like """" & name & """" to set the double quotes. The outer double quotes "..." in the expression """" define a valid string. The two inner double quote characters "" force VBScript to insert one " into the string.

The *Quit* Method

The *Quit* method terminates the *WScript* object (and thus terminates the script). In a JScript script, you can call this method by using the following statement:

```
WScript.Quit();
```

In VBScript, this is the equivalent statement:

```
WScript.Quit
```

The object name is followed by a dot and then the name of the method. Both statements use the *WScript* object, which causes the script to terminate.

Quit accepts an optional parameter, which in JScript must be set in parentheses following the method's name. The JScript sample shown doesn't pass parameters to the *Quit* method; the parentheses in the statement are empty.

The parameter used in the *Quit* method defines the process exit code. If no value is passed, WSH returns the value 0 to the operating system. Alternatively, you can insert an integer value (such as 0 or 1) as a parameter to indicate to the operating system whether the process terminates with an error. The value 0 indicates that the process terminates regularly. All positive values indicate an error that causes the process to terminate. Windows doesn't check this code, but you can check the termination code yourself—for example, by using the host CScript.exe to execute the script in the Command Prompt window. You can check the error code by using the *ERRORLEVEL* function in a batch program. Or you can use the *Run* method as described in the next section to get the exit code.

> **NOTE** You don't have to insert the *Quit* statement before the script's end. When the language engine reaches the last line of a script, the process terminates automatically. You can use the *Quit* method to terminate a script at a specified point, however.

Waiting for process termination and checking the exit code

The sample code in Listing 7-18 launches an external application and waits until the process terminates. If the process returns an error code as it terminates, the parent script examines the process exit code (which is shown in a dialog box).

```
'***************************************************
' File:    Test.vbs (WSH sample in VBScript)
' Author:  (c) G. Born
'
' Returning an error code
'***************************************************
Option Explicit

WScript.Echo "Test script", vbCrLf, _
             "We return error code 2"


WScript.Quit 2

'*** End
```

Listing 7-18 *Test.vbs*

We still need the parent script to execute Test.vbs. Listing 7-19 does this. The script waits until the child process terminates, and then it reads the termination code and displays it in a dialog box.

Before we look at Run1.vbs, I'd like to make a few remarks about the *GetPath* function. The parent script must know the path in order to execute the child script Test.vbs. We'll assume that Test.vbs is stored in the same folder as Run1.vbs, so we can use the *WScript.ScriptFullName* property to determine its path. The function *GetPath* reads the *ScriptFullName* property, removes the filename from the path, and returns the path. The filename of the second script, Test.vbs, is appended to the path, and the resulting command string is used to execute the script.

The Run1.vbs sample also demonstrates how you can call up a script from a second script and how to exchange simple information such as an error code (a value between 0 and 255) between a child and a parent script.

NOTE You can pass information from the parent script to the child script by using script arguments. You insert the arguments into the command to be executed. The child script must read the script arguments to obtain the information.

Setting the third parameter in the *Run* method to *True* creates a new process and executes the command given in the first parameter in the address space of the new process. The script then waits until the new process terminates. The *Run* method returns the process exit code of the new process:

```
ErrCode = WshShell.Run(name, 1, True)
```

You can then use the content of *ErrCode* to check the error code.

```
'************************************************************
' File:    Run1.vbs (WSH sample in VBScript)
' Author:  (c) G. Born
'
' Launching a script as a second process, waiting for the
' return code, and showing the value in a dialog box
'************************************************************
Option Explicit

Dim WshShell, name, ErrCode

' We need this object for the Run method.
Set WshShell = WScript.CreateObject("WScript.Shell")

' Now we get the path to the executable program.
' The second script must be in the same folder
' as Run1.vbs.
name = """" & GetPath & "Test.vbs" & """"

ErrCode = WshShell.Run(name, 1, True)    ' Just wait!

WScript.Echo "Error code received: ", ErrCode ' Show error code.

Function GetPath
    ' This function determines the path of the current script.
    ' Read the path and remove the script filename, and then return
    ' the result of the requested path.
    Dim path
    path = WScript.ScriptFullName  ' Script name
    GetPath = Left(path, InStrRev(path, "\"))
End Function

'*** End
```

Listing 7-19 *Run1.vbs*

When *bWaitOnReturn* fails

You can set *bWaitOnReturn* to *True* to pause your script until the launched process terminates. This feature fails, however, if you try to use it with the program Explorer.exe. Listing 7-20 demonstrates this behavior.

```
'*************************************************
' File:    Run2.vbs (WSH sample in VBScript)
' Author:  (c) G. Born
'
' Launching Calculator using the Run method,
' waiting until the Calculator is closed, and then
' trying to do the same with Windows Explorer
'*************************************************
Option Explicit

Const command1 = "Calc.exe"
Const command2 = "Explorer.exe"

Dim WshShell

Set WshShell = WScript.CreateObject("WScript.Shell")

WScript.Echo "Launch Calculator and pause script", vbCrLf & _
             "until Calculator terminates"

WshShell.Run command1, 1, True    ' Wait until app is closed.

WScript.Echo command1, "closed", vbCrLf, vbCrLf & _
             "Launch Explorer and try to pause the script", _
             vbCrLf & "until the Explorer window terminates"

WshShell.Run command2, 1, True    ' Won't work

WScript.Echo "The Explorer window is still open, " & _
             "so bWaitOnReturn doesn't work"

'*** End
```

Listing 7-20 *Run2.vbs*

The script in Listing 7-20 shows an introductory dialog box that must be closed. It then launches Calculator and pauses until the user closes the Calculator window. Obviously, the *bWaitOnReturn* parameter works. The script then tries to do the same with Windows Explorer. The following command launches Explorer, but the script doesn't pause:

```
WshShell.Run command2, 1, True
```

Instead, the next dialog box appears. At first glance, this behavior looks like a bug, but in fact it is by design. Explorer.exe is part of the Windows shell, and the shell is already running (as the desktop folder, for example). Therefore, only a new instance of the shell is used to show the Explorer window. And in this case, no new process is executed using *Run*, so *bWaitOnReturn* fails.

Using the *Run* Method to Execute MS-DOS Commands

You can execute an MS-DOS command from a script by using the *Run* method, just as you execute Windows applications. For example, in Windows 95 and Windows 98, you can use the following JScript command:

```
WshShell.Run("Edit.com");
```

This statement opens the window of the MS-DOS Editor. If you append the name of a document file to the command, the document is loaded in the editor window.

Because the path is missing, Windows searches the directories in the *PATH* environment variable for the program file.

> **TIP**   To set the properties of an MS-DOS program in Windows 95 and Windows 98, you create a .pif file. Right-click on the program file, choose Properties from the shortcut menu, select the Program property page, and set the properties on this page. After you close the page by clicking the OK button, Windows creates a .pif file containing the program's MS-DOS properties. The file has the same name as the program and the (hidden) filename extension .pif, and it's stored in the program's folder. When the application starts, Windows loads the .pif file and sets the new properties for the MS-DOS session in the Command Prompt window.

Let's get back to executing an MS-DOS command from a script. Can you use the *Run* method, as shown here?

```
WshShell.Run "Dir C:\"
```

This statement won't work because there's no program file named Dir.com or Dir.exe. The *Run* method requests an executable file (a file with an .exe, .com, .bat, or .pif extension). In Windows 95 and Windows 98, internal MS-DOS commands such as *Dir*, *Copy*, and *Rename* are stored in the MS-DOS command processor Command.com (unlike external commands such as *Edit.com*). Command.com is in the Windows folder. Windows NT uses cmd.exe as the command processor for MS-DOS commands. To execute an internal MS-DOS command, you execute the command processor and pass the internal MS-DOS command to the command processor. (The command is executed in the Command Prompt window.)

In Windows 95 and Windows 98, you can write a command to display the folder as follows:

```
C:\Windows\Command.com /k dir *.*
```

This statement assumes that Windows is installed in the C:\Windows folder. The switch /*k* is important because it tells the command processor not to close the MS-DOS window. If you want to close the MS-DOS window automatically after termination, you must use the switch /*c* instead.

> **TIP** If you type the command *Command.com* /? on the command line, you get a list of all options supported in Command.com.

The command shown on the preceding page causes two problems, however. First, you should make the statement independent of the Windows installation folder, which you could do by using the environment variable *%WINDIR%* instead of C:\Windows. But there's a second issue as well. Windows 95 and Windows 98 use Command.com as the command processor, and Windows NT and Windows 2000 use Cmd.exe. These command processors are also in different locations. To ensure that the script runs on all platforms, you can insert the environment variable *%COMSPEC%* into the command, as shown below. This environment variable contains the command processor and its location. It therefore ensures that the command string always contains the correct command processor.

```
command = "%COMSPEC% /k ";
```

The variable *dos_command* is used to store the MS-DOS command, and you can use the variable *option* to append options to the MS-DOS command. In the sample code in Listing 7-21, I inserted the | character and the *more* command into *option* to use the MS-DOS filter. This combination causes the MS-DOS command processor to redirect the *Dir* output to the *more* filter. This filter shows the results page by page.

> **TIP** You can use the > character in a similar way as | to redirect the output of the *Dir* command to a printer (to print the content of a directory, for example) or into a file.

```
//*****************************************************
// File:    RunDOS.js (WSH sample in JScript)
// Author:  (c) G. Born
//
// Executing an MS-DOS command using the Run method
//*****************************************************

var command, dos_command, option

// Get WshShell object.
var WshShell = WScript.CreateObject("WScript.Shell");

// Create a command to show the contents of
// the Windows folder.
```

Listing 7-21 *RunDOS.js*   *(continued)*

Listing 7-21 *continued*

```
// Subcommand to call the command processor
// Tip: Using the environment variable %COMSPEC% ensures that
// the script runs in Windows 95 and Windows 98 and in Windows NT
// and Windows 2000 because %COMSPEC% contains the name and path
// of the command processor.
command = "%COMSPEC% /k ";

// Here comes the MS-DOS command.
dos_command = "dir " + "%WINDIR%";

// You can append other options:
// | more      forces a page-oriented display
// > PRN:      redirection to printer
// > Dir.txt  redirection into file
//
option = "| more";   // Use page-oriented display.

// Execute command.
WshShell.Run(command + dos_command + option);

//*** End
```

Chapter 8

Retrieving User Input in WSH Scripts

In Chapter 6, I introduced a few techniques for creating simple user dialog boxes. In this chapter, I'll describe several ways to invoke a dialog box for gathering user input in Microsoft Windows Script Host (WSH) scripts. VBScript supports the *InputBox* function to invoke an input dialog box, but WSH and JScript don't support such a function, so you have to be creative to get the same kind of input dialog box.

INVOKING AN INPUT DIALOG BOX IN VBSCRIPT

VBScript supports the *InputBox* function to invoke an input dialog box. The function has the following syntax:

```
result = InputBox(prompt[, [title], [default], [xpos], [ypos]])
```

The dialog box has a message, title bar text, and a simple text box, as shown in Figure 8-1. The user can enter text in the text box and click either of the command buttons.

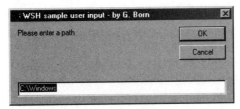

Figure 8-1 *An input dialog box created using the* InputBox *function*

The *InputBox* function has the following parameters:

- **prompt** A required parameter that defines the message shown in the dialog box. In Figure 8-1, this is the string Please Enter A Path.

- **title** An optional parameter that defines the title bar text for the dialog box.

- **default** An optional parameter that specifies the default value shown in the text box.

- **xpos** and **ypos** Optional parameters that define the position of the upper left corner of the dialog box.

NOTE *InputBox* supports a sixth (*helpfile*) and seventh (*context*) parameter. Both parameters are optional and can be used to connect a help file (in .hlp format) to an input dialog box. Because creating custom help files is beyond the scope of this book, I omitted those parameters.

If an optional parameter is omitted, VBScript uses a default value. To omit an optional parameter between other parameters, you must use a pair of empty commas, as shown here:

```
InputBox("Hello", "Test", , 100, 200)
```

The *InputBox* function has no *buttons* parameter (as *MsgBox* does). When the user closes the dialog box, *InputBox* returns a result value that depends on the button the user clicked to close the dialog box. The OK button returns the content of the text box (the user input). The Cancel button aborts the dialog box and returns an empty string. You can use the *result* value to check whether the user input is valid.

The following code sequence checks the *result* value and uses an *If* statement to show the result:

```
If result = "" Then    ' Test for Cancel.
    WScript.Echo "Canceled"
Else
    WScript.Echo "You entered: " & result
End If
```

The VBScript program shown in Listing 8-1 displays an input dialog box containing a text box with a default value, which the user can change. After the user closes the dialog box, the script displays a second dialog box showing the result (Figure 8-2, left) or a cancellation message (Figure 8-2, right).

Figure 8-2 *User input retrieved using* InputBox

The text shown in the dialog box is declared in the script's header using global variables. Storing the text in variables keeps the *InputBox* function call as simple as possible. Input.vbs also uses the VBScript constant *vbCrLf* to split the output string onto two lines. (Like the other samples shown in this chapter, Input.vbs is in the \WSHDevGuide\Chapter08 folder on the book's companion CD.)

```
'************************************************
' File:    Input.vbs (WSH sample in VBScript)
' Author:  (c) G. Born
'
' Retrieving user input in VBScript
'************************************************
Option Explicit

Dim Message, result
Dim Title, Text1, Text2

' Define dialog box variables.
Message = "Please enter a path"
Title = "WSH sample user input - by G. Born"
Text1 = "User input canceled"
Text2 = "You entered:" & vbCrLf

' Ready to use the InputBox function
' InputBox(prompt, title, default, xpos, ypos)
' prompt:    The text shown in the dialog box
' title:     The title of the dialog box
' default:   Default value shown in the text box
' xpos/ypos: Upper left position of the dialog box
' If a parameter is omitted, VBScript uses a default value.

result = InputBox(Message, Title, "C:\Windows", 100, 100)

' Evaluate the user input.
If result = "" Then     ' Canceled by the user
    WScript.Echo Text1
Else
    WScript.Echo Text2 & result
End If

'*** End
```

Listing 8-1 *Input.vbs*

INVOKING AN INPUT DIALOG BOX IN JSCRIPT

JScript doesn't support the VBScript *InputBox* function, and WSH doesn't provide a method for user input. For example, you can't use a command such as the following, which you might recognize from HTML scripts:

```
var txt = window.prompt("WSH sample ", "Name: ");
```

You can't use this command because WSH doesn't provide a *window* object or a *prompt* method. To overcome these limitations, you can use the solutions described in the following sections.

A WSH 2 Solution: Combining VBScript and JScript

In WSH 2, you can combine multiple scripts in a single .wsf file. If JScript doesn't support a particular function but VBScript does, you can combine the two languages in one .wsf file. For example, you can write a user-defined VBScript function to expose the *InputBox* function to a JScript script program that's included in the .wsf file, as shown here:

```
Function WSHInputBox(Message, Title, Value)
    ' Provides an InputBox function for JScript
    ' Can be called from JScript as:
    ' var result = WSHInputBox("Enter a name", "Input", test);
    WSHInputBox = InputBox(Message, Title, Value)
End Function
```

This code uses an ordinary user-defined VBScript function named *WSHInputBox*. (The function has this name to avoid a naming conflict with the original VBScript *InputBox* function.) The user-defined function has three parameters: *Message* contains the text shown in the dialog box, *Title* contains the title bar text, and *Value* is the default value shown in the text box. *WSHInputBox* passes the parameters received from the caller to the corresponding parameters of the VBScript *InputBox* function. The following line assigns the result obtained from the *InputBox* function to *WSHInputBox*, which defines the return value of the user-defined function *WSHInputBox*:

```
WSHInputBox = InputBox(Message, Title, Value)
```

After defining the *WSHInputBox* function, you can use it in JScript. The following code snippet defines two variables and calls the new function:

```
var title = "InputBox function for JScript";
var prompt = "Enter a name:";
var result = WSHInputBox(prompt, title, "New York");
```

The user input obtained from the dialog box is returned in the variable *result*. If the value is *null*, the user clicked the Cancel button. If *result* has any other value, the user clicked the OK button.

Listing 8-2, which runs only in WSH 2, assembles all these parts in one .wsf file. Both scripts are kept in one *<job>* element but in two separate *<script>* elements. Using one *<job>* element is required because the scope of a function or procedure is limited to the job in which the function or procedure is defined. The processing instruction on the first line forces validation of the file's content as a valid XML document:

```
<?xml version="1.0" encoding="ISO-8859-1"?>
```

As a result, the content of the *<script>* elements must be inserted into CDATA elements (as described in Chapter 1). Figure 8-3 shows the input dialog box and two dialog boxes with input results.

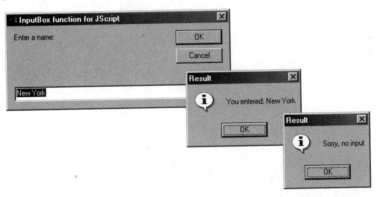

Figure 8-3 *An input dialog box and results created from a WSH 2 script*

```
<?xml version="1.0" encoding="ISO-8859-1"?>

<job id="IncludeExample">

    <script language="VBScript">
    <![CDATA[
        Function WSHInputBox(Message, Title, Value)
            ' Provides an InputBox function for JScript
            ' Can be called from JScript as:
            ' var result = WSHInputBox("Enter a name", "Input", test);
            WSHInputBox = InputBox(Message, Title, Value)
        End Function
    ]]>
    </script>
```

Listing 8-2 *WSH2Input.wsf*   *(continued)*

Listing 8-2 *continued*

```
    <script language="JScript">
    <![CDATA[
        // This is the JScript script, which reads user input
        // and displays it in a dialog box. It uses the
        // VBScript function WSHInputBox to create the
        // dialog box.
        var vbOKOnly = 0;                       // Constants for Popup
        var vbInformation = 64;

        var title = "InputBox function for JScript";
        var prompt = "Enter a name:";

        // Create the WshShell object (needed for using Popup).
        var WshShell = WScript.CreateObject("WScript.Shell");

        // Open the input dialog box using a function in the .wsf file.
        var result = WSHInputBox(prompt, title, "New York");

        // Test whether the Cancel button was clicked.
        if (result != null)
        {   // Cancel wasn't clicked, so get input.
            var intDoIt = WshShell.Popup("You entered: " + result,
                                         0,
                                         "Result",
                                         vbOKOnly + vbInformation);
        }
        else
        {   // Cancel button was clicked.
            var intDoIt = WshShell.Popup("Sorry, no input",
                                         0,
                                         "Result",
                                         vbOKOnly + vbInformation);
        }

        //*** End
    ]]>
    </script>
</job>
```

Using the *prompt* Method from Internet Explorer

The solution you've learned so far for retrieving user input in JScript works well in WSH 2. Because WSH is designed to act as the "glue" for assembling objects and methods into one application, you can use other ways to retrieve user input in JScript.

To prepare for Chapter 9, which deals with forms, let's now look at how to access Microsoft Internet Explorer and use an input box method.

If you've programmed scripts in HTML documents using JavaScript, you're probably familiar with the *prompt* method, which retrieves user input as shown here:

```
var result = prompt("Please enter a name", "Chicago");
```

The *prompt* method has two parameters: the first contains the string shown in the input dialog box, and the second is the default value in the text box.

The Internet Explorer object model supports the *prompt* method, but the WSH object model doesn't provide a similar method, so to use *prompt* in your WSH JScript programs you need a technique to "incorporate" Internet Explorer objects into your WSH scripts. (You can also use this technique for other objects, and it works for either WSH 1 or WSH 2 as long as the objects are accessible.)

To use Internet Explorer and its objects from a WSH script, you must obtain a reference to the Internet Explorer *Application* object. You can use the following JScript statement to create the object:

```
var oIE = WScript.CreateObject("InternetExplorer.Application");
```

This statement does two things. First, it loads an instance of the object into memory, which means that an instance of Internet Explorer is launched. Second, it stores a reference to this object in the object variable *oIE*, which you can use later to access the properties and methods of the *Application* object.

Unfortunately, the *prompt* method isn't part of the *Application* object; it's a method of the *Script* object, which is a subobject of the *Document* object, which is in turn a subobject of the *Application* object. Therefore, you must obtain a reference to the *Script* object. This part of the Internet Explorer object model is depicted in Figure 8-4.

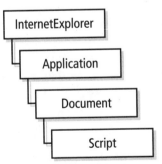

Figure 8-4 *Part of the Internet Explorer 4 and Internet Explorer 5 object model*

Before you can create a reference to the *Document* object, a document must be loaded into the *Application* object. The *Script* subobject is supported automatically whether or not the document contains script code (because Internet Explorer also supports internal script commands). Therefore, you can use the object hierarchy to access the *prompt* method of the *Script* object.

We haven't yet reached our final destination. The browser requires that the document be loaded before the *Document* object is accessible. Also, you don't want to see the browser window on the desktop—you need only the input dialog box. Loading a document and hiding the browser window might seem complicated, but the solution is rather simple. To load a document into the Internet Explorer *Application* object, you can use the *navigate* method of the *Application* object. To use a method, you simply write the object name, a dot, the method name, and then the required parameters. Thus, you can load a document into Internet Explorer using the following (JScript) statement:

```
oIE.navigate("about:blank");
```

This command uses the *navigate* method of the object variable *oIE* (which contains a reference to Internet Explorer's *Application* object instance). The parameter submitted to the method uses a little trick: because you don't need a real document, you can submit the internal resource *"about:blank"* to force Internet Explorer to display a blank document page (the same thing you'd get if you typed the URL *about:blank* in Internet Explorer's address bar).

To hide or show the browser window, you can use the *Visible* property of the *Application* object:

```
oIE.Visible = 0;
```

In this statement, the *Visible* property is set to 0, which hides the browser window. The value *Visible = 1* shows the browser window. Because the default value for *Visible* is 0, you need no *oIE.Visible* statement within your code.

After these preliminary steps, you could try to get a reference to the *Script* object in order to call the *prompt* method. Unfortunately, *Script* objects are children of the *Document* object, and the *Document* object is inaccessible while Internet Explorer loads a document. Because you have two processes (the script and the browser) running asynchronously, any attempt to retrieve a reference to the *Script* object might fail. Instead, the script should wait until the browser has loaded the document.

You could use the *Busy* property, which the browser uses to flag its internal state. This property provides a simple and reliable way to check whether the browser is ready to call methods. If Busy is set to true, the browser is loading the document (and no calls are allowed).

The loop used within the following statement delays the script until Internet Explorer is ready to load the document:

```
while (oIE.Busy) {}
```

If the browser is ready for further queries, you can create a reference to the *Script* object using the following JScript statement:

```
var obj = oIE.Document.Script;
```

After this statement is executed, the object variable *obj* contains a reference to the *Script* object. You can then use a statement such as the following to call the *prompt* method:

```
var input = obj.prompt("Enter a name", "Chicago");
```

The first parameter defines the text in the dialog box, and the second parameter contains the default input value, as shown in Figure 8-5.

Figure 8-5 *An input dialog box invoked using the* prompt *method in JScript*

The title bar is filled from Internet Explorer, and the string *"JavaScript Prompt:"* is inserted from the browser (Internet Explorer 5 in this example).

> **NOTE** I've discussed this Internet Explorer example in depth because many macro programmers don't understand the advantages of programming with objects. When I began programming with objects, I had similar doubts. But once I realized that you need only six JScript statements to embed a feature from another application into a WSH script, I decided that programming with objects is the best thing since sliced bread. In my book *Advanced Development with Microsoft Windows Script Host 2.0*, I'll introduce scripts that use features from Microsoft Word, Microsoft Excel, Microsoft Outlook, and other applications using similar techniques.

To simplify the use of the *prompt* method in JScript, I put all the code that interacts with Internet Explorer into a simple function, *MyPrompt*. (I chose the name *MyPrompt*, and not *Prompt*, to avoid naming conflicts with the *prompt* method itself.) The following JScript code uses this function.

```
// A helper function to view a prompt window
function MyPrompt(text, value)
{
    // Create Internet Explorer application object.
    var oIE = WScript.CreateObject("InternetExplorer.Application");
    oIE.navigate("about:blank");  // Empty HTML document
    oIE.Visible = 0;              // Keep Internet Explorer invisible.
```

(continued)

```
        while (oIE.Busy) {}            // Important: Wait until Internet
                                       // Explorer is ready.

    var obj = oIE.Document.Script;        // Get scripting object.
    var input = obj.prompt(text, value); // Open prompt window.
    oIE.Quit();                        // Close Internet Explorer object.
    return input;
}
```

In addition to the statements discussed earlier, the function calls the *Quit* method of the Internet Explorer *Application* object using the following statement to terminate Internet Explorer and release the object:

```
oIE.Quit();
```

The next statement is required to return the user input obtained from *prompt* to the calling script:

```
return input;
```

Using the function *MyPrompt* requires one statement:

```
var temp = MyPrompt("Enter a name", "Chicago");
```

MyPrompt returns a string containing the user input if the user clicked the OK button. If the user clicked the Cancel button, *MyPrompt* returns the value *null*. You can use the following code to check the return value:

```
if (temp != null)    // Check return value.
```

Listing 8-3 contains a full implementation of these code snippets. The script invokes an input dialog box, examines the user input, and shows it in a second dialog box.

```
//*******************************************************
// File:     Input1.js (WSH sample in JScript)
// Author:   (c) G. Born
//
// Retrieving user input in JScript using the prompt
// method. The script uses Internet Explorer.
//*******************************************************

// A helper function to view a prompt window
function MyPrompt(text, value)
{
    // Create Internet Explorer application object.
    var oIE = WScript.CreateObject("InternetExplorer.Application");
    oIE.navigate("about:blank");  // Empty HTML document
    oIE.Visible = 0;              // Keep Internet Explorer invisible.
```

Listing 8-3 *Input1.js*

```
    while (oIE.Busy) {}              // Important: Wait until Internet
                                     // Explorer is ready.


    var obj = oIE.Document.Script;       // Get scripting object.
    var input = obj.prompt(text, value); // Open prompt window.
    oIE.Quit();                          // Close Internet Explorer object.
    return input;
}


// Here goes the main program.
var temp = MyPrompt("Enter a name", "Chicago");
if (temp != null)    // Check return value.
{
    WScript.Echo(temp);
}
else
    WScript.Echo("No input");


//*** End
```

Chapter 9

Working with Forms

Even though the Microsoft Windows Script Host (WSH) object model and the JScript and VBScript languages don't support methods or functions for creating or showing forms, you can still implement user forms in scripts. In this chapter, I'll first explain how to use Microsoft Internet Explorer as a front end to display the content of an HTML file as a kind of advanced About dialog box. Then I'll explain how to use Internet Explorer as a front end to display the content of an HTML form under the control of a WSH script. You'll also learn how to use event handling in WSH scripts.

USING INTERNET EXPLORER TO CREATE AN ABOUT DIALOG BOX

In previous chapters, you learned how to show simple dialog boxes in JScript and VBScript using methods such as *Echo* and *Popup*. But unfortunately, these dialog boxes don't allow you to show lengthy text (that can be scrolled) or add such features as hyperlinks and icons. In Chapter 8, you learned a technique for accessing Internet Explorer from a WSH script. In this chapter, you'll learn how to create and display forms using Internet Explorer as a front end, but let's first look at a simpler example. We'll use Internet Explorer and an HTML file to create a simple About dialog box that needs no user input. Within the HTML file, you can add any features that you want.

Using the *showModalDialog* Method to Display an HTML File

You can use Internet Explorer's *showModalDialog* method to display an HTML file. This method, which is exposed from the *window* object, creates a simple dialog box that displays the content of an HTML file. Listing 9-1 shows a simple HTML file that contains script code to load a second HTML file and display its content as a dialog box. (This sample and the others in this chapter are in the \WSHDevGuide\Chapter09 folder on the book's companion CD.)

```
<html>
    <script>
        function init()
        {
            window.showModalDialog("Test1.htm");
        }
    </script>
    <body onload="init()">
    </body>
</html>
```

Listing 9-1 *Test.htm*

The script in the HTML page contains the *init* function, which uses a *showModalDialog* call. The *window* object is exposed automatically from Internet Explorer. The *showModalDialog* method requires a path to an HTML file, which is displayed in a modal dialog box. (A modal dialog box is a dialog box that must be dismissed before switching back to the main application.) The HTML file displayed in the modal dialog box can contain any valid HTML content.

NOTE   If the path to the second HTML file is missing, the browser searches the directory from the parent HTML document that was loaded for the given file name.

Listing 9-2 shows HTML code for creating the content of the About dialog box.

```
<html>
    <head>
        <meta http-equiv="Content-Type"
            content="text/html; charset=ISO-8859-1">
        <meta name="GENERATOR"
            content="Microsoft FrontPage Express 2.0">
        <title>About dialog</title>
    </head>
```

Listing 9-2 *About.htm*

```
<body bgcolor="#FEFFE8" bgproperties="fixed">
    <h2 align="center">About WSH Scripting Tools</h2>
    <p align="center">
        <a href="http://www.borncity.de">
            <font size="2">
                by G. Born
            </font>
        </a>
    </p>
    <p align="center">
        <font size="2">
            <img src="Line.gif" width="472" height="26">
        </font>
    </p>
    <h2 align="center">Help</h2>
    <p align="center">
        <strong>
            Sorry, we are (still) thinking
        </strong>
    </p>
    <p align="center">
        <font size="2">try: </font>
        <a href="http://msdn.microsoft.com">
            <font size="2">msdn.microsoft.com/scripting</font>
        </a>
        <font size="2"> instead</font>
    </p>
    <form>
        <p align="center">
            <input type="button" name="B1"
                   value="Close" onclick="window.close()">
        </p>
    </form>
</body>
</html>
```

The HTML code in Listing 9-2 creates the dialog box shown in Figure 9-1. The *<title>* tag defines the first part of the title text. Other tags create the static title bar text. The About dialog box contains hyperlinks that are inserted into the document using the *<a>* tag. The graphical line is inserted using the *<img>* tag.

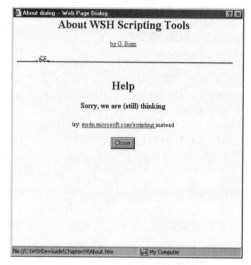

Figure 9-1 *An About dialog box in Internet Explorer*

ADDING A CLOSE BUTTON

You can add a Close button to the HTML code by using a *<form>* tag in combination with an *<input>* tag:

```
<form>
    <p align="center">
        <input type="button" name="B1"
               value="Close" onclick="window.close()">
    </p>
</form>
```

It's important to use the *button* type rather than the *submit* type within the *<input>* tag; otherwise, in Internet Explorer 5, a click on the Close button opens a second window.

When the user clicks the Close button, the *onclick* event is raised and the *onclick* event handler calls *window.close*. Unfortunately, calling *window.close* opens a dialog box that says that the Web page is trying to close the window and asks the user whether to close it. Because of this behavior, I converted the HTML file to an HTML application (HTA). An HTA file can be executed in Internet Explorer 5, but because it's a local HTML application, several Internet Explorer security settings are lowered. Clicking the Close button in an HTA page closes the window immediately. Turning an HTML document into an HTA file is simple: you simply change the .htm or .html extension to .hta.

Displaying the About Dialog Box Using VBScript

I wrote a short script in VBScript to access the *showModalDialog* method from a WSH script without displaying the Internet Explorer window. As you learned in previous chapters, you invoke Internet Explorer using the following statements:

```
Set oIE = WScript.CreateObject("InternetExplorer.Application")
oIE.Navigate "about:blank"  ' Empty document

Do While (oIE.Busy)  ' Important: wait until Internet Explorer is ready.
    WScript.Sleep 200
Loop
```

The *WScript.Sleep* statement within the loop suspends the script for 200 milliseconds during each pass. This lowers the CPU load (as I'll discuss in Chapter 13).

Because the browser window is hidden, you need only fetch the object reference and set the *Navigate* property to a blank document window. The *Visible* property of the Internet Explorer *Application* object is left at the default of 0 (invisible). When the browser is ready, the *showModalDialog* method is called with the following code:

```
oIE.Document.Script.showModalDialog path & "About.hta"
```

The *showModalDialog* method is a method of Internet Explorer's *Script* object, which is contained in the *Document* object of the *Application* object. To access the method, the script must build the object path from Internet Explorer's *Application* object to the *Script* object. The object variable *oIE* still contains a reference to the *Application* object. Therefore, you simply append the *Document.Script* object names and the *showModalDialog* method name to the *oIE* object variable name. The method requires the path to the HTML document as a parameter. (As an optional parameter, you can pass the width and/or height of the dialog box.)

The script can pass an absolute path (such as *"C:\Test\About.hta"*) in the URL to the method. If the user moves the HTML file to another folder or drive, the WSH script fails with a run-time error. A much better approach is to store the HTML document in the same folder as the WSH script. Then you can determine the path of the HTML document by retrieving the path of the WSH script. The user can thus move the files to other folders as long as the HTML file is in the WSH script's folder. You can determine the script's path by using these two VBScript statements:

```
path = WScript.ScriptFullName
path = Left(path, InStrRev(path, "\"))
```

The first statement reads the path and the script filename using the *ScriptFullName* property of the *WScript* object. You use the second line with the *InStrRev* function to search the string in reverse, from the last character to the first occurrence of \. If this character is found, the substring from the first character to the current position in the string is derived using the *Left* function. The function requires the string and a pointer to the last valid character in the string. The position of the last valid character is returned from the *InStrRev* function. The filename is stripped from the string and the result is assigned to the *path* variable. The advantage of using *showModalDialog* is that after the method call, the script pauses until the user closes the dialog box. The script uses the following command to display a message (which appears after the browser window is closed):

```
WScript.Echo "Dialog box is closed"
oIE.Quit              ' Close Internet Explorer.
```

Using the browser's *Quit* method in the second line terminates the browser. Otherwise, an Internet Explorer instance will remain in memory until the script terminates. Listing 9-3 shows the complete code for using the *showModalDialog* method. (To use this sample with Internet Explorer 4, you must change the filename in the load command to *About.htm.*)

```
'**************************************************
' File:      About.vbs (WSH sample in VBScript)
' Author:    (c) G. Born
'
' Using Internet Explorer 5 to display a modal
' About dialog box containing an HTML document.
'**************************************************
Option Explicit

Dim oIE              ' Internet Explorer object
Dim path
Dim Title

' Get path to the script file because the HTML
' document displayed in the dialog box must be
' located in the same folder.
path = WScript.ScriptFullName
path = Left(path, InStrRev(path, "\"))

' Launch Internet Explorer.
Set oIE = WScript.CreateObject("InternetExplorer.Application")
oIE.navigate "about:blank"  ' Empty document

' Window is hidden (default), so there's no need to set further
' window options.

' Important: wait until Internet Explorer is ready.
Do While (oIE.Busy)
    WScript.Sleep 200       ' Suspend for 200 milliseconds.
Loop
```

Listing 9-3 *About.vbs*

```
' Display the dialog box using showModalDialog.
' For Internet Explorer 4, change About.hta to About.htm.
oIE.Document.Script.showModalDialog path & "About.hta"

' This message is displayed after the dialog box is closed.
WScript.Echo "Dialog box is closed"

' Clean up.
oIE.Quit             ' Close Internet Explorer.
Set oIE = Nothing    ' Reset object variable.

'*** End
```

Displaying the About Dialog Box Using JScript

Porting the VBScript sample to JScript is fairly simple. Listing 9-4 shows the implementation details.

```javascript
//*************************************************
// File:    About.js (WSH sample in JScript)
// Author:  (c) G. Born
//
// Using Internet Explorer 5 to display a modal
// About dialog box containing an HTML document
//*************************************************

// Get path to the script file because the HTML
// document displayed in the dialog box must be
// located in the same folder.
var path = WScript.ScriptFullName;  // Script name
path = path.substr(0, path.lastIndexOf("\\") + 1);

// Launch Internet Explorer.
var oIE = WScript.CreateObject("InternetExplorer.Application");
oIE.navigate("about:blank");  // Empty document

// Window is hidden (default), so there's no need to set further
// window options.

// Important: wait till IE is ready.
while (oIE.Busy) {WScript.Sleep(200);}

// Display the dialog box using showModalDialog.
// For Internet Explorer 4, change About.hta to About.htm.
oIE.Document.Script.showModalDialog(path + "About.hta");
```

Listing 9-4 *About.js*

(continued)

Listing 9-4 *continued*

```
// This message is displayed after the dialog box is closed.
WScript.Echo("Dialog box is closed");

// Clean up.
oIE.Quit();              // Close Internet Explorer.

//*** End
```

USING INTERNET EXPLORER
AND WSH TO CREATE A FORM

Now let's apply the techniques we just discussed to create a form for user input. Again, we'll use Internet Explorer and an HTML page. An HTML form can contain text boxes, option buttons, check boxes, and numerous other features. (Figure 9-2 shows a simple form with two text boxes.) The only difficult part is accessing the form in the browser window from your WSH script.

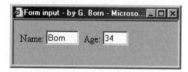

Figure 9-2 *An input form*

HTML Code for the Form

An HTML form is an HTML document with a few special HTML tags. You can use Microsoft FrontPage Express or any other HTML editor to insert the items for the form into the document.

The HTML code in Listing 9-5 creates the form shown in Figure 9-2.

```
<html>
    <head>
        <title>Form input - by G. Born</title>
    </head>
    <body bgcolor="silver" scroll="no">
        <form name="ValidForm">
            Name:
            <input name="fName" type="TEXT" size="5"> 
            Age:
            <input name="fAge" type="TEXT" size="3">
        </form>
    </body>
</html>
```

Listing 9-5 *HTML code for creating a form*

The title of the form's window is defined in the *<head>* block using the *<title>* tag. The background color of the form is specified in the *<body>* tag using the *bgcolor* attribute, which is set to *"silver"*. This sets a gray background for the form. The attribute *scroll="no"* causes Internet Explorer to hide the vertical scroll bar. The commands for creating the form are embedded in the *<form> ...</form>* tags. The *name* attribute of the starting tag gives the form a unique name. We'll need this name later.

The two controls in the form are created using *<input>* tags. The *<input>* tag has the following syntax:

```
<input name="fName" type="TEXT" size="5">
```

The *name* attribute defines the name of the control. The *type* attribute defines the type of control (text box, button, and so forth). The *size* attribute defines the size (character length) of a control. If you store these HTML tags in an HTML file and load this file in Internet Explorer, a form is displayed.

> **NOTE** I omitted a Close button (as shown in the About dialog box sample) because if an *onclick* event on a Close button calls the *window.close* method, a browser dialog box appears asking the user whether to close the window. Converting the .htm file to .hta doesn't change this behavior because Windows won't load an HTA application in the requested order. I decided to just let the user close the form using the default Close button in the upper right corner of the browser window. Later I'll show a different solution that includes a Close button in the form.

Displaying the Form

Now let's write a WSH script, implemented in VBScript, to use the form. The script launches Internet Explorer, loads the HTML file containing the form, and reads the user input from the form.

The following code sequence loads Internet Explorer and displays the form:

```
Set oIE = CreateObject("InternetExplorer.Application", "IE_")

oIE.Left = 50              ' Window position and other properties
oIE.Top = 100
oIE.Height = 100
oIE.Width = 280
oIE.MenuBar = 0            ' Disable some bars.
oIE.ToolBar = 0
oIE.StatusBar = 0
' oIE.Resizable = 0        ' Disable resizing.

oIE.navigate path & "Form1.htm"  ' Form

oIE.Visible = 1            ' Show document window.
```

The *Set* keyword in the first line assigns a reference to Internet Explorer's *Application* object. This object variable allows you to access the Internet Explorer object model with all its properties. The second parameter submitted to the *CreateObject* method defines the prefix used in event handling procedures. It enables WSH to connect events raised from the object to the event handlers in the script. (See also the Chapter 7 sections dealing with *CreateObject* and *DisconnectObject*.) I'll use this technique here to detect when the user has closed the form.

You can set the window position and size in the WSH script using the *Left*, *Top*, *Height*, and *Width* properties. To disable the menu bar, the status bar, and so on, you set the associated Internet Explorer properties (*MenuBar*, *ToolBar*, and *StatusBar*) to 0.

> **NOTE**   The statement *oIE.Resizable = 0* disables document window resizing. I commented out this statement because Internet Explorer versions 4 and 5 render the form's border incorrectly on my system if the property is set.

You load the HTML file using the following statement:

```
oIE.navigate GetPath() & "Form1.htm"
```

I moved the statements (used in the previous sample) that extract the current folder into a procedure named *GetPath*. I mentioned earlier that the *Script* object isn't accessible until Internet Explorer loads a document. Therefore, you must use the following code to test Internet Explorer's *Busy* property. The following loop is processed in the WSH script until Internet Explorer reports that the form has been loaded:

```
Do While (oIE.Busy)
    WScript.Sleep 200
Loop
```

Internet Explorer sets this property to *True* when it loads a document and resets it to *False* when the document finishes loading. The *WScript.Sleep* call suspends the script during each pass (which lowers the CPU load).

After loading the form, we have a slight problem: the WSH script and the browser window displaying the form are two independent processes, so the WSH script must wait until the user closes the form. I decided to use the following strategy:

■   Within the main routine, I set the *ready* variable to *False*. The script loops until this variable becomes *True*.

■   Within the *IE_OnQuit* event handling procedure, I set the *ready* variable to *True*. *IE_OnQuit* is called when the user closes the form's window. This event is raised automatically from Internet Explorer, which is why I connected the script to the outgoing interface of the browser object using the "*IE_*" parameter in *CreateObject*.

You can then query the form's state by using the following code:

```
Do While (Not ready)
    WScript.Sleep 500    ' Suspend for 0.5 second.
Loop
```

Closing the browser window raises the *onclose* event. The script's event handling procedure reads the user input and sets the variable *ready* to *True*. After exiting the loop, the script uses a simple *MsgBox* call to display the user input. (See Figure 9-3.)

Figure 9-3 *The results shown in a WSH script dialog box*

Now let's take a closer look at the event handling procedure. It contains the following script code:

```
Sub IE_OnQuit()
    ' Event handler is called if IE terminates.
    ' This happens if the user clicks the OK button.
    ' Retrieve the values.
    name = "Name: " & oIE.Document.ValidForm.fName.Value
    age = "Age: " & oIE.Document.ValidForm.fAge.Value
    ready = True        ' Indicate form is closed.
End Sub
```

The first statement retrieves the user input in the Name text box and stores it in the global variable *name*. You can use this global variable in the script's main routine.

I'd like to say a word about how to obtain the user input from the text box. The statement uses the following object hierarchy:

```
oIE.Document.ValidForm.fName.Value
```

oIE is the object variable pointing to Internet Explorer's application object, and the form is loaded in its subobject *Document*. I assigned the object name *ValidForm* to the form using the *name* attribute in the HTML code. I did the same with the *name* attribute of each control element. *ValidForm.fName* identifies the first text box in the form, and the *Value* attribute of this object contains the user input as a text string. After reading both values and saving them in global variables, the event handler sets the *ready* state to *True*. Then it terminates and allows Internet Explorer to close the browser window.

The entire WSH script source code is shown in Listing 9-6.

```
'**************************************************
' File:    Form1.vbs (WSH sample in VBScript)
' Author:  (c) G. Born
'
' Using Internet Explorer 4 or 5 to retrieve
' form input
'**************************************************
Option Explicit

Const Title = "WSH sample form input - by G. Born"
Dim oIE       ' Internet Explorer object
Dim path      ' Path to script file
Dim ready     ' State of the form (True = form closed)

Dim Text2
Dim name, age ' Values obtained from form

Text2 = "You entered:" & vbCrLf

' Launch Internet Explorer, and connect event handler.
Set oIE = WScript.CreateObject("InternetExplorer.Application", "IE_")

oIE.Left = 50           ' Window position and other properties
oIE.Top = 100
oIE.Height = 100
oIE.Width = 280
oIE.MenuBar = 0         ' No menu
oIE.ToolBar = 0
oIE.StatusBar = 0
' Commented out because it causes a corrupted window border.
' oIE.Resizable = 0     ' Disable resizing.
oIE.navigate GetPath() & "Form1.htm"  ' Load form.
oIE.Visible = 1         ' Keep visible.

' Important: wait until Internet Explorer is ready.
Do While (oIE.Busy)
    WScript.Sleep 200   ' Suspend for 200 milliseconds.
Loop

ready = False           ' Form is still open.

' Wait until the user closes the form using
' the Close button in the upper right corner of the window.
' This sets ready to True in the onclose event.
```

Listing 9-6 *Form1.vbs*

```
Do While (Not ready)     ' Wait until form is closed.
    WScript.Sleep 500    ' Suspend for 500 milliseconds.
Loop

' Display the data obtained in the event handling procedure.
MsgBox Text2 & vbCrLf & name & vbCrLf & age, _
            vbOKOnly + vbInformation + vbSystemModal, Title

' We're ready now. The sample script terminates.
' Here you can add script-specific code.

' Event handler and helper

Sub IE_OnQuit()
    ' Event handler is called if IE terminates.
    ' This happens if the user clicks the Close button.
    ' Retrieve the values.
    name = "Name: " & oIE.Document.ValidForm.fName.Value
    age = "Age: " & oIE.Document.ValidForm.fAge.Value
    ready = True         ' Indicate form is closed.
End Sub

Function GetPath()
    ' Get script path because the form (HTML file)
    ' must be in the same folder.
    Dim path
    path = WScript.ScriptFullName
    GetPath = Left(path, InStrRev(path, "\"))
End Function

'*** End
```

A JScript WSH Script for Displaying the Form

If you prefer to use JScript for WSH scripts, you can port the VBScript program to JScript. You simply have to consider the different syntax. The only changes you have to make are to the WSH script because the script in the HTML document is independent. You must also pay attention to case sensitivity in method and object names.

By the way, JScript doesn't support some VBScript functions, such as *Left* for extracting the path. You must use the *substr* method of the *String* object instead. The position of the last \ character is returned from the *lastIndexOf* method of the *String* object. Listing 9-7 shows the JScript equivalent of Form1.vbs.

```
//**************************************************
// File:    Form1.js (WSH sample in JScript)
// Author:  (c) G. Born
//
// Using Internet Explorer 4 or 5 to retrieve
// form input
//**************************************************
var Text2 = "You entered:\n";

// Launch Internet Explorer, and connect event handler.
var oIE = WScript.CreateObject("InternetExplorer.Application", "IE_");

oIE.Left = 50;            // Window position and other properties
oIE.Top = 100;
oIE.Height = 100;
oIE.Width = 280;
oIE.MenuBar = 0;          // No menu
oIE.ToolBar = 0;
oIE.StatusBar = 0;
// Commented out because it causes a corrupted window border.
// oIE.Resizable = 0      // Disable resizing.
oIE.navigate(GetPath() + "Form1.htm");  // Load form.
oIE.Visible = 1;          // Keep visible.

// Important: Wait until IE is ready.
while (oIE.Busy) {WScript.Sleep(200)}  // Suspend

var ready = false;        // Form is still open.

// Wait until the user closes the form using
// the Close button in the upper right corner of the window.
// This sets ready to true in the onclose event.
while (!ready) {WScript.Sleep(500)}  // Suspend

// Display the data obtained in the event handling procedure.
WScript.Echo(Text2 + "\n" + name + "\n" + age);

// We're ready now. The sample script terminates.
// Here you can add script-specific code.

// Event handler and helper
```

Listing 9-7 *Form1.js*

```
function IE_OnQuit()
{
    // Event handler is called if IE terminates.
    // This happens if the user clicks the Close button.
    // Retrieve the values.
    name = "Name: " + oIE.Document.ValidForm.fName.value;
    age = "Age: " + oIE.Document.ValidForm.fAge.value;
    ready = true;          // Indicate form is closed.
}

function GetPath()
{
    // Get script path because form (HTML file)
    // must be in the same folder.
    var path = WScript.ScriptFullName;
    path = path.substr(0, path.lastIndexOf("\\") + 1);
    return path;
}

//*** End
```

Displaying a File Selection Dialog Box

Sometimes a script needs a way to let the user select a file for further processing. WSH doesn't offer a method that displays a file selection dialog box. In Chapter 12, I'll discuss how to use the Browse For Folder dialog box to select drives, files, or folders, but this isn't the best solution. Now that you know how to use Internet Explorer as a front end, you can use a neat trick: you can use a form with a Browse button that allows the user to select a file using the default Windows dialog box. (See Figure 9-4.) You can write the HTML tag to display the text box and the *Browse* button as follows:

```
<input type="file" size="75" name="fFile">
```

The *<input>* tag is the same one we used in the previous sample to create a text box. If the *type* attribute is set to *"file"*, a text box and a Browse button are shown in the form. The *size* attribute defines the length of the text box, and the *name* attribute defines an object name for this control. The caption *Browse* is already rendered by the browser. (The caption depends on the localized browser version.)

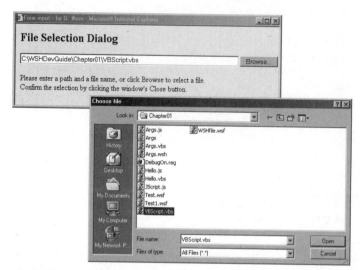

Figure 9-4 *Displaying a Choose File dialog box from a WSH script*

The form includes a text box and a Browse button. (See Figure 9-4, left.) If the user clicks the Browse button, the browser opens the Choose File dialog box (Figure 9-4, right) and allows the user to select a file. After the user closes the dialog box, the selected file, including its path, is shown in the text box.

The code for handling the Choose File dialog box is based on the previous sample. I changed only a few messages and the name of the text box control. Listing 9-8 shows the implementation in JScript.

```
//*****************************************************
// File:    Form2.js (WSH sample in JScript)
// Author:  (c) G. Born
//
// Using Internet Explorer 4 or 5 to display
// a file selection dialog
//*****************************************************
var Text2 = "File selected:\n";

// Launch Internet Explorer, and connect event handlers.
var oIE = WScript.CreateObject("InternetExplorer.Application", "IE_");
var file = "";              // Initialize file name.

oIE.Left = 50;              // Window position and other properties
oIE.Top = 100;
oIE.Height = 200;
oIE.Width = 580;
oIE.MenuBar = 0;            // No menu
```

Listing 9-8 *Form2.js*

```
oIE.ToolBar = 0;
oIE.StatusBar = 0;
// Commented out because it causes a corrupted window border.
// oIE.Resizable = 0        // Disable resizing.
oIE.navigate(GetPath() + "Form2.htm");  // Load form.
oIE.Visible = 1;            // Keep visible.


// Important: Wait till IE is ready
while (oIE.Busy) {WScript.Sleep(200)}  // Suspend


var ready = false;          // Form still open


// Wait until the user closes the form using
// the Close button in the upper right window corner.
// This sets ready to true in the onclose event.
while (!ready) {WScript.Sleep(500)}   // Suspend


// Display the file name obtained in the event handling procedure.
WScript.Echo(Text2 + "\n" + file);


// We are ready now; the sample script terminates here.
// Here you can add script-specific code.


// Event handler and helper

function IE_OnQuit()
{
    // Event handler called when IE terminates.
    // This is the case if the user clicked the Close button.
    // Retrieve the values.
    file = oIE.Document.ValidForm.fFile.value;
    ready = true;           // Indicate form is closed
}


function GetPath()
{
    // Get script path because form (HTML file)
    // must be in the same folder.
    var path = WScript.ScriptFullName;
    path = path.substr(0, path.lastIndexOf("\\") + 1);
    return path;
}

//*** End
```

Improving the Form

The problem with the preceding samples is that they don't include an OK button that allows the user to confirm the input. An improved solution should follow these guidelines:

- The HTML document should provide the form with the controls and only a minimal script that supports handling from WSH.

- The WSH script should handle the form and read all data entered in the form.

Using this approach, the HTML document contains only a small script, which provides the rudimentary functions for retrieving the form's state. You access the form's values directly from the WSH script (as shown previously).

Creating the HTML form

The first step in implementing a user input form is to create an HTML document that provides the necessary form elements. The simplest method is to use an HTML editor such as Microsoft FrontPage or FrontPage Express to create an HTML document containing the form. After you design the form, you must alter the HTML source code and add a few scripts. Figure 9-5 shows an extended HTML form and a WSH dialog box with the user input retrieved from that form.

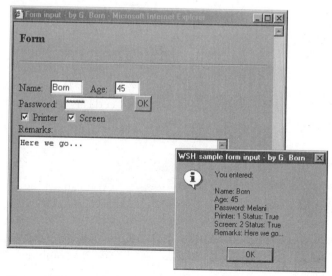

Figure 9-5 *An extended form and the results in a WSH script dialog box*

Here are the HTML tags for creating the form:

```
<form name="ValidForm">
    <p>
        Name:  
        <input type="text" size="5" name="fName">  
        Age:  
        <input type="text" size="3" name="fAge">
        <br>

        Password:  
        <input type="password" size="12" maxlength="8" name="fPassw">
           
        <input type="button" name="Button1" value="OK">
        <br>

        <input type="checkbox" name="fPrinter" value="1" checked>
        Printer  
        <input type="checkbox" name="fScreen" value="2">
        Screen
        <br>

        Remarks:
        <br>

        <textarea cols="40" rows="5" name="fRemark">
        </textarea>
    </p>
</form>
```

The form is embedded in the *<form>* ... *</form>* tags. The *name* attribute of the *<form>* tag specifies the object name (which you'll need later to access the form items in your scripts). Each form element is given a unique name in its own HTML tag.

You insert a text box using this code:

```
<input type="text" size="5" name="fName">
```

The *type* attribute specifies the form element's type. You can set the *size* attribute to restrict the size of the text box. The *name* attribute is required for each tag because it allows you to identify the item later in the scripts.

A text area input field requires the *<textarea>* ... *</textarea>* tags. The *<textarea>* tag is ideal for collecting large amounts of text data. By combining *<input>* and *<textarea>* tags, you should be able to create any desired form.

After building your form, you need a few helper functions in the HTML document. You can initialize the form items when the document is loaded by using this procedure:

```
Sub Window_OnLoad()
    ' Here we can initialize the form (optional).
    Set TheForm = Document.ValidForm  ' Retrieve object.
    TheForm.fName.Value = ""    ' Initialize fName control value.
    ready = 0 ' User input not ready.
End Sub
```

The *Window_OnLoad* event procedure is invoked when the HTML document is loaded. The procedure shown above uses the (optional) statement to retrieve the form's object reference and assign it to the object variable *TheForm*. You can use this (optional) code to set the content of the first text box (with the name *fName*) to an empty string:

```
TheForm.fName.Value = ""       ' Initialize fName control value.
```

If necessary, you can add statements to initialize the other form items. (This example doesn't need them.)

The last statement is required:

```
ready = 0 ' User input not ready.
```

The browser containing the form runs as an asynchronous process, so you need some mechanism to coordinate the browser and the VBScript/JScript program. This sample uses the variable *ready* as a flag to indicate whether the user clicked the form's OK button. When the form is loaded, *ready* is set to 0 (which means that the form is still in input mode).

The user can fill in the fields in the form and click the OK button to release the form and return control to the script. I mentioned that the HTML document browser process runs independently of the WSH script process. To force Internet Explorer to close the browser window (after first displaying a warning dialog box and asking the user for confirmation), you can add the following to the *<input>* tag of the OK button:

```
onclick = "window.close()"
```

As mentioned earlier, I wasn't successful in using an HTA form from a script to avoid this behavior, so I decided to take a different approach: having the *onclick* event be handled within the HTML script in the document itself. As a result, the WSH script must close the form.

The next HTML sample uses a simple trick to tell the WSH script that the user has clicked the OK button. The *OnClick* event procedure of the *Button1* object is called when the user clicks the OK button, and the *ready* value is set to *1*.

```
Sub Button1_OnClick
    ' If the user clicks OK, we must signal the polling
    ' WSH script by setting the ready flag.
    ready = 1 ' User input is ready.
End Sub
```

To have the WSH script check the internal state of the *ready* value, you can implement another small function, *CheckVal*:

```
Public Function CheckVal()
    ' This function is called from the host to check whether
    ' the user clicked the OK button.
    CheckVal = ready
End Function
```

CheckVal returns the *ready* value. If this value is set to *1*, the WSH script knows that the OK button was clicked.

The entire HTML source code is shown in Listing 9-9.

```
<html>
    <head>
        <meta http-equiv="Content-Type"
              content="text/html; charset=iso-8859-1">
        <meta name="GENERATOR"
              content="Microsoft FrontPage Express 2.0">
        <title>
            Form input - by G. Born
        </title>
    </head>

    <body bgcolor="#C0C0C0" scroll="no">
        <script language="VBScript">
        <!--
            Dim ready
            Public TheForm

            Sub Button1_OnClick
                ' If the user clicks OK, we must signal the polling
                ' WSH script by setting the ready flag.
                ready = 1 ' User input is ready.
            End Sub

            Sub Window_OnLoad()
                ' Here we can initialize the form.
                Set TheForm = Document.ValidForm
                TheForm.fName.Value = ""
                ready = 0 ' User input not ready.
            End Sub
```

Listing 9-9 *Form3.htm*

(continued)

Listing 9-9 *continued*

```
          Public Function CheckVal()
              ' This function is called from the host to check
              ' whether the user clicked the OK button.
              CheckVal = ready
          End function

      '-->
      </script>

      <h3>
          Form
      </h3>

      <hr>
          <form name="ValidForm">
              <p>
                  Name:  
                  <input type="text" size="5" name="fName">  
                  Age:  
                  <input type="text" size="3" name="fAge">
                  <br>

                  Password:  
                  <input type="password" size="12" maxlength="8"
                      name="fPassw">
                     
                  <input type="button" name="Button1" value="OK">
                  <br>

                  <input type="checkbox" name="fPrinter" value="1"
                      checked>
                  Printer  
                  <input type="checkbox" name="fScreen" value="2">
                  Screen
                  <br>

                  Remarks:
                  <br>

                  <textarea cols="40" rows="5" name="fRemark">
                  </textarea>
              </p>
          </form>
      </hr>
  </body>
</html>
```

TIP After you've created the form, you can store it as a template (because it already contains the necessary script code). To create a new form, load the script in a tool such as Microsoft FrontPage and alter or add the necessary controls to the form. After storing the result in a new HTML file, all you need to do is customize the WSH script to handle the controls of this form. But the HTML script code remains unaltered.

Displaying the HTML form

Now that you have an HTML document containing a form and a few script functions, you need a WSH script to invoke the form and retrieve the user input. The script must launch an instance of Internet Explorer, load the HTML document into the browser, and scan the *ready* state of the HTML document. You've already seen the basic techniques in earlier samples.

The user can fill in all the form's text boxes and click the OK button to close the form. At this point, you need a trick for the WSH script to recognize that the user has clicked the OK button. Earlier I introduced the *CheckVal* function, which returns the *ready* value to the caller. The following code sequence in the WSH script loops until the *ready* value is set to *1*, which indicates that the user has clicked OK.

```
' Wait until the user clicks the OK button.
' Use the CheckVal function.
Do ' Wait for results.
Loop While (oIE.Document.Script.CheckVal() = 0)
```

The *oIE* object variable points to the *Application* object of the Internet Explorer process, which is the parent object of the *Document.Script* objects.

After the loop exits, all the user input is accessible. You'll recall from previous samples how to access the form's input value. To access the first text box, *fName*, you can use the following statement:

```
oIE.Document.ValidForm.fName.value
```

The *value* property contains the value the user entered into the text box *fName*. (Note that the names are case-sensitive if you use JScript to access the form's data.) This value is always provided as a string. Using similar code, you can access any form item from your WSH script. If you need to check user input, you can evaluate the values. If a value is unacceptable, you can display a message box to that effect.

By the way, you can also use this technique to write data to the form's control elements. You can do this to initialize the text box values from the script.

After you retrieve all values from the form, you can close the form by using this command:

```
oIE.Quit
```

This command executes the *Quit* method provided by the object referenced in the *oIE* object variable, causing Internet Explorer to close the HTML document and

217

terminate the application. The values obtained from the form are displayed using a *MsgBox* call. By the way, the constant *vbSystemModal* used within the *MsgBox* call forces Windows to always display the dialog box in the foreground. Listing 9-10 is the entire VBScript program.

```vbscript
'***************************************************
' File:    Form3.vbs (WSH sample in VBScript)
' Author:  (c) G. Born
'
' Using Internet Explorer 4 or 5 to retrieve
' form input
'***************************************************
Option Explicit

Const Title = "WSH sample form input - by G. Born"

Dim oIE      ' Internet Explorer object

' Global variables for form values
Dim name, age, password, printer, screen, remark
Dim Text2

Text2 = "You entered:" & vbCrLf

' *** Launch Internet Explorer. ***
Set oIE = WScript.CreateObject("InternetExplorer.Application")

oIE.Left = 50            ' Window position and other properties
oIE.Top = 100
oIE.Height = 380
oIE.Width = 450
oIE.MenuBar = 0          ' No menu
oIE.ToolBar = 0
oIE.StatusBar = 0
' Commented out because it causes a corrupted window.
' oIE.Resizable = 0      ' Disable resizing.
oIE.navigate GetPath() & "Form3.htm" ' Form
oIE.Visible = 1          ' Keep visible.

' Important: wait until Internet Explorer is ready.
Do While (oIE.Busy)
    WScript.Sleep 200    ' Suspend for 0.2 second.
Loop

' Try to initialize the text box value from the script.
oIE.Document.ValidForm.fRemark.Value = "No remarks"
```

Listing 9-10 *Form3.vbs*

```
' Wait until the user clicks the OK button.
' Use the CheckVal function.
On Error Resume Next   ' Handle case in which IE is closed.
Do                     ' Wait until the OK button is clicked.
    WScript.Sleep 200  ' Suspend for 0.2 second.
Loop While (oIE.Document.Script.CheckVal() = 0)

' If an error occurs because the form is closed, quit the
' script.
If Err <> 0 Then
    WScript.Echo "Sorry, a run-time error occurred while checking" & _
                 " the OK button " & vbCrLf & _
                 "Error: " & Err.Number & " " & _
                 "I guess the form was closed; no input values..."
    WScript.Quit         ' End script.
End If

On Error GoTo 0    ' Switch off error handling.

' User clicked the OK button; retrieve the values.
name = "Name: " & oIE.Document.ValidForm.fName.Value
age = "Age: " & oIE.Document.ValidForm.fAge.Value
password = "Password: " & oIE.Document.ValidForm.fPassw.Value
printer = "Printer: " & oIE.Document.ValidForm.fPrinter.Value _
          & " Status: " & oIE.Document.ValidForm.fPrinter.Checked
screen = "Screen: " & oIE.Document.ValidForm.fScreen.Value _
          & " Status: " & oIE.Document.ValidForm.fScreen.Checked
remark = "Remarks: " & oIE.Document.ValidForm.fRemark.Value
MsgBox Text2 & vbCrLf & name & vbCrLf & _
       age & vbCrLf & password & vbCrLf & _
       printer & vbCrLf & screen & vbCrLf & _
       remark, vbOKOnly + vbInformation + vbSystemModal, Title

oIE.Quit             ' Close Internet Explorer.
Set oIE = Nothing    ' Reset object variable.

' We're ready.

Function GetPath()
' Get script path because the form (HTML file)
' must be in the same folder.
    Dim path
    path = WScript.ScriptFullName
    GetPath = Left(path, InStrRev(path, "\"))
End Function

'*** End
```

The JScript implementation

The JScript implementation (Listing 9-11) uses a similar approach. Note the case sensitivity of variable names.

```
//***************************************************
// File:    Form3.js (WSH sample in JScript)
// Author:  (c) G. Born
//
// Using Internet Explorer 4 or 5 to retrieve
// form input
//***************************************************

var vbOKOnly = 0;                // Pop-up dialog box VB constants
var vbInformation = 64;
var vbSystemModal = 4096;

var Title = "WSH sample form input - by G. Born";
var Text2 = "You entered:\n";

// *** Launch Internet Explorer. ***
var oIE = WScript.CreateObject("InternetExplorer.Application");
oIE.left=50;              // Window position
oIE.top = 100;            // and other properties
oIE.height = 380;
oIE.width = 450;
oIE.menubar = 0;          // No menu
oIE.toolbar = 0;
oIE.statusbar = 0;
oIE.navigate (GetPath() + "Form3.htm");  // Form
oIE.visible = 1;          // Keep visible

// Important: wait until Internet Explorer is ready.
while (oIE.Busy) {WScript.Sleep(200);}

// Try to initialize the text box value from the script.
oIE.Document.ValidForm.fRemark.value = "No remarks";

// Wait until the user clicks the OK button.
// Use the CheckVal function.
try
{
    while (oIE.Document.Script.CheckVal()==0)
        {WScript.Sleep(200);}  // Wait.
}
```

Listing 9-11 *Form3.js*

```
catch (e)
{
    WScript.Echo("Sorry, a run-time error occurred while checking" +
                 " the OK button \n" +
                 "I guess the form was closed; no input values...");
    WScript.Quit();         // End script
}
// User has clicked the OK button; retrieve the values.
name = "Name: " + oIE.Document.ValidForm.fName.value;
age = "Age: " + oIE.Document.ValidForm.fAge.value;
password = "Password: " + oIE.Document.ValidForm.fPassw.value;
printer = "Printer: " + oIE.Document.ValidForm.fPrinter.value +
          " Status: " + oIE.Document.ValidForm.fPrinter.checked;
screen = "Screen: " + oIE.Document.ValidForm.fScreen.value +
         " Status: " + oIE.Document.ValidForm.fScreen.checked;
remark = "Remarks: " + oIE.Document.ValidForm.fRemark.value;

var WshShell = WScript.CreateObject("WScript.Shell");
WshShell.Popup (Text2 + "\n" + name + "\n"+ age + "\n" +
               "\n" + password + "\n" + printer + "\n" +
               screen + "\n" + remark,0, Title,
               vbOKOnly + vbInformation + vbSystemModal);

oIE.Quit();              // Close Internet Explorer.

function GetPath ()
{
    // Retrieve the script path.
    var path = WScript.ScriptFullName;  // Script name
    path = path.substr(0, path.lastIndexOf("\\") + 1);
    return path;
}

//*** End
```

You now know about the basic techniques for extending WSH scripts with a user interface. In *Advanced Development with Microsoft Windows Script Host 2.0,* I'll extend this technology with ActiveX forms (a topic beyond the scope of this book). I'll also show you how to use progress bars, bar graphs, and so on from scripts.

Part III

Power Scripting

Chapter 10

Creating Shortcuts

This chapter explains how to use the methods of the *WshShell* object to create shortcuts on the Desktop, the Start menu, and other places in Microsoft Windows. You'll also learn how to map URLs as shortcuts.

SHORTCUT BASICS

In Windows, shortcuts provide a way to link to an application, a file, or a folder. Usually, the user creates a shortcut in Windows by right-clicking on a file or folder and dragging it to another folder, the Desktop, or the Start menu. A shortcut menu appears with the Create Shortcut(s) Here command. Alternatively, you can right-click on the file or folder and choose Create Shortcut from the shortcut menu.

These techniques create a shortcut file with the .lnk extension. This file contains properties such as the shortcut icon and paths to the target directory and the working directory. When you right-click on a shortcut icon and choose Properties, a property sheet appears. Figure 10-1 shows the Shortcut property page for a shortcut file.

In Windows, you use API functions to manipulate shortcut files and their properties. In Microsoft Windows Script Host (WSH), you use methods of the *WshShell* object to create shortcuts.

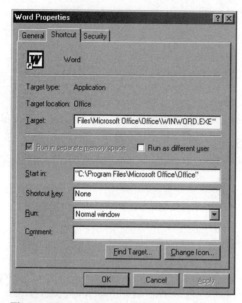

Figure 10-1 *Shortcut properties*

Using the *CreateShortcut* Method

To create a new shortcut, you use the *CreateShortcut* method of the *WshShell* object in WSH, which has the following syntax:

```
Set WshShell = WScript.CreateObject("WScript.Shell")
Set object = WshShell.CreateShortcut("shortcut_file.lnk")
```

The first VBScript statement creates an object instance of the *WshShell* object and stores the reference in the object variable *WshShell*. The second statement applies the *CreateShortcut* method to the *WshShell* object.

The *CreateShortcut* method requires a parameter for the filename of the shortcut file to be created. This method creates a *WshShortcut* object but doesn't create an actual shortcut file. It also assigns an object instance to an object variable. In subsequent statements, you can set the properties of this shortcut object. When you create a new shortcut file or update an existing file, you must apply the *Save* method of the shortcut object to finalize any changes.

> **NOTE**   If you apply the *CreateShortcut* method with the name of a new shortcut, no .lnk file is created until you call the *Save* method. If the .lnk file specified in the *CreateShortcut* parameter already exists, the properties of this file are changed to the corresponding properties of the *WshShortcut* object.

Creating a shortcut to the current script file

For simplicity, our sample will create a shortcut to its own source code file. The .lnk file will be stored in the same folder as the script file. After the script starts, the program will ask the user whether to create the shortcut file. If the user clicks the Yes button, the script determines the path to the current script file by using the following two lines of VBScript code:

```
path = WScript.ScriptFullName
path = Left(path, InStrRev(path, "\"))
```

These two statements read the name of the script file, including the path, and strip off the filename.

You also need the name of the script file without the filename extension:

```
Lnk_Title = WScript.ScriptName
Lnk_Title = Left(Lnk_Title, InStrRev(Lnk_Title, ".") - 1)
```

The first statement reads the script filename. In the second statement, the string is searched in reverse order for the period separating the filename from the extension. The extension is then removed from the string using the VBScript *Left* function.

To create the shortcut, you need the *WshShell* object:

```
Set WshShell = WScript.CreateObject("WScript.Shell")
```

This object is a subobject of *WScript* (and has nothing to do with the Windows *Shell* object, which we'll discuss in later chapters). Now you can apply the *CreateShortcut* method to the *WshShell* object:

```
Set Shortcut = WshShell.CreateShortcut(path & Lnk_Title & ".lnk")
```

The parameter of the *CreateShortcut* method of the *WshShell* object defines the path and the name of the new .lnk file. This information is located in the variables *path* and *Lnk_Title*. When the *CreateShortcut* method is executed, a reference to the new *WshShortcut* object is assigned to the *Shortcut* object variable.

> **NOTE** At this point, you don't have a shortcut file on the hard disk. All you have is a *WshShortcut* object instance that's specified in an object variable. You can then set the properties of the *WshShortcut* object. To create the actual shortcut file, you must apply the *Save* method.

After creating a *WshShortcut* object instance, you can set the *WshShortcut* properties:

```
Shortcut.TargetPath = WScript.ScriptFullName
```

The *TargetPath* property defines the path to the target file, which is specified in the shortcut file. Our sample specifies the current script file by assigning the *ScriptFullName* property of the *WScript* object to *TargetPath*.

In a second statement, you assign the working directory for this shortcut:

```
Shortcut.WorkingDirectory = path
```

Any properties not set in the script (such as window style or hot keys) are automatically set to default values.

Now you use the *Save* method to create the new .lnk file for the shortcut object:

```
Shortcut.Save
```

This method requires no further parameters. Listing 10-1 shows the full implementation details. (Like the other samples in this chapter, this file is in the \WSHDevGuide\Chapter10 folder on the book's companion CD.)

```
'*************************************************
' File:    Shortcut.vbs (WSH sample in VBScript)
' Author:  (c) G. Born
'
' Creating a shortcut to the current file in
' the script file's folder
'*************************************************
Option Explicit

Dim Text, Title, Lnk_Title, Shortcut
Dim WshShell     ' Object variable
Dim status, Ready_txt, path

' Define user messages.
Ready_txt = "Shortcut created"
Text = "Creates a shortcut to this script file in the current folder"
Title = "WSH sample - by G. Born"

status = MsgBox(Text, _
                vbOKCancel + vbInformation, _
                Title)

If (status <> vbOK) Then
    WScript.Quit 1          ' Cancel selected.
End if

' *** Get script file path.
path = WScript.ScriptFullName
path = Left(path, InstrRev(path, "\"))
```

Listing 10-1 *Shortcut.vbs*

```
' Get script filename without extension.
Lnk_Title = WScript.ScriptName
Lnk_Title = Left(Lnk_Title, InStrRev(Lnk_Title, ".") - 1)

' Create new WshShell object, whose CreateShortcut method we need.
Set WshShell = WScript.CreateObject("WScript.Shell")

' Use the CreateShortcut method to create a shortcut.
Set Shortcut = WshShell.CreateShortcut(path & Lnk_Title & ".lnk")

' Set the shortcut properties. First set the target folder.
Shortcut.TargetPath = WScript.ScriptFullName

' Set working directory.
Shortcut.WorkingDirectory = path

Shortcut.Save              ' Create shortcut.

WScript.Echo Ready_txt     ' Ready message

'*** End
```

The JScript implementation

The JScript version, shown in Listing 10-2, uses the same objects, methods, and properties; only the syntax is different.

```
//************************************************
// File:    Shortcut.js (WSH sample in JScript)
// Author:  (c) G. Born
//
// Creating a shortcut to the current file in
// the script file's folder
//************************************************

var vbOKCancel = 1;        // Create variables.
var vbInformation = 64;
var vbCancel = 2;

var L_Welcome_MsgBox_Message_Text =
    "Creates a shortcut to this script file in the current folder";
var L_Welcome_MsgBox_Title_Text = "WSH sample - by G. Born";

Welcome();     // Welcome dialog box
```

Listing 10-2 *Shortcut.js*   *(continued)*

Listing 10-2 *continued*

```
// Get script path.
var path = WScript.ScriptFullName;
path = path.substr(0, path.lastIndexOf("\\") + 1);

// Get script filename and strip off extension.
var Lnk_Title = WScript.ScriptName
Lnk_Title = Lnk_Title.substr(0, Lnk_Title.lastIndexOf("."));

// Get WshShell object.
var WshShell = WScript.CreateObject("WScript.Shell");

// Create shortcut object.
var Shortcut = WshShell.CreateShortcut(path + Lnk_Title + ".lnk");

// Set shortcut properties.
Shortcut.TargetPath = WScript.ScriptFullName;
Shortcut.WorkingDirectory = path;
Shortcut.Save();        // Store shortcut file.

WScript.Echo("Shortcut created");

//////////////////////////////////////////////////////////////////
//
// Welcome
//
function Welcome()
{
    var WshShell = WScript.CreateObject("WScript.Shell");
    var intDoIt;

    intDoIt = WshShell.Popup(L_Welcome_MsgBox_Message_Text,
                             0,
                             L_Welcome_MsgBox_Title_Text,
                             vbOKCancel + vbInformation);
    if (intDoIt == vbCancel)
    {
        WScript.Quit(1);    // Cancel selected.
    }
}

//*** End
```

SHORTCUTS: BEYOND THE BASICS

Now that you know the basic steps involved in creating a shortcut using WSH, let's look at how to use the *WshShortcut* object and other objects to create shortcuts in one of the folders predefined by Windows, such as the Desktop, the Start menu, and so on, which are collectively known as *special folders*.

Using the *SpecialFolders* Object

The *CreateShortcut* method requires that you specify the path to the target folder, such as the folder for the Desktop or the Start menu. But here you run into a problem: the exact location of a special folder isn't obvious.

Because the Windows folder (in Windows 95 and Windows 98) has subfolders called Start Menu and Desktop for all Start and Desktop menu items, you might think that you can simply expand the environment variable *WINDIR* and extract the path to the subfolder you need. But if multiuser settings are enabled on Windows 95 or Windows 98, the Windows shell creates user-specific folders in the \Profiles subfolder, which itself has subfolders for the individual user's Desktop, Start menu, and so on.

In addition, programs such as the Tweak UI utility and even Microsoft Internet Explorer let you change the location of a special folder, and Windows 2000 keeps some special folders in different locations.

Fortunately, there's a way to find special folders. You can use the *SpecialFolders* property of the *WshShell* object. This property returns a *WshSpecialFolders* object containing a collection with the paths of all special folders. Using this collection, you can get the path of any folder for which you want to create a shortcut on the Desktop or the Start menu.

Table 10-1 shows the special folder names the *WshSpecialFolders* object uses, all of which you'll find on Microsoft Windows NT 4 and Windows 2000.

Table 10-1 SPECIAL FOLDERS IN WINDOWS

Folder Name(s)	*Description*
AllUsersDesktop AllUsersStartMenu AllUsersPrograms AllUsersStartup	Store data for all users. Some of the subfolders are specific to Windows NT and Windows 2000. Some are also found in Windows 98.
Desktop	Defines all user-defined shortcuts for the Desktop of the current user.

(continued)

Table 10-1 *continued*

Folder Name(s)	Description
Favorites	Points to the Favorites menu.
Fonts	Points to the folder containing all installed fonts (files and shortcut files to font files in other folders).
MyDocuments	Points to the user-specific folder named My Documents.
NetHood	An empty folder used as a placeholder for the network environment.
PrintHood	An empty folder used for printer mapping in the network.
Programs	Points to the subfolder for the user-defined entries in the Programs command on the Start menu.
Recent	Points to the Recent Files folder.
SendTo	Points to the SendTo folder.
StartMenu	Points to the user-defined Start Menu folder.
Startup	Points to the user-defined Startup folder.
Templates	Points to the ShellNew folder, which contains the templates for new files.

You use these names to get the location of a special folder from the *WshSpecial-Folders* collection. The actual folder name returned by *WshSpecialFolders* might differ from the one in Table 10-1.

NOTE *WshShell.SpecialFolders(strFolderName)* returns the value *Null* if the folder requested in *strFolderName* doesn't exist. For example, Windows 95 doesn't have an AllUsers\Desktop folder; for *strFolderName = AllUsersDesktop*, the *SpecialFolders* property returns *Null*.

Displaying all special folders

The following sample displays a dialog box that lists all special folders on the local machine. As you can see in Figure 10-2, the machines in this sample keep special folders in different locations. Also, the folder names depend on the localized version of Windows being used. The dialog box on the left belongs to a German Windows 98 version, and the dialog box on the right is from Windows 2000 (logged in as an administrator). The Windows 2000 dialog box shows two special folders for the Desktop and the Start menu.

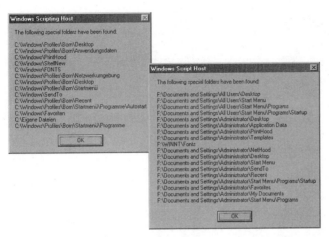

Figure 10-2 *Paths to special folders in Windows 98 (left) and Windows 2000 (right)*

To access the *SpecialFolders* property, you need the *WshShell* object, which you create by using the following VBScript statement:

```
Set WshShell = WScript.CreateObject("WScript.Shell")
```

The *CreateObject* method instantiates a copy of the *WshShell* object and assigns a reference to this object to the *WshShell* object variable. You can use this object variable to retrieve the *SpecialFolders* property, which contains a *WshSpecialFolders* collection.

The *Count* and *length* properties of the *WshSpecialFolders* object both contain the number of entries in the collection.

NOTE The *WshSpecialFolders* object offers both the *Count* and *length* properties for compatibility with VBScript and JScript. Commonly, *Count* is used in VBScript and *length* in JScript.

To process all elements in a collection, you can use a *For Each...In* loop in VBScript:

```
For Each i In WshShell.SpecialFolders
    WScript.Echo i
Next
```

This loop displays all special folders in the collection in separate dialog boxes. The variable *i* contains an item (pathname) retrieved from the *WshSpecialFolders* collection.

Listing 10-3 retrieves the paths to all special folders and displays them in a dialog box.

```
'*********************************************************
' File:    SpecialFolder.vbs (WSH sample in VBScript)
' Author:  (c) G. Born
'
' Using the SpecialFolders property of the WshShell
' object to list all special folders in a dialog box
'*********************************************************
Option Explicit

Dim Text, Title, i
Dim WshShell        ' Object variable

Text = "The following special folders have been found:" & _
    vbCrLf & vbCrLf
Title = "WSH sample - by G. Born"

' Create WshShell object, which we'll use to access the
' WshSpecialFolders object.
Set WshShell = WScript.CreateObject("WScript.Shell")

' Get the paths to the special folders.
For Each i In WshShell.SpecialFolders
    Text = Text & i & vbCrLf
Next

WScript.Echo Text          ' Show result.

'*** End
```

Listing 10-3 *SpecialFolder.vbs*

The JScript implementation

Listing 10-4 shows the JScript implementation.

```
//*********************************************************
// File:    SpecialFolder.js (WSH sample in JScript)
// Author:  (c) G. Born
//
// Using the SpecialFolders property of the WshShell
// object to list all special folders in a dialog box
//*********************************************************
```

Listing 10-4 *SpecialFolder.js*

```
var Text = "The following special folders have been found:\n\n";
var Title = "WSH sample - by G. Born";

// Create WshShell object, which we'll use to access the
// WshSpecialFolders object.
var WshShell = WScript.CreateObject("WScript.Shell");

// Show paths to special folders.
var objAdr = WshShell.SpecialFolders

/// Attention: The next for loop doesn't work
/// for (var i in objAdr).
/// {
///     WScript.Echo ("*" + i + "\n");
/// }
/// Therefore, we'll use

for (var i = 0; i < objAdr.length; i++)
{
    Text = Text + objAdr(i) + "\n";
}

WScript.Echo(Text);        // Show result.

//*** End
```

Finding the path to a special folder

You can also use the *SpecialFolders* property to retrieve the path of a specific special folder. The *WshSpecialFolders* collection not only gets the path but also returns the localized folder names, so your script is independent from localized Windows versions.

These two VBScript statements display the path to the Desktop folder:

```
Set WshShell = WScript.CreateObject("WScript.Shell")
WScript.Echo "Desktop: " & WshShell.SpecialFolders("Desktop")
```

The first line creates a *WshShell* object instance, which exposes the *SpecialFolders* property. The second line accesses an item in the *WshSpecialFolders* collection through the *SpecialFolders* property. Our sample uses the folder name *Desktop* as an index, which causes the *WshSpecialFolders* object to return just that one item from the collection. Because *Item* is the default property of the *WshSpecialFolders* object, you don't need to specify the *Item* property name to get the path to the Desktop folder.

The VBScript program in Listing 10-5 uses this approach to retrieve a few special folders and show the results in a dialog box, as shown in Figure 10-3.

```
'*********************************************************
' File:     SpecialFolder1.vbs (WSH sample in VBScript)
' Author:  (c) G. Born
'
' Using the SpecialFolders property of the WshShell
' object to list specific special folders in a
' dialog box
'*********************************************************
Option Explicit

Dim Text, Title
Dim WshShell

Text = "The following special folders have been found:" & _
    vbCrLf & vbCrLf
Title = "WSH sample - by G. Born"

' Create the WshShell object, which we'll use to access the
' WshSpecialFolders object.
Set WshShell = WScript.CreateObject("WScript.Shell")

' Get the paths to the special folders.
Text = Text & "Desktop: " & _
    WshShell.SpecialFolders("Desktop") & vbCrLf
Text = Text & "Startmenu: " & _
    WshShell.SpecialFolders("Startmenu") & vbCrLf
Text = Text & "Startup: " & _
    WshShell.SpecialFolders("Startup") & vbCrLf
Text = Text & "MyDocuments: " & _
    WshShell.SpecialFolders("MyDocuments") & vbCrLf
Text = Text & "Templates: " & _
    WshShell.SpecialFolders("Templates") & vbCrLf

WScript.Echo Text          ' Show results.

'*** End
```

Listing 10-5 *SpecialFolder1.vbs*

Figure 10-3 *The paths to some special folders*

The JScript implementation

The JScript version is shown in Listing 10-6.

```
//******************************************************
// File:    SpecialFolder1.js (WSH sample in JScript)
// Author:  (c) G. Born
//
// Using the SpecialFolder property of the WshShell
// object to list specific special folders in a
// dialog box
//******************************************************

var Text = "The following special folders have been found:\n\n";
var Title = "WSH sample - by G. Born";

// Create WshShell object, which we'll use to access the
// WshSpecialFolders object.
var WshShell = WScript.CreateObject("WScript.Shell");

// Get the paths to the special folders.
Text = Text + "Desktop: " +
    WshShell.SpecialFolders("Desktop") + "\n";
Text = Text + "Startmenu: " +
    WshShell.SpecialFolders("Startmenu") + "\n";
Text = Text + "Startup: " +
    WshShell.SpecialFolders("Startup") + "\n";
Text = Text + "MyDocuments: " +
    WshShell.SpecialFolders("MyDocuments") + "\n";
Text = Text + "Templates: " +
    WshShell.SpecialFolders("Templates") + "\n";

WScript.Echo(Text);          // Result

//*** End
```

Listing 10-6 *SpecialFolder1.js*

Creating a Shortcut on the Desktop

Now let's create a shortcut on the Desktop. Our sample will create a shortcut to the Windows Editor. The sample will display a dialog box that asks the user whether to create this shortcut. If the user clicks Yes, the script takes these steps:

1. It creates a *WshShell* object to access the *SpecialFolders* property and the *CreateShortcut* method.

2. It retrieves the path to the current Desktop folder using the *SpecialFolders* property of the *WshShell* object.

3. It creates the *WshShortcut* object.

The following VBScript code sequence creates a reference to the *WshShell* object, retrieves the path to the Desktop folder, sets the title of the shortcut file, and calls the *CreateShortcut* method:

```
Set WshShell = WScript.CreateObject("WScript.Shell")
DesktopPath = WshShell.SpecialFolders("Desktop")
Lnk_Title = "\Editor.lnk"
Set Shortcut = WshShell.CreateShortcut(DesktopPath & Lnk_Title)
```

The *DesktopPath* variable contains the path to the Desktop folder, and *Lnk_Title* contains the name of the shortcut .lnk file. Next, you define a few properties of the *WshShortcut* object. You use the *TargetPath* property of the new *WshShortcut* object to set the command to be executed after a double-click on the shortcut icon:

```
Shortcut.TargetPath = _
    WshShell.ExpandEnvironmentStrings("%WINDIR%\Notepad.exe")
```

The *ExpandEnvironmentStrings* method expands the content of the environment variable *%WINDIR%*. In other words, the method retrieves the Windows folder that contains the Windows Editor, Notepad.exe. Once you append the string "*Notepad.exe*" to this folder, the executable command is complete.

You now specify the working directory for the shortcut. Applications use this directory to store temporary files and other files.

```
Shortcut.WorkingDirectory = _
    WshShell.ExpandEnvironmentStrings("%WINDIR%\Temp")
```

Our sample sets this property to the Windows subfolder \Temp because the editor doesn't need a working directory. The *WindowStyle* property determines the mode in which the application window is shown after the shortcut is activated:

```
Shortcut.WindowStyle = 1
```

This property can have three possible values:

- 1 = normal
- 3 = maximized
- 7 = minimized

These styles are applicable only if the application window was terminated in Normal mode in the previous session.

The *IconLocation* property defines the link to the icon for the shortcut:

```
Shortcut.IconLocation = _
    WshShell.ExpandEnvironmentStrings("%WINDIR%\Notepad.exe, 0")
```

The command uses the first icon in Notepad.exe as the shortcut icon.

> **NOTE** In Windows, EXE and DLL files can contain one or more icons, which are counted from 0. Alternatively, you can use icon libraries such as Moricons.dll and Shell32.dll in the Windows folder or in the \System subfolder. Keep in mind, however, that the location of those files depends on the operating system. In Windows 2000, the files are in the \System32 subfolder, and in Windows 95 and Windows 98 they're in the Windows folder and the \System subfolder. You can also assign the path to a .bmp or .ico file to the *IconLocation* property.

Once you set the properties, you can use the *Save* method to create the shortcut file. The full VBScript implementation is shown in Listing 10-7.

```
'***********************************************
' File:    Shortcut1.vbs (WSH sample in VBScript)
' Author:  (c) G. Born
'
' Creating a shortcut to the Windows Editor on
' the Desktop
'***********************************************
Option Explicit

Dim Text, Title, Lnk_Title
Dim WshShell    ' Object variable
Dim status, Ready_txt
Dim Shortcut, DesktopPath

Ready_txt = "Shortcut to the Windows Editor on the Desktop"
Text = "Creates a shortcut to the Windows Editor on the Desktop"
Title = "WSH sample - by G. Born"
```

Listing 10-7 *Shortcut1.vbs*   *(continued)*

Listing 10-7 *continued*

```
' Ask the user whether to create shortcut.
status = MsgBox(Text, _
                vbOKCancel + vbInformation, _
                Title)
If (status <> vbOK) Then
    WScript.Quit 1        ' Cancel selected.
End If


' Create a new WshShell object, which we'll need for
' the WshSpecialFolders object.
Set WshShell = WScript.CreateObject("WScript.Shell")

' Get path to the Desktop folder using the
' WshSpecialFolders object.
DesktopPath = WshShell.SpecialFolders("Desktop")

' We know the path to the Desktop folder, so we'll use the
' CreateShortcut method to create the shortcut.
Lnk_Title = "\Editor.lnk"
Set Shortcut = WshShell.CreateShortcut(DesktopPath & Lnk_Title)

' Set shortcut properties.
' Target folder
Shortcut.TargetPath = _
    WshShell.ExpandEnvironmentStrings("%WINDIR%\Notepad.exe")

' Working directory
Shortcut.WorkingDirectory = _
    WshShell.ExpandEnvironmentStrings("%WINDIR%")

' Windows style 1 = normal, 3 = maximized, 7 = minimized
Shortcut.WindowStyle = 1

' Shortcut icon
Shortcut.IconLocation = _
    WshShell.ExpandEnvironmentStrings("%WINDIR%\\Notepad.exe, 0")

Shortcut.Save              ' Create shortcut file.

WScript.Echo Ready_txt     ' Ready message

'*** End
```

The JScript implementation

The JScript version is shown in Listing 10-8.

```
//**************************************************
// File:    Shortcut1.js (WSH sample in JScript)
// Author:  (c) G. Born
//
// Creating a shortcut to the Windows Editor on
// the Desktop
//**************************************************

var vbOKCancel = 1;        // Define variables.
var vbInformation = 64;
var vbCancel = 2;

var L_Welcome_MsgBox_Message_Text =
    "Creates a shortcut to the Windows Editor on the Desktop";
var L_Welcome_MsgBox_Title_Text =
    "WSH sample - by G. Born";

Welcome();   // Show welcome dialog box.

// Method for creating a shortcut
var WshShell = WScript.CreateObject("WScript.Shell");

// Get Desktop path using the WshSpecialFolders object.
var DesktopPath = WshShell.SpecialFolders("Desktop");

// Create shortcut file on Desktop.
var Shortcut =
    WshShell.CreateShortcut(DesktopPath + "\\Editor.lnk");

// Set object properties; %WINDIR% specifies the Windows folder.
Shortcut.TargetPath =
    WshShell.ExpandEnvironmentStrings("%WINDIR%\\Notepad.exe");
Shortcut.WorkingDirectory =
    WshShell.ExpandEnvironmentStrings("%WINDIR%");
Shortcut.WindowStyle = 1;   // Windows style normal
Shortcut.IconLocation =
    WshShell.ExpandEnvironmentStrings("%WINDIR%\\Notepad.exe, 0");

Shortcut.Save();    // Store shortcut.

WScript.Echo("Shortcut to the Windows Editor on the Desktop");
```

Listing 10-8 *Shortcut1.js*

(continued)

Listing 10-8 *continued*

```
///////////////////////////////////////////////////////////////
//
// Welcome
//
function Welcome()
{
    var WshShell = WScript.CreateObject("WScript.Shell");
    var intDoIt;

    intDoIt =  WshShell.Popup(L_Welcome_MsgBox_Message_Text,
                              0,
                              L_Welcome_MsgBox_Title_Text,
                              vbOKCancel + vbInformation );
    if (intDoIt == vbCancel)
    {
        WScript.Quit();
    }
}

//*** End
```

Creating a Shortcut on the Start Menu

Now let's create a shortcut on the Start menu. We'll create a new entry (also known as a *group*) named *Born* on the Start menu's Programs group. We'll use the new group to create a shortcut to Notepad.

> **NOTE** Creating a shortcut in a new group instead of using an existing entry such as Accessories requires a few additional steps. You must verify that the new group exists before you can apply the *CreateShortcut* method.

In principle, this task shouldn't be more complicated than the previous samples. You simply use the *CreateShortcut* method and submit the path to the destination folder and the shortcut filename as a parameter. You can use the filename Editor.lnk for the shortcut file. All that's missing is the path to the destination folder for the shortcut file. The path must point to the Start menu group \Programs\Born.

You can use the *SpecialFolders* property of the *WshShell* object to retrieve the path to Startmenu\Programs. But because this sample will use the Born group for the shortcut, the path must be extended to include this subfolder name.

> **WARNING** When you create a shortcut, you can't apply the *Save* method of the *WshShortcut* object if the target path doesn't exist. You'll get a run-time error.

How do you make sure the destination folder exists, and how do you create a folder for the new program group? You could call the *Run* method and create a new folder using something like the MS-DOS *MD* command. But here's a better approach (in VBScript):

```
Sub MakePath(pathx)
    On Error Resume Next
    ' Create a folder if one doesn't exist.
    Dim fso, f
    Set fso = CreateObject("Scripting.FileSystemObject")
    Set f = fso.CreateFolder(pathx)
    Set fso = Nothing
    Set f = Nothing
    On Error GoTo 0
End Sub
```

You must call this procedure with a parameter containing the whole path to the folder, as in *"C:\Windows\Born\"*. If a run-time error occurs, the *On Error Resume Next* statement causes the program to continue with the next statement.

NOTE For details on using the *FileSystemObject* object, see Chapter 12.

A *FileSystemObject* object is then created. The methods of this object allow you to handle files and folders. The *CreateFolder* method creates the folder passed as an argument. If the folder already exists, a run-time error occurs and the *On Error Resume Next* statement forces the script to continue with the next statement. Nothing changes in the file system. If the folder doesn't exist, no run-time error is generated and the new folder is created.

You call the *MakePath* procedure with the path to the subfolder Born as an argument, and then you apply the *CreateShortcut* method:

```
MakePath Path
Set Shortcut = WshShell.CreateShortcut(Path & "Editor.lnk")
```

Once you have the *WshShortcut* object, you can set its properties. Notepad is in the Windows folder in the file Notepad.exe, so you can get the path to this file as shown in the previous examples.

In addition to the shortcut object properties you learned about earlier in the chapter, you can set the *Hotkey* property, which defines a hot key for executing a shortcut:

```
Shortcut.Hotkey = "Alt+Ctrl+E"
```

In this code, the key combination Alt+Ctrl+E invokes Notepad.

IMPORTANT You can use hot keys only for shortcuts in the Desktop or Start Menu folder. Windows processes those folders if a hot key is detected. You must make sure that the key combination you specify for the hot key isn't already used for other purposes. Otherwise, the hot key won't work or will affect other applications.

If you call the *Save* method of the *WshShortcut* object, the shortcut is created on the Start menu. You can verify the existence of this shortcut by opening the Start menu. The branch Programs/Born should contain a new entry for the Windows Editor. The VBScript implementation is shown in Listing 10-9.

```
'*****************************************************
' File:     Startmenu.vbs (WSH sample in VBScript)
' Author:   (c) G. Born
'
' Creating a shortcut to Notepad in the
' Start menu group Born
'*****************************************************
Option Explicit

Dim Text, Title
Dim WshShell     ' Object variable
Dim status, Ready_txt
Dim Shortcut, Path

Ready_txt = "Shortcut created"
Text = _
    "Creates a shortcut to Notepad on the Start menu (Group ""Born"")"
Title = "WSH sample - by G. Born"

' Ask user whether to create shortcut.
status =  MsgBox(Text, _
                 vbOKCancel + vbInformation, _
                 Title)
If (status <> vbOK) Then
    WScript.Quit 1          ' Cancel selected.
End If

' Create WshShell object, which is needed for the
' WshSpecialFolders object.
Set WshShell = WScript.CreateObject("WScript.Shell")

' Get path to the folder Startmenu/Programs using
' the WshSpecialFolders object.
Path = WSHShell.SpecialFolders("Programs")
```

Listing 10-9 *Startmenu.vbs*

```
' Important: Entry goes into Programs\Born.
Path = Path & "\Born\"

' Check whether path exists; if not, create group.
MakePath Path

' We know the path to the Start menu; create shortcut using
' the CreateShortcut method.
Set Shortcut = WshShell.CreateShortcut(Path & "Editor.lnk")

' Set shortcut properties.
' Target path
Shortcut.TargetPath = _
    WshShell.ExpandEnvironmentStrings("%WINDIR%\Notepad.exe")

' Working directory
Shortcut.WorkingDirectory = _
    WshShell.ExpandEnvironmentStrings("%WINDIR%")

' Windows style 1 = normal, 3 = maximized, 7 = minimized
Shortcut.WindowStyle = 1

' Shortcut icon
Shortcut.IconLocation = _
    WshShell.ExpandEnvironmentStrings("%WINDIR%\Notepad.exe, 0")

' Hot key for shortcut
Shortcut.Hotkey = "Alt+CtrL+E"

Shortcut.Save              ' Create shortcut.

WScript.Echo Ready_txt     ' Show ready message.

Sub MakePath(pathx)
    On Error Resume Next
    ' Create folder if it doesn't exist.

    Dim fso, f
    Set fso = CreateObject("Scripting.FileSystemObject")
    Set f = fso.CreateFolder(pathx)
    Set fso = Nothing
    Set f = Nothing
    On Error GoTo 0
End Sub

'*** End
```

The JScript implementation

The JScript version is shown in Listing 10-10. Within the function *MakePath*, I used the *FolderExists* method (discussed in Chapter 12) to check whether the folder exists. An alternative might be to use the *try...catch* statement in JScript (available since version 5.0) to catch run-time errors (similar to *On Error Resume Next* in VBScript).

```
//*************************************************
// File:    Startmenu.js (WSH sample in JScript)
// Author:  (c) G. Born
//
// Creating a shortcut to Notepad in the
// Start menu group Born
//*************************************************

var vbOKCancel = 1;          // Declare variables.
var vbInformation = 64;
var vbCancel = 2;

var L_Welcome_MsgBox_Message_Text =
    "Creates a shortcut on the Start menu";
var L_Welcome_MsgBox_Title_Text =
    "WSH sample - by G. Born";

Welcome();    // Show welcome dialog box.

// Get object with method for creating shortcut.
var WshShell = WScript.CreateObject("WScript.Shell");

// Get path to the folder Startmenu/Programs using
// the WshSpecialFolders object.
var Path = WshShell.SpecialFolders("Programs");

// Important: Entry goes into Programs\Born.
Path = Path + "\\Born\\";

// Test whether path exists; if not, create group.
MakePath(Path);

// We know the path to the Start menu; use the
// CreateShortcut method to create the shortcut.
var Shortcut = WshShell.CreateShortcut(Path + "Editor.lnk");

// Set shortcut properties; first comes the target path.
Shortcut.TargetPath =
    WshShell.ExpandEnvironmentStrings("%WINDIR%\\Notepad.exe");
```

Listing 10-10 *Startmenu.js*

```
// Working directory
Shortcut.WorkingDirectory =
    WshShell.ExpandEnvironmentStrings("%WINDIR%");

// Windows style 1 = normal, 3 = maximized, 7 = minimized
Shortcut.WindowStyle = 1;

// Shortcut icon
Shortcut.IconLocation =
    WshShell.ExpandEnvironmentStrings("%WINDIR%\\Notepad.exe, 0");

// Hot key for shortcut
Shortcut.Hotkey = "Alt+Ctrl+E";

Shortcut.Save();                 // Create shortcut file.

WScript.Echo("Shortcut file created");

/////////////////////////////////////////////////////////
//
// Welcome
//
function Welcome()
{
    var WshShell = WScript.CreateObject("WScript.Shell");
    var intDoIt;

    intDoIt =  WshShell.Popup(L_Welcome_MsgBox_Message_Text,
                          0,
                          L_Welcome_MsgBox_Title_Text,
                          vbOKCancel + vbInformation );
    if (intDoIt == vbCancel)
    {
        WScript.Quit();
    }
}

function MakePath(pathx)
{
    // Create folder if it doesn't exist.
    var fso = new ActiveXObject("Scripting.FileSystemObject")
    if (!fso.FolderExists(pathx))
    {
        var f = fso.CreateFolder(pathx);
        f = null;
    }
    fso = null;
}

//*** End
```

You can use similar techniques to create shortcuts in other special folders (such as My Documents or Favorites). You simply use the *WshShell.SpecialFolders* property to get the path to the special folder.

> **TIP** If you want to create a shortcut on the Start menu in Windows NT or Windows 2000, you can do so for the current user, for a group of users, or for all users. You can modify the preceding script so that it retrieves the location of the current user's Start Menu special folder and add the shortcut there. To create a shortcut for a group of users, you start by retrieving the location of the current user's Start Menu and then moving two levels up in the folder hierarchy and enumerating all subfolders. Each subfolder belongs to a user account. You can retrieve the appropriate user's Start Menu folder and update the shortcut to ensure that the Start menu of selected users is updated. If you follow the sample above but use the All Users\Start Menu folder as a target, all users will see the shortcut on their Start menu.

Creating a Shortcut Using Arguments

If you manually open the property sheet of a shortcut, you can append several options to the Target text box. For example, the command *C:\Windows\Notepad.exe C:\Text\Born.txt* launches Notepad and loads Born.txt into it.

To append additional arguments to the shortcut command, you use the *Arguments* property. This property has nothing to do with the *Arguments* property exposed from the *WScript* object. Rather, it is a property of the *WshShortcut* object. The following sample creates a shortcut to Notepad in the Start menu's Programs/Born group. If the user chooses this Start menu command, the source code of the script is loaded. The shortcut must therefore contain the path and the script filename as extra arguments.

You can specify argument values for the shortcut object by using the *Arguments* property:

```
Shortcut.Arguments = WScript.ScriptFullName
```

This code assigns the name of the script file to the *Arguments* property. The Start menu entry Programs/Born/... created from the script file invokes Notepad and loads the script's source code. The *Save* method creates the shortcut filename from the *Shortcut* object and appends the *Arguments* property to the shortcut command.

The VBScript code in Listing 10-11 creates a shortcut to Notepad on the Start menu and includes the name of the script file in the command.

```
'***************************************************
' File:    Startmenu1.vbs (WSH sample in VBScript)
' Author:  (c) G. Born
'
' Creating a shortcut to Notepad in the
' Start menu group Born
'***************************************************
Option Explicit

Dim Text, Title
Dim WshShell      ' Object variable
Dim status, Ready_txt
Dim Shortcut, Path

Ready_txt = "Shortcut created"
Text = "Creates a shortcut to Notepad in the Start menu group Born"
Title = "WSH sample - by G. Born"

' Ask user whether to create shortcut.
status = MsgBox(Text, _
                vbOKCancel + vbInformation, _
                Title)
If (status <> vbOK) Then
    WScript.Quit 1         ' Cancel selected.
End If

' Create WshShell object, which is needed for the
' WshSpecialFolders object.
Set WshShell = WScript.CreateObject("WScript.Shell")

' Get path to the Start Menu/Programs folder using
' the WshSpecialFolders object.
Path = WshShell.SpecialFolders("Programs")

' Important: entry goes into Programs\Born.
Path = Path & "\Born\"

' Check whether path exists; if not, create group.
MakePath Path
```

Listing 10-11 *Startmenu1.vbs* *(continued)*

Listing 10-11 *continued*

```
' We know the path to the Start menu. Create shortcut using the
' CreateShortcut method.
Set Shortcut = WshShell.CreateShortcut(Path & "Editor.lnk")

' Set shortcut properties.
' Target path
Shortcut.TargetPath = _
    WshShell.ExpandEnvironmentStrings("%WINDIR%\Notepad.exe")

' Set arguments for program execution.
' Load the script file into Notepad.
Shortcut.Arguments = WScript.ScriptFullName

Shortcut.WorkingDirectory = _
    WshShell.ExpandEnvironmentStrings("%WINDIR%")

' Windows style 1 = normal, 3 = maximized, 7 = minimized
Shortcut.WindowStyle = 1

' Shortcut icon
Shortcut.IconLocation = _
    WshShell.ExpandEnvironmentStrings("%WINDIR%\Notepad.exe, 0")

' Hot key for shortcut
Shortcut.Hotkey = "Alt+CtrL+E"

Shortcut.Save               ' Create shortcut.

WScript.Echo Ready_txt      ' Show ready message.

Sub MakePath(pathx)
    On Error Resume Next
    ' Create folder if it doesn't exist.
    Dim fso, f
    Set fso = CreateObject("Scripting.FileSystemObject")
    Set f = fso.CreateFolder(pathx)
    Set fso = Nothing
    Set f = Nothing
    On Error GoTo 0
End Sub

'*** End
```

TIP The *Save* method stores the properties set in the script into the shortcut .lnk file. You need not set all *Shortcut* properties in the script. Any property not defined in the script stays unchanged in the .lnk file. You can test this by executing Startmenu1.vbs and then Startmenu.vbs. Both script programs create one shortcut file. The second program simply updates the existing file because Startmenu.vbs doesn't set the *Arguments* property. If you open the Start menu and choose the command for Born\Editor, Notepad is launched and Startmenu1.vbs is loaded. Obviously, the old property set in Startmenu1.vbs already exists. To prevent this behavior, you must set the property explicitly to an empty string.

The JScript implementation

The JScript implementation is shown in Listing 10-12.

```jscript
//**************************************************
// File:     Startmenu1.js (WSH sample in JScript)
// Author:   (c) G. Born
//
// Creating a shortcut to Notepad in the
// Start menu group Born
//**************************************************

var vbOKCancel = 1;        // Declare variables.
var vbInformation = 64;
var vbCancel = 2;

var L_Welcome_MsgBox_Message_Text =
    "Creates a shortcut on the Start menu";
var L_Welcome_MsgBox_Title_Text =
    "WSH sample - by G. Born";

Welcome();    // Show welcome dialog box.

// Get object with method for creating shortcut.
var WshShell = WScript.CreateObject("WScript.Shell");

// Get path to the Start Menu/Programs folder using
// the WshSpecialFolders object.
var Path = WshShell.SpecialFolders("Programs");

// Important: entry goes into Programs\Born.
Path = Path + "\\Born\\";

// Test whether path exists; if not, create group.
MakePath(Path);
```

Listing 10-12 *Startmenu1.js*   *(continued)*

Listing 10-12 *continued*

```javascript
// We have the path to the Start menu; use the
// CreateShortcut method to create the shortcut.
var Shortcut = WshShell.CreateShortcut(Path + "Editor.lnk");

// Set shortcut properties; first, the target path.
Shortcut.TargetPath =
    WshShell.ExpandEnvironmentStrings("%WINDIR%\\Notepad.exe");

// Here are the arguments for the script.
// Load the script file into Notepad.
Shortcut.Arguments = WScript.ScriptFullName;

// Working directory
Shortcut.WorkingDirectory =
    WshShell.ExpandEnvironmentStrings("%WINDIR%");

// Windows style 1 = normal, 3 = maximized, 7 = minimized
Shortcut.WindowStyle = 1;

// Shortcut icon
Shortcut.IconLocation =
    WshShell.ExpandEnvironmentStrings("%WINDIR%\\Notepad.exe, 0");

// Hot key for shortcut
Shortcut.Hotkey = "Alt+CtrL+E";

Shortcut.Save();                 // Create shortcut file.

WScript.Echo("Shortcut file created.");

/////////////////////////////////////////////////////////
//
// Welcome
//
function Welcome()
{
    var WshShell = WScript.CreateObject("WScript.Shell");
    var intDoIt;

    intDoIt = WshShell.Popup(L_Welcome_MsgBox_Message_Text,
                             0,
                             L_Welcome_MsgBox_Title_Text,
                             vbOKCancel + vbInformation );
    if (intDoIt == vbCancel)
    {
        WScript.Quit();
    }
}
```

```
function MakePath(pathx)
{
    // Create folder if it doesn't exist.
    var fso = new ActiveXObject("Scripting.FileSystemObject")
    if (!fso.FolderExists(pathx))
    {
        var f = fso.CreateFolder(pathx);
        f = null;
    }
    fso = null;
}

//*** End
```

NOTE Are you looking for a way to enumerate all shortcuts on the Desktop or in a Start menu group? We won't discuss how to do this until Chapter 12, which covers file-handling features that use the *FileSystemObject* object. For now, you can achieve the same thing by getting the path to the destination folder and using the *FileSystemObject* object to enumerate all files with the .lnk extension in the special folder. You can then manipulate the .lnk files (rename or delete them, for example).

Reading Shortcut Properties

If you want to read and alter properties of an existing shortcut file, studying the Windows Script Host Reference won't help because it doesn't include any property access functions such as *GetShortcut* or *ReadShortcut*. After playing with the samples shown in this chapter, however, I found that applying the *CreateShortcut* method to an existing shortcut file doesn't alter its properties. This realization brought me to the clever idea of using the *CreateShortcut* object to access existing shortcut files.

Take a look at these statements:

```
Set Shortcut = WshShell.CreateShortcut(lnk_file)
WScript.Echo Shortcut.TargetPath
```

The first line creates a shortcut object whose name is submitted to the *CreateShortcut* method. The second line reads the *TargetPath* property of this object. If the shortcut file given in the variable *lnk_file* already exists, the *CreateShortcut* method reads the settings of the associated .lnk file. The line thus invokes a dialog box that shows the target path already defined for the shortcut.

The *Arguments* property contains extra arguments set in the shortcut. The *Description* property is supported by the *WshShortcut* object, but only Windows 2000 has a property sheet that displays it; Windows 95 and Windows 98 have no such item on their property sheets for shortcut files.

> **NOTE** The *WshShortcut* object doesn't support the properties used in Windows 2000 to run the process in a separate address space or under another user account. (See Figure 10-1.)

The following VBScript sample uses *CreateShortcut* to retrieve all properties from an existing shortcut file and display the results in a dialog box (Figure 10-4). If a property isn't set, the line is left blank in the dialog box. The *IconLocation* property returns the value *",0"* if no icon is specified. In this case, the shortcut uses the default icon from the associated EXE program.

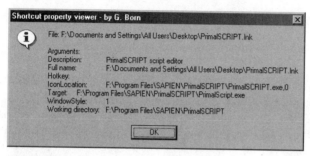

Figure 10-4 *Displaying shortcut properties*

The sample script comes with drag-and-drop support. The user can drag an existing shortcut file's icon to the script. After the user releases the left mouse button, the script is invoked with the name of the dragged file. The script then displays the properties of the file if it's a .lnk file.

The techniques for retrieving arguments submitted to a script are discussed in Chapter 7 (in the section "Accessing Script Arguments"). The following code checks whether the script was called with at least one argument:

```
Set objArgs = WScript.Arguments      ' Create object.

If objArgs.Count < 1 Then  ' No argument found; warn user and
                           ' end script.
    WScript.Echo  " Sorry, no arguments were found!" , _
        vbCrLf & vbCrLf, _
        "Please drag the shortcut to the script's icon", _
        "or call the script using:", vbCrLf & vbCrLf, _
        "<host> GetShortcutProperties.vbs shortcut_file", _
        vbCrLf & vbCrLf, _
        "(Example: CScript.exe GetShortcutProperties.vbs C:\Editor.lnk)"
    WScript.Quit  ' Quit script.
End If
```

After you retrieve the *Arguments* property, you can access the *Arguments* collection by using the object variable *objArgs*. The *Count* property of this object tells you whether the collection contains objects. If no objects are found, the script terminates with a simple dialog box that tells the user how to invoke the script program (Figure 10-5).

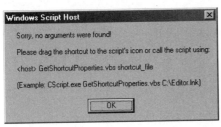

Figure 10-5 *The dialog box that appears if no arguments were submitted*

If an argument is obtained from the *WScript.Arguments* collection (the sample script supports only one filename at a time), you must at least check whether it's a shortcut file. Our sample simply checks to see whether the filename ends with the .lnk extension, using the following function:

```
Function IsLnk(name)
    ' Checks whether the extension is .lnk.
    ' Returns True or False.
    If (LCase(Right(name, 4)) = ".lnk") Then
        IsLnk = True
    Else
        IsLnk = False    ' ".lnk" not found
    End If
End Function
```

The function must be called with a valid filename. It returns *True* or *False*, depending on the file's extension. The function extracts the last four characters of the filename, converts them to lowercase, and compares them with "*.lnk*". The main script verifies the filename as follows:

```
If Not IsLnk(objArgs(0)) Then    ' Check whether file has .lnk extension.
    WScript.Echo "Sorry, but '" & objArgs(0) & _
        "' isn't a shortcut file."
    WScript.Quit
End If
```

The *IsLnk* function is called with the first item in the *Arguments* collection. If more than one argument is submitted, all other arguments are ignored. But it might be easy to extend the script to process multiple files dragged to the script file's icon.

NOTE If the user drags a file to the script, you can assume that the filename is valid and a file exists, so the script checks only the filename extension. But it's much better also to check whether the filename belongs to an existing file. You do this by using the *FileSystemObject* object. We'll discuss this object in later chapters. For now, we'll omit this step. Another helpful step would be to check whether the file is a valid shortcut. This test involves using methods of the Windows *Shell* object.

After these tests are run, the script is ready to access the (hopefully) existing shortcut file with the following statement:

```
Set Shortcut = WshShell.CreateShortcut(objArgs(0))
```

At this point, you're ready to read and display the properties of the *WshShortcut* object, which are specified in the *Shortcut* object variable.

Listing 10-13 shows the entire script.

```
'************************************************************
' File:    GetShortcutProperties.vbs (WSH sample in VBScript)
' Author:  (c) G. Born
'
' Retrieving the properties of a shortcut file submitted
' as an argument
'************************************************************
Option Explicit

Const Title = "Shortcut property viewer - by G. Born"
Dim WshShell     ' Object variable
Dim objArgs, Shortcut

' Create a new WshShell object.
Set WshShell = WScript.CreateObject("WScript.Shell")
' Try to retrieve the arguments.
Set objArgs = WScript.Arguments    ' Create object.

If objArgs.Count < 1 Then  ' No argument found; warn user and
                           ' end script.
    WScript.Echo  " Sorry, no arguments were found!" , _
        vbCrLf & vbCrLf, _
        "Please drag the shortcut to the script's icon", _
        "or call the script using:", vbCrLf & vbCrLf, _
        "<host> GetShortcutProperties.vbs shortcut_file", _
        vbCrLf & vbCrLf, _
        "(Example: CScript.exe GetShortcutProperties.vbs C:\Editor.lnk)"
    WScript.Quit  ' Quit script.
End If
```

Listing 10-13 *GetShortcutProperties.vbs*

```
' Try to get the argument submitted to the script.
If Not IsLnk(objArgs(0)) Then  ' Check whether file has .lnk extension.
    WScript.Echo "Sorry, but '" & objArgs(0) & _
        "' isn't a shortcut file."
    WScript.Quit
End If


' Try to create a shortcut file at the given location
' using the CreateShortcut method; if we don't use the Save
' method, no update is done.
Set Shortcut = WshShell.CreateShortcut (objArgs(0))

MsgBox "File: " & objArgs(0) & vbCrLf & vbCrLf & _
        "Arguments: " & vbTab & Shortcut.Arguments & vbCrLf & _
        "Description: " & vbTab & Shortcut.Description & vbCrLf & _
        "Full name: " & vbTab & Shortcut.FullName & vbCrLf & _
        "Hotkey: " & vbTab & Shortcut.Hotkey & vbCrLf & _
        "IconLocation: " & vbTab & Shortcut.IconLocation & vbCrLf & _
        "Target: " & vbTab & Shortcut.TargetPath & vbCrLf & _
        "WindowStyle: " & vbTab & Shortcut.WindowStyle & vbCrLf & _
        "Working directory: " & vbTab & Shortcut.WorkingDirectory & _
        vbCrLf, vbOKOnly + vbInformation, Title


Function IsLnk(name)
    ' Checks whether the extension is .lnk.
    ' Returns True or False.
    If (LCase(Right(name, 4)) = ".lnk") Then
        IsLnk = True
    Else
        IsLnk = False    ' ".lnk" not found
    End If
End Function

'*** End
```

The JScript implementation

In the JScript version in Listing 10-14, only the *IsLnk* function uses a new feature: the *GetExtensionName* method of the *FileSystemObject* object. The filename must be submitted as a parameter. This sample implements the *IsLnk* function in such a way that two parameters (the filename and the .lnk extension) must be submitted.

```
//***********************************************************
// File:    GetShortcutProperties.js (WSH sample in JScript)
// Author:  (c) G. Born
//
// Retrieves the properties of a shortcut file submitted
// as an argument.
//***********************************************************

// Create a new WshShell object.
var WshShell = WScript.CreateObject("WScript.Shell");

// Try to retrieve the arguments.
var objArgs = WScript.Arguments;      // Create object.

if (objArgs.length < 1)   // No argument found; warn user and
                          // end script.
{
    WScript.Echo(" Sorry, no arguments were found!\n\n",
        "Please drag the shortcut to the script's icon",
        "or call the script using:\n\n",
        "<host> GetShortcutProperties.vbs shortcut_file\n\n",
        "(Example: CScript.exe GetShortcutProperties.vbs C:\Editor.lnk)");
    WScript.Quit();        // Quit script.
}

// Try to get the argument submitted to the script.
if (!IsLnk(objArgs(0), "lnk")) // Check whether file has
                               // .lnk extension.
{
    WScript.Echo("Sorry, but \'" + objArgs(0) +
        "\' isn't a shortcut file");
    WScript.Quit();
}

// Try to create a shortcut file at the given location
// using the CreateShortcut method; if we don't use the Save
// method, no update is done.
var Shortcut = WshShell.CreateShortcut(objArgs(0));

WScript.Echo("File: " + objArgs(0) + "\n",
    "\nArguments: " + Shortcut.Arguments,
    "\nDescription: " + Shortcut.Description,
    "\nFull name: " + Shortcut.FullName,
    "\nHotkey: " + Shortcut.Hotkey,
    "\nIconLocation: " + Shortcut.IconLocation,
```

Listing 10-14 *GetShortcutProperties.js*

```
        "\nTarget: " + Shortcut.TargetPath,
        "\nWindowStyle: " + Shortcut.WindowStyle,
        "\nWorking directory: " + Shortcut.WorkingDirectory);


/////////////////////////////////////////////////////////////
//
// IsLnk
//
// Checks whether the file has the given extension.
// Returns true or false.
function IsLnk(name, ext)
{
    var fso = new ActiveXObject("Scripting.FileSystemObject");
    var s = fso.GetExtensionName(name);
    var s1 = s.toLowerCase();
    if (s1 == ext)
    {
        return (true);
    }
    else
    {
        return (false);
    }
}

//*** End
```

> **TIP** The *GetShortcutProperties* sample is handy for finding out the icon number for a shortcut file. Windows itself doesn't provide a feature to find this number.

Updating a Shortcut

Updating a shortcut is simple. You can apply the *CreateShortcut* method to an existing shortcut and then read a property or set a new value. The *Save* method updates the shortcut file.

The following VBScript sample accepts a shortcut filename as a parameter. The icon used for this shortcut file is then set to a new value. You can submit the parameter in WSH 2 by dragging a shortcut file to the script's icon. For simplicity, our sample sets the icon by default to an image contained in the file Shell32.dll, which is available in all Windows versions.

> **NOTE** The location of Shell32.dll depends on the Windows version. In Windows 95 and Windows 98, the file is in the \System subfolder. In Windows NT and Windows 2000, it's in \System32.

The script must start by checking the version of the operating system. This sample implements the *IsWinNT* function for this purpose:

```
' IsWinNT checks whether the operating system is Windows 95 or
' Windows 98, or Windows NT or Windows 2000. Returns True or
' False. Needs WshShell object.
Function IsWinNT
    Dim objEnv
    Set objEnv = WshShell.Environment("Process")
    If objEnv("OS") = "Windows_NT" Then
        IsWinNT = True
    Else
        IsWinNT = False
    End If
End Function
```

For the function to work, the main script must declare a *WshShell* variable and set that variable to an instance of the *WshShell* object. The function uses the *WshShell* variable to retrieve the environment variables for the process. The function then queries for the environment variable *OS*. This environment variable exists only in Windows NT and Windows 2000 and is set to *Windows_NT* in both operating systems. Depending on the value found, the function returns the value *True* or *False*.

The other techniques used in this sample are the same as in the previous sample. The script accepts two arguments. The first must be the filename of the shortcut file. The second argument is optional and can define the path and name of an icon file. The following are valid commands for invoking the script:

```
WScript.exe D:\ChangeShortcutIcon.vbs D:\C.lnk F:\WINNT\Explorer.exe,0
WScript.exe D:\ChangeShortcutIcon.vbs D:\C.lnk D:\B.ico
```

If the user drags a .lnk file to the script's icon, a default icon is obtained from Shell32.dll. After obtaining the parameters, the script creates a shortcut object (which contains the properties of an existing .lnk file). Then the *IconLocation* property is set to the second argument, and this modification is stored using the *Save* method.

Listing 10-15 shows the entire script. I'll leave it to you to implement the sample in JScript.

```
'**********************************************************
' File:     ChangeShortcutIcon.vbs (WSH sample in VBScript)
' Author:   (c) G. Born
'
' Changing the shortcut icon of the Registry Editor's
' shortcut on the Desktop
'**********************************************************
Option Explicit
```

Listing 10-15 *ChangeShortcutIcon.vbs*

```
Const Ready_txt = "Shortcut icon changed"
Const Text = "Change shortcut icon?"
Const Title = "Shortcut icon changer - by G. Born"
Dim WshShell     ' Object variable
Dim objArgs, Shortcut
Dim Arg(2)
Dim status, i

' Create a new WshShell object.
Set WshShell = WScript.CreateObject("WScript.Shell")

' Initialize icon path (if only one argument is submitted).
' Expand environment variable to get default icon (from Explorer).
Arg(1) = WshShell.ExpandEnvironmentStrings("%WINDIR%")
' Try to detect the operating system.
If IsWinNT Then
    Arg(1) = Arg(1) & "\System32\Shell32.dll, 19"
Else
    Arg(1) = Arg(1) & "\System\Shell32.dll, 19"
End If

' Try to retrieve the arguments.
Set objArgs = WScript.Arguments     ' Create object.

If objArgs.Count < 1 Then  ' No argument found; warn user and
                           ' end script.
    WScript.Echo   "Changes the icon of a given shortcut", _
        vbCrLf & vbCrLf, _
        "Sorry, no arguments were found!" , vbCrLf, _
        "Please drag the shortcut to the script's icon", _
        "or call the script using:", vbCrLf & vbCrLf, _
        "<host> ChangeShortcutIcon.vbs shortcut_file icon_file", _
        vbCrLf & vbCrLf, _
        "(Example: CScript.exe ChangeShortcutIcon.vbs C:\Editor.lnk " & _
        "D:\Bmp\Book.bmp)"
    WScript.Quit   ' Quit script.
End If

' Try to get the arguments submitted to the script. If only one
' argument is present, use the default icon specified above.
For i = 0 to objArgs.Count - 1       ' Loop through all arguments.
    Arg(i) = objArgs(i)              ' Get argument.
Next

If Not IsLnk(Arg(0)) Then  ' Check whether file has .lnk extension.
    WScript.Echo "Sorry, but '" & Arg(0) & "' isn't a shortcut file."
    WScript.Quit
End If
```

(continued)

Listing 10-15 *continued*

```
' Ask the user whether the shortcut icon should be modified.
status =  MsgBox(Text, _
                vbYesNo + vbQuestion, _
                Title)
If (status <> vbYes) Then
    WScript.Quit 1          ' Cancel selected.
End If


' We know the path to the shortcut file and the icon location.
' Use the CreateShortcut method to update the shortcut.
Set Shortcut = WshShell.CreateShortcut(Arg(0))

' Change shortcut icon.
Shortcut.IconLocation = Arg(1)

Shortcut.Save              ' Update shortcut file.

WScript.Echo Ready_txt     ' Ready message

Function IsLnk(name)
    ' Checks whether the extension is .lnk.
    ' Returns True or False.
    If (LCase(Right(name, 4)) = ".lnk") Then
        IsLnk = True
    Else
        IsLnk = False    ' ".lnk" not found
    End If
End Function


' IsWinNT checks whether the operating system is Windows 95 or
' Windows 98, or Windows NT or Windows 2000. Returns True or
' False. Needs WshShell object.
Function IsWinNT
    Dim objEnv
    Set objEnv = WshShell.Environment("Process")
    If objEnv("OS") = "Windows_NT" Then
        IsWinNT = True
    Else
        IsWinNT = False
    End If
End Function

'*** End
```

Creating a Shortcut to a Web Site

A link to a Web site placed on the Desktop is a special version of a shortcut. If you use the filename extension .url rather than .lnk, Windows creates a link to the Web site. You'll recognize this type of shortcut because it uses an icon for Web documents.

WSH has a few features for creating this type of shortcut. You can use the *CreateShortcut* method and *TargetPath* property of the *WshShell* object. The VBScript program in Listing 10-16 creates a link to a Web site on the Desktop. It differs from the previous samples in that the shortcut file has a .url extension and the *TargetPath* property doesn't contain a path. Instead, the property is set to the URL of the Web site.

```
'*******************************************************
' File:    URLShortcut.vbs (WSH sample in VBScript)
' Author:  (c) G. Born
'
' Creating a shortcut to a URL on the desktop
'*******************************************************
Option Explicit

Dim Text, Title, oURL
Dim WshShell     ' Object variable
Dim status, Ready_txt, path

Ready_txt = "URL shortcut created"
Text = "Create URL shortcut on the Desktop?"
Title = "WSH sample - by G. Born"

' Ask user before creating the shortcut.
status = MsgBox(Text, _
                vbYesNo + vbInformation, _
                Title)
If (status <> vbYes) Then
    WScript.Quit 1          ' User clicked No.
End If

' Create WshShell object, which we need for the
' WshSpecialFolders object.
Set WshShell = WScript.CreateObject("WScript.Shell")

' Get path to the Desktop folder using the
' WshSpecialFolders object.
Path = WshShell.SpecialFolders("Desktop")

' Use CreateShortcut method to create shortcut.
Set oURL = WshShell.CreateShortcut(path & "\Microsoft.URL")
```

Listing 10-16 *URLShortcut.vbs*   *(continued)*

Listing 10-16 *continued*

```
' Set shortcut properties.
oURL.TargetPath = "http://www.microsoft.com"

oURL.Save                ' Create shortcut.

WScript.Echo Ready_txt    ' Ready message

'*** End
```

The JScript implementation

The JScript version is shown in Listing 10-17.

```
//************************************************
// File:    URLShortcut.js (WSH sample in JScript)
// Author:  (c) G. Born
//
// Creating a shortcut to a URL on the Desktop
//************************************************

var vbOKCancel = 1;
var vbInformation = 64;
var vbCancel = 2;

var L_Welcome_MsgBox_Message_Text =
    "Creates a URL shortcut on the Desktop";
var L_Welcome_MsgBox_Title_Text =
    "WSH sample - by G. Born";

Welcome();    // Welcome dialog box

// Get object with method for creating shortcut.
var WshShell = WScript.CreateObject("WScript.Shell");

// Get Desktop path using WshSpecialFolders object.
var Path = WshShell.SpecialFolders("Desktop");

// Create shortcut on Desktop.
var oURL = WshShell.CreateShortcut(Path + "\\Microsoft.URL");

//  Set shortcut properties. First, the target path.
oURL.TargetPath = "http://www.microsoft.com";
oURL.Save();          // Store shortcut.
```

Listing 10-17 *URLShortcut.js*

```
WScript.Echo("Shortcut created");

/////////////////////////////////////////////////////////////
//
// Welcome
//
function Welcome()
{
    var WshShell = WScript.CreateObject("WScript.Shell");
    var intDoIt;

    intDoIt =  WshShell.Popup(L_Welcome_MsgBox_Message_Text,
                              0,
                              L_Welcome_MsgBox_Title_Text,
                              vbOKCancel + vbInformation );
    if (intDoIt == vbCancel)
    {
        WScript.Quit();
    }
}

//*** End
```

Chapter 11

Using Advanced WSH Features

In this chapter, we'll look at additional advanced features of Microsoft Windows Script Host (WSH). You'll learn how to retrieve the name of the current user, domain, or computer in a network and how to map network devices such as drives and printers and connect to them during logon. You'll also find out how to use WSH scripts to access the Microsoft Windows Registry so that you can extend Windows with new features and automate tasks.

RETRIEVING THE USER, DOMAIN, OR COMPUTER NAME

Windows allows you to retrieve the user name, domain name, or computer name from property pages of your Network Neighborhood property sheet. You can also use properties of the *WshNetwork* object to retrieve these names. You can create the object as a *WScript* subobject:

```
Set WshNetwork = WScript.CreateObject("WScript.Network")
```

You then access the properties of the object by using this *WshNetwork* object variable. The properties are as follows:

- **ComputerName**   The name of the workstation.
- **UserName**   The name of the user currently logged on at the workstation.

UserDomain is valid only if the machine is connected to a domain-oriented network such as Microsoft Windows NT Server or Microsoft Windows 2000 Server. If a Windows 95 or Windows 98 workstation is connected to a workgroup network, WSH returns an empty string (Figure 11-1, right). On a Windows 2000 machine, the property contains the name of the workstation, not the name of the workgroup (Figure 11-1, left).

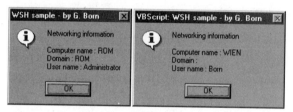

Figure 11-1 *Network properties (Windows 2000, left; Windows 98, right)*

PROBLEMS RETRIEVING THE USER NAME

Several postings in the WSH newsgroup have reported problems retrieving the user name. When used in a domain logon script, *UserName* is blank. This is a limitation of Windows 95 and Windows 98 because the logon script is running before you're physically logged on to the network. You can use a loop such as the following, which waits until the property is nonblank:

```
Set WshNetwork = WScript.CreateObject("WScript.Network")
User = ""    ' Initialize value.
Do While User = ""           ' Loop until user name is returned.
    User = WshNetwork.UserName    ' Read property.
    WScript.Sleep 200             ' Suspend to lower CPU load.
Loop
```

I used the *Sleep* method within this loop to lower the CPU load while the loop executes. For more details about *Sleep*, see Chapter 13.

The VBScript program shown in Listing 11-1 retrieves these properties and shows them in a dialog box. (Like the other samples shown in this chapter, Network.vbs is in the \WSHDevGuide\Chapter11 folder on the book's companion CD.)

```
'*************************************************
' File:    Network.vbs (WSH sample in VBScript)
' Author:  (c) G. Born
'
' Showing the user name, domain name, and
' workgroup name
'*************************************************
Option Explicit

Dim Text, Title
Dim WshNetwork           ' Object variable

Text = "Networking information" & vbCrLf & vbCrLf
Title = "WSH sample - by G. Born"

' Create a new WshNetwork object to access network properties.
Set WshNetwork = WScript.CreateObject("WScript.Network")

Text = Text & "Computer name : " & WshNetwork.ComputerName & vbCrLf
Text = Text & "Domain : " & WshNetwork.UserDomain & vbCrLf
Text = Text & "User name : " & WshNetwork.UserName & vbCrLf

MsgBox Text, vbOKOnly + vbInformation, Title

'*** End
```

Listing 11-1 *Network.vbs*

The JScript Implementation

The JScript version, Network.js, is shown in Listing 11-2.

```
//*************************************************
// File:    Network.js (WSH sample in JScript)
// Author:  (c) G. Born
//
// Showing the user name, domain name, and
// workgroup name
//*************************************************

var Text = "Networking information\n\n";
```

Listing 11-2 *Network.js*

(continued)

Listing 11-2 *continued*

```
// Create WshNetwork object to access network properties.
var WshNetwork = WScript.CreateObject("WScript.Network");

Text = Text + "Computer name : " + WshNetwork.ComputerName + "\n";
Text = Text + "Domain : " + WshNetwork.UserDomain + "\n";
Text = Text + "User name : " + WshNetwork.UserName + "\n";

WScript.Echo(Text);

//*** End
```

CONNECTING TO A NETWORK PRINTER

Within a network, you can connect a local workstation to a network printer. This task is commonly known as *printer mapping*. Windows can connect directly to a network printer or map a local port to a remote printer. (The latter approach is recommended only if you need support for network printing for an MS-DOS program.)

In WSH 2, the *WshNetwork* object provides two methods, *AddPrinterConnection* and *AddWindowsPrinterConnection*, for adding a network printer connection to Windows. *AddWindowsPrinterConnection* is the recommended method for connecting to a network printer (unless you need network printing support for MS-DOS applications).

First you retrieve an instance of the *WshNetwork* object using the following (VBScript) command:

```
Set WshNetwork = WScript.CreateObject("WScript.Network")
```

Then you use the following syntax for *AddWindowsPrinterConnection* in Windows 95 and Windows 98:

```
WshNetwork.AddWindowsPrinterConnection(strPrinterPath,
                                strDriverName[, strPort])
```

The first parameter must contain the printer path in UNC format (as in *\\ROM\HP500*). The second parameter specifies the name of the printer driver, and the third (optional) parameter specifies the local port to be remapped (such as LPT1).

> **NOTE**   In Windows 95 and Windows 98, the printer driver must be installed on the local machine in order for the *AddWindowsPrinterConnection* method to work. Otherwise, Windows returns the error message "Unknown printer driver."

In Windows NT and Windows 2000, the *AddWindowsPrinterConnection* method has just one parameter:

```
WshNetwork.AddWindowsPrinterConnection(strPrinterPath)
```

This parameter must contain the path to the network printer (as in *\\ROM\HP500*). No local port or printer driver is required.

If you intend to print from MS-DOS programs, you can also map a local printer port to a network printer in a WSH script using the *AddPrinterConnection* method of the *WshNetwork* object, as follows:

```
Set WshNetwork = WScript.CreateObject("WScript.Network")
WshNetwork.AddPrinterConnection "LPT1", "\\ROM\HP500"
```

The first line creates an instance of the *WshNetwork* object and assigns it to the object variable *WshNetwork*. The next line applies the *AddPrinterConnection* method to this object. This method requires at least two parameters. The first parameter contains the name of the local resource (such as *LPT1* or *LPT2*) as a string, and the second parameter defines the remote name of the network resource to be mapped, in UNC notation. (UNC stands for Universal Naming Convention, which specifies a reference to a network in the format *\\station name\path*.) For example, on my test machine, I can select the resource *\\ROM\HP500*, which references the printer *\HP500*, which is released on the workstation *\\ROM* for sharing.

Printer Mapping Using *AddWindowsPrinterConnection*

Listing 11-3 shows how to use VBScript to connect a printer to a network device in Windows NT or Windows 2000.

```
'**********************************************************
' File:    MapPrinter1.vbs (WSH sample in VBScript)
' Author:  (c) G. Born
'
' Connecting a printer to a network printer using
' the AddWindowsPrinterConnection method in
' Windows NT or Windows 2000
'**********************************************************
Option Explicit

' Const printer = "\\ROM\HP500"
Const printer = "\\Wien\HPLJ"

Dim Text, Title, icon
Dim WshNetwork            ' Object variable

Title = "WSH sample - by G. Born"

' Create a new WshNetwork object to access network properties.
Set WshNetwork = WScript.CreateObject("WScript.Network")

On Error Resume Next
```

Listing 11-3 *MapPrinter1.vbs*   *(continued)*

Listing 11-3 *continued*

```
WshNetwork.AddWindowsPrinterConnection printer

Select Case Err.Number
    Case 0
        Text = "Printer connected to """ & printer & """."
        icon = vbInformation
    Case -2147023688
        Text = "Error: Network resource """ & _
            printer & """ doesn't exist."
        icon = vbCritical
    Case -2147024811
        Text = "Error: Mapping to """ & printer & """ already exists."
        icon = vbCritical
    Case Else
        Text = "Error: Code " & Err.Number & " " & Err.Description
        icon = vbCritical
End Select

On Error GoTo 0      ' Enable run-time error handling.

MsgBox Text, vbOKOnly + icon, Title

'*** End
```

Printer Mapping Using *AddPrinterConnection*

To map a network printer to a local port (to support MS-DOS programs with network printing), you can use the *AddPrinterConnection* method of the *WshNetwork* object:

```
WshNetwork.AddPrinterConnection "LPT1", "\\ROM\HP500"
```

The first parameter in the VBScript statement is the name of the local port, and the second parameter is a valid network resource in UNC format. You can establish a printer mapping permanently, over several sessions, or temporarily (where the mapping is lost during reboot). You can select the Reconnect At Logon check box in the Capture Printer Port dialog box during a manual printer mapping to force permanent printer capturing. You can also use the *AddPrinterConnection* method's third, optional, parameter for this purpose. If this parameter is set to *True*, the method establishes a persistent connection that's set up during each logon. The preceding statement establishes a temporary connection for the local user.

You can also use the *AddPrinterConnection* method to set up a printer mapping for any user. You pass the user's name in a fourth parameter and a password in an optional fifth parameter, as shown in the following statement, which creates a connection for the user *Bill*.

```
WshNetwork.AddPrinterConnection "LPT1", "\\ROM\HP500", , _
                                "Bill", "Pegasus"
```

This statement omits the third parameter, so you must use a comma as a place-holder for the missing parameter. The method inserts the value *False* for the missing parameter, and you get a temporary mapping.

> **NOTE** It might seem useful to specify a user name and a password, but because these values are in a readable format in your script, anyone who has access to the script's source can see them. Therefore, it's better simply not to include passwords in a script.

RUN-TIME ERROR HANDLING

Using *AddPrinterConnection* to connect a local port to a network resource can lead to problems if the printer capture already exists. In this case, the method causes a run-time error. Whether or not you try to remap the port to the same resource, you get a message saying that the local resource is already being used.

You can use VBScript's *On Error Resume Next* statement to get around the problem:

```
Set WshNetwork = WScript.CreateObject("WScript.Network")
On Error Resume Next
WshNetwork.AddPrinterConnection "LPT1", "\\ROM\HP500"
On Error GoTo 0
    :
```

The *On Error Resume Next* statement in the second line means that if the printer mapping already exists, the third line causes a run-time error but the interpreter must continue with the next line of code.

The script can inform the user of the error, however. You can use VBScript's *Err* object for this purpose. If a run-time error occurs, the library assigns an error code to the *Err* object. You can retrieve this error code by using the object's *Number* property, as shown in the following statements:

```
On Error Resume Next ' Handle run-time errors.
WshNetwork.AddPrinterConnection "LPT1", \\ROM\HP500
If Err.Number <> 0 Then
    WScript.Echo "Error: " & CStr(Err.Number)
End If
On Error GoTo 0      ' Disable run-time error handling.
```

This code shows an error message if a run-time error occurs in the *Add-PrinterConnection* method.

The VBScript sample in Listing 11-4 uses *AddPrinterConnection* to establish a printer capture provided by the network client between the local port defined in the constant *port* and the network printer given in the constant *printer*. The script uses the *On Error Resume Next* statement to catch run-time errors. If the printer port is already captured, the script informs the user that the connection can't be made. You can extend this listing to force WSH to delete the current connection and establish a new mapping.

```
'****************************************************************
' File:    MapAddPrinterConnection.vbs (WSH sample in VBScript)
' Author:  (c) G. Born
'
' Mapping the printer port LPT1 to a network
' printer
'****************************************************************
Option Explicit

' Const printer = "\\ROM\HP500"
Const printer = "\\Wien\HP500"
Const port = "LPT1"

Dim Text, Title, icon
Dim WshNetwork           ' Object variable

Title = "WSH sample - by G. Born"

' Create a new WshNetwork object to access network properties.
Set WshNetwork = WScript.CreateObject("WScript.Network")

On Error Resume Next
WshNetwork.AddPrinterConnection port, printer

Select Case Err.Number
    Case 0
        Text = "Printer """ & port & """ connected to """ & _
            printer & """."
        icon = vbInformation
    Case -2147023688
        Text = "Error: Network resource """ & printer & _
            """ doesn't exist."
        icon = vbCritical
    Case -2147024811
        Text = "Error: Mapping """ & port & """ to """ & _
            printer & """ already exists."
        icon = vbCritical
```

Listing 11-4 *MapAddPrinterConnection.vbs*

```
    Case Else
        Text = "Error: Code " & Err.Number & " " & Err.Description
        icon = vbCritical
End Select

On Error Goto 0        ' Disable run-time error handling.

MsgBox Text, vbOKOnly + icon, Title

'*** End
```

NOTE If the script encounters an unknown error, the error code is reported. A negative error number (such as –2147023688) indicates a COM object error (because the high bit is set). Sometimes it's helpful to subtract *vbObjectError* from the negative value to get a more meaningful error code. Alternatively, you can convert the original decimal error number to a hexadecimal value. If the error isn't described in the VBScript help, you can search the Microsoft Knowledge Base (at *http://www.microsoft.com*) for error codes.

The JScript implementation

You can use the same methods for printer mapping in JScript. JScript 5 supports a *try ... catch* block that you can use to trap run-time errors, as shown here:

```
try
{
    WshNetwork.AddPrinterConnection("LPT1", "\\\\ROM\\HP500");
}
catch (err)
{
    if (err != 0)    // Check error object.
        WScript.Echo("Error: " + err);
}
```

The *try { ... }* block contains all the statements that might cause run-time errors. You must enclose the statements within the block in braces. If one of the statements causes a run-time error, the error dialog box of the run-time system is suppressed and control is transferred to the *catch* statement, which assigns the error code to the error variable given as the parameter of the *catch (err)* statement. You can define any variable name for *err*.

The statements within the *catch* branch must also be enclosed in braces, to create a block. These statements handle the run-time error. The sequence just shown uses an *if* statement to check whether the content of the variable *err* is equal to *0*. The sequence displays a user-defined error dialog box only if a run-time error occurs.

Listing 11-5 establishes a printer mapping. If a run-time error occurs, a user-defined error dialog box is shown.

```
//***************************************************
// File:     MapPrinter.js (WSH sample in JScript 5)
// Author:   (c) G. Born
//
// Mapping the printer port LPT1 to a network
// printer and trapping run-time errors
//***************************************************

var port = "LPT1"
var printer = "\\\\WIEN\\HPLJ"

// Create a new WshNetwork object to access network properties.
var WshNetwork = WScript.CreateObject("WScript.Network");

// Catch run-time errors.
try
{            // Try to add the connection.
    WshNetwork.AddPrinterConnection(port, printer);
}
catch (e)      // Catch a possible run-time error.
{
    if (e != 0)   // Display a possible error message.
        WScript.Echo("Error connecting printer", port,
                    "to", printer, "\n\nError code: " + e);
    WScript.Quit();
}
WScript.Echo("Printer port \"" + port +
            "\" connected to  \"" + printer);

//*** End
```

Listing 11-5 *MapPrinter.js*

Removing a Printer Mapping

You can remove a printer connection by using the *RemovePrinterConnection* method of the *WshNetwork* object. This method has the following syntax:

```
object.RemovePrinterConnection strName, [bForce], [bUpdateProfile]
```

The parameter *strName* can be a local resource (such as a printer port) or a remote printer. You can set the optional second parameter to a Boolean value of *True* or *False* to specify whether the connection should be removed if it's in use. You can also set the third parameter, *bUpdateProfile*, which is also optional, to *True* or *False*. If it's set to *True*, the mapping is removed from the user profile.

Listing 11-6 uses the *RemovePrinterConnection* method to remove a mapping from the local printer port LPT1.

```vbscript
'********************************************************
' File:    UnMapPrinter.vbs (WSH sample in VBScript)
' Author:  (c) G. Born
'
' Removing a printer mapping
'********************************************************
Option Explicit

Const port = "LPT1"

Dim Text, Title, icon
Dim WshNetwork          ' Object variable

Title = "WSH sample - by G. Born"

' Create a new WshNetwork object to access network properties.
Set WshNetwork = WScript.CreateObject("WScript.Network")

On Error Resume Next

WshNetwork.RemovePrinterConnection port

Select Case Err.Number
    Case 0
        Text = "Printer """ & port & """ connection removed"
        icon = vbInformation
    Case -2147023688
        Text = "Error: Network resource """ & printer & _
                """ doesn't exist."
        icon = vbCritical
    Case Else
        Text = "Error: Code " & Err.Number & " " & Err.Description
        icon = vbCritical
End Select

On Error Goto 0     ' Disable run-time error handling.

MsgBox Text, vbOKOnly + icon, Title

'*** End
```

Listing 11-6 *UnMapPrinter.vbs*

Listing All Mapped Printers

You can use the *EnumPrinterConnections* property to display a list of mapped printers on a machine. This property returns a collection containing the currently defined printer mappings. The following code statement retrieves the printer mappings:

```
Set oDevices = WshNetwork.EnumPrinterConnections
```

Once you retrieve the collection, you can use the variable *oDevices(0)* to find the name of the first printer port. The *oDevices(1)* variable contains the UNC name of the mapped network resource. This pattern continues, with the printer port in the even-numbered elements and the corresponding mapped network resource name in the odd-numbered elements.

Listing 11-7 uses a loop to process all entries in the collection and show the printer mappings in a dialog box (Figure 11-2). The step width in the loop is set to 2, and the local port and the network mapping are retrieved within each step.

```vbscript
'************************************************************
' File:     ListPrinterMapping.vbs (WSH sample in VBScript)
' Author:   (c) G. Born
'
' Listing printer mappings using EnumPrinterConnections
'************************************************************
Option Explicit

Dim Text, Title, i
Dim WshNetwork, oDevices        ' Object variable

Title = "WSH sample - by G. Born"

' Create a new WshNetwork object to access network properties.
Set WshNetwork = WScript.CreateObject("WScript.Network")

' List mappings.
Text = "Printer mapping" & vbCrLf

Set oDevices = WshNetwork.EnumPrinterConnections

For i = 0 To oDevices.Count - 1 Step 2
    Text = Text & oDevices(i) & "      " & oDevices(i+1) & vbCrLf
Next

MsgBox Text, vbOKOnly + vbInformation, Title

'*** End
```

Listing 11-7 *ListPrinterMapping.vbs*

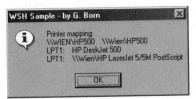

Figure 11-2 *A list of printer mappings (in Windows 2000)*

The JScript implementation

The JScript version, ListPrinterMapping.js, is shown in Listing 11-8.

```
//***********************************************************
// File:    ListPrinterMapping.js (WSH sample in JScript)
// Author:  (c) G. Born
//
// Showing printer mappings using EnumPrinterConnections
//***********************************************************

// Create a new WshNetwork object to access network properties.
var WshNetwork = WScript.CreateObject("WScript.Network");

// List mappings.
Text = "Printer mapping \n";

var oDevices = WshNetwork.EnumPrinterConnections();

for (var i = 0; i <= oDevices.length-2; i = i+2)
{
    Text = Text + oDevices(i) + "    " + oDevices(i+1) + "\n";
}

WScript.Echo(Text);

//*** End
```

Listing 11-8 *ListPrinterMapping.js*

Setting the Default Printer

WSH 2 also provides a *SetDefaultPrinter* method, whose parameter specifies a printer as the default printer:

```
Set WshNetwork = WScript.CreateObject("WScript.Network")
WshNetwork.SetDefaultPrinter "\\Wien\HP500"
```

NOTE While experimenting with this method in Windows 2000, I found an irregularity. If the printer doesn't exist, the method causes a run-time error. My attempt to handle this run-time error using *On Error Resume Next* failed. If a run-time error occurs, the script terminates without any further messages even if you insert statements (such as *If Err <> 0 Then* or *WScript.Echo Err.Code*) to test the error code. As a result, the sample in Listing 11-9 doesn't contain any error handling.

Listing 11-9 lists in an input dialog box (shown in Figure 11-3) all printers found on a system. The user can enter a number to select a valid entry. The associated printer is then set as the default printer, and a dialog box reports this result.

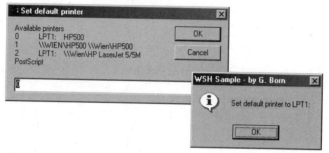

Figure 11-3 *Setting the default printer*

```
'***********************************************************
' File:    DefaultPrinter.vbs (WSH sample in VBScript)
' Author: (c) G. Born
'
' Setting the default printer (in WSH 2)
'***********************************************************
Option Explicit

Dim Text, Title, i, j, tmp, printer
Dim WshNetwork, oDevices          ' Object variable

Title = "WSH sample - by G. Born"

' Create a new WshNetwork object to access network properties.
Set WshNetwork = WScript.CreateObject("WScript.Network")

' Read all printers.
Set oDevices = WshNetwork.EnumPrinterConnections

Text = "Available printers" & vbCrLf
j = oDevices.Count
```

Listing 11-9 *DefaultPrinter.vbs*

```
For i = 0 To j - 1 Step 2
    Text = Text & (i/2) & vbTab
    Text = Text & oDevices(i) & vbTab & oDevices(i+1) & vbCrLf
Next

' Show all available printers and allow a user selection.
tmp = InputBox(Text, "Set default printer", 0)
If tmp = "" Then
    WScript.Echo "No user input, aborted"
    WScript.Quit
End If

tmp = CInt(tmp)
If (tmp < 0) Or (tmp > (j/2 - 1)) Then
    WScript.Echo "Wrong value, aborted"
    WScript.Quit
End If

printer = oDevices(tmp*2 + 1)  ' Select printer name.

' Set the default printer.
WshNetwork.SetDefaultPrinter printer

MsgBox "Set default printer to " & printer, _
        vbOKOnly + vbInformation, Title

'*** End
```

MAPPING NETWORK DRIVES

Just as you can share printers, you can share drives or folders within a network. In Windows, you can map these network resources to local drives, which is useful if you use older software that doesn't support UNC network paths or if you prefer to use a drive such as D: or E: to access a device.

In this section, we'll look at a simple script that maps three shareable network resources to the X:, Y:, and Z: drives. The program then displays a list of all mapped drives in a dialog box (Figure 11-4).

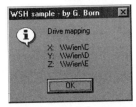

Figure 11-4 *Drive mapping*

You can map a network resource (such as a drive or a folder) to a local drive by using the *MapNetworkDrive* method of the *WshNetwork* object. The method's first parameter is the name of the local drive (the drive letter and the colon). The second parameter specifies a network resource in UNC format.

Two other, optional, parameters specify the user name and the password to establish the mapping. If you use these two parameters, you run the risk that the password won't be secure. For more details on the syntax of the *MapNetworkDrive* method, see the Windows Script Host Reference.

> **NOTE** The *MapNetworkDrive* method causes a run-time error if the local drive is already mapped or if the UNC path to the network resource isn't valid.

The following VBScript sequence catches run-time errors while creating the mapping:

```
Set WshNetwork = WScript.CreateObject("WScript.Network")
On Error Resume Next
WshNetwork.MapNetworkDrive "X:", \\ROM\C
ErrCheck Err.Number
```

The first statement creates the *WshNetwork* object. *On Error Resume Next* forces the interpreter to continue with the next statement in the script. The third line uses the *MapNetworkDrive* method to map a network drive to a local drive. The *ErrCheck* procedure in the last line ensures that a run-time error is reported to the user in a customized dialog box (not a run-time error dialog box, which terminates the script).

To list all mapped local drives, this sample uses the *EnumNetworkDrives* method, which returns an object containing a collection with all mapped drives. The following statement creates the collection:

```
Set oDrives = WshNetwork.EnumNetworkDrives
```

You can then use the following loop to process all items in the collection:

```
For i = 0 To oDrives.Count - 1 Step 2
    If oDrives(i) <> " " Then
        Text = Text & oDrives(i) & "    " & oDrives(i+1) & vbCrLf
    End If
Next
```

The first entry in the collection returns the local drive name, and the second entry contains the UNC path to the mapped network resource. Therefore, the loop uses a step width of 2.

The full VBScript implementation is shown in Listing 11-10.

```vbscript
'***************************************************
' File:    MapDrives.vbs (WSH sample in VBScript)
' Author:  (c) G. Born
'
' Mapping network drives and listing them in a
' dialog box
'***************************************************
Option Explicit

Const machine = "\\Wien"

Dim Text, Title, i
Dim WshNetwork, oDrives          ' Object variable

Text = "Drive mapping" & vbCrLf & vbCrLf
Title = "WSH sample - by G. Born"

' Create a new WshNetwork object to access Network properties.
Set WshNetwork = WScript.CreateObject("WScript.Network")

' Map some drives.
On Error Resume Next
WshNetwork.MapNetworkDrive "X:", machine & "\C"
ErrCheck Err.Number

WshNetwork.MapNetworkDrive "Y:", machine & "\D"
ErrCheck Err.Number

WshNetwork.MapNetworkDrive "Z:", machine & "\E"
ErrCheck Err.Number

' Get collection from EnumNetworkDrives property.
Set oDrives = WshNetwork.EnumNetworkDrives

For i = 0 To oDrives.Count - 1 Step 2
    If oDrives(i) <> " " Then
        Text = Text & oDrives(i) & "    " & oDrives(i+1) & vbCrLf
    End If
Next

MsgBox Text, vbOKOnly + vbInformation, Title
```

Listing 11-10 *MapDrives.vbs*

(continued)

Listing 11-10 *continued*

```
'################
' Show error.
Sub ErrCheck(nr)
    Select Case nr
        Case 0
            ' No error
        Case -2147024829
            WScript.Echo "Error: Network resource doesn't exist"
        Case -2147024811
            WScript.Echo "Error: Drive already mapped"
        Case Else
            WScript.Echo "Error: " & CStr(nr)
    End Select
End Sub

'*** End
```

The JScript Implementation

To prevent run-time errors when using the *MapNetworkDrive* method on an already mapped drive, you can use the following statements:

```
WshNetwork.RemoveNetworkDrive("X:");
WshNetwork.MapNetworkDrive("X:", "\\\\ROM\\C");
```

The command removes the mapping of a drive and creates a new assignment. If a mapping doesn't exist, the *RemoveNetworkDrive* method raises a run-time error. To establish run-time error handling, you can move the *RemoveNetworkDrive* and *MapNetworkDrive* methods into separate procedures. These procedures use *try...catch* error handling to force script execution and show run-time errors. Listing 11-11 shows the full code listing.

```
//****************************************************
// File:    MapDrives.js (WSH sample in JScript)
// Author:  (c) G. Born
//
// Mapping network drives and listing them in a
// dialog box
//****************************************************

var machine = "\\\\Wien\\";
```

Listing 11-11 *MapDrives.js*

```
// Create a new WshNetwork object, which we need
// to access network properties.
var WshNetwork = WScript.CreateObject("WScript.Network");

// Remove mapping to prevent run-time errors.
DisconnectDrive("X:");
DisconnectDrive("Y:");
DisconnectDrive("Z:");

// Create some mappings for network drives.
ConnectDrive("X:", machine + "C");
ConnectDrive("Y:", machine + "D");
ConnectDrive("Z:", machine + "E");

// List all mapped drives.
Text = "Mapped drives \n";

var oDevices = WshNetwork.EnumNetworkDrives();

for (var i = 0; i <= oDevices.length - 2; i = i + 2)
{
    Text = Text + oDevices(i) + "      " + oDevices(i+1) + "\n";
}

WScript.Echo(Text);

function DisconnectDrive(drive)
{
    try
    {
        WshNetwork.RemoveNetworkDrive(drive);
    }
    catch (e)
    {
        if (e != 0)          // Display a possible error message.
            WScript.Echo("Remove " + drive, "\nError code : ",
                        e.number, e.description);
    }
}
```

(continued)

Listing 11-11 *continued*

```
function ConnectDrive(drive, resource)
{
    try
    {
        WshNetwork.MapNetworkDrive(drive, resource);
    }
    catch (e)
    {
        if (e != 0)              // Display a possible error message.
            WScript.Echo("Map " + drive + " to " + resource,
                         "\nError code : ", e.number, e.description);
    }
}

//*** End
```

Logon Scripts

You can execute WSH scripts in Windows during logon to customize the user environment (map network drives and printers, for example). In Windows 2000, an administrator can also set up scripts to be executed during startup, shutdown, logon, and logoff (using the Microsoft Management Console). I'll come back to this topic in Chapter 13.

ACCESSING THE WINDOWS REGISTRY

You can use methods of the *WshShell* object to access the Registry. The Registry is a database that stores internal configuration data.

> **WARNING** Altering the Registry can seriously damage your Windows system. Use and modify the upcoming scripts at your own risk. For tips on backing up the Registry, see my book *Inside the Microsoft Windows 98 Registry* (Microsoft Press, 1998).

You don't need to deal directly with these data files because Windows provides API functions for accessing the Registry. These functions organize the Registry as hierarchical trees of keys, subkeys, and values. The tree structure is also shown in the Registry Editor.

Figure 11-5 shows part of the Registry in the Registry Editor. The left pane contains the key's hierarchy, and the right pane contains the value of the current key. The Registry in Windows 95 and Windows 98 consists of six root keys. In Windows NT and Windows 2000, only five root keys (sometimes called hives) are used. All root keys start with *HKEY_*, and they group subkeys into categories. The root keys of the Windows 2000 Registry are shown in the figure.

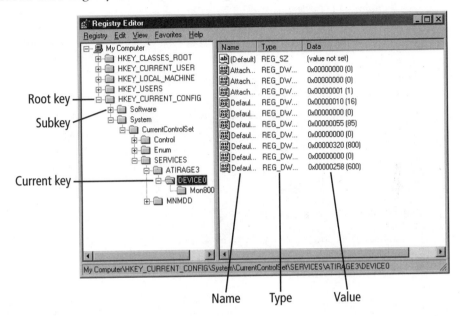

Root key

Subkey

Current key

Name   Type   Value

Figure 11-5 *Keys and values in the Registry Editor*

Each key can contain zero or more subkeys. A key can have a default value associated with it; if this default value isn't set, *(Default)* and the string *(value not set)* are shown in the right pane of the Registry Editor. In the Registry Editor, you can define your own values using letters, the numerals 0 to 9, and the underscore character (_). Values can be of several data types for storing the content:

- *String (REG_SZ)*   Contains string values. The content must be enclosed in double quotes (as in "*C:\WINDOWS\EXPLORER.EXE*").

- *Binary (REG_BINARY)*   Some drivers and applications need binary code values stored with this data type. The Registry Editor displays binary data as a hexadecimal byte sequence (as in *01 03 01 00 AB 00...*). The data in a binary value can be a sequence between 1 byte and 64 KB long. Binary data are stored in little endian order (with the least significant byte first).

TIP   The WSH *RegWrite* method supports only write access for binary values with up to 4 bytes. If you need to write a Registry value of the type *Binary* that contains more than 4 bytes, use the following trick: write a .reg file (using the *FileSystemObject* object discussed in the next chapter) with the necessary entries. Then use the *Run* method to shell the Registry Editor, which imports the file (as in *WshShell.Run "RegEdit.exe D:\Data.reg", ,True*).

■   *DWORD (REG_DWORD)*   A special binary data type that always contains 32 bits. DWORD values are shown as hexadecimal and decimal values in the Registry Editor.

Windows NT and Windows 2000 also support two other data types. *REG_EXPAND_SZ* contains expandable strings, and *REG_MULTI_SZ* contains multiple strings. Windows 2000 also has a new data type, *REG_FULL_RESOURCE_DESCRIPTOR*, that describes hardware resources. (It isn't supported in WSH.)

> **WARNING**   The user shouldn't modify binary entries (or any Registry entries for that matter) because this data is coded specifically to a program. The risk of writing the wrong data into the Registry and damaging the system is simply too high. I recommend that you use Control Panel or install programs to update binary Registry values.

Accessing the Registry in WSH

You can access the Registry (keys and values) from a WSH script by using the methods of the *WshShell* object: *RegRead*, *RegWrite*, and *RegDelete*. To create a new key, you use the following statement:

```
WshShell.RegWrite "HKCR\.1G_BORN\", ""
```

Here, the *RegWrite* method creates the subkey *.1G_BORN* in the root key *HKEY_CLASSES_ROOT*. The first parameter of the *RegWrite* method passes the name of a key or value, which should be written. The name must begin with one of the six root keys or the abbreviation of that name (if there is one), as shown in Table 11-1.

Table 11-1   **NAMES OF ROOT KEYS**

Short Name	*Long Name*
HKCU	HKEY_CURRENT_USER
HKLM	HKEY_LOCAL_MACHINE
HKCR	HKEY_CLASSES_ROOT
	HKEY_USERS
	HKEY_CURRENT_CONFIG
	HKEY_DYN_DATA

The subkeys must be separated with backslashes. Because the first parameter of *RegWrite* passes either a key name or a value name and because these are very different types of data, the system must determine whether a key or value is provided:

■   If the string in the first parameter ends with a backslash, the WSH run-time system assumes that a key should be written. If the key doesn't exist, it is created. If the key exists, the method terminates without further processing.

■   If the string ends without a backslash (as in *"HKCR\.1G_BORN\Test"*), it's a value. The method interprets this as a command to write a value. In this case, the *RegWrite* method writes the value into the key given in the string. If the value doesn't exist, a new entry with the name and the data is created.

> **NOTE**   Uppercase and lowercase are preserved when you create an entry. When you access the keys or values, the names are case insensitive.

The method's second parameter contains the data for the entry (key or value) whose name is defined in the first parameter. A third parameter defines the data type used for a value:

```
WshShell.RegWrite "HKCR\.1G_BORN\Test", "Hello, world", "REG_SZ"
```

The statement creates the value *Test* in the key *HKEY_CLASSES_ROOT\.1G_BORN* and writes the string *"Hello, world"*. Thus, the value's data type, passed in the third parameter, should be set to *REG_SZ*. Other data types are *REG_EXPAND_SZ*, *REG_DWORD*, and *REG_BINARY*. Windows 95 and Windows 98 support only *REG_SZ*, *REG_DWORD*, and *REG_BINARY*.

> **NOTE**   For more information on the data types of Registry entries, see the Platform SDK. (See *http://msdn.microsoft.com/library/default.asp*, for example.)

To read a value, you use the *RegRead* method with the following syntax:

```
sregval = WshShell.RegRead("HKCR\.1G_BORN\Test")
```

The method requires the name of the key, including the value's name, and returns the value. If the key doesn't exist, the method causes a run-time error. Later, I'll show you how to catch such run-time errors and how to test whether a key exists.

To delete a value or a key, you can use the *RegDel* method with the following syntax:

```
WshShell.RegDelete "HKCR\.1G_BORN\Test"
```

The parameter contains the path to a value or a key. If the string ends with a backslash, the parameter contains a key name. The key or value is deleted. If a key contains other subkeys or values, all entries are deleted automatically.

> **WARNING**   If a key or value doesn't exist, the method causes a run-time error (as described shortly).

Accessing the Registry in VBScript

Let's look at a simple example that applies the methods we just discussed. The script first creates a new key and then a new value. After starting, the script asks whether the key *.1G_BORN* in the branch *HKEY_CLASSES_ROOT* should be created. If the user clicks Yes, a new key is created (or an existing key is retained). Because the key *.1G_BORN* isn't normally present in Windows, there should be no problem with Registry access. Another dialog box is shown before the value is written and before the value of the key is deleted.

The dialog boxes enable you to check each step. They also allow you to skip the functions to delete the value or the key. After creating the key and the value, you can examine the branch *HKEY_CLASSES_ROOT* using the Registry Editor (Figure 11-6).

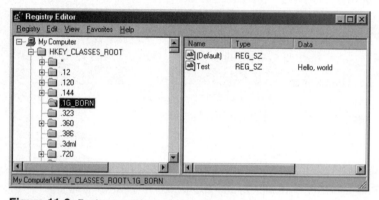

Figure 11-6 *Registry entries*

IMPORTANT In Windows NT and Windows 2000, the script needs the right to access the key (read, write, and delete), which it has if the script is executed using the administrator account. In Windows 2000, you can create a shortcut to the script file. On the shortcut's property page, you can select the option to execute the script under another user account. An administrator can thus allow scripts to be executed at user level but grant the script administrator-level access rights.

The full VBScript implementation is shown in Listing 11-12. By the way, in this sample, the key is always present in the Registry, so your script probably won't cause a run-time error. After you do your tests, you should remove the entries from the Registry using the Registry Editor or the script itself.

```vbscript
'**************************************************
' File:    Registry.vbs (WSH sample in VBScript)
' Author:  (c) G. Born
'
' Accessing the Registry
'**************************************************
Option Explicit

Dim Root, key, valname, valx, Response, sregval

' Initialize variables.
Root = "HKEY_CLASSES_ROOT"
key = "\.1G_BORN\"
valname = "Test"
valx ="Hello, world"

' Create WshShell object.
Dim WshShell
Set WshShell = WScript.CreateObject("WScript.Shell")

' Ask user before creating a key.
Response = MsgBox("Create key?", vbYesNo + vbQuestion _
                  + vbDefaultButton2, "Registry access")

If Response = vbYes Then    ' Selected Yes
    ' Create key/value.
    WshShell.RegWrite Root & Key, ""
    ' Show success.
    MsgBox "Key " & Root & Key & " created"
End If

' Ask user before creating a value.
Response = MsgBox("Create value?", vbYesNo + vbQuestion _
                  + vbDefaultButton2, "Registry access")

If Response = vbYes Then     ' Selected Yes
    ' Create string entry.
    WshShell.RegWrite Root & Key & valname, valx, "REG_SZ"
    WshShell.Popup "Value " & Root & Key & valname & " created"

    ' Try to read value.
    sregval = WshShell.RegRead(Root & Key & valname)
    MsgBox "Value " & valname & ": " & sregval
End If
```

Listing 11-12 *Registry.vbs*   *(continued)*

Listing 11-12 *continued*

```
' Ask before deleting value.
Response = MsgBox("Delete value?", vbYesNo + vbQuestion + _
                 vbDefaultButton2, "Registry access")
If Response = vbYes Then     ' Yes selected.
    WshShell.RegDelete Root & Key & valname
    MsgBox "Value " & valname & " deleted"
End If

' Ask before deleting the key.
Response = MsgBox("Delete key?", vbYesNo + vbQuestion + _
                 vbDefaultButton2, "Registry access")
If Response = vbYes Then     ' Yes selected.
    WshShell.RegDelete Root & Key
    MsgBox "Key " & key & " deleted"
End If

'*** End
```

The JScript implementation

The only difference between the VBScript and JScript implementations is that in JScript you must use a double backslash instead of a single backslash in the string because the single backslash is an escape character in JScript. The JScript implementation is shown in Listing 11-13.

```
//*************************************************
// File:    Registry.js (WSH sample in JScript)
// Author:  (c) G. Born
//
// Accessing the Registry
//*************************************************

var vbOKCancel = 1;
var vbInformation = 64;
var vbCancel = 2;

// Initialize variables.
var Root = "HKEY_CLASSES_ROOT";
var key = "\\.1G_BORN\\";
var valname = "Test";
var valx ="Hello, world";
var result;

// Create WshShell object.
var WshShell = WScript.CreateObject("WScript.Shell");
```

Listing 11-13 *Registry.js*

```
// Ask user before the key is created.
result = WshShell.Popup("Create key?",
                        0,
                        "Registry access",
                        vbOKCancel + vbInformation);
if (result != vbCancel)
{  // Use "REG_SZ" or "REG_BINARY" or "REG_BINARY" as type
   WshShell.RegWrite(Root + key + valname, valx, "REG_SZ");
   WshShell.Popup("Inserted: " + Root + key + valname);

   // Try to read value back.
   sregval = WshShell.RegRead(Root + key + valname);
   WshShell.Popup("Value: " + sregval);
}

// Ask before deleting the value.
result = WshShell.Popup("Delete value?",
                        0,
                        "Registry access",
                        vbOKCancel + vbInformation);
if (result != vbCancel)
{
   WshShell.RegDelete(Root + key + valname);
   WshShell.Popup("Deleted: " + Root + key + valname);
}

// Ask before deleting the key.
result = WshShell.Popup("Delete key?",
                        0,
                        "Registry access",
                        vbOKCancel + vbInformation);
if (result != vbCancel)
{
   WshShell.RegDelete(Root + key);
   WshShell.Popup("Deleted: " + Root + key);
}

//*** End
```

Run-Time Error Handling for Registry Access

The Registry.vbs and Registry.js examples don't encounter problems when reading from the Registry because they create the *.1G_BORN* key before they try to read it. In the real world, however, you'll run into the following trap sooner or later: if the key or value specified in a Registry read operation doesn't exist, *WshShell.RegRead* produces a run-time error. In VBScript, you can use the *On Error Resume Next* statement to catch run-time errors, and you can use the *Err* object's *Number* property to analyze the error code. The code to read a Registry key with error handling can look like this:

```
On Error Resume Next
' Try to read the value. If value doesn't exist, catch run-time error.
sregval = WshShell.RegRead(Root & Key & valname)
If Err.Number <> 0 Then
    MsgBox "Value doesn't exist"
    WScript.Quit     ' Terminate script.
End If
```

The next code listing uses this approach and tries to read a key in VBScript. The sample contains error-handling code to detect whether a key exists. To test the sample, execute the script Registry1.vbs and click No in the dialog boxes that ask whether the key or the value should be created. The required key and value aren't created, and a run-time error occurs during read access of the nonexistent value. The script handles this run-time error by displaying a message that the key doesn't exist.

The full implementation is shown in Listing 11-14.

```
'*************************************************
' File:    Registry1.vbs (WSH sample in VBScript)
' Author:  (c) G. Born
'
' Accessing the Registry and catching run-time
' errors while accessing missing keys
'*************************************************
Option Explicit

' Warning: Enable run-time error handling for the entire script.
On Error Resume Next

Dim Root, key, valname, valx, Response, sregval

' Initialize variables.
Root = "HKEY_CLASSES_ROOT"
key = "\.1G_BORN\"
valname = "Test"
valx ="Hello, world"

' Create WshShell object.
Dim WshShell
Set WshShell = WScript.CreateObject("WScript.Shell")
```

Listing 11-14 *Registry1.vbs*

```
' Ask user before creating a key.
Response = MsgBox("Create key?", vbYesNo + vbQuestion _
                  + vbDefaultButton2, "Registry access")

If Response = vbYes Then    ' Yes selected.
    ' Create key/value.
    WshShell.RegWrite Root & Key, ""
    ' Show success.
    WshShell.Popup "Key " & Root & Key & " created"
End If

' Ask user before creating a value.
Response = MsgBox("Create value?", vbYesNo + vbQuestion _
                  + vbDefaultButton2, "Registry access")

If Response = vbYes Then     ' Yes selected.
    ' Create string entry.
    WshShell.RegWrite Root & Key & valname, valx, "REG_SZ"
    MsgBox "Value " & Root & Key & valname & " created"
    ' Get value.
    sregval = WshShell.RegRead(Root & Key & valname)
    MsgBox "Value " & valname & ": " & sregval
Else
    ' Try to read value back. If the value doesn't exist,
    ' catch the run-time error using the Err object.
    sregval = WshShell.RegRead(Root & Key & valname)
    If Err.Number <> 0 Then
        MsgBox "Value doesn't exist"
        WScript.Quit
    Else
        MsgBox "Value " & valname & ": " & sregval
    End If
End If

' Ask before deleting value.
Response = MsgBox("Delete value?", vbYesNo + vbQuestion + _
                  vbDefaultButton2, "Registry access")
If Response = vbYes Then    ' Yes selected.
    WshShell.RegDelete Root & Key & valname
    MsgBox "Value " & valname & " deleted"
End If

' Ask before deleting key.
Response = MsgBox("Delete key?", vbYesNo + vbQuestion + _
                  vbDefaultButton2, "Registry access")
```

(continued)

Listing 11-14 *continued*

```
If Response = vbYes Then      ' Yes selected.
    WshShell.RegDelete Root & Key
    MsgBox "Key " & key & " deleted"
End If

'*** End
```

Checking the Existence of a Key

The error handling shown above is too much work because you have to add all the error-handling code to each Registry read statement. It's much more convenient to use a function that tests for the existence of a key or value. In VBScript, you can implement such a function with just a few lines of code.

```
Function KeyExists(key)
    Dim key2
    On Error Resume Next
    key2 = WshShell.RegRead(key)
    If Err <> 0 Then
        KeyExists = False
    Else
        KeyExists = True
    End If
    On Error GoTo 0
End Function
```

You pass the expression containing the key or value name as a parameter to the function, which then tries to read the key or value. Depending on the value of the *Err* object, the function returns the value *True* or *False*.

This new function is shown in Listing 11-15. The program asks the user to enter the name of a key or a value. After the user closes the input dialog box, the program tests whether the key or value exists. If an entry exists, its value is shown in a dialog box (Figure 11-7, top). Otherwise, an error dialog box is shown (Figure 11-7, bottom).

Key names must end with a backslash. Using *HKCR\.bmp* results in a message that the key doesn't exist because the *RegRead* method requires the terminating slash for keys. Using *HKCR\.bmp* forces the program to read the content of the key *.bmp* in the branch *HKEY_CLASSES_ROOT*. This entry defines the .bmp file type within the Registry.

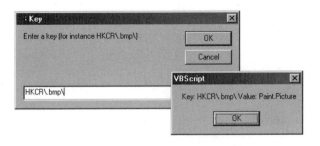

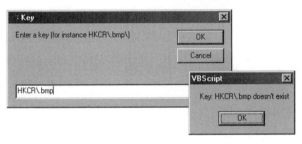

Figure 11-7 *Dialog boxes for accessing a Registry key*

```
'*************************************************
' File:    Registry2.vbs (WSH sample in VBScript)
' Author:  (c) G. Born
'
' Accessing the Registry and using KeyExist to
' check whether a key or value exists
'*************************************************
Option Explicit

Dim key1
Dim WshShell

' Get WshShell object for Registry methods.
Set WshShell = WScript.CreateObject("WScript.Shell")

' Query user for new key.
key1 = InputBox("Enter a key (for instance HKCR\.bmp\)", "Key", "HKCR\")
If KeyExists(key1) = True Then
    MsgBox "Key: " & key1 & " Value: " & WshShell.RegRead(key1)
Else
    MsgBox "Key: " & key1 & " doesn't exist"
End If
```

Listing 11-15 *Registry2.vbs*   *(continued)*

Listing 11-15 *continued*

```
Function KeyExists(key)
    Dim key2
    On Error Resume Next
    key2 = WshShell.RegRead(key)
    If Err <> 0 Then
        KeyExists = False
    Else
        KeyExists = True
    End If
    On Error GoTo 0
End Function


'*** End
```

The JScript implementation

JScript doesn't have an input function, so the sample in Listing 11-16 is implemented as a .wsf file using the technique I described in Chapter 8 to retrieve user input. The function to test a Registry key's existence is implemented in JScript.

```
<?xml version="1.0" encoding="ISO-8859-1"?>
<!--
    File:   Registry2.wsf (WSH 2)
    Author: (c) G. Born
-->

<job id="T1">
    <script language="VBScript">
    <![CDATA[
        Function WSHInputBox(Message, Title, Value)
            ' Provides an InputBox function for JScript
            ' It can be called from JScript as follows:
            ' var result = WSHInputBox("Enter a name", "Input", test);
            WSHInputBox = InputBox(Message, Title, Value)
        End Function
    ]]>
    </script>

    <script language="JScript">
    <![CDATA[
        function KeyExists(obj, key)
        {
            // Checks whether a key exists.
```

Listing 11-16 *Registry2.wsf*

```
        try
        {
            var key2 = obj.RegRead(key);
        }
        catch (e)
        {
            if (e != 0)    // Error
                return false;
        }
        return true;
    }
  ]]>
</script>

<script language="VBScript">
<![CDATA[
    Dim key1
    Dim WSHShell

    ' Get WSHShell object for Registry methods.
    Set WSHShell = WScript.CreateObject("WScript.Shell")

    ' Query key name for new key.
    key1 = WSHInputBox("Enter a key (for instance HKCR\.bmp\) ", _
                        "Key", "HKCR\")
    If KeyExists(WSHShell, key1) = True Then
        MsgBox "Key: " & key1 & " Value: " & WSHShell.RegRead(key1)
    Else
        MsgBox "Key: " & key1 & " doesn't exist"
    End If
  ]]>
    </script>
</job>
```

Techniques for Registry Access in WSH

In Listing 11-16, only simple values are read from Registry keys. According to the Windows Script Host Reference, the methods to read from and write to the Registry support several data types:

■ **REG_SZ** A simple string value is written.

■ **REG_MULTI_SZ** A value with multiple string entries is written. This data type is supported only in Windows NT and Windows 2000. WSH 2 doesn't support this value.

- ■ ***REG_EXPAND_SZ***   An expandable string value is written. This data type is supported only in Windows NT and Windows 2000.

- ■ ***REG_DWORD***   A DWORD value is written. The value passed to *RegWrite* must be an integer.

- ■ ***REG_BINARY***   A binary data stream is written. The value passed to *RegWrite* must be an integer that contains the data stream.

You can use these types to read values, and you can use some of them to create a value, as I'll demonstrate shortly.

At this point, I should mention what happens when a new key is created. If you create a new key using the Registry Editor, the default value is undefined. Writing a new Registry key by using *RegWrite* sets the default value to a zero string:

```
WshShell.RegWrite "HKCR\.123\", ""
```

If you need similar behavior in a script, you have to use a trick. Don't create a new key; instead, insert a new value and a key into the Registry. Then you can delete the value, and a new key with a *(Default)* value set to *"value not set"* is left. You can create a new value, including the hosting key, by using the following statement:

```
' Create a value directly, forcing an empty default value.
WshShell.RegWrite "HKCR\.123\Test", "Hello, world", "REG_SZ"
```

This statement creates the value *Test* in the key *HKEY_CLASSES_ROOT\.123*. If the key is created when the value is created, the default value is undefined.

Using *RegRead* to read the values can also cause a few problems. First, if you attempt to read a default value of a given key, WSH 2 forces a run-time error if the value isn't defined. The error code is the same as for a nonexistent key. In a moment, I'll show a sample program, RegAccessTest.vbs, that allows you to test this behavior. (See Listing 11-19 on pages 303–4.)

Dealing with binary values

When you use WSH to write *REG_BINARY* values in the Registry, you're limited to 4-byte entries because the parameter passed for the value must be a long integer. When you read values containing *REG_BINARY*, you use *RegRead* to return a byte array, which can be extracted within a *For Each* loop. Listing 11-17 writes a *REG_BINARY* value and reads it back.

```
'*************************************************
' File:   BinaryRead.vbs (WSH sample in VBScript)
' Author: (c) G. Born
'
' Reading a binary entry from the Registry and
' displaying it
'*************************************************
Option Explicit

Dim WshShell, value, entry, text

' Create WshShell object to access Registry.
Set WshShell = WScript.CreateObject("WScript.Shell")

' Add a binary value using the REG_BINARY type.
WshShell.RegWrite "HKCR\.123\Binary", 123456789, "REG_BINARY"

' Read value.
value = WshShell.RegRead("HKCR\.123\Binary")

' Extract array values.
text = "Entry is of type " & typename(value) & vbCrLf
For Each entry In value
    text = text & entry & vbCrLf
Next

MsgBox text, vbOKOnly, "Read REG_BINARY entry"

WshShell.RegDelete "HKCR\.123\"

WScript.Echo "Key removed"

'*** End
```

Listing 11-17 *BinaryRead.vbs*

Dealing with *REG_MULTI_SZ* values

WSH doesn't support *REG_MULTI_SZ* values. You can create a value of type *REG_MULTI_SZ*, but you can't set a true multistring entry. You can read a *REG_MULTI_SZ* value by using the *RegRead* method, which returns an array containing strings. To show these values in a dialog box, the script must process this array. Listing 11-18 reads a *REG_MULTI_SZ* value (using a predefined key from the Registry).

```
'**********************************************************
' File:   MultiStrRead.vbs (WSH sample in VBScript)
' Author: (c) G. Born
'
' Reading a REG_MULTI_SZ entry from the Registry
' and displaying it
'**********************************************************
Option Explicit

Dim WshShell, val, entry, text

' Create WshShell object to access Registry.
Set WshShell = WScript.CreateObject("WScript.Shell")

' Read a REG_MULTI_SZ entry.
val = WshShell.RegRead _
    ("HKLM\System\CurrentControlSet\Control\ServiceGroupOrder\list")

' Process values.
text = "Entry is of type " & typename(val) & vbCrLf
For Each entry In val
    text = text & entry & vbCrLf
Next

MsgBox text, vbOKOnly, "Read REG_MULTI_SZ entry"

'*** End
```

Listing 11-18 *MultiStrRead.vbs*

Accessing Registry values and keys

The VBScript program in Listing 11-19 accesses Registry values and keys in WSH. The script creates a new key called *HKCR\.123* and adds some values of type *REG_SZ*, *REG_DWORD*, *REG_BINARY*, and *REG_EXPAND_SZ*. In each step, the values added to the Registry are shown in a dialog box. You can thus inspect the Registry using the Registry Editor. Next, the script creates a new value in the key *HKCR\.123* in one step, causing the *(Default)* value of the key to be undefined. The *RegRead* method causes a run-time error. You can use this script to test the behavior of the methods for accessing the Registry.

```
'********************************************************
' File:   RegAccessTest.vbs (WSH sample in VBScript)
' Author: (c) G. Born
'
' Accessing different types in the Registry (in WSH 2)
'********************************************************
Option Explicit

Dim WshShell
Dim value

' Create WshShell object to access the Registry.
Set WshShell = WScript.CreateObject("WScript.Shell")

' First, create a simple key. Note that the
' default value is set implicitly to ""
WshShell.RegWrite "HKCR\.123\", ""
value = WshShell.RegRead("HKCR\.123\")
WScript.Echo "Key HKCR\.123 written ..." & vbCrLf & _
           "Default value: ", value

' Now set the default value to "Default value".
WshShell.RegWrite "HKCR\.123\", "Default value"
value = WshShell.RegRead("HKCR\.123\")
WScript.Echo "Key HKCR\.123 default value written ..." & vbCrLf & _
           "Default value: ", value

' Now add a Text value using the REG_SZ type.
WshShell.RegWrite "HKCR\.123\Test", "Hello, world", "REG_SZ"
value = WshShell.RegRead("HKCR\.123\Test")
WScript.Echo "Key HKCR\.123 value 'Test' written ..." & vbCrLf & _
           "Test value: ", value

' Now add a Number value using the REG_DWORD type.
WshShell.RegWrite "HKCR\.123\Number", 8000, "REG_DWORD"
value = WshShell.RegRead("HKCR\.123\Number")
WScript.Echo "Key HKCR\.123 value 'Number' written ..." & vbCrLf & _
           "Number value: ", value
```

Listing 11-19 *RegAccessTest.vbs*   *(continued)*

Listing 11-19 *continued*

```
' Now add a Binary value using the REG_BINARY type.
WshShell.RegWrite "HKCR\.123\Binary", 123456789, "REG_BINARY"
' We can't read a binary value; RegRead returns an error value
' that can't be used.
'value = WshShell.RegRead ("HKCR\.123\Binary")
value = "not readable"
WScript.Echo "Key HKCR\.123 value 'Binary' written ..." & vbCrLf & _
             "Binary value: ", value


' Now add the expandable TextEx value using the REG_EXPAND_SZ type.
WshShell.RegWrite "HKCR\.123\TestEx", "%WINDIR%\Notepad.exe", _
                  "REG_EXPAND_SZ"
value = WshShell.RegRead("HKCR\.123\TestEx")
WScript.Echo "Key HKCR\.123 value 'TestEx' written ..." & vbCrLf & _
             "Test value: ", value


WshShell.RegDelete "HKCR\.123\"
WScript.Echo "Key HKCR\.123 removed ..."


' ### Now make a second attempt. ###
' Create a value directly; this forces an empty Default value.
WshShell.RegWrite "HKCR\.123\Test", "Hello, world", "REG_SZ"
value = WshShell.RegRead("HKCR\.123\Test")
WScript.Echo "Key HKCR\.123 value 'Test' written ..." & vbCrLf & _
             "Test value: ", value


' Try to read the default value. This causes a run-time error.
On Error Resume Next
value = WshShell.RegRead("HKCR\.123\")
If Err <> 0 Then
    WScript.Echo "Error ", Err.Number, Err.Description
Else
    WScript.Echo "Key HKCR\.123 read ..." & vbCrLf & _
                 "Default value: ", value
End If

On Error GoTo 0

WshShell.RegDelete "HKCR\.123\"
WScript.Echo "Key HKCR\.123 removed ..."

'*** End
```

Enumerating Registry Keys and Values

You can't enumerate values and subkeys within a given key in WSH. But several API functions are available that let you retrieve the necessary information. Microsoft offers a small module named Regobj.dll that allows a script to access API functions via an object model.

> **NOTE** Regobj.dll is available on the companion CD in the \Tools\RegObj folder. An accompanying Microsoft Word file briefly introduces the *RegObj* object model. The object model not only lets you enumerate a key but also lets you access the Registry of remote computers. You can also download Regobj.dll free from Microsoft's Web site (*http://www.microsoft.com*) if you have a valid Microsoft Visual Basic license. (Search on *Regobj.dll*.)

You can retrieve an instance of the object by using the following command:

```
Set objReg = WScript.CreateObject("RegObj.Registry")
```

If the DLL is registered on the system, a reference to the object instance is associated with the object variable *objReg*. The script can then use the properties and methods of the *RegObj* object. The *RegKeyFromString* method retrieves the content of a given key. This method requests the key name as a parameter:

```
Set RootKey = objReg.RegKeyFromString(key1)
```

You can then use a simple *For Each...In* loop to process the collection returned from the method. To enumerate all subkeys of a given key, use the following sequence:

```
For Each oVal In RootKey.SubKeys ' Loop through collection.
    name = name & oVal.Name & vbCrLf
Next
```

The *SubKeys* collection contains all keys of a given parent key. The *Name* property of a collection item contains the name of the key. If you want to read the values of a given key, you must use the following loop:

```
For Each oVal In RootKey.Values  ' Loop through collection.
    name = name & oVal.Name & vbTab & oVal.Value & vbCrLf
Next
```

The loop uses the *Values* property, which returns a collection containing all values of a given key. You can then use the *Name* property of a given item to retrieve the value name. The *Value* property of an item returns the value itself.

> **IMPORTANT** Windows 2000 uses a new value type called *REG_FULL_RESOURCE_DESCRIPTOR*, which Regobj.dll doesn't support. If this value is retrieved, a run-time error occurs.

The VBScript sample in Listing 11-20 enumerates the subkeys in a specified key. In a second step, it enumerates the values of the key.

```
'****************************************************
' File:   Enumerate.vbs (WSH sample in VBScript)
' Author: (c) G. Born
'
' Using Regobj.dll to enumerate the subkeys in a
' Registry key and then enumerating the values
' of the key
'****************************************************
Option Explicit

' Define the two keys.
Const key1 = "\HKEY_Classes_Root\Folder"
Const key2 = _
    "\HKEY_LOCAL_MACHINE\SOFTWARE\Microsoft\Windows\CurrentVersion\Run"

Dim objReg
Dim RootKey
Dim name
Dim oVal

' Create object reference to Regobj.dll.
Set objReg = WScript.CreateObject("RegObj.Registry")

' Retrieve property of parent key object.
Set RootKey = objReg.RegKeyFromString(key1)

name = "Registry key " & key1 & " entries are" & vbCrLf

For Each oVal In RootKey.SubKeys ' Loop through collection.
    name = name & oVal.Name & vbCrLf
Next

MsgBox name, vbOKOnly, "WSH Registry Enumerate sample"

' Retrieve property of key object.
Set RootKey = objReg.RegKeyFromString(key2)

name = "Registry key " & key2 & " value entries are" & vbCrLf
```

Listing 11-20 *Enumerate.vbs*

```
For Each oVal In RootKey.Values  ' Loop through collection.
    name = name & oVal.Name & vbTab & oVal.Value & vbCrLf
Next

MsgBox name, vbOKOnly, "WSH Registry Enumerate sample"

'*** End
```

NOTE To use the Enumerate.vbs file, you must register Regobj.dll using the Regsvr32.exe program. (See Chapter 2.) Regobj.dll is in the \Tools\RegObj folder on the companion CD.

Accessing the Registry Remotely

WSH doesn't support remote Registry access. Fortunately, the Regobj.dll file provides this feature. After retrieving an object instance to *RegObj*, you can use the following statement to obtain an object instance of the remote Registry object:

```
Set objRemote = objReg.RemoteRegistry(host)
```

The *RemoteRegistry* method has one parameter, which contains the host name (such as *Rom*). You can then use the object variable *objRemote* to call other methods:

```
Set RootKey = objRemote.RegKeyFromString(key1)
```

You call the *RegKeyFromString* method in the same way that you do for local Registry access. The only difference is that you use the *objRemote* object variable, which contains an instance of the remote object. Listing 11-21 contains the same functionality as the sample in Listing 11-20. The only difference is that it connects to the remote Registry of the host \\Wien. To execute the script in your environment, you must adapt the settings for the host.

```
'**************************************************
' File:   RemoteReg.vbs (WSH sample in VBScript)
' Author: (c) G. Born
'
' Using Regobj.dll to enumerate the subkeys in a
' Registry key and then enumerating the values
' of the key
'**************************************************
Option Explicit
```

Listing 11-21 *RemoteReg.vbs*   *(continued)*

Listing 11-21 *continued*

```
' Define the two keys.
Const key1 = "\HKEY_CLASSES_ROOT\Folder"
Const key2 = _
    "\HKEY_LOCAL_MACHINE\SOFTWARE\Microsoft\Windows\CurrentVersion\Run"
Const host = "\\Wien"

Dim objReg
Dim RootKey, objRemote
Dim name
Dim oVal

' Create object reference to Regobj.dll.
Set objReg = WScript.CreateObject("RegObj.Registry")

' ### Connect to remote Registry. ###
Set objRemote = objReg.RemoteRegistry(host)

' Retrieve property of parent key object.
Set RootKey = objRemote.RegKeyFromString(key1)

name = "Registry key " & key1 & " entries on " & _
       host & " are" & vbCrLf

For Each oVal In RootKey.SubKeys ' Loop through collection.
    name = name & oVal.Name & vbCrLf
Next

MsgBox name, vbOKOnly, "WSH Registry Enumerate sample"

' Retrieve property of key object.
Set RootKey = objRemote.RegKeyFromString(key2)

name = "Registry key " & key2 & " value entries on" & _
       host & " are" & vbCrLf

For Each oVal In RootKey.Values  ' Loop through collection.
    name = name & oVal.Name & vbTab & oVal.Value & vbCrLf
Next

MsgBox name, vbOKOnly, "WSH Registry Enumerate sample"

'*** End
```

NOTE Accessing the Registry on a remote machine requires that the machine supports remote Registry access. In Windows 2000, remote Registry access is part of the operating system, but in Windows 95 and Windows 98 you must install the optional Remote Registry service. If the script raises the run-time error "An unexpected error has been returned from the registration database," the remote machine isn't reachable (because of either a missing connection or a missing service). Also, if the script doesn't have sufficient user privileges, a run-time error reporting that the key isn't available occurs. In this case, try to execute the script with administrator privileges.

Changing the Windows 98 Installation Path

During the setup process, Windows 98 stores the path to the source that contains the installation files in the Registry. The path is located in the branch *HKEY-_LOCAL_MACHINE* in the following key:

```
\SOFTWARE\Microsoft\Windows\CurrentVersion\Setup
```

This key contains the value *SourcePath*, which stores the installation path. If you want to add a Windows component to the system, the Setup program retrieves the library files from the source specified in this path. If the path isn't valid (because the source is now on a different drive), Windows asks you for a new path. If the operating system was installed from a CD, you're asked to put the CD in the drive.

Some users are unnerved by this behavior and copy the Windows 98 CD content to a local folder on the hard disk in the hope that Windows will use these files during the next installation. Unfortunately, Windows continues to request the CD. A similar thing happens if you install a new hard disk or a new ZIP drive because Windows assigns a new drive letter for the CD. When you try to reinstall Windows components, an error message appears because the source can't be found on the requested drive.

OEM systems often keep the installation files in a folder on the local hard disk. If you delete this folder to free up space, Setup reports an error when you try to add Windows components.

NOTE These scenarios force you to enter the installation path in a dialog box each time you add a Windows component because Windows doesn't store the path used in the last session.

If you run into this sort of trouble, you might want to use the script shown in Listing 11-22. This program reads the installation path contained in the Registry. The user can overwrite this path in an input dialog box (Figure 11-8).

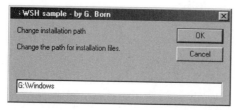

Figure 11-8 *Dialog box for reading the installation path*

After the user closes the dialog box, the new path is written to the Registry. During the next setup process, Windows uses the new path to retrieve the library files.

```
'****************************************************
' File:    SetInstPath.vbs (WSH sample in VBScript)
' Author:  (c) G. Born
'
' Setting the path for locating the Windows
' installation CD (Use this at your own risk!)
'****************************************************
Option Explicit

Dim WshShell
Dim Root, key, valname, valx
Dim text, title

' Variables for Registry access.
Root = "HKEY_LOCAL_MACHINE"
key = "\SOFTWARE\Microsoft\Windows\CurrentVersion\Setup\"
valname = "SourcePath"
valx =""

text = "Change installation path" & vbCrLf & vbCrLf & _
       "Change the path for installation files."
title = "WSH sample - by G. Born "

' Create WshShell object.
Set WshShell = WScript.CreateObject("WScript.Shell")

' Get installation path from Registry.
valx = WshShell.RegRead(Root & key & valname)
```

Listing 11-22 *SetInstPath.vbs*

```
' Allow user to change the path.
valx = InputBox(text, title, valx)

If valx <> "" Then    ' Test for empty string.
    WshShell.RegWrite Root & Key & valname, valx, "REG_SZ"
End If


'*** End
```

Hiding the Last User Name at Logon

During Windows logon, the name of the last user is shown in the logon dialog box. Most administrators prefer to hide this name because unauthorized users might use it to enter the system. Both the Tweak UI utility and the System Policy Editor that ship with Windows support a function to show or hide the last user name in the logon dialog box. Windows 95 and Windows 98 store this information in the Registry in the branch *HKEY_LOCAL_MACHINE* in the following key:

`\SOFTWARE\Microsoft\Windows\CurrentVersion\Winlogon`

If the key contains the value *DontDisplayLastUserName* and if this value is set to *0x0000001*, the last user name is hidden in the logon dialog box. (See *Inside the Microsoft Windows 98 Registry*.)

The JScript program shown in Listing 11-23 hides the last user name. When the script starts, you see a dialog box asking whether the last user name should be shown or hidden.

```
//*****************************************************
// File:    HideUserName.js (WSH sample in JScript)
// Author:  (c) G. Born
//
// Showing or hiding the last user's logon name
//*****************************************************

var vbYesNo = 4;
var vbOK = 0;
var vbInformation = 64;
var vbCancel = 2;
var vbYes = 6
```

Listing 11-23 *HideUserName.js*

(continued)

Listing 11-23 *continued*

```
// Initialize variables.
var Root = "HKEY_LOCAL_MACHINE";
var key = "\\SOFTWARE\\Microsoft\\Windows\\CurrentVersion\\Winlogon\\";
var valname = "DontDisplayLastUserName";
var result;

var WshShell = WScript.CreateObject("WScript.Shell");

result = WshShell.Popup(
    "hide last user in logon dialog box?\n\n\r" +
    "Hide last user's name in logon dialog box",
    0,
    "Windows 98 - powered by G. Born",
    vbYesNo + vbInformation );

if (result == vbYes)
{
    WshShell.RegWrite(Root + key + valname, "1", "REG_SZ");
    WshShell.Popup("Show user name disabled" +
                "\n\n\rHide last user's logon name",
                0,
                "http://www.borncity.de",
                vbOK);
}
else
{
    WshShell.RegWrite(Root + key + valname, "1", "REG_SZ");
    WshShell.RegDelete(Root + key + valname);
    WshShell.Popup("Enable user name" +
                "\n\n\rShow last user's logon name",
                0,
                "http://www.borncity.de",
                vbOK);
}

//*** End
```

Retrieving the Workgroup Name in Windows 98

If your machine is part of a workgroup network, you might want to retrieve information about which workgroup the current user belongs to. Unfortunately, WSH doesn't offer any methods for retrieving workgroup information. But you can use the methods of the *WshNetwork* object to retrieve networking information such as user name, domain name, and computer name.

Let's look at a sample in Windows 98. Information about the domain is kept in the Windows 98 Registry in the branch *HKEY_LOCAL_MACHINE* in the following key:

```
\SYSTEM\CurrentControlSet\Services\VxD\VNETSUP
```

The value *Workgroup* contains the workgroup name as a string, which you can easily retrieve and display (Figure 11-9).

Figure 11-9 *Dialog box showing networking information (in Windows 98)*

The VBScript sample in Listing 11-24 is fairly simple. It uses the sample file Network.vbs as a foundation and adds the *KeyExists* function (which we used earlier). The sample retrieves the information provided by the *WshNetwork* properties. In a second step, it looks for the *Workgroup* value in the Registry. If the value exists, the name is inserted into a string. The results are then displayed in a dialog box.

```
'*****************************************************
' File:    GetDomain.vbs (WSH sample in VBScript)
' Author:  (c) G. Born
'
' Showing the user name, domain name, computer
' name, and workgroup name
'*****************************************************
Option Explicit

Dim Text, Title
Dim WshNetwork          ' Object variable
Dim key1
Dim WshShell

' Get WshShell object for Registry access.
Set WshShell = WScript.CreateObject("WScript.Shell")

Text = "Networking information" & vbCrLf & vbCrLf
Title = "WSH sample - by G. Born"
```

Listing 11-24 *GetDomain.vbs*   *(continued)*

Listing 11-24 *continued*

```
' Create a new WshNetwork object to access network properties.
Set WshNetwork = WScript.CreateObject("WScript.Network")

Text = Text & "Computer name : " & WshNetworK.ComputerName & vbCrLf
Text = Text & "Domain : " & WshNetworK.UserDomain & vbCrLf
Text = Text & "User name : " & WshNetworK.UserName & vbCrLf
Text = Text & "Workgroup name : "

' Check whether Workgroup entry (a value) exists.
key1 = "HKEY_LOCAL_MACHINE\System\CurrentControlSet" & _
       "\Services\VxD\VNETSUP\Workgroup"
If (KeyExists(key1) = True) Then
    Text = Text & WshShell.RegRead(key1)
End If

Text = Text & vbCrLf

MsgBox Text, vbOKOnly + vbInformation, Title

'##############################################
' Helper function tests whether the key exists.
'##############################################
Function KeyExists(key)
    Dim key2
    On Error Resume Next
    key2 = WshShell.RegRead(key)
    If Err <> 0 Then
        KeyExists = False
    Else
        KeyExists = True
    End If
    On Error GoTo 0
End Function

'*** End
```

The JScript implementation

Listing 11-25 shows how to retrieve a user name, domain name, computer name, and workgroup name using JScript. The *KeyExists* function is the JScript implementation of the VBScript *KeyExists* function.

```
//**************************************************
// File:    GetDomain.js (WSH sample in JScript 5)
// Author:  (c) G. Born
//
// Showing the user name, domain name, computer
// name, and workgroup name
//**************************************************

// Get WshShell object for Registry access.
var WshShell = WScript.CreateObject("WScript.Shell");

var Text = "Networking information\n\n";
var Title = "WSH sample - by G. Born";

// Create a new WshNetwork object to access network properties.
var WshNetwork = WScript.CreateObject("WScript.Network");

Text = Text + "Computer name : " + WshNetwork.ComputerName + "\n";
Text = Text + "Domain : " + WshNetwork.UserDomain + "\n";
Text = Text + "User name : " + WshNetwork.UserName + "\n";
Text = Text + "Workgroup name : ";

// Check whether Workgroup entry (a value) exists.
key1 = "HKEY_LOCAL_MACHINE\\System\\CurrentControlSet\\" +
       "Services\\VxD\\VNETSUP\\Workgroup";
if (KeyExists(WshShell, key1))
    Text = Text + WshShell.RegRead(key1)

Text = Text + "\n";

WScript.Echo(Text);

//#################################################
// Helper function tests whether the key exists.
//#################################################
function KeyExists(obj, key)
{
    var key2;
    try
    {
        key2 = obj.RegRead(key)
    }
```

Listing 11-25 *GetDomain.js*   *(continued)*

Listing 11-25 *continued*

```
    catch(e)
    {
        if (e != 0)
            return false;
    }
    return true;  // Key found.
}

//*** End
```

Chapter 12

Using File System and I/O Commands

In this chapter, you'll learn how to use the *FileSystemObject* object in Microsoft Windows Script Host (WSH) to access drives, files, and folders. You'll also find out how to use methods and properties of the object to copy, rename, move, and delete files or folders. Then you'll see how WSH 2 supports methods for reading and writing text files. Finally, you'll learn about shell support for file select dialog boxes.

THE *FILESYSTEMOBJECT* OBJECT MODEL

The *FileSystemObject* (*fso* for short) object is available in both VBScript and JScript. Its subobjects, methods, and properties are listed in Table 12-1.

Table 12-1 THE *FILESYSTEMOBJECT* OBJECT MODEL

Object or Collection	Description
Drives	A collection of all drives (logical or physical) known on the machine, including drives with removable media (such as floppy disks)
Drive	An object whose methods and properties you can use to access a drive (fixed disk, mapped network drive, CD-ROM drive, or floppy disk drive), retrieve free space on the medium, and so on
Folders	A collection of all subfolders in a given folder

(continued)

Table 12-1 *continued*

Object or Collection	Description
Folder	An object whose methods you can use to create, move, rename, and delete folders and whose properties you can use to retrieve folder names, paths, and so on
Files	A collection of all files in a folder
File	An object whose methods you can use to create, delete, rename, and move files and whose properties you can use to retrieve filenames and paths
FileSystemObject	The main object of the *FileSystemObject* object model, which provides all methods and properties for file system access
TextStream	An object whose methods you can use to read and write text files

The *FileSystemObject* object (which is provided in the file Scrrun.dll) doesn't have any binary file access methods. You can read or write a binary file only by using the text file methods, with all the accompanying disadvantages: You'll need to convert all data within your script, you'll have no direct methods for handling binary data types, and so on. The VBScript and JScript language references for the version 5 script engines contain detailed, up-to-date information on the *FileSystemObject* object model.

Creating a *FileSystemObject* Object

Before you can access the objects, methods, and properties of the *FileSystemObject* object model, you must create an object variable and assign a reference to the *FileSystemObject* object. This object is part of the language itself, so you can also use the native methods of VBScript or JScript to retrieve the object reference.

As you'll recall, the syntax for creating an object reference and assigning a reference looks like this in VBScript:

```
Dim fso
Set fso = WScript.CreateObject("Scripting.FileSystemObject")
```

The second line uses the *CreateObject* method of *WScript* to load an object instance and assign a reference to it to the object variable *fso*.

In JScript, you can use the following line to create a reference to the *FileSystemObject* object:

```
var fso = WScript.CreateObject("Scripting.FileSystemObject");
```

This statement creates the object variable *fso*, creates an object instance, and assigns the reference to this object instance to the object variable.

NATIVE METHODS FOR CREATING A *FILESYSTEMOBJECT* OBJECT

Instead of using the *WScript.CreateObject* method to assign the reference to the *FileSystemObject* object variable, you can use a native VBScript or JScript method (as described in Chapter 7).

In VBScript, you use the native *CreateObject* function:

```
Set fso = CreateObject("Scripting.FileSystemObject")
```

In JScript, you apply the *new* method to the *ActiveXObject* object to create a new object instance and assign a reference to an object variable:

```
var fso = new ActiveXObject("Scripting.FileSystemObject");
```

Methods of the *FileSystemObject* Object

After you create the *FileSystemObject* object, you can access its methods, properties, and subobjects. To create a new folder, you use the *CreateFolder* method. To create a new text file, you use the *CreateTextFile* method—and so on. You can delete items such as files and folders by using the *DeleteFile* and *DeleteFolder* methods, respectively. *FileSystemObject* also has methods for copying and moving files and folders.

> **NOTE** The *FileSystemObject* object duplicates some of the functionality of its subobjects so that programmers have more flexibility when writing scripts. For example, you can copy files by using the *CopyFile* method of the *FileSystemObject* object or the *Copy* method of the *File* object. The corresponding methods of the various file and folder objects use slightly different parameters, so you might have to check the language reference for the correct parameters of each method you want to use.

You use the *GetDrive*, *GetFolder*, and *GetFile* methods of the *FileSystemObject* object to access drives, folders, or files. The following VBScript statements create a reference to a file:

```
Dim fso, oFile
Set fso = CreateObject("Scripting.FileSystemObject")
Set oFile = fso.GetFile("C:\Test.txt")
```

Here's the JScript equivalent:

```
var fso = new ActiveXObject("Scripting.FileSystemObject");
var oFile = fso.GetFile("C:\\Test.txt");
```

Both code sequences use the *GetFile* method of the *FileSystemObject* object (which is kept in the object variable *fso*). The method returns a reference to the object variable *oFile*. You can use this *oFile* variable to access the file.

ACCESSING DRIVES

The *FileSystemObject* object provides a way to access all drives known on your machine (all drives that can be accessed from Windows, including floppy disk drives, CD-ROM drives, hard disks, and network drives that are mapped to logical drive letters).

Listing All Drives on a Machine

Let's use *FileSystemObject* in a WSH script to display the drive letters, drive types, and label names of all drives known on a machine. Drives that support removable media must be checked for whether a medium (such as a CD or floppy disk) is in the drive. If a network drive is found, the script displays the UNC network path. The dialog box in Figure 12-1 lists the drives on one of my test systems.

Figure 12-1 *A list of drives on a machine*

NOTE Some of the drives shown in Figure 12-1 (such as drive F) are listed without a label name because I didn't assign a label to these drives. The drives A and G are listed without a label because a floppy disk or CD wasn't inserted in the drive.

To list all drives available in the system, you need an instance of the *FileSystem-Object* object as well as a reference to the *Drives* object. You create the *FileSystemObject* object instance as follows:

```
Set fso = WScript.CreateObject("Scripting.FileSystemObject")
```

Then you use the object variable *fso* to read the *Drives* property, which returns a collection of *Drive* objects. The following statement retrieves the *Drives* collection, which contains all drives found on the local machine:

```
Set oDrive = fso.Drives
```

You can use a simple loop to access the drives in the collection:

```
For Each i In oDrive
    ⋮
Next
```

The object variable *i* receives one drive object on each pass, so you can use this variable within the loop to access the properties of a drive. For example, to retrieve the drive letter, you can use the following statement:

```
driveletter = i.DriveLetter
```

To get the drive type, you use the *DriveType* property of the object referenced in the object variable *i*:

```
Type = i.DriveType
```

The drive type is coded as an integer value in the range between 0 and *n*. Table 12-2 lists the codes for valid drive types.

Table 12-2 **DRIVE TYPES**

Constant*	Value	Description
Unknown	0	Unknown drive type. (Drive type couldn't be detected.)
Removable	1	A drive with removable media (such as a floppy disk drive or a ZIP drive).
Fixed	2	A fixed disk. This type includes removable hard disks.
Remote	3	Network drive. Indicated only for mapped resources (shared drives and folders).
CDROM	4	CD-ROM drive. There's no difference between CD-R and CD-RW.
RAMDisk	5	A RAM drive. A RAM disk is created within memory using a special driver.

* The Constant column lists the constant names used for the drive types in the Scrrun.dll type library. The Value column lists the values returned in the *DriveType* property. VBScript and JScript don't support the constants defined in the type library, so you must define these named constants explicitly in your .vbs and .js script files. In WSH 2, you can use the *<reference>* element in a .wsf file to create a reference to a type library. I'll show you an example of this shortly.

You can use the *VolumeName* property to retrieve the label (also called the volume name) that's assigned to a medium when it's formatted. If the drive type supports removable media, the medium must be inserted in the drive for you to retrieve the volume name. If the drive contains no medium, it makes no sense to retrieve the *VolumeName* property. However, you can use the *IsReady* property to check whether the medium is available. If it is, *IsReady* returns the value *True*.

For mapped network drives, the drive name contains no information about the real resource name because the user assigns the associated drive letter manually. You can, however, use the *ShareName* property of the drive (object) to determine the UNC path to the resource.

The program in Listing 12-1 lists all drives found on a machine. (This sample, like the others in this chapter, is in the \WSHDevGuide\Chapter12 folder on the book's companion CD.)

```
'****************************************************
' File:    ListDrives.vbs (WSH sample in VBScript)
' Author:  (c) G. Born
'
' Listing the drives of a machine by using
' FileSystemObject
'****************************************************
Option Explicit

' Drive type constants
Const Unknown = 0
Const Removable = 1   ' Removable medium
Const Fixed = 2       ' Fixed medium (hard disk)
Const Remote = 3      ' Network drive
Const CDROM = 4       ' CD-ROM
Const RAMDisk = 5     ' RAM disk

Dim Text, Title
Dim fso, oDrive, curDrive    ' Object variables

Dim drtype(6)
drtype(0) = " Unknown "
drtype(1) = " Removable "
drtype(2) = " Fixed "
drtype(3) = " Remote "
drtype(4) = " CDROM "
drtype(5) = " RAMDisk "

Text = "Drives" & vbCrLf & vbCrLf
Title = "WSH sample - by G. Born"

' Create FileSystemObject object to access the file system.
Set fso = WScript.CreateObject("Scripting.FileSystemObject")

Set oDrive = fso.Drives    ' Get Drives collection.
```

Listing 12-1 *ListDrives.vbs*

```
For Each curDrive In oDrive         ' All drive objects
    Text = Text & curDrive.DriveLetter & vbTab  ' Drive letter
    Text = Text & drtype(curDrive.DriveType)
    Select Case curDrive.DriveType      ' Identify drive type.
        Case Removable·                 ' Removable medium
            If curDrive.IsReady Then
                Text = Text & curDrive.VolumeName ' Local drive
            End If

        Case CDROM                      ' CD-ROM
            If curDrive.IsReady Then
                Text = Text & curDrive.VolumeName ' Local drive
            End If

        Case Remote
            Text = Text & curDrive.ShareName  ' Network drive

        Case Else                       ' Other medium
            Text = Text & curDrive.VolumeName  ' Local drive
    End Select
    Text = Text & vbCrLf
Next

MsgBox Text, vbOKOnly + vbInformation, Title

'*** End
```

TIP In VBScript, the *vbTab* named constant inserts a tab character into a string so that the output in the dialog box is formatted in columns.

The JScript implementation

In JScript, you also use the *FileSystemObject* object to list all drives. The following statements create a *FileSystemObject* object and a *Drives* collection:

```
var fso = new ActiveXObject("Scripting.FileSystemObject");
var oDrives = new Enumerator(fso.Drives);  // Get Drives collection.
```

The native *new ActiveXObject* statement creates the object instance. The second line contains the JScript keyword *Enumerator*, which creates a new object variable that contains the *Drives* collection. After retrieving this collection, you can use the *atEnd* and *moveNext* methods of the *Enumerator* object to access all items in the collection using a *for* loop. You can get the object from the *item* property by using this statement:

```
oDrive.item();
```

The loop shown here accesses all items in the collection:

```
for (; !oDrives.atEnd(); oDrives.moveNext())
{
    var drive = oDrive.item();    // Fetch object.
    ⋮
}
```

You can then use properties of the *Drive* object, such as *DriveLetter*, *DriveType*, *ShareName*, and *VolumeName*. To avoid defining the drive type constants explicitly within the script, you can add a reference to the type library by adding the following *<reference>* definition to the .wsf file:

```
<reference guid='{420B2830-E718-11CF-893D-00A0C9054228}'/>
```

The reference above uses the guid value of the *FileSystemObject* object. Listing 12-2 shows the full JScript implementation using a .wsf file.

```
<?xml version="1.0" encoding="ISO-8859-1"?>
<!--
    File:    ListDrives.wsf (WSH 2)
    Author:  (c) G. Born
    Listing the drives of a machine
-->

<job id="ListDrives">
    <reference guid='{420B2830-E718-11CF-893D-00A0C9054228}'/>

    <script language="JScript">
    <![CDATA[
        // List all drives on a machine. The drive type values are
        // obtained from the FileSystemObject type library.

        var drtype = new Array(5);

        drtype[0] = " Unknown ";
        drtype[1] = " Removable ";
        drtype[2] = " Fixed ";
        drtype[3] = " Remote ";
        drtype[4] = " CDROM ";
        drtype[5] = " RAMDisk ";

        Text = "Drives \n\n";
        Title = "WSH sample - by G. Born";
```

Listing 12-2 *ListDrives.wsf*

```
// Create FileSystemObject object to access the file system.
// Here we use the native method provided by JScript.
var fso = new ActiveXObject("Scripting.FileSystemObject");

// Get drives enumerator.
var oDrive = new Enumerator(fso.Drives);

for (; !oDrive.atEnd(); oDrive.moveNext())
{
    var drive = oDrive.item();                   // Fetch object.
    Text = Text + drive.DriveLetter + " \t "; // Drive letter
    Text = Text + drtype[drive.DriveType];

    if (drive.DriveType == Remote)
        Text = Text + drive.ShareName;           // Network drive

    if ((drive.DriveType == Removable) ||
        (drive.DriveType == CDROM))              // Removable medium
        if (drive.IsReady)
            Text = Text + drive.VolumeName;   // Local drive

    if (drive.DriveType == Fixed)
        Text = Text + drive.VolumeName;          // Local drive

    Text = Text + "\n";
}

// Show result.
var objAdr = WScript.CreateObject("WScript.Shell");
objAdr.Popup(Text, 0, Title);
]]>
</script>
</job>
```

TIP In JScript, the escape character \t inserts a tab character into a string so that the output in the dialog box is formatted in columns. The JScript implementation, *ListDrives.js*, is also on the companion CD.

Showing Drive Properties

Now let's write a script to query the user for a drive letter via an input dialog box (Figure 12-2). After the user enters a valid drive letter (without the colon), the script retrieves the drive's properties (such as the file system, the free space, and so on) and shows them in a second dialog box (Figure 12-3).

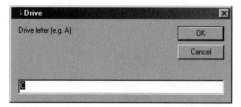

Figure 12-2 *Querying the user for a drive letter*

Figure 12-3 *Drive properties*

This sample shows the necessary tests that you must make in a script before you can access a drive. If you omit these tests, a run-time error will probably occur.

The following statement queries for the drive letter using the VBScript *InputBox* function:

```
drive = InputBox("Drive letter (e.g. A)", "Drive", "C")
```

> **NOTE** The script uses the statement *drive = Left(drive, 1)* to extract the first character (the drive letter) the user enters.

After you retrieve the user input, it makes sense to check whether the drive letter is valid. For example, the drive *"0"* doesn't make sense. You can use an *If* statement such as the following to check the user input:

```
If Asc(UCase(drive)) < Asc("A") Or _
   Asc(UCase(drive)) > Asc("Z") Then …
```

If a valid drive letter between A and Z is detected, the script must create a reference to the *FileSystemObject* object:

```
Set fso = WScript.CreateObject("Scripting.FileSystemObject")
```

Before you can access the drive's properties, you must check whether the drive exists. You can do this by using the *DriveExists* method:

```
If (Not fso.DriveExists(drive)) Then
    WScript.Echo "The drive " & drive & " doesn't exist"
    WScript.Quit
End If
```

Only if the method returns the value *True* can you access the drive from the script. In this case, you can create a *Drive* object by using the following statement:

```
Set oDrive = fso.GetDrive(drive)
```

The *GetDrive* method returns an object, so you must use the *Set* keyword in the assignment statement. (Otherwise, the script causes a run-time error.) Before you can access the object's properties, you must check whether the drive is ready. If you omit this check, each attempt to access a drive that doesn't contain a medium will cause a run-time error. You can use the following statement to perform the check:

```
If (drive.IsReady) Then
    ⋮
End If
```

The *IsReady* property returns the value *True* if the drive contains a medium and is ready.

> **TIP** The sample code doesn't differentiate between drive types when check-ing *IsReady*, which means that *IsReady* is sometimes checked unnecessarily. For example, the *IsReady* property always returns *True* on a (formatted) hard disk. Of course, checking *IsReady* on hard disks doesn't do any harm, and after this one check, you can access the media/drive properties freely, regardless of the drive type.

Another interesting property is *TotalSize*, which returns the medium capacity, as shown here:

```
WScript.Echo "Capacity: " & _
            FormatNumber(oDrive.TotalSize/(1024*1024), 0) & _
            " MB" & vbCrLf
```

This statement uses the VBScript function *FormatNumber* to format the result using a separator for thousands. By dividing the result by 1024 * 1024, you get the capacity in megabytes. To retrieve the free drive capacity, use this statement:

```
WScript.Echo "Free: " & FormatNumber(oDrive.FreeSpace/1024, 0) & _
            " KB" & vbCrLf
```

The full VBScript program is shown in Listing 12-3. It uses a .wsf file to allow references to the type library. The pure VBScript solution is in the file GetDriveX.vbs.

> **NOTE** You can use the *FreeSpace* and *AvailableSpace* properties to retrieve the free space on a medium. Both properties return the same value unless the operating system (such as Windows 2000) supports quotas. Then the adminis-trator can set a space quota for each user on the medium. In such cases, the *FreeSpace* property specifies the free space for the volume (the entire disk), and the *AvailableSpace* property specifies the free space for the current user. Because of bugs in Windows 95 OSR 2, problems occur with the *FreeSpace* and *AvailableSpace* properties on that platform if the drive is bigger than 2 GB. Wrong values for the capacity are returned.

```
<?xml version="1.0" encoding="ISO-8859-1"?>
<!--
    File:    GetDriveX.wsf (WSH 2)
    Author:  (c) G. Born
    Showing the properties of a drive by using
    FileSystemObject and a reference to the type library
-->

<job id="GetDriveX">
    <reference guid='{420B2830-E718-11CF-893D-00A0C9054228}'/>

    <script language="VBScript">
    <![CDATA[
        Option Explicit

        Dim Text, Title, drive
        Dim fso, oDrive                    ' Object variable

        Dim drtype(6)
        drtype(0) = " Unknown "
        drtype(1) = " Removable "
        drtype(2) = " Fixed "
        drtype(3) = " Remote "
        drtype(4) = " CDROM "
        drtype(5) = " RAMDisk "

        Text = "Drive" & vbCrLf & vbCrLf
        Title = "WSH sample - by G. Born"

        drive = ""
        Do                          ' Query drive letter.
            drive = InputBox("Drive letter (e.g. A)", "Drive", "C")

            If drive = "" Then  ' Test for Cancel button.
                WScript.Quit
            End If

            drive = Left(drive, 1)  ' Extract drive letter.

            ' Valid drive name (between A and Z)?
            If Asc(UCase(drive)) < Asc("A") Or _
               Asc(UCase(drive)) > Asc("Z") Then
                MsgBox "Drive " & drive & " is illegal"
                drive = ""
            End If
        Loop Until drive <> ""
```

Listing 12-3 *GetDriveX.wsf*

```
        ' Create FileSystemObject object to access the file system.
        Set fso = WScript.CreateObject("Scripting.FileSystemObject")

        ' Check whether drive exists.
        If (Not fso.DriveExists(drive)) Then
            WScript.Echo "The drive " & drive & " doesn't exist"
            WScript.Quit
        End If

        Set oDrive = fso.GetDrive(drive)     ' Get Drive object.

        If (oDrive.IsReady) Then
            Text = Text & UCase(drive) & " - " & _
                    oDrive.VolumeName & vbCrLf
            Text = Text & "Drive type: " & _
                    drtype(oDrive.DriveType) & vbCrLf
            Text = Text & "File system: " & _
                    oDrive.FileSystem & vbCrLf
            Text = Text & "Capacity: " & _
                    FormatNumber(oDrive.TotalSize/(1024*1024), 0) & _
                    " MB" & vbCrLf
            Text = Text & "Free: " & _
                    FormatNumber(oDrive.FreeSpace/1024, 0) & _
                    " KB" & vbCrLf
        Else
            Text = Text & "Drive not ready" & vbCrLf
        End If

        MsgBox Text, vbOKOnly + vbInformation, Title
    ]]>
    </script>
</job>
```

The JScript implementation

The JScript version uses the same methods and properties. You must replace a few functions with their JScript counterparts, however. For example, the JScript version uses *WSHInputBox* (a VBScript function introduced in Chapter 8) to implement a user input dialog box. Also, to convert lowercase characters to uppercase, you must apply the JScript *toUpperCase* method to a *String* object instead of using the VBScript *UCase* function. In addition, the format function used in the VBScript sample isn't available in JScript, so I have added a small VBScript function, *JsFormatNumber*, that provides the missing functionality. The full JScript implementation (as a .wsf file) is shown in Listing 12-4.

```
<?xml version="1.0" encoding="ISO-8859-1"?>
<!--
    File:    GetDriveXJS.wsf (WSH 2)
    Author:  (c) G. Born
    Showing the properties of a drive by using
    FileSystemObject and a reference to the type library
    and using a VBScript function to obtain user input
-->

<job id="ListDrives">
    <reference guid='{420B2830-E718-11CF-893D-00A0C9054228}'/>

    <script language="VBScript">
    <![CDATA[
        Function WSHInputBox(Message, Title, Value)
            ' Provides an InputBox function for JScript
            ' It can be called from JScript as follows:
            ' var result = WSHInputBox("Enter a name","Input",test);
            WSHInputBox = InputBox(Message, Title, Value)
        End Function
    ]]>
    </script>

    <script language="VBScript">
    <![CDATA[
        Function JsFormatNumber (value, decimals)
            ' Formats a number
            JsFormatNumber = FormatNumber(value, decimals)
        End Function
    ]]>
    </script>

    <script language="JScript">
    <![CDATA[
        // JScript part to retrieve and show drive properties
        // Define an array with drive type text constants.
        var drivetype = new Array(" Unknown ", " Removable ",
                                  " Fixed ", " Remote ",
                                  " CDROM ", " RAMDisk ");

        var Text = "Drive\n\n";
        var Title = "WSH sample - by G. Born";

        // Query drive letter.
        var drive = WSHInputBox("Drive letter (e.g. A)",
                                "Drive", "C");
```

Listing 12-4 *GetDriveXJS.wsf*

```
    if (drive == "")    // Test for Cancel button.
        WScript.Quit();

    drive = drive.substr(0, 1);   // Extract drive letter.

    // Create FileSystemObject object to access the file system.
    var fso = new ActiveXObject("Scripting.FileSystemObject");

    // Check whether drive exists.
    if (!fso.DriveExists(drive))
    {
        WScript.Echo("The drive " + drive + " doesn't exist");
        WScript.Quit();
    }

    var oDrive = fso.GetDrive(drive);         // Get drive object.

    if (oDrive.IsReady)
    {
        Text = Text + drive.toUpperCase() + ": " +
                oDrive.VolumeName + "\n";
        Text = Text + "Drive type: " +
                drivetype[oDrive.DriveType] + "\n";
        Text = Text + "File system: " + oDrive.FileSystem + "\n";
        Text = Text + "Capacity: " +
                JsFormatNumber(oDrive.TotalSize/1024/1024, 0) +
                " MB\n";
        Text = Text + "Free: " +
                JsFormatNumber(oDrive.FreeSpace/1024, 0) + " KB\n";
    }
    else
        Text = Text + "Drive not ready\n";

    var objAdr = WScript.CreateObject("WScript.Shell");
    objAdr.Popup(Text, 0, Title);
    ]]>
    </script>
</job>
```

ACCESSING FILES AND FOLDERS

This section introduces the objects, methods, and properties of the *FileSystemObject* object that you can use to access files and folders.

Listing All Subfolders in a Folder

If you need a list of all subfolders in a given folder, you can use the *Folders* collection of the *FileSystemObject* object. We'll write a simple script that retrieves the subfolders of the Windows \System folder and lists them in a dialog box (Figure 12-4).

Figure 12-4 *A list of the \System subfolders in Windows 98*

NOTE   You can select any folder for this experiment, but our sample uses the \System folder to restrict the number of subfolders shown in the dialog box. If you select a folder such as the Windows folder, the dialog box becomes larger than the Desktop and the user can't close the dialog box by clicking the OK button. Later in this book and in *Advanced Development with Microsoft Windows Script Host 2.0,* I'll introduce a more advanced solution that uses a browser window to display file entries.

The path to the target folder is set in a named constant in the program's header:

```
Const path = "%WINDIR%\System"
```

To access the folder, you create a *FileSystemObject* object by using the following statement:

```
Set fso = WScript.CreateObject("Scripting.FileSystemObject")
```

You then use the *GetFolder* method to access the folder. Because the named constant *path* contains the placeholder *%WINDIR%*, you must expand this environment variable by using *ExpandEnvironmentStrings*:

```
Set oFolders = fso.GetFolder(wsh.ExpandEnvironmentStrings(path))
```

The *GetFolder* method of the *FileSystemObject* object variable *fso* returns a reference to the current folder as an object. You can then use the *SubFolders* property of the object variable *oFolders* to get the subfolders collection:

```
Set oSubFolders = oFolders.SubFolders
```

You can retrieve the name of a subfolder by using the *Name* property of a collection item. The following loop processes all folders in the collection and adds the folder name to the *Text* variable:

```
For Each oFolder In oSubFolders          ' All folders
    Text = Text & oFolder.Name & vbCrLf
Next
```

When the loop terminates, the variable *Text* contains the names of all subfolders found in the current folder. (Of course, you can use different code within the loop to implement a function to evaluate the folder names. This sample adds the name to a string for simplicity.) The full VBScript program is shown in Listing 12-5.

```
'**************************************************
' File:    Folders.vbs (WSH sample in VBScript)
' Author:  (c) G. Born
'
' Listing all subfolders of a folder by using
' FileSystemObject
'**************************************************
Option Explicit

Const path = "%WINDIR%\System"       ' For Windows 95 and Windows 98
' Const path = "%WINDIR%\System32"   ' For Windows NT and Windows 2000

Dim Text, Title
Dim fso, oFolders, oFolder, oSubFolders, wsh ' Object variables

Text = "Folders" & vbCrLf & vbCrLf
Title = "WSH sample - by G. Born"

Set wsh = WScript.CreateObject("WScript.Shell")

' Create FileSystemObject object to access the file system.
Set fso = WScript.CreateObject("Scripting.FileSystemObject")

' Get Folders collection.
Set oFolders = fso.GetFolder(wsh.ExpandEnvironmentStrings(path))
Set oSubFolders = oFolders.SubFolders

For Each oFolder In oSubFolders          ' All folders
    Text = Text & oFolder.Name & vbCrLf
Next

MsgBox Text, vbOKOnly + vbInformation, Title

'*** End
```

Listing 12-5 *Folders.vbs*

The JScript implementation

The JScript version has a similar structure. The most important difference is in the way the collection is processed. The following statements create the folder object and then the collection by using the *SubFolders* property:

```
var oFolders = fso.GetFolder(wsh.ExpandEnvironmentStrings(path));
var oSubFolders = new Enumerator(oFolders.SubFolders);
```

You must then use the *for* loop to process all entries in the collection:

```
for (; !oSubFolders.atEnd(); oSubFolders.moveNext())    // All folders
{
    var oFolder = oSubFolders.item();
    Text = Text + oFolder.name + "\n";
}
```

Notice that the code uses the *moveNext* method to access the next item in the collection. This method is particular to JScript because a construction such as *for (oFolder in oSubFolders)* doesn't work. You must retrieve an item from the collection by using the *item* property, as shown in the following statement:

```
var oFolder = oSubFolders.item();
```

The *name* property of this object returns the folder's name. In addition to the folder name, you can access properties such as the file attribute and creation date.

Alternatively, you can retrieve the path to the system folder in such a way that the script is independent of the operating system. The VBScript sample above uses the *path* constant to define the path to the operating system's system folder. This folder is the subfolder of the Windows folder and is named \System in Windows 95, Windows 98, and Windows Millennium Edition and \System32 in Windows NT and Windows 2000. Instead, you can use the *FileSystemObject* object's *GetSpecialFolder* method to retrieve the path to a special folder:

```
var path = fso.GetSpecialFolder(1);
```

If the value 1 is passed to the method, *GetSpecialFolder* returns the path to the system folder. The value 0 returns the path to the Windows folder, and the value 2 retrieves the path to the Temp folder.

The full JScript program is shown in Listing 12-6.

```
//************************************************
// File:    Folders.js (WSH sample in JScript)
// Author:  (c) G. Born
//
// Listing the contents of a subfolder
// by using the FileSystemObject
//************************************************
```

Listing 12-6 *Folders.js*

```
var Text = "Folders\n\n";

var wsh = WScript.CreateObject ("WScript.Shell");

// Create FileSystemObject object to access file system.
var fso = WScript.CreateObject("Scripting.FileSystemObject");

// Retrieve the operating system's system folder.
var path = fso.GetSpecialFolder(1);   // 1 = system folder

// Fetch Folders collection.
var oFolders = fso.GetFolder(wsh.ExpandEnvironmentStrings(path));
// Subfolders collection
var oSubFolder = new Enumerator(oFolders.SubFolders);

for (; !oSubFolder.atEnd(); oSubFolder.moveNext())   // All folders
{
    var oFolder = oSubFolder.item();
    Text = Text + oFolder.name + "\n";
}

WScript.Echo(Text);

//*** End
```

Creating, Moving, Renaming, and Deleting Folders

The next sample creates a folder, shows the subfolders of the parent folder, and removes at least the new folder.

Creating a new folder

In VBScript, you can use the *InputBox* function to create a new folder. The following lines also ask for the new folder's name (path):

```
path = InputBox("Enter folder name (e.g. C:\Born).", _
            Title, "C:\Born")
If path = "" Then
    WScript.Quit        ' Canceled by the user.
End If
```

The code sequence examines the user input. The script terminates if the user clicks the Cancel button. In JScript, you can use the *WSHInputBox* method to implement the same input dialog box (as shown in previous chapters).

Now you can create the new folder. Our sample also uses the *FolderExists* method of the *FileSystemObject* object to check whether the folder already exists:

```
Set fso = WScript.CreateObject("Scripting.FileSystemObject")
If (Not fso.FolderExists(path)) Then
    ⋮
End If
```

The *FolderExists* method requests the path to the folder as a parameter. If the folder exists, the method returns the value *True*; otherwise, it returns *False*.

NOTE   If the user types an illegal pathname (such as *C:\Born\\test*, which contains invalid characters), WSH raises a run-time error. I omitted run-time error handling from the sample for simplicity.

If you're sure that the folder doesn't exist, you can use the *CreateFolder* method to create the empty folder by using the following code:

```
Set oNewFolder = fso.CreateFolder(path)
```

The method is applied to the object variable *fso*, which contains the *FileSystemObject* object. The method requests a path (which includes the folder name, as in *C:\Born*) as a parameter. The method creates the folder and returns the object reference (containing the handle) to this folder. You must use this object reference to access the folder.

NOTE   You must be sure that the path (including the folder name) is valid. The target medium must also be writable.

Retrieving the parent folder

A folder usually belongs to a parent folder. You can separate the parent folder name from the path, but the *FileSystemObject* object provides a method for this purpose:

```
parent = fso.GetParentFolderName(path)
```

The *GetParentFolderName* method requires the path to the current folder as a parameter. By default, the method returns the path to the parent folder. If no parent folder exists (for example, if the path points to the root), the method returns an empty string. You can determine whether a parent folder exists by using the following code:

```
If (parent = "") Then
    MsgBox "No parent folder"
    ⋮
End If
```

The sample uses this method to retrieve the parent folder and show the path in a dialog box.

NOTE   As mentioned earlier, if you select a parent folder that contains too many subfolders, the dialog box showing the folder can get larger than the Desktop and the user won't be able to use the OK button to close the dialog box. Later in this chapter, I'll introduce a solution that uses a browser window instead of a dialog box to display large amounts of information.

Renaming, copying, or moving a folder

You can use the *CopyFolder* method of the *FileSystemObject* object to copy an entire folder with its content:

```
Object.CopyFolder source, destination[, overwrite]
```

The *Object* identifier is the placeholder for the object variable of the *FileSystem-Object* object. The three method parameters specify the source, the destination folder, and the overwrite mode:

- ■ *source*   A mandatory parameter that passes a string containing the name (path) of the source folder. The string can contain wildcards to copy multiple folders.

- ■ *destination*   A mandatory parameter that holds the destination folder as a string. The method copies the source folder to the destination. This parameter can't contain wildcards.

- ■ *overwrite*   An optional parameter that can be set to *True* or *False*. If it's set to *True* (the default), the *CopyFolder* method overwrites existing files in the target folder.

You can use wildcard characters only in the last name in the path. For example, you can use this statement:

```
FileSystemObject.CopyFolder "C:\Document\*", "C:\temp\"
```

But this command causes a run-time error:

```
FileSystemObject.CopyFolder "C:\Document\*\*", "C:\temp\"
```

If the source folder contains wildcard characters or if the path to the target folder ends with a \ character, the method assumes that the target folder exists and that the folder, files, and subfolders should be copied. Otherwise, a new target folder is created.

The success of a *CopyFolder* call depends on the particular combination of source and target folders. If the target folder doesn't exist, it is created and the content of the source folder is copied. This is the default action. If the destination path points to an existing file, a run-time error occurs. If it points to a folder, the method tries to copy the content of the source folder to the destination folder. If a file from the source folder already exists in the target folder and if the *overwrite* parameter is set to *False*, a run-time error occurs. If *overwrite* is set to *True*, existing files in the target folder are overwritten. If the *Read-only* file attribute is set for the target folder, a run-time error occurs unless the *overwrite* parameter is set to *True*. A run-time error also occurs if the source folder contains wildcards that don't match a folder in the source path.

> **IMPORTANT** When the *CopyFolder* method detects an error, execution terminates. The method doesn't support a rollback feature; files and folders already copied aren't deleted in the target folder. Basically, this method behaves the same way Windows or MS-DOS behaves when copying folders.

You rename and move folders by using the *MoveFolder* method, which uses the same parameters as the *CopyFolder* method. The files are moved and the content of the source folder is deleted.

> **NOTE** You can also set the *name* attribute of a folder to a new value to rename that folder. Let's say that the statement *Set oFolder = fso.GetFolder("C:\Test")* is used to retrieve a reference to the given folder. You can rename the folder *Test1* by using the command *oFolder.name = "Test1"*. The statement fails if a folder with the new name already exists.

Our sample uses the *MoveFolder* method to rename a folder. The original folder name is passed in the source path parameter, and the target path parameter must contain the new folder name:

```
If (MsgBox("Rename folder " & path & " ?", _
          vbYesNo + vbQuestion, Title) = vbYes) Then
    ' Yes
    newpath = path & "New"
    fso.MoveFolder path, newpath

    MsgBox "Folder renamed to " & newpath
End If
```

Before the folder is renamed, the script asks the user to confirm the action. This request for confirmation prevents the accidental renaming of important folders (such as the Windows folder). The variable *path* contains the source path, and the variable *newpath* contains the path to the target folder. (The name of the target folder is created by appending the string *"New"* to the old folder name.)

TIP The *MoveFolder* method terminates if an error occurs. This behavior leaves the source and target folders in an indeterminate state because *MoveFolder* deletes each item (file or subfolder) from the source folder as it is copied. If you want to restore the source folder, you have to do the rollback manually. Therefore, I recommend using the *CopyFolder* method instead of *MoveFolder*. If the content of the source folder is copied successfully, you can delete its content. Using the *CopyFolder* method ensures that if an error occurs, the content of the source folder is kept intact.

Deleting a folder

You use the *DeleteFolder* method of the *FileSystemObject* object to delete a folder. The method requires a string as a parameter; the string must contain the folder name and the path to the folder, as shown here:

```
If (MsgBox("Delete folder " & newpath & "?", _
        vbYesNo + vbQuestion, Title) = vbYes) Then _
   fso.DeleteFolder(newpath)
```

The method supports a second (optional) parameter, *force*, which isn't used in the statement shown above. If this parameter is set to *True*, files with the *Read-only* attribute are also deleted. The method deletes the entire folder, including files and subfolders.

Listing 12-7 uses all the methods for manipulating folders that we've covered so far—except the *CopyFolder* method. The script asks the user for a folder name and then creates the folder. The subfolders of the parent folder are then shown in a dialog box. The folder can be renamed and deleted in later steps. The script creates several user dialog boxes to keep the user informed.

```
'*****************************************************
' File:    Folder1.vbs (WSH sample in VBScript)
' Author:  (c) G. Born
'
' Creating a folder
'*****************************************************
Option Explicit

Dim isnew
Dim path, newpath, parent
Dim Text, Text1, Title, oFolder
Dim fso, oFolders, oSubFolder, wsh        ' Object variables
```

Listing 12-7 *Folder1.vbs*   *(continued)*

Listing 12-7 *continued*

```
Text = "Folders" & vbCrLf & vbCrLf
Title = "WSH sample - by G. Born"

' Query folder name.
path = InputBox("Enter folder name (e.g. C:\Born).", _
                Title, "C:\Born")
If path = "" Then
    WScript.Quit               ' Canceled by the user.
End If


newpath = path                 ' Save path (for deletion).


' Create FileSystemObject object to access file system.
Set fso = WScript.CreateObject("Scripting.FileSystemObject")

' Check whether the folder exists.
If (Not fso.FolderExists(path)) Then
    ' Folder doesn't exist; create it.
    Set oFolders = fso.CreateFolder(path)
    MsgBox "Folder " & path & " created"
    isnew = True          ' Keep in mind that the folder is new.
Else
    isnew = False         ' Keep in mind that the folder already exists.
End If


If (MsgBox("List parent folders?", _
          vbYesNo + vbQuestion, Title) = vbYes) Then
    ' Fetch parent folder.
    parent = fso.GetParentFolderName(path)

    If (parent = "") Then
        MsgBox "No parent folder"
    Else
        ' Get Folders collection.
        Set oFolders = fso.GetFolder(parent)
        Set oSubFolder = oFolders.SubFolders

        For Each oFolder In oSubFolder            ' All folders
            Text = Text & oFolder.Name & vbCrLf
        Next

        MsgBox Text, vbOKOnly + vbInformation, Title
    End If
End If
```

```
If isnew = False Then
    MsgBox "Attention! The next steps might delete your folder " & _
        newpath & vbCrLf & _
        "Do not delete system folders!", _
        vbYes + vbExclamation, Title
End If

' Rename folder using the MoveFolder method.
If (MsgBox("Rename folder " & path & " ?", _
        vbYesNo + vbQuestion, Title) = vbYes) Then
    ' Yes, the user agrees.
    newpath = path & "New"
    fso.MoveFolder path, newpath

    MsgBox "Folder renamed " & newpath
End If

' Delete folder.
If (MsgBox("Delete folder " & newpath & " ?", _
        vbYesNo + vbQuestion, Title) = vbYes) Then
    ' User has accepted.
    fso.DeleteFolder(newpath)
End If

'*** End
```

The JScript implementation

In JScript, the *Popup* method has an additional time-out parameter (which isn't present in the VBScript *MsgBox* function). The full JScript implementation is shown in Listing 12-8.

```
//***************************************************
// File:    Folder1.js (WSH sample in JScript)
// Author:  (c) G. Born
//
// Creating a folder
//***************************************************

var vbOKCancel = 1;        // Declare variables.
var vbOK = 1;
var vbYes = 6;
var vbCancel = 2;
```

Listing 12-8 *Folder1.js*   (continued)

Listing 12-8 *continued*

```
var vbYesNo = 4;
var vbQuestion = 32;
var vbInformation = 64;

var Text = "Folders\n\n";
var Title = "WSH sample - by G. Born";

// Get a few objects that we need here.
var wsh = WScript.CreateObject("WScript.Shell");
var objAdr = WScript.CreateObject("WSHExtend.WinExt");
var fso = new ActiveXObject("Scripting.FileSystemObject");

// Query folder name.
var path = objAdr.WSHInputBox("Enter folder name (e.g. C:\\Born).",
                              Title, "C:\\Born");
if (path == "")
    WScript.Quit();           // Canceled by the user.

var newpath = path;           // Save path (for deletion).

// Check whether the folder exists.
if (!fso.FolderExists(path))
{
    // Folder doesn't exist; create it.
    var fo = fso.CreateFolder(path);
    WScript.Echo("Folder " + path + " created");
    var isnew = true;    // Keep in mind that the folder is new.
}
else
    var isnew = false;  // Keep in mind that the folder
                        // already exists.

if (wsh.Popup("List parent folders?", 0, Title,
            vbYesNo + vbQuestion) == vbYes)
{
    var parent = fso.GetParentFolderName(path) // Parent folder
    if (parent == "")
        WScript.Echo("No parent folder")
    else
    {   // Get Folders collection.
        var oFolders = fso.GetFolder(parent);
        var oSubFolder = new Enumerator(oFolders.SubFolders);
```

```
        // All folders
        for (; !oSubFolder.atEnd(); oSubFolder.moveNext())
        {
            var i = oSubFolder.item();
            Text = Text + i.name + "\n";
        }

        WScript.Echo(Text);
    }
}

if (!isnew)
    WScript.Echo(
        "Attention! The next steps might delete your folder " +
        newpath + "\n" +
        "Do not delete system folders!");

// Rename folder using the MoveFolder method.
if (wsh.Popup("Rename folder " + path + " ?", 0, Title,
            vbYesNo + vbQuestion) == vbYes)
{ // User has accepted.
    newpath = path + "New";
    fso.MoveFolder(path, newpath);

    WScript.Echo("The folder was renamed " + newpath);
}

// Delete folder.
if (wsh.Popup("Delete folder " + newpath, 0, Title,
            vbYesNo + vbQuestion) == vbYes)
    // User has accepted.
    fso.DeleteFolder(newpath);

//*** End
```

Listing All Files in a Folder

The preceding sample lists all folders in a given folder. You can use the *Files* collection of the *FileSystemObject* object to list all files in a given folder in a similar way. The next sample lists all files in the Windows folder \ShellNew in a dialog box (Figure 12-5).

You can specify the path to the target folder in a named constant in the program header:

```
Const path = "%WINDIR%\ShellNew"
```

Figure 12-5 *A list of files in a given folder*

To access the folder's content, you must first create the *FileSystemObject* object:

```
Set fso = WScript.CreateObject("Scripting.FileSystemObject")
```

You can then retrieve an object reference to the folder by using the *GetFolder* method. In this step, you can submit the path to the method. Because the path defined in the constant *path* contains the environment variable *%WINDIR%*, you must expand the expression by using the *ExpandEnvironmentStrings* method. You can do this with the following nested statements:

```
Set oFolder = fso.GetFolder(wsh.ExpandEnvironmentStrings(path))
```

After this line of code, the variable *oFolder* holds an object reference to the current folder. You can use this object to retrieve the *Files* property, which returns a collection containing all files in the given folder:

```
Set oFiles = oFolder.Files
```

You can extract the name of a file from the collection by using the *Name* property. The following loop retrieves all filenames and their size from the current folder:

```
For Each i In oFiles            ' All files
    Text = Text & i.Name & vbTab
    Text = Text & FormatNumber(i.Size, 0) & vbCrLf
Next
```

When the loop terminates, the variable *Text* contains the names of all files. To separate the filename and its size, the sample uses the named VBScript constant *vbTab*. If the text is shown in a dialog box, the filename and size are listed in columns.

Unfortunately, the tab stops are set to default locations; I haven't found a way to adjust them (as you can see in Figure 12-6). The full sample is shown in Listing 12-9.

```
'*********************************************************
' File:     Files.vbs (WSH sample in VBScript)
' Author:   (c) G. Born
'
' Listing all files in the Windows folder ShellNew
'*********************************************************
Option Explicit

Const path = "%WINDIR%\ShellNew"

Dim Text, Title, oFile
Dim fso, oFolder, oFiles, wsh          ' Object variables

Text = "Folder "
Title = "WSH sample - by G. Born"

Set wsh = WScript.CreateObject("WScript.Shell")

' Create FileSystemObject object to access the file system.
Set fso = CreateObject("Scripting.FileSystemObject")

' Get Folder object.
Set oFolder = fso.GetFolder(wsh.ExpandEnvironmentStrings(path))

Text = Text & oFolder & vbCrLf & vbCrLf
Text = Text & "Name" & vbTab & vbTab & "Size" & vbCrLf
Set oFiles = oFolder.Files          ' Get Files collection.

For Each oFile In oFiles            ' All files
    Text = Text & oFile.Name & vbTab
    Text = Text & FormatNumber(oFile.Size, 0) & vbTab
    ' List the short filename (but comment out for VBScript 3.1)
    ' Text = Text & oFile.ShortName & vbCrLf
    Text = Text & vbCrLf
Next

MsgBox Text, vbOKOnly + vbInformation, Title

'*** End
```

Listing 12-9 *Files.vbs*

The JScript implementation

Listing 12-10 shows the JScript version.

```
//***************************************************
// File:     Files.js (WSH sample in JScript)
// Author:   (c) G. Born
//
// Listing all files in the Windows folder ShellNew
//***************************************************

var path = "%windir%\\ShellNew";
var Text = "Folder ";
var wsh = WScript.CreateObject ("WScript.Shell");

// Create FileSystemObject object to access the file system.
var fso = WScript.CreateObject("Scripting.FileSystemObject");

// Get Folders collection.
var oFolder = fso.GetFolder(wsh.ExpandEnvironmentStrings(path));
var oFiles = new Enumerator(oFolder.Files);    // Files collection

Text = Text + oFolder + "\n\n";
Text = Text + "Name\t\tSize\n";

for (; !oFiles.atEnd(); oFiles.moveNext())    // All folders
{
    var oFile = oFiles.item();
    Text = Text + oFile.name + "\t";
    Text = Text + oFile.size + "\t";
    // Text = Text + oFile.ShortName + "\n";
    Text = Text + "\n";
}

WScript.Echo(Text);

//*** End
```

Listing 12-10 *Files.js*

Retrieving File Attributes and Dates

Once you obtain the *Files* collection, you can extract the file object and its properties, as shown in the previous sample. The *Name* property of a *File* object returns the name of a file. The *Attributes* property returns a binary value indicating the attributes set for the file. The values are shown in Table 12-3.

Table 12-3 CONSTANTS FOR FILE ATTRIBUTES

Constant*	Value	Description
Normal	0	Normal file without attributes set.
ReadOnly	1	Read-only attribute is set.
Hidden	2	Hidden attribute is set.
System	4	System file.
Directory	16	Folder or directory. (Attribute can be read-only.)
Archive	32	Archive attribute is set; the file was changed since the last backup.
Alias	1024	Shortcut (.lnk) file.
Compressed	2048	Compressed file (Windows NT and Windows 2000 only).

* These constants are valid for Scrrun.dll as shipped with WSH 2.

You can combine the constant values within the *Attributes* property. You can obtain the file creation date, file modification date, or file last accessed date by using the *DateCreated*, *DateLastAccessed*, or *DateLastModified* properties, respectively, of the *File* or *Folder* objects.

The next sample retrieves some information about a file. It uses the Autoexec.bat file (which is always present in Windows 95 and Windows 98) as the default. Windows NT and Windows 2000 users can use any other text file. The sample supports drag-and-drop, so if the user drags a file's icon to the script file's icon, the script returns information about that file. Figure 12-6 shows the dialog box the script creates. It contains the values (date and attribute information) retrieved from the Autoexec.bat file.

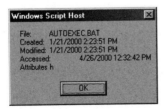

Figure 12-6 *Information about Autoexec.bat*

A Problem with *DateCreated*

While developing this script, I encountered a problem: *CStr(j.DateCreated)* caused an "Invalid procedure call or argument" run-time error on my test machine. At first, I thought it was just a bug because the sample ran without any trouble under version 3.1 of the language engines (on another machine). After debugging for a while, I discovered that *DateCreated* was causing the run-time error. On the General page of the Autoexec.bat property sheet on that other machine (Figure 12-7), I found the reason: the creation date of the Autoexec.bat file was undefined on the machine. If you want your script to be foolproof, you must implement a kind of error handling in case any entries in the file's date fields are undefined. The same is true for folders. (Alas, sometimes it's hard to be a programmer.)

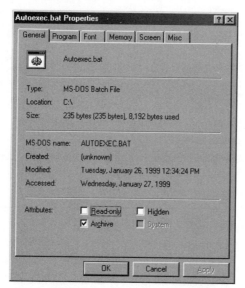

Figure 12-7 *Properties of Autoexec.bat*

The script in Listing 12-11 reads the Autoexec.bat file attributes and the create, modify, and access dates. The script then displays the information in a dialog box.

```
'*************************************************
' File:     File1.vbs (WSH sample in VBScript)
' Author:   (c) G. Born
'
' Reading the attributes, creation date, modify
' date, and access date of the Autoexec.bat file
' (Windows NT users must modify the "file"
' constant.)
'*************************************************
Option Explicit

Dim fso, oFile, objArgs, Text, attrib, file

file = "C:\Autoexec.bat" ' Specify default file.

' Try to get a file as an argument.
Set objArgs = WScript.Arguments    ' Create object.
If objArgs.Count > 0 Then _
    file = objArgs(0)              ' First argument

' Create FileSystemObject object to access the file system.
Set fso = WScript.CreateObject("Scripting.FileSystemObject")

If fso.FileExists(file) Then       ' Check whether file exists.
    Set oFile = fso.GetFile(file) ' Get file handle object.
    ' Now we try to retrieve the file information.
    Text = "File: " & vbTab & oFile.Name & vbCrLf ' Retrieve filename.

    ' File dates (created, modified, accessed)
    Text = Text & "Created: " & vbTab & oFile.DateCreated & vbCrLf
    Text = Text & "Modified: " & vbTab & oFile.DateLastModified & vbCrLf
    Text = Text & "Accessed: " & vbTab & _
           oFile.DateLastAccessed & vbCrLf

    ' Decode attributes.
    Text = Text & "Attributes " & vbTab
    attrib = oFile.Attributes
```

Listing 12-11 *File1.vbs*   *(continued)*

Listing 12-11 *continued*

```
' This is the read-only attribute.
If (attrib And &H01) > 0 Then Text = Text & "r "
' This is the hidden attribute.
If (attrib And &H02) > 0 Then Text = Text & "h "
' This is the system attribute.
If (attrib And &H04) > 0 Then Text = Text & "s "
' This is the archive attribute.
If (attrib And &H20) > 0 Then Text = Text & "a "
' This is the compressed attribute in Windows NT.
If (attrib And &H800) > 0 Then Text = Text & "c "

    WScript.Echo Text              ' Show result.
Else
    WScript.Echo "Error: File " & file & " not found"
End If

'*** End
```

The JScript implementation

The JScript version is shown in Listing 12-12. The script reads the attributes and the dates and displays the information in a dialog box (Figure 12-8).

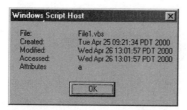

Figure 12-8 *File properties displayed by JScript*

By default, the script displays the Autoexec.bat properties. In WSH 2, a user can drag a file to the script file's icon to display the file's properties. You'll notice that this script creates a slightly different message box than that shown in Figure 12-6. In particular, the date properties return a value in long format (including the day of the week). Also, the *CStr* function isn't available in JScript. String concatenation using the + operator causes an automatic type conversion.

```
//*************************************************
// File:    File1.js (WSH sample in JScript)
// Author:  (c) G. Born
//
// Reading the attributes, creation date, modify
// date, and access date of the Autoexec.bat file
// (Windows NT users must modify the "file"
// variable.)
//*************************************************

var file = "C:\\Autoexec.bat";  // Specify file.

// Try to retrieve parameters submitted;
// only one filename is supported.
var objArgs = WScript.Arguments; // Create object.
if (objArgs.length > 0)          // Arguments?
    file = objArgs(0);           // Get first argument.

// Create FileSystemObject object to access file system.
var fso = WScript.CreateObject("Scripting.FileSystemObject");

if (!fso.FileExists(file))
{
    WScript.Echo("Error", file, "doesn't exist");
    WScript.Quit(1);
}

var j = fso.GetFile(file);       // Get file handle object.

// Now we try to retrieve the file information.
var Text = "File: \t\t" + j.name + "\n";   // Filename

// File dates (created, modified, accessed)
Text = Text + "Created: \t\t" + j.DateCreated + "\n";
Text = Text + "Modified: \t\t" + j.DateLastModified + "\n";
Text = Text + "Accessed: \t" + j.DateLastAccessed + "\n";

// Decode attributes.
Text = Text + "Attributes\t\t";
var attrib = j.Attributes;
```

Listing 12-12 *File1.js*

(continued)

Listing 12-12 *continued*

```
if ((attrib & 0x01) != 0)     // Read-only attribute
    Text = Text + "r ";
if ((attrib & 0x02) != 0)     // Hidden attribute
    Text = Text + "h ";
if ((attrib & 0x04) != 0)     // System attribute
    Text = Text + "s ";
if ((attrib & 0x20) != 0)     // Archive attribute
    Text = Text + "a ";
if ((attrib & 0x800) != 0)    // Compressed attribute (Windows NT)
    Text = Text + "c ";

WScript.Echo(Text);           // Show result.

//*** End
```

> **TIP** The File1.wsf file on the companion CD uses a reference to the type library. This enables the program to use named constants for attributes such as *ReadOnly*, *Hidden*, and *System* within the code.

Solving the problem of undefined *CreationDate* entries

I mentioned earlier that on some of my machines the creation date of several files was undefined, causing the script to fail with a run-time error. However, there's a way to get a *Files* collection and process all files within a loop (to show all file properties within a folder, for example). For each item in the collection, you can access and manipulate several properties, as shown in Figure 12-9. If the date value isn't defined, the script recovers from the run-time error.

Figure 12-9 *A file list with undefined file properties*

Let's extend the first part of our earlier sample that lists the files of the Windows subfolder \ShellNew so that we also get the attributes and the creation date. After retrieving the files collection of this folder, you can use a simple *For Each file In oFiles* loop to process all files:

```
For Each file In oFiles
    Text = Text & file.Name              ' Add filename.
    Text = Text & " " & file.DateCreated ' Creation date
Next
```

The statement *Text = Text & file.Name* uses the *Name* property to append the filename to a string. The statement *Text = Text & " " & file.DateCreated* should add the file's creation date to the string. Unfortunately, the code still causes a run-time error ("Invalid procedure call or argument") if the *DateCreated* value of the file is undefined. You need something to make the *file.DateCreated* statement tolerant of undefined date values.

The following procedure handles this situation. The *DateCreated* property is retrieved in a function:

```
Function DateCreatedEx(obj)
    On Error Resume Next
    Dim datex
    ' Retrieves the file creation date
    datex = i.DateCreated     ' Created
    If Err.Number <> 0 Then datex = "unknown"
    DateCreatedEx = datex
    On Error Goto 0
End Function
```

The *On Error Resume Next* statement catches all run-time errors and causes the interpreter to continue with the next statement. If an attempt to access the *DateCreated* property fails, *Err.Number* contains a value not equal to 0. When *DateCreated* fails, our sample returns the string "*unknown*," so a run-time error caused by a missing creation date entry isn't possible. The *On Error GoTo 0* statement disables inline run-time error handling. The script code is stored in a .wsf file containing a reference to the type library, so we can use named constants (such as *ReadOnly*, *Hidden*, and *System*) within the code to decipher the attribute values. The full implementation is shown in Listing 12-13.

```
<?xml version="1.0" encoding="ISO-8859-1"?>
<!--
    File:     File2.wsf (WSH 2 sample)
    Author:   (c) G. Born

    Reading the attributes, creation date, modify
    date, and access date of the files in ShellNew
-->

<job id="File2">
    <reference guid='{420B2830-E718-11CF-893D-00A0C9054228}'/>

    <script language="VBScript">
    <![CDATA[
        Option Explicit

        Const path = "%WINDIR%\ShellNew"

        Dim Text, attrib
        Dim wsh, fso, oFolder, oFiles, oFile

        Set wsh = WScript.CreateObject("WScript.Shell")

        ' Create the FileSystemObject to access file system.
        Set fso = WScript.CreateObject("Scripting.FileSystemObject")

        Set oFolder = _
            fso.GetFolder(wsh.ExpandEnvironmentStrings(path))

        Set oFiles = oFolder.Files          ' Get Files collection.

        ' Set header text.
        Text = "File" & vbTab & vbTab & "Creation Date" & vbTab _
            & vbTab & "Attributes" & vbCrLf

        ' Now we try to retrieve the file information.
        For Each oFile In oFiles
            Text = Text & oFile.name & vbTab & " ["      ' Filename
            Text = Text & DateCreatedEx(oFile) & "] "    ' Date created
            Text = Text & vbTab                          ' Tab
            ' Decode attributes.
            If (oFile.Attributes And ReadOnly) > 0 Then _
                Text = Text & "r "
            If (oFile.Attributes And Hidden) > 0 Then _
                Text = Text & "h "
```

Listing 12-13 *File2.wsf*

```
            If (oFile.Attributes And System) > 0 Then _
                Text = Text & "s "
            If (oFile.Attributes And Archive) > 0 Then _
                Text = Text & "a "
            If (oFile.Attributes And Compressed) > 0 Then _
                Text = Text & "c "
            Text = Text & vbCrLf              ' New line
        Next

        WScript.Echo Text             ' Display results.


        ' Helper function for preventing run-time errors
        Function DateCreatedEx(obj)
            On Error Resume Next        ' Error handling on
            Dim datex
            ' Retrieves the file creation date
            datex = obj.DateCreated        'Created
            If Err.Number <> 0 Then datex = "          unknown        "
            DateCreatedEx = datex
            On Error Goto 0             ' Error handling off
        End Function
    ]]>
    </script>
</job>
```

Copying and Deleting Files

You can use methods of the *File* object to copy, move, and delete files. Before you can access the *File* object, you must create the *FileSystemObject* object:

```
Set fso = CreateObject("Scripting.FileSystemObject")
```

To prevent run-time errors, you must check whether the file to be copied already exists. You can use the *FileExists* method (which we used in an earlier sample) for this purpose:

```
If (fso.FileExists(file1)) Then
    ⋮
```

The method returns the value *True* if the file passed in the parameter *file1* exists. The parameter *file1* must contain the entire path, including the filename. If you've already checked that the source file exists, you can retrieve a *File* object reference using the *GetFile* method of the *FileSystemObject* object:

```
Set oFile = fso.GetFile(file1)
```

The *file1* parameter must also contain the path and the source filename. You can use the *File* object reference, contained in the object variable *oFile*, to apply the *Copy* method:

```
oFile.Copy file2
```

The *Copy* method requires at least one parameter containing the name of the target file. An optional second parameter, *overwrite*, can be set to *True* or *False*. If it's set to *True*, an existing file in the target folder is overwritten during the copy operation. If it's set to *False*, a run-time error occurs if the target exists.

To move or rename a file, you can use the *Move* method of the *File* object. This method has the same syntax as the *Copy* method. (Unlike the *Copy* method, it deletes the source file after the copy operation is finished.)

To delete a file, you use the *Delete* method:

```
Set oFile = fso.GetFile(file2)
oFile.Delete
```

The first line retrieves the object reference to the file specified in the parameter *file2*. This object reference is returned as a *File* object, so you can apply the *Delete* method to the *oFile* object variable to delete the file. The *Delete* method has an optional parameter, *force*. If this parameter is set to *True*, WSH also deletes files with the *Read-only* attribute set. If *force* is set to *False* and if the file is read-only, the *Delete* method raises a run-time error. Instead of using the two lines given above, you can combine the commands into one line:

```
fso.DeleteFile file2
```

> **NOTE**   If you move or delete a file, be aware that the object reference to the original file is no longer valid after the method is executed.

The *Copy* and *Move* methods don't support wildcard characters. Nor does *Delete*, which allows you to delete only one file at a time. However, you can use a collection containing all files in a folder to process multiple files. You can also execute an MS-DOS command by using the *Run* method to copy, delete, move, or rename several files at a time. This command launches the MS-DOS *Copy* command, which supports wildcards:

```
wsh.Run "%COMSPEC% /c Copy C:\Born\Text*.txt C:\Born\Backup"
```

Setting the *bWaitOnReturn* parameter in the method to *True* (see Chapter 7) causes the script to wait until the command is finished and the process terminates. This approach has one disadvantage: the script can't handle errors caused by the commands.

Besides the methods used in the next listing, the *FileSystemObject* object contains other objects and methods for file handling. *CopyFile* also supports file copying. The first parameter (which can include wildcards) specifies the source files, and the second parameter specifies the target file.

Listing 12-14 uses these methods in VBScript. The script requires that the folder C:\Born containing the file Test.txt already exists. The file Test.txt is copied within the folder to Test1.txt. On request, the file is also deleted.

```vbscript
'****************************************************
' File:    File3.vbs (WSH sample in VBScript)
' Author:  (c) G. Born
'
' Copying and deleting files
'****************************************************
Option Explicit

Const path = "C:\Born"                ' Test folder (must exist)
Const file1 = "C:\Born\Test.txt"      ' Source file (must exist)
Const file2 = "C:\Born\Test1.txt"     ' Target file

Dim Text, Title, i
Dim fso, oFile, oFolder               ' Object variables

Text = "File copied" & vbCrLf
Title = "WSH sample - by G. Born"

' Create FileSystemObject object to access file system.
Set fso = CreateObject("Scripting.FileSystemObject")

' Check whether file exists.
If (fso.FileExists(file1)) Then
    ' Copy file1 to file2 (or use fso.CopyFile file1, file2).
    Set oFile = fso.GetFile(file1)    ' Get File object.
    oFile.Copy file2, True            ' Overwrite existing target.

    Set oFolder = fso.GetFolder(path)
    Set oFile = oFolder.Files         ' Get Files collection.
    For Each i In oFile               ' All files
        Text = Text & i.Name & vbCrLf
    Next
```

Listing 12-14 *File3.vbs* *(continued)*

Listing 12-14 *continued*

```
    MsgBox Text, vbOKOnly + vbInformation, Title
Else
    WScript.Echo "File " & file1 & " doesn't exist"
    WScript.Quit
End If


' Delete file upon request.
If (MsgBox("Delete file?", vbYesNo, Title) = vbYes) Then
    Set oFile = fso.GetFile(file2)      ' Fetch File object.
    oFile.Delete          ' (or use fso.CopyFile file2)
    WScript.Echo "File " & file2 & " deleted"
End If


'*** End
```

The JScript implementation

The JScript implementation, shown in Listing 12-15, uses the same methods as the VBScript sample. The Test.txt file in the C:\Born folder is copied to Test1.txt, and then the file is deleted if the user clicks Yes.

```
//*************************************************
// File:    File3.js (WSH sample in JScript)
// Author:  (c) G. Born
//
// Copying and deleting files
//*************************************************
var vbYesNo = 4;
var vbYes = 6;
var vbInformation = 64;
var vbCancel = 2;

var path = "C:\\Born";
var file1 = "C:\\Born\\Test.txt";
var file2 = "C:\\Born\\Test1.txt";

var Text = "File copied\n";
var Title = "WSH sample - by G. Born";

var obj = WScript.CreateObject("WScript.Shell");

// Create FileSystemObject object to access file system.
var fso = WScript.CreateObject("Scripting.FileSystemObject");
```

Listing 12-15 *File3.js*

```
// Check whether file exists.
if (fso.FileExists(file1))
{
    // Copy file1 to file2.
    var oFile = fso.GetFile(file1);          // Get File object.
    oFile.Copy (file2, true);                // Overwrite target.

    var oFolder = fso.GetFolder(path);
    var oFile = new Enumerator(oFolder.Files); // Files collection
    for (; !oFile.atEnd(); oFile.moveNext())   // All files
    {
        var i = oFile.item();
        Text = Text + i.Name + "\n";
    }
    WScript.Echo(Text);
}
else
{
    WScript.Echo("File " + file1 + " doesn't exist");
    WScript.Quit(1);
}

// Delete file on request.
if (obj.Popup("Delete file?", 0, Title, vbYesNo) == vbYes)
{
    var oFile = fso.GetFile(file2);    // Get File object.
    oFile.Delete();
    WScript.Echo("File " + file2 + " deleted");
}

//*** End
```

Backing Up Folders

Using a few statements, you can create your own folders for a daily backup. The folder names can include the current date. The next sample, a simple VBScript program, asks whether a folder should be backed up (Figure 12-10, left). The script assumes that the source folder C:\Born exists. If the folder is missing, the script terminates with a message dialog box (Figure 12-10, middle).

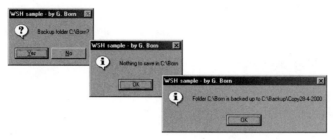

Figure 12-10 *Dialog boxes of the backup program*

If the source folder exists, the script determines whether the folder contains files. If the folder is empty, no backup is necessary and a message box to that effect is shown. If the folder contains files, the script creates the target folder C:\Backup\Copy*xx-yy-zzzz*, copies the files to that folder, and displays a dialog box confirming the copy (Figure 12-10, right). The characters *xx-yy-zzzz* are a placeholder for the current date in the format *day-month-year*. For every day, a target folder is created as a subfolder of C:\Backup. If you do several backups per day, the files are overwritten in the target folder. The script assumes that the files aren't in use; it doesn't include run-time error handling in case the files are in use.

You set the paths for the target and destination folders in the constants *path1* and *path2* in the program's header, so it's easy to customize this script for your own purposes. The files should be backed up to the target folder whose name includes the current date.

You set the path to the folder by using the following statement:

```
file2 = path2 & Day(Date) & "-" & Month(Date) & "-" & Year(Date)
```

The constant *path2* is set in the program's header to *C:\Backup\Copy*. The functions *Day(Date)*, *Month(Date)*, and *Year(Date)* append the current date to this path.

You might wonder why I didn't use this statement to create the path:

```
file2 = path2 & Date
```

This command is short, but it causes a problem: the user can define separators within the date format at the operating-system level, and not all of these separator characters (such as the backslash, \) are valid filename characters. In the previous statement, the *Date* function doesn't return valid filenames. The path *C:\Backup\Copy2\22\1998*, for example, would be interpreted as a folder hierarchy. This folder hierarchy would be created automatically, but the result wouldn't be what you'd expect. The statement above extracts the day, month, and year from the date value and inserts the separators manually. It's up to you to combine the date to create a valid directory name. (I write the date in European format, in which the day precedes the month, and merge it into a folder name.)

Next, you must check whether the source folder exists. If it doesn't, the script terminates with an error message. The following sequence uses the *FolderExists* method for this purpose:

```
If (Not fso.FolderExists(path1)) Then
    Text = "Folder " & path1 & " doesn't exist."
    MsgBox Text, vbOKOnly + vbInformation, Title
    WScript.Quit
End If
```

You also need to check whether the source folder is empty. (If it is, you don't need to copy any files.) Applying the *CopyFile* method to an empty folder causes a run-time error. I tried to use the *oFiles.Count* item of the collection to get the number of entries, but I got a run-time error. To test whether a folder is empty, you should use the following sequence:

```
If FolderEmpty(path1) Then
    ⋮

Function FolderEmpty(name)
    Dim fso, oFolder, oFiles        ' Object variables
    Dim i, flag

    Set fso = CreateObject("Scripting.FileSystemObject")
    Set oFolder = fso.GetFolder(path1)    ' Get folder.
    Set oFiles = oFolder.Files            ' All files
    flag = True                           ' Set flag to "no files."
    For Each i In oFiles
        flag = False                      ' File found; toggle flag.
        Exit For
    Next
    FolderEmpty = flag
End Function
```

The function *FolderEmpty* requests the folder's name—a string containing a valid path, including the folder name. You use this path to obtain a *Files* collection. A *For Each i In oFiles* loop is processed only if the collection contains files. In this case, the variable *flag* is set to *False* (indicating that a file was found). If the folder doesn't contain files, the function returns *True*.

NOTE The function doesn't check whether the folder exists. You can extend the sample to include this error check as well. I also omitted a test for subfolders because the *FileCopy* method can be applied only to files in the current folder.

Before doing the backup, you must check whether the target folder exists. If the folder doesn't exist, you must create it. First, you create the root folder C:\Backup. Then you create the new destination subfolder by using *CreateFolder*:

```
If (Not fso.FolderExists(file2)) Then
    ' Does parent folder exist?
    If (Not fso.FolderExists(path3)) Then _
        fso.CreateFolder(path3) ' First step

    fso.CreateFolder(file2)      ' Create backup folder.
End If
```

The *FolderExists* method of the *FileSystemObject* object requires the folder name as a parameter. The method checks whether the folder is available in the given (valid) path and returns the value *True* for an existing folder. After these checks, you use this command to copy the files:

```
fso.CopyFile path1 & "\*.*", file2
```

The CopyFile method is applied to the *FileSystemObject* object. The first parameter passed to the method contains the source (which in this sample is the path to the source folder, ending with wildcard characters). This parameter ensures that all files in the source folder are copied. Be aware that the method doesn't process subfolders. Also, the source folder must contain at least one file. The mandatory second parameter specifies the target. If this parameter contains a filename appended to the path, the method renames the copied files.

To execute the script, you must create a folder C:\Born that contains at least one file. After the script runs, your hard disk should contain a new folder named Backup that contains a subfolder with the current date in its name (Figure 12-11).

Figure 12-11 *Source and target folders*

The full VBScript implementation is shown in Listing 12-16.

```
'*******************************************************
' File:    Backup.vbs (WSH sample in VBScript)
' Author:  (c) G. Born
'
' Searching the folder C:\Born and, if the folder
' contains files, backing it up to the target folder
' C:\Backup\Copyxx-yy-zzzz (where xx-yy-zzzz stands
' for the current date)
'*******************************************************
Option Explicit

Const path1 = "C:\Born"
Const path2 = "C:\Backup\Copy"
Const path3 = "C:\Backup\"

Dim Text, Title,  destination
Dim fso                        ' Object variable
Dim flag

Text = "Backup folder " & path1 & "?"
Title = "WSH sample - by G. Born"

If (MsgBox(Text, vbYesNo + vbQuestion, Title) = vbNo) Then
    WScript.Quit          ' Cancel selected.
End If

' Create the name of the destination folder. Because
' localized versions of Windows can use illegal filename
' characters (such as \ and :) in the date format,
' create the name manually from the date.
destination = path2 & Day(Date) & "-" & Month(Date) & _
              "-" & Year(Date)

' Create FileSystemObject object to access the file system.
Set fso = CreateObject("Scripting.FileSystemObject")

' Test whether the source folder exists.
If (Not fso.FolderExists(path1)) Then
    Text = "Folder " & path1 & " not found!"
    MsgBox Text, vbOKOnly + vbInformation, Title
    WScript.Quit
End If
```

Listing 12-16 *Backup.vbs*   *(continued)*

Listing 12-16 *continued*

```
' Check whether there are files in the source folder. If
' not, the copy operation causes a run-time error.
' We don't need to create the destination folder if the
' source is empty.
If FolderEmpty(path1) Then
    Text = "Nothing to save in " & path1
    MsgBox Text, vbOKOnly + vbInformation, Title
    WScript.Quit
End If


' Check whether the target folder exists.
If (Not fso.FolderExists(destination)) Then
    ' Does parent folder exist?
    If (Not fso.FolderExists(path3)) Then _
        fso.CreateFolder(path3)     ' First step

    fso.CreateFolder(destination)  ' Create backup folder.
End If


' Copy files from source to target.
fso.CopyFile path1 & "\*.*", destination

Text = "Folder " & path1 & " is backed up to " & destination
MsgBox Text, vbOKOnly + vbInformation, Title


' Check for an empty folder.
Function FolderEmpty (name)
    Dim fso, oFolder, oFiles          ' Object variables
    Dim i, flag

    Set fso = CreateObject("Scripting.FileSystemObject")
    Set oFolder = fso.GetFolder(path1)  ' Get folder.
    Set oFiles = oFolder.Files           ' Get Files collection.
    flag = True                          ' No files
    For Each i In oFiles                 ' A file is found if
        flag = False                     ' the loop is processed.
    Next
    FolderEmpty = flag                   ' Return result.
End Function

'*** End
```

I'll leave the JScript implementation up to you as an exercise.

NOTE As I mentioned earlier, the *FileSystemObject* object has several methods and subobjects that you can use to copy files or folders. Keep in mind that the *Copy* method provided by the subobjects requires only the target as a parameter—the source is implied by the subobject. If a method raises a run-time error during a copy or move operation, you should check whether a backslash character terminates the folder's path, even if the folder and files exist.

ACCESSING TEXT FILES

You can use methods of the *FileSystemObject* object to read from and write to text files.

Reading from a Text File

You use the *FileSystemObject* object's *OpenTextFile* method to access a text file. Let's look at a simple script that accesses text files. If the script is called without a parameter, it tries to read the file C:\Autoexec.bat. A dialog box allows the user to specify whether the file's content should be shown in a dialog box or in a browser window (Figure 12-12).

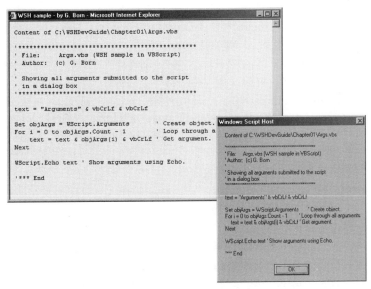

Figure 12-12 *Content of a text file shown in a browser window and in a dialog box*

To read from a text file, you must first create the *FileSystemObject* object:

```
Set fso = CreateObject("Scripting.FileSystemObject")
```

You should also check whether the file exists because the script causes a run-time error if a file is missing:

```
If fso.FileExists(file) Then
  ⋮
```

If the file exists, you can try to open the file by using the *OpenTextFile* method of the *FileSystemObject* object:

```
Set txtStream = fso.OpenTextFile(file)
```

The parameter *file*, which contains the path (including the name of the text file), must be passed to the method. If the file doesn't exist, a run-time error occurs. The statement above uses only one parameter, which contains the filename. The method supports some optional parameters to control how text files are opened, as shown here:

```
Object_name.OpenTextFile(filename[, iomode[, create[, format]]])
```

This statement has the following parameters:

- **filename**   The name of an existing text file.

- **iomode**   An optional parameter that specifies the I/O mode for the file operation. The parameter can contain the constants *ForReading* (with a value of 1 for read-only access), *ForWriting* (with a value of 2 for write access only), and *ForAppending* (with a value of 8 for write access and appending data at the end of the file).

  NOTE You must declare the *OpenTextFile* constants explicitly in your script because WSH doesn't use predefined names for them. In WSH 2, you can use a .wsf file with a *<reference>* element that defines a reference to the type library to obtain these constants. (This technique is demonstrated several times in this chapter.)

- **create**   An optional parameter that contains the Boolean value. The value *True* causes a missing file to be created. The value *False* doesn't create the file.

- **format**   An optional parameter that specifies the format of the text file to be opened. If the parameter is omitted, an ASCII file is defined for the format. You can set the value to *TristateUseDefault* (with a value of −2 to open the file with default settings), *TristateTrue* (with a value of −1 to open the file in Unicode format), and *TristateFalse* (with a value of 0 to open the file in ASCII format).

To read the lines in a text file, you must apply the *ReadLine* method to the file object. During reading, you must use the *atEndOfStream* method to check whether the file's end has been reached. The following loop reads a file line by line into a string:

```
Do While Not (txtStream.atEndOfStream)
    Text = Text & txtStream.ReadLine & vbCrLf
Loop
```

After you read the file's content, you can use the variable *Text* for further processing.

The sample script sets C:\Autoexec.bat as the default file. If no other filename is specified, this file is read and its content is shown. It can be helpful, however, if the user can drag another file to the script file's icon so that the script shows the content of the dragged file. You can do this in VBScript by using the following statements:

```
file = "C:\Autoexec.bat"          ' Default test file
' Try to get a filename from the Arguments collection.
Set objArgs = WScript.Arguments ' Create object.
If objArgs.Count > 0 Then        ' Argument found.
    file = objArgs(0)             ' Set filename to first argument.
End If
```

After these statements are processed, the variable *file* contains either the name *C:\Autoexec.bat* or the path and name of the file dragged to the script's icon. Before you can access the file, you must check whether the file exists:

```
Set fso = CreateObject("Scripting.FileSystemObject")
If fso.FileExists(file) Then ' Check whether file exists.
    ⋮
End If
```

The first line creates a reference to the *FileSystemObject* object. Then you apply the *FileExists* method to this object to check whether the file exists. If the file doesn't exist, the script can terminate by using the *Quit* method. If the script exists, you can read the file's content:

```
Set txtStream = fso.OpenTextFile(file) ' Open text file.
Do While Not (txtStream.atEndOfStream)
    Text = Text & txtStream.ReadLine & vbCrLf
Loop
```

The *OpenTextFile* method opens the file. The sample omits optional parameters because you need only read access. Then it uses a loop to read the file by using the *ReadLine* method. To test whether the end of the file has been reached, the *atEndOfStream* method is used. This method returns *False* if the file's end hasn't been reached. After exiting the loop, the string variable *Text* contains the entire file. The script then shows the file's content in a simple dialog box or a browser window.

Pitfalls of Using Dialog Boxes and Browser Windows to View Text Files

To show a simple dialog box in VBScript, you can use this statement:

```
WScript.Echo Text
```

Or you can use a command such as this:

```
MsgBox Text, vbOKOnly + vbInformation, Title
```

If the content of the variable *Text* contains only a few characters, no problems occur. But if you show the content of a lengthy text file by using the *Echo* method, the window will be larger than the Desktop. The lower part of the dialog box, which contains the text's trail and the OK button, will be hidden under the taskbar.

Using the VBScript *MsgBox* call causes a different problem: the text isn't shown in its entirety. The VBScript help says that *MsgBox* can display a parameter *prompt* with a maximum length of 1024 characters. If you attempt to show a lengthy text file, however, you see a dialog box that displays only the first part of the file.

The following sample solves this problem by showing a simple dialog box that allows the user to specify a browser window or a dialog box for viewing the file's content (Figure 12-13).

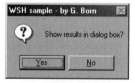

Figure 12-13 *Dialog box for selecting the file viewer (browser window or dialog box)*

To use Microsoft Internet Explorer to display the content, you can use the following procedure:

```
ShowWindow Text, Title
```

In the samples that follow, the *ShowWindow* procedure contains the following statements:

```
Sub ShowWindow(txt, title)
    Dim oIE, doc1
    ' Create Internet Explorer Application object.
    Set oIE = WScript.CreateObject("InternetExplorer.Application")
    oIE.Navigate "about:blank"  ' Empty HTML document
    oIE.Visible = 1             ' Internet Explorer is visible.
    oIE.ToolBar = 0
    oIE.StatusBar = 0
    ' oIE.Width=600
    oIE.Height = 500
```

```
Do While (oIE.Busy): Loop      ' Important: Wait until Internet
                               ' Explorer is ready.


Set doc1 = oIE.Document        ' Get Document object.
doc1.open                      ' Open document.
' Write script into the Document object.
doc1.writeln "<html><head><title>" & Title & "</title></head>"
doc1.writeln "<body bgcolor='#FAF0F0'><pre>"
doc1.writeln txt               ' Text output
doc1.writeln "</pre></body></html>"
doc1.close                     ' Close document for write access.
End Sub
```

The procedure invokes an Internet Explorer window, writes a valid HTML
header, and inserts the content of the submitted string in the browser window. The
text itself is formatted using the tags *<pre>...</pre>*. Then the document is completed
with a valid HTML file end (the tags *</body></html>*). The content of the text file is
then shown in a browser window.

Did you notice that the *Width* property of the browser window isn't set in the
procedure? Because the statement to set this property begins with a comment character ('), the browser adjusts the window width based on the length of the lines in
the text file.

After implementing the procedure in the sample file, I noticed that some files
cause "wrong" results in the browser window. As you can see in Figure 12-14, some
lines are shown in bold. Other files (such as HTML files containing forms) are shown
as a form in the browser window. I analyzed the HTML source code and found the
cause: the *ShowWindow* procedure simply writes the content of the file to the browser's
document window. If the variable *Text* contains HTML commands embedded in the
source code, the browser applies these commands. The results are unpredictable.

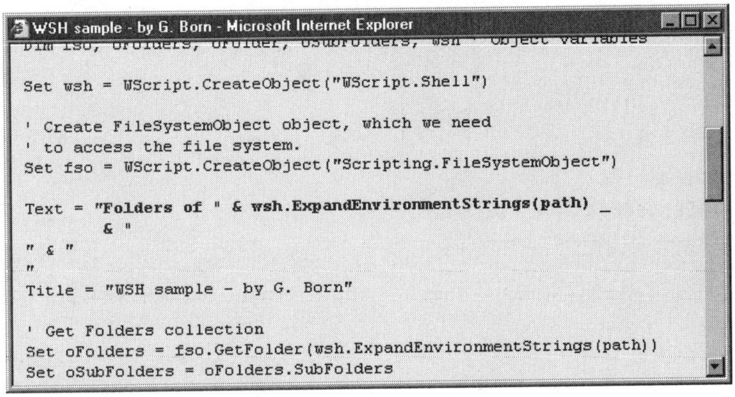

Figure 12-14 *Text shown in bold in the browser window*

For example, if you show a script file that contains statements for writing HTML code to the browser window, these statements affect the browser window. Therefore, you need a "filter" that converts the HTML. First, the tag characters < and > must be converted to *<* and *>*.

I decided to write my own filter function, *MakeHTMLCode*, to convert the string to a format that can be displayed as an HTML document. Besides the tag characters < and >, I decided also to filter all carriage return/line feed codes in the string and convert them to *
* tags so that you can display text in the browser window without inserting all of it into *<pre>...</pre>* tags. Unfortunately, in HTML a space character is treated as a "white space" character, which means that multiple spaces are stripped off the HTML code and the browser displays only a blank. I then tried to convert the blanks in the string to * * entities, but the result of several * * entities in an HTML file depends on the browser used. In Internet Explorer 5, multiple blanks are treated as one blank. I then decided to use a second parameter in the filter function *MakeHTMLCode*, which controls the filter options. A value of 0 forces the filter to convert all < and > characters. A value of 1 processes the string (as the value 0 does) and converts all line breaks to *
* tags. A value of 2 works like a value of 1 but also forces the filter to convert blanks to * * entities.

At this point, I'd like to make a few remarks about converting patterns in a string. Version 5 of VBScript and JScript support a regular expression object. You can create this object in VBScript as follows:

```
Set oReg = New RegExp
```

You can then set the properties of this object by using methods such as *Replace* to convert patterns in a string. If all matches in a string are to be processed, you can set the *Global* property to *True*:

```
oReg.Global = True
```

The following command specifies that pattern matching not be case sensitive:

```
oReg.IgnoreCase = True
```

To replace all < characters in a string, you can use the following statements:

```
oReg.Pattern = "<"
txt = oReg.Replace(txt, "&lt;")
```

The first line sets the pattern, and the second line applies the *Replace* method to the string *txt*. The string *<* is the replacement expression. Here is the entire source code:

```
Sub MakeHTMLCode(txt, flag)
    ' Convert text file to HTML structure.
    ' Flag controls which elements are converted.
    ' Use the following values:
    ' 0: Convert all < and > characters to &lt; and &gt;.
    ' 1: Like flag = 0, but also sets vbCrLf to <br> tag
    '    (forces line wrap).
    ' 2: Like flag = 1, but also sets blanks to  .
    ' ### Be careful of the order of pattern replacement. ###
    Dim oReg
    Set oReg = New RegExp          ' Create regular expression.
    oReg.Global = True             ' All matches
    oReg.IgnoreCase = True         ' Make case insensitive.

    ' Replace all < with &lt;.
    oReg.Pattern = "<"             ' Set pattern.
    txt = oReg.Replace(txt, "&lt;")

    ' Replace all ">" with "&gt;"
    oReg.Pattern = ">"             ' Set pattern.
    txt = oReg.Replace(txt, "&gt;")

    If flag > 0 Then               ' Replace vbCrLf?
        ' Now we're ready to replace all vbCrLf with <br>.
        oReg.Pattern = vbCrLf      ' Set pattern.
        oReg.Global = True         ' All matches
        txt = oReg.Replace(txt, "<br>")
    End If

    If flag > 1 Then               ' Replace blanks?
        ' Now we're ready to replace all blanks with  .
        oReg.Pattern = " "         ' Set pattern.
        oReg.Global = True         ' All matches
        txt = oReg.Replace(txt, " ")
    End If
End Sub
```

You can use the *MakeHTMLCode* function to control how the string is filtered. In the sample, the second parameter is set to 0, which forces the filter to simply convert the < and > characters. The carriage return line feed codes remain in the string. Because the text is embedded in *<pre>...</pre>* tags in the document area, all blanks are unchanged.

The full VBScript implementation is shown in Listing 12-17.

```vbscript
'*************************************************
' File:    ReadTxt.vbs (WSH sample in VBScript)
' Author:  (c) G. Born
'
' Reading the content of a text file and
' displaying it in a dialog box. The script
' uses defaults for "iomode."
'*************************************************
Option Explicit

Dim Text, Title
Dim fso, objArgs              ' Object variables
Dim txtStream                 ' Text stream
Dim file                      ' Filename

file = "C:\Autoexec.bat"      ' Default test file

' Try to get a filename from the Arguments collection.
Set objArgs = WScript.Arguments ' Create object.
If objArgs.Count > 0 Then      ' Argument found.
    file = objArgs(0)          ' Set filename to first argument.
End If

Text = "Content of " & file & vbCrLf & vbCrLf
Title = "WSH sample - by G. Born"

' Create FileSystemObject object to access the file system.
Set fso = CreateObject("Scripting.FileSystemObject")
' Check whether file exists.
If fso.FileExists(file) Then
    Set txtStream = fso.OpenTextFile(file) ' Open text file.
    Do While Not (txtStream.atEndOfStream)
        Text = Text & txtStream.ReadLine & vbCrLf
    Loop
Else                          ' Terminate.
    MsgBox "File '" & file & "' not found", _
           vbOKOnly + vbCritical, Title
    WScript.Quit 1            ' Terminate with error code.
End If

If MsgBox("Show results in dialog box?", vbYesNo, Title) _
    = vbYes Then              ' Show result in message box.
    MsgBox Text, vbOKOnly + vbInformation, Title
Else                          ' Use browser window for results.
    MakeHTMLCode Text, 0      ' Convert text to HTML (only < and >).
    ShowWindow Text, Title    ' Show result in HTML window.
End If
```

Listing 12-17 *ReadTxt.vbs*

```
Sub ShowWindow(txt, title)
    Dim oIE, doc1
    ' Create Internet Explorer Application object.
    Set oIE = WScript.CreateObject("InternetExplorer.Application")
    oIE.Navigate "about:blank"    ' Empty HTML document
    oIE.Visible = 1               ' Internet Explorer is visible.
    oIE.ToolBar = 0
    oIE.StatusBar = 0
    'oIE.Width = 600
    oIE.Height = 500

    Do While (oIE.Busy): Loop     ' Important: Wait until Internet
                                  ' Explorer is ready.

    Set doc1 = oIE.Document       ' Get Document object.
    doc1.open                     ' Open document.
    ' Write script to the Document object.
    doc1.writeln "<html><head><title>" & Title & "</title></head>"
    doc1.writeln "<body bgcolor='#FAF0F0'><pre>"
    doc1.writeln txt              ' Text output
    doc1.writeln "</pre></body></html>"
    doc1.close                    ' Close document for write access.
End Sub

Sub MakeHTMLCode(txt, flag)
    ' Convert text file to HTML structure.
    ' Flag controls which elements are converted.
    ' Use the following values:
    ' 0: Convert all < and > characters to &lt; and &gt;.
    ' 1: Like flag = 0, but also sets vbCrLf to <br> tag
    '    (forces line wrap).
    ' 2: Like flag = 1, but also sets blanks to  .
    ' ### Be careful of the order of pattern replacement. ###
    Dim oReg
    Set oReg = New RegExp         ' Create regular expression.
    oReg.Global = True            ' All matches
    oReg.IgnoreCase = True        ' Make case insensitive.

    ' Replace all < with &lt;.
    oReg.Pattern = "<"            ' Set pattern.
    txt = oReg.Replace(txt, "&lt;")

    ' Replace all ">" with "&gt;"
    oReg.Pattern = ">"            ' Set pattern.
    txt = oReg.Replace(txt, "&gt;")
```

(continued)

Listing 12-17 *continued*

```
        If flag > 0 Then                ' Replace vbCrLf?
            ' Now we're ready to replace all vbCrLf with <br>.
            oReg.Pattern = vbCrLf        ' Set pattern.
            oReg.Global = True           ' All matches
            txt = oReg.Replace(txt, "<br>")
        End If

        If flag > 1 Then                ' Replace blanks?
            ' Now we're ready to replace all blanks with  .
            oReg.Pattern = " "           ' Set pattern.
            oReg.Global = True           ' All matches
            txt = oReg.Replace(txt, " ")
        End If
End Sub

'*** End
```

The JScript implementation

The following JScript version uses a regular expression object to replace patterns such as < and > with *<* and *>*. The JScript *exchange* method is applied to a text object and requests two parameters. The first parameter must be a regular expression pattern (such as */>/ig*). The / character encloses the search string; the letter *i* in *ig* stands for ignore case, and the *g* causes a global replace of that pattern in the string object. The second parameter contains the replacement string. The entire JScript version is shown in Listing 12-18.

```
//**************************************************
// File:    ReadTxt.js (WSH sample in JScript)
// Author:  (c) G. Born
//
// Reading the content of a text file and
// displaying it in a dialog box
//**************************************************

var vbYesNo = 4;
var vbYes = 6;
var vbInformation = 64;
var vbQuestion = 32;
var vbCancel = 2;

var file = "C:\\Autoexec.bat";
var Title = "WSH sample - by G. Born";
```

Listing 12-18 *ReadTxt.js*

```javascript
// Try to get a filename from the Arguments collection.
var objArgs = WScript.Arguments; // Create object.
if (objArgs.length > 0)          // Argument found.
    file = objArgs(0);           // Set filename to first argument.
var Text = "Content of " + file + "\n\n";

// Create FileSystemObject object to access the file system.
var fso = WScript.CreateObject("Scripting.FileSystemObject");

// Check whether file exists.
if (fso.FileExists(file))
{
    var txtStream = fso.OpenTextFile(file);  // Open text file.
    while (!txtStream.atEndOfStream)
        Text = Text + txtStream.ReadLine() + "\n";
}
else
{
    WScript.Echo(" File \'" + file + "\' not found");
    WScript.Quit(1);
}

var wsh = WScript.CreateObject("WScript.Shell");
if (wsh.Popup("Show results in dialog box?",0,Title,
             vbYesNo + vbQuestion) == vbYes)
{
    WScript.Echo(Text);
}
else
{
    Text = MakeHTMLCode(Text, 0); // Convert text to HTML
    ShowWindow(Text, Title);      // (only < and >) in browser window.
}

// Helper functions
function ShowWindow(txt, title)
{
    // Create Internet Explorer Application object.
    var oIE = WScript.CreateObject("InternetExplorer.Application");
    oIE.navigate("about:blank"); // Empty HTML document
    oIE.visible = 1;             // Internet Explorer is visible.
    oIE.toolbar = 0;
    oIE.statusbar = 0;
    oIE.width=400;
    oIE.height=500;
    while (oIE.Busy) {}          // Important: Wait until Internet
                                 // Explorer is ready.
```

(continued)

Listing 12-18 *continued*

```
        var doc1 = oIE.Document;      // Get Document object.
        doc1.open;                    // Open document.
        // Write script to the document object.
        doc1.writeln("<html><head><title>");
        doc1.writeln(Title);
        doc1.writeln("</title></head>");
        doc1.writeln("<body bgcolor=\'#FAF0F0\'><pre>");
        doc1.writeln(txt);            // Text output
        doc1.writeln("</pre></body></html>");
        doc1.close;                   // Close document for write access.
}

function MakeHTMLCode(txt, flag)
{
    // Convert text file to HTML structure.
    // Flag controls which elements are converted.
    // Use the following values:
    // 0: Convert all < and > characters to &lt; and &gt;.
    // 1: Like flag = 0, but also sets \n to <br> tag
    //     (forces line wrap).
    // 2: Like flag = 2, but also sets blanks to  .
    // ### Be careful of the order of pattern replacement. ###

  // Replace all < with &lt;. (Use regular expression.)
    txt = txt.replace(/</ig, "&lt;");

    // Replace all > with &gt;.
    txt = txt.replace(/>/ig, "&gt;");

    if (flag > 0)                     // Replace \n?
        txt = txt.replace(/\n/ig, "<br>");

    if (flag > 1)                     // Replace blanks?
        txt = txt.replace(/ /ig, " ");
    return txt;
}

//*** End
```

Writing to a Text File

The following short sample opens the Autoexec.bat file, copies the content to a new file, and appends the line *Set Born=Hello* to the new file. This line causes Windows 95 or Windows 98 to create the environment variable *Born* at the next system startup.

> **NOTE** In Windows NT and Windows 2000, you can simply create a test file named C:\Autoexec.bat and add a few text lines to enable the script to run.

To access the text file, you need the *FileSystemObject* object. The file must be opened using the *OpenTextFile* method. As mentioned earlier, you can use the parameters passed to the method to control the access mode. The following statement opens the text file for write access. (The named constant *ForWriting* must be set to 2.)

```
Set txtStreamOut = fso.OpenTextFile(file2, ForWriting, True)
```

If a value of *True* is passed in the third parameter, the text file is created if it doesn't exist.

> **NOTE** VBScript doesn't recognize the constant *ForWriting*, so you must either declare it in the script (if you use .vbs or .js files) or use a .wsf file and define a reference to the type library (as shown in several previous samples).

During the write process (using *ForWriting* mode), the output file is filled line by line, starting from the beginning of the file. The following sequence copies the content of the text file *txtStream* to *txtStreamOut*. Then a new line is appended to the output file.

```
Do While Not (txtStream.atEndOfStream)    ' Copy file content.
    Text = txtStream.ReadLine              ' Read line.
    txtStreamOut.WriteLine Text            ' Write line.
Loop

' Append a new line.
txtStreamOut.WriteLine "Set Born=Hello"
```

The *WriteLine* method inserts the new line of code automatically during each write access.

The script in Listing 12-19 reads the Autoexec.bat file, creates the output file Autoexec.xx1, copies the content of Autoexec.bat to the output file, and appends the new statement to the output file. After processing, a message box indicates that the file was created (Figure 12-15). If you execute the script several times, the same output file is always created because the write process rewrites the file each time.

Figure 12-15 *Dialog box that appears after the Autoexec.bat file is copied*

```
'****************************************************
' File:    WriteTxt.vbs (WSH sample in VBScript)
' Author:  (c) G. Born
'
' Copying the content of a text file and appending
' a new line
'****************************************************
Option Explicit

Const file1 = "C:\Autoexec.bat"   ' Our test file
Const file2 = "C:\Autoexec.xx1"   ' The output file

' We must define ForWriting because the
' iomode constants are unknown to VBScript.
Const ForWriting = 2              ' iomode: write access

Dim Text
Dim fso                           ' Object variable
Dim txtStream, txtStreamOut       ' TextStream objects

' Create a FileSystemObject object to access the file system.
Set fso = CreateObject("Scripting.FileSystemObject")

' Check whether the file exists.
If fso.FileExists(file1) Then
    Set txtStream = fso.OpenTextFile(file1) ' Open input file.
    Set txtStreamOut = fso.OpenTextFile(file2, _
             ForWriting, True)          ' Open output file.

    Do While Not (txtStream.atEndOfStream) ' Copy folder content.
        Text = txtStream.ReadLine          ' Read line.
        txtStreamOut.WriteLine Text        ' Write line.
    Loop

    txtStreamOut.WriteLine "Set Born=Hello" ' Append a line.

    Set txtStream = Nothing                 ' Release objects.
    Set txtStreamOut = Nothing

    WScript.Echo "Text file " & file1 & _
              " copied and extended in " & file2
Else
    WScript.Echo "File " & file & " not found."
End If

'*** End
```

Listing 12-19 *WriteTxt.vbs*

The JScript implementation

The JScript version (Listing 12-20) has the same structure as the VBScript program. The script creates the output text file Autoexec.xx1 using the Autoexec.bat content and then appends a new line (Figure 12-16).

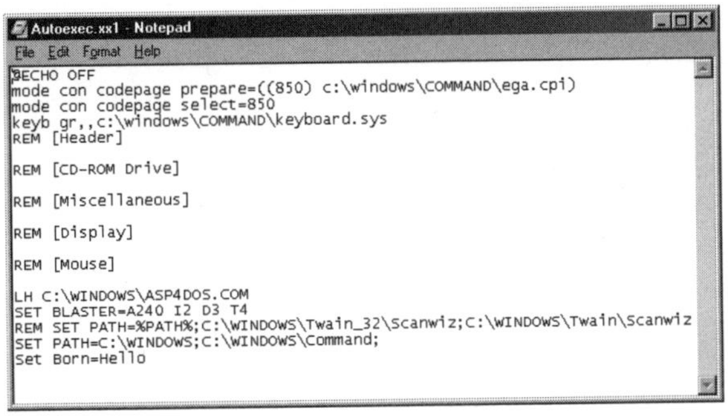

Figure 12-16 *Autoexec.xx1 shown in Notepad*

```
//*****************************************************
// File:    WriteTxt.js (WSH sample in JScript)
// Author:  (c) G. Born
//
// Copying the content of a text file and appending
// a new line
//*****************************************************

var file1 = "C:\\Autoexec.bat";    // Input file
var file2 = "C:\\Autoexec.xx1";    // Output file
var ForWriting = 2;                // iomode: write access
var Text;

// Create a FileSystemObject object to access the file system.
var fso = WScript.CreateObject("Scripting.FileSystemObject");

if (fso.FileExists(file1))         // Check whether the file exists.
{
    var txtStream = fso.OpenTextFile(file1);  // Open input file.
    var txtStreamOut = fso.OpenTextFile(file2,
            ForWriting, true);              // Open output file.

    while (!txtStream.atEndOfStream)        // Copy folder content.
    {
        Text = txtStream.ReadLine();        // Read line.
        txtStreamOut.WriteLine(Text);       // Write line.
    }
```

Listing 12-20 *WriteTxt.js*   *(continued)*

Listing 12-20 *continued*

```
        txtStreamOut.WriteLine("Set Born=Hello"); // Append line.

        WScript.Echo("Text file " + file1 +
                    " copied and extended in " + file2);
    }
    else
        WScript.Echo("File " + file + " not found.");

    //*** End
```

Appending New Text to an Existing File

You might want to append some information to a text file when you process log files and in other situations. You can append new text to an existing text file by using the *WriteLine* method of the *FileSystemObject* object. Unlike in the preceding sample, you must set the second parameter to append mode. The following statement causes all data written to the text file to be appended. (The named constant *ForAppend* must be set to 8 if you use a .vbs or .js file, or else you need to use a .wsf file and define a reference to the type library, as shown in the following sample.)

```
Set txtStream = fso.OpenTextFile(file2, ForAppend, True)
```

The value *True* in the third parameter forces the method to create a new file if the output text file is missing.

Listing 12-21 opens the C:\Autoexec.xx1 file and appends the text line *Set Born=Hello*. (The file C:\Autoexec.xx1 is created by the script called WriteTxt.vbs, shown in Listing 12-19.) If you execute the sample several times, the new line is appended each time to the existing file.

```
<?xml version="1.0" encoding="ISO-8859-1"?>
<!--
    File:    WriteTxt1.wsf (WSH 2)
    Author:  (c) G. Born
    Appending a line to a text file by using a reference
    to the FileSystemObject type library
-->

<job id="WriteTxt1">
    <reference guid='{420B2830-E718-11CF-893D-00A0C9054228}'/>

    <script language="VBScript">
    <![CDATA[
        Option Explicit
```

Listing 12-21 *WriteTxt1.wsf*

```
        Const file1 = "C:\Autoexec.xx1"

        '*** Const ForAppending = 8  ' Obtained from type library

        Dim Text
        Dim fso              ' Object variable
        Dim txtStream        ' Text stream

        ' Create a FileSystemObject object to access the file system.
        Set fso = CreateObject("Scripting.FileSystemObject")

        If fso.FileExists(file1) Then  ' Check whether the file exists.
            Set txtStream = _
                fso.OpenTextFile(file1, ForAppending)    ' Output file

            txtStream.WriteLine "Set Born=Hello" ' Append line.

            Set txtStream = Nothing     ' Release object.
            WScript.Echo "Text file " & file1 & " extended."
        Else
            WScript.Echo "File " & file1 & " not found."
        End If

        '*** End
    ]]>
    </script>
</job>
```

The JScript implementation

The JScript version is shown in Listing 12-22. This solution uses a simple .js file, so the constant *ForAppending* must be set to 8 within the script. However, you can easily use the code from Listing 12-21 and exchange the VBScript part with the code in this JScript listing and import the named constant *ForAppending* from the *FileSystemObject* type library.

```
//***********************************************
// File:    WriteTxt1.js (WSH sample in JScript)
// Author:  (c) G. Born
//
//  Appending a line to a text file
//***********************************************

var file1 = "C:\\Autoexec.xx1";
var ForAppending = 8;                  // Writing
var Text = "Set Born=Hello";
```

Listing 12-22 *WriteTxt1.js*

(continued)

Listing 12-22 *continued*

```
// Create a FileSystemObject object to access the file system.
var fso = WScript.CreateObject("Scripting.FileSystemObject");

if (fso.FileExists(file1))    // Check whether the file exists.
{
    var txtStream = fso.OpenTextFile(file1,
            ForAppending, true); // Output file

    txtStream.WriteLine(Text);         // Append line.

    WScript.Echo("Text file " + file1 + " extended.");
}
else
    WScript.Echo("File " + file + " not found.");

//*** End
```

Replacing Text in a File

The next sample combines some of the knowledge you gained in the previous sections to read data from an input file, search for patterns, replace all matches with a string, and write the result to another file. The sample reads the TestFile.txt file (which must be in the same folder as the script file) and then changes all occurrences of the ' character to //#. The result is written to a second file, TestFile1.txt.

All you need to do is combine code snippets from previous examples. To get the path to the script file, you can use the following line:

```
path = GetPath
```

The *GetPath* function contains the following statements:

```
Function GetPath
    ' Retrieve the script path.
    Dim path
    path = WScript.ScriptFullName  ' Script name
    GetPath = Left(path, InStrRev(path, "\"))
End Function
```

After retrieving the path, you can open the input file and create the output file by using the following sequence:

```
Set fso = CreateObject("Scripting.FileSystemObject")
If Not fso.FileExists(fileIn) Then WScript.Quit 1
Set oFileIn = fso.OpenTextFile(path & "TestFile.txt")
Set oFileOut = fso.OpenTextFile(path & "TestFile1.txt", _
                        ForWriting, True)
```

The first line creates an instance of the *FileSystemObject* object. The second line checks whether the input file exists. If it does, it's opened using the *OpenTextFile* method in the third line. Because you need only read access to the file, just the filename is passed as a parameter. The last statement opens the output file. The second parameter submitted to the *OpenTextFile* method is set to *ForWriting* so that you can write to the file.

You process the input file and replace all matches with the replacement text by using the following code sequence:

```
Do While Not (oFileIn.atEndOfStream)
    Text = oFileIn.ReadLine                 ' Read a line.
    Text = Filter(Text, pattern, replacement)
    oFileOut.WriteLine Text                 ' Write text.
Loop
```

The *Do While* loop terminates if the *atEndOfStream* method of the input file returns the value *True*. If the file is empty, *atEndOfStream* returns *True* immediately and the loop is skipped; otherwise, *atEndOfStream* returns *True* only after *ReadLine* reads the last line in the file. The second statement within the loop calls the user-defined function *Filter*, which has three parameters: the first parameter contains the string to be processed, the second parameter specifies the search pattern, and the third parameter specifies the replacement string. The sample specifies the parameters *pattern* and *replacement* as constants. The last line within the loop simply writes the text returned from the *Filter* function to the output file.

The *Filter* function contains the code that does the replacement. We used a similar approach earlier in the chapter in the ReadTxt.vbs sample, so I reused most of the code for this sample.

```
Function Filter(txt, expr1, expr2)
    ' Replaces expr1 with expr2 in text.
    Dim oReg

    Set oReg = New RegExp          ' Create regular expression.
    oReg.Global = True             ' All matches
    oReg.IgnoreCase = True         ' Make case insensitive.

    ' Replace all expr1 with expr2
    oReg.Pattern = expr1           ' Set pattern.
    Filter = oReg.Replace(txt, expr2)
End Function
```

The function creates a regular expression object *oReg*. Then the properties of this object are set to force a global operation. The *Replace* method ensures that all occurrences of the parameter *expr1* are replaced by the string contained in *expr2*.

Listing 12-23 shows the full VBScript program.

```
'*****************************************************
' File:    ReplaceTxt.vbs (WSH sample in VBScript)
' Author:  (c) G. Born
'
' Reading a file, replacing a given pattern in the
' file, and writing the result to another file
'*****************************************************
Option Explicit

' We must define ForWriting because the
' iomode constants are unknown to VBScript.
Const ForWriting = 2                ' iomode: write access

Const inF = "TestFile.txt"
Const outF = "TestFile1.txt"

' Here are the strings for replacement.
Const pattern = "'"
Const replacement = "//#"

Dim Text
Dim fso                  ' Object variable
Dim oFileIn, oFileOut    ' Text stream
Dim path, fileIn, fileOut

path = GetPath()         ' Retrieve current path to script.
fileIn = path & inF      ' Create filenames.
fileOut = path & outF

' Create a FileSystemObject object to access the file system.
Set fso = CreateObject("Scripting.FileSystemObject")

If Not fso.FileExists(fileIn) Then  ' Input file exists?
    WScript.Echo "File '" & fileIn & "' not found"
    WScript.Quit 1
End If

' Input file present; open file and create output file.
Set oFileIn = fso.OpenTextFile(fileIn)   ' Open input file.
Set oFileOut = fso.OpenTextFile(fileOut, _
               ForWriting, True)    ' Open output file.
```

Listing 12-23 *ReplaceTxt.vbs*

```
Do While Not (oFileIn.atEndOfStream)
    Text = oFileIn.ReadLine                    ' Read a line.
    Text = Filter(Text, pattern, replacement)
    oFileOut.WriteLine Text                    ' Write text.
Loop

WScript.Echo "Text file: " & fileIn & vbCrLf & _
             "Written into: " & fileOut

Function GetPath
    ' Retrieve the script path.
    Dim path
    path = WScript.ScriptFullName  ' Script name
    GetPath = Left(path, InStrRev(path, "\"))
End Function

Function Filter(txt, expr1, expr2)
    ' Replace expr1 with expr2 in text.
    Dim oReg

    Set oReg = New RegExp         ' Create regular expression.
    oReg.Global = True            ' All matches
    oReg.IgnoreCase = True        ' Make case-insensitive.

    ' Replace all expr1 with expr2.
    oReg.Pattern = expr1          ' Set pattern.
    Filter = oReg.Replace(txt, expr2)
End Function

'*** End
```

NOTE You can extend ReplaceTxt.vbs in a number of ways. For example, you can extend it so that it accepts a matching pattern, a replacement pattern, and one or several filenames. Then you can apply the program to a group of files to replace a given string with a second string.

USING THE BROWSE FOR FOLDER DIALOG BOX

Handling files and folders interactively requires that the user specify the pathnames of files and folders at run time. In previous chapters, we used the *InputBox* function or the *WSHInputBox* method to implement an input dialog box. But how do you implement file dialog boxes in WSH scripts? Let's look at two approaches.

Using *BrowseForFolder* to Select Folders

If you need the path to a folder, Windows provides the dialog box shown in Figure 12-17. The user can easily select a drive and the folder. The good news is that you can invoke this dialog box from a WSH script.

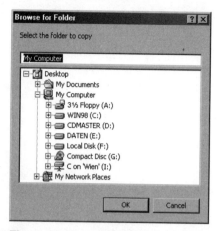

Figure 12-17 *Dialog box for selecting a folder*

NOTE The dialog box is provided by a function contained in the file Shdocvw.dll, which is part of Internet Explorer versions 4 and 5. You also need Shell32.dll version 4.71 or later, which is available in Windows 98 (version 4.72) and Windows 2000 (version 5). In Windows 95 and Windows NT 4, Shell32.dll version 4.71 is available if Internet Explorer 4 is installed with the Active Desktop update. In Windows 95 and Windows NT, installing Internet Explorer 5 doesn't update Shell32.dll. You must install Internet Explorer 4 with Active Desktop and then upgrade to Internet Explorer 5.

Before you can access the methods of the Internet Explorer 4 or 5 *Application* object, you must create an object reference by using the following command:

```
Set objDlg = WScript.CreateObject("Shell.Application")
```

You can then use the methods of the *Application* object and its subobjects.

To invoke the dialog box shown in Figure 12-17, you use the *BrowseForFolder* method:

```
Set objF = objDlg.BrowseForFolder(hWnd, Title, Options[, Root])
```

This method returns a reference to an object of the Windows shell's namespace (which is different from the *FileSystemObject* object). The parameters of this method are not well documented, but I've collected the following information:

■   The first parameter submits a window handle to the dialog box. You should always use the value 0 for this parameter because the script has no handle.

■   The second parameter specifies the string shown in the dialog box below the title bar (as shown in Figure 12-17).

■   The third parameter is a 32-bit flag that specifies internal features of the dialog box. Table 12-4 shows the constants that can be passed to the method. You can also combine some constants (such as *&H0010* and *&H0001*).

■   The fourth parameter is optional and can be used to preselect a folder in the dialog box. You can submit a string with the folder's path (such as *C:\Born*) or you can use one of the values in Table 12-5 to select a special folder object in the shell's namespace.

Table 12-4 CONSTANTS FOR THE THIRD PARAMETER OF *BROWSEFORFOLDER**

Constant	*Description*
&H0001	Only file system folders can be selected. If this bit is set, the OK button is disabled if the user selects a folder that doesn't belong to the file system (such as the Control Panel folder).
&H0002	The user is prohibited from browsing below the domain within a network (during a computer search).
&H0004	Room for status text is provided under the text box. (I haven't found a way to show the status, however.)
&H0008	Returns file system ancestors only.
&H0010	Shows an edit box in the dialog box for the user to type the name of an item.
&H0020	Validate the name typed in the edit box.
&H1000	Enables the user to browse the network branch of the shell's namespace for computer names.
&H2000	Enables the user to browse the network branch of the shell's namespace for printer names.
&H4000	Allows browsing for everything.

* Values are documented in the file Shlobj.h, which is part of the Platform SDK.

Table 12-5 CONSTANTS FOR THE
FOURTH PARAMETER OF *BROWSEFORFOLDER*

Constant	Description
0	The Desktop (virtual) folder is the root directory. Using this constant along with *&H0001* for the third parameter circumvents problems with the OK button.
1	Internet Explorer is the root.
2	The Programs folder of the Start menu is the root.
3	The Control Panel folder is the root. The third parameter must be set to *&H4000* (browse for everything).
4	The Printers folder is the root. The third parameter must be set to *&H4000* (browse for everything).
5	The Documents folder of the Start menu is the root.
6	The Favorites folder of the Start menu is the root.
7	The Startup folder of the Start menu is the root. The third parameter must be set to *&H4000* (browse for everything).
8	The Recent folder is the root. The third parameter must be set to *&H4000* (browse for everything).
9	The SendTo folder is the root. The third parameter must be set to *&H4000* (browse for everything).
10	The Recycle Bin folder is the root. The third parameter must be set to *&H4000* (browse for everything).
11	The Start menu folder is the root.
16	The Desktop (physical) folder is the root.
17	My Computer is the root.
18	Network Neighborhood is the root.
19	The Nethood folder is the root.
20	The Fonts folder is the root.
21	The Templates folder is the root.

NOTE The *BrowseForFolder* method is powerful but potentially dangerous because it can retrieve shell namespace objects. Changing these objects in your script can cause a lot of problems on your machine. If you use the method only to browse file system folders, there's no risk.

The next sample uses only three parameters, and the third parameter is set to *&H0010* (show edit box) + *&H0001* (only file system objects). If the user selects a folder and closes the dialog box using the OK button, the method returns the selected folder name.

Detecting Whether the User Has Clicked the Cancel Button

How do you detect whether the user has clicked the Cancel button? Because *BrowseForFolder* returns an object reference to the shell's namespace, you can't use something like this:

```
If objF <> "" Then
```

If the Cancel button has been clicked, nothing is returned. If you access the object variable containing the result, a run-time error occurs because the value is undefined.

This test doesn't work either because it always evaluates to "canceled":

```
If objF Is Nothing Then
```

The following test always returns the value *True*:

```
If IsObject(objF) Then
```

I therefore implemented the user-defined function *IsValue*, which checks whether a value has been returned:

```
Function IsValue(obj)
    ' Check whether a value has been returned.
    Dim tmp
    On Error Resume Next
    tmp = " " & obj
    If Err <> 0 Then
        IsValue = False
    Else
        IsValue = True
    End If
    On Error GoTo 0
End Function
```

If the Cancel button was used to close the dialog box, the *obj* variable contains the value *Nothing*, in which case the command *tmp = " " & obj* causes a run-time error that you can detect by using the value of the *Err* object.

In the WSH newsgroup, I found another suggestion: checking *Type-Name(objF)*. If the string *"Folder"* is found, the object variable contains a valid folder name. Unfortunately, the string returned depends on the operating system. Windows 95, Windows 98, and Windows NT return the string *"Folder"*, but Windows 2000 returns the string *"Folder2"*. Therefore, you must do a string comparison to detect whether the Cancel button was clicked.

Listing 12-24 invokes a Browse For Folder dialog box. After the user closes the dialog box, the script uses both methods described in this section to detect whether the user clicked the OK button or the Cancel button. Therefore, two dialog boxes with the results are shown. Note that the following sample doesn't return the full path to the selected object. (The next sample has a *BrowseForFolder* function, which derives the full path to the object.)

```vbscript
'*************************************************
' File:    Dialog.vbs (WSH sample in VBScript)
' Author:  (c) G. Born
'
' Using the shell dialog box to select a folder
'*************************************************
Option Explicit

' Flags for the options parameter
Const BIF_returnonlyfsdirs   = &H0001
Const BIF_dontgobelowdomain  = &H0002
Const BIF_statustext         = &H0004
Const BIF_returnfsancestors  = &H0008
Const BIF_editbox            = &H0010
Const BIF_validate           = &H0020
Const BIF_browseforcomputer  = &H1000
Const BIF_browseforprinter   = &H2000
Const BIF_browseincludefiles = &H4000

Dim wsh, objDlg, objF

' Get Application object of the Windows shell.
Set objDlg = WScript.CreateObject("Shell.Application")

' Use the BrowseForFolder method.
' For instance: Set objF = objDlg.BrowseForFolder _
'     (&H0, "Select the folder to copy", &H10, "C:\Born")

Set objF = objDlg.BrowseForFolder (&H0, _
    "Select the folder to copy", _
    BIF_editbox + BIF_returnonlyfsdirs)

' Here we use the first method to detect the result.
If IsValue(objF) Then
    MsgBox "Selected folder: " & objF.Title
Else
    MsgBox "Canceled"
End If
```

Listing 12-24 *Dialog.vbs*

```
' Here we use TypeName to detect the result.
If InStr(1, TypeName(objF), "Folder") > 0 Then
    MsgBox "Selected folder: " & objF.Title
Else
    MsgBox "Canceled"
End If

Function IsValue(obj)
    ' Check whether the value has been returned.
    Dim tmp
    On Error Resume Next
    tmp = " " & obj
    If Err <> 0 Then
        IsValue = False
    Else
        IsValue = True
    End If
    On Error GoTo 0
End Function

'*** End
```

TIP The Shdocvw.dll file contains additional objects, properties, and methods for accessing the Windows shell. (See also Chapter 14 for more information on accessing the Windows shell.) You can find descriptions at *http://msdn.microsoft.com/library/default.asp.* You can also inspect the methods by using the Object Browser in Microsoft Script Editor, Microsoft Visual Basic Editor (which is available in each Microsoft Office application), or Microsoft Visual Basic 5 Control Creation Edition (CCE) if you define a reference to this DLL file. (See *Advanced Development with Microsoft Windows Script Host 2.0* for details.)

Using *BrowseForFolder* to Select Files

Listing 12-24 doesn't support the path to a given object, and if the user selects a drive, the volume name is retrieved along with the drive letter. The sample also doesn't allow you to select files in the Browse For Folder dialog box.

Let's extend the program a bit. A value of *&H4000* (the constant *BIF_browseincludefiles*) also allows you to use *BrowseForFolder* to select files. The following command invokes the Browse For Folder dialog box and allows file selection:

```
Set oItem = WshShell.BrowseForFolder( _
        &H0, "Select a file or folder to copy", _
        BIF_returnonlyfsdirs + BIF_browseincludefiles, "C:\")
```

BIF_browseincludefiles must be defined and the variable *WshShell* must be a valid object variable pointing to the *WshShell* object. The method returns an object, which is assigned to the variable *oItem*. This object variable doesn't contain the path to the folder, so you need something to retrieve the full path and the name of a selected object. You can use the following command:

```
name = oItem.ParentFolder.ParseName(oItem.Title).Path
```

Within this statement, the *ParentFolder* method is applied to the object. This method returns an object that hosts the parent folder. Then you apply the *ParseName* method to select an entry in the collection. The method retrieves the name of the selected object, which is returned by the *oItem.Title* property. The *Path* property of the object contains the entire path, including the name.

At this point, you're done (if you're omitting error checking). Unfortunately, if the user closes the dialog box by clicking the Cancel button, the preceding statement doesn't return a valid path and object name, and a run-time error (code 424) occurs. Also, the *BrowseForFolder* method causes a run-time error (code 5) in Windows 2000 if a file is selected from the root folder of a drive. In addition, if the user selects a drive, you have to extract the drive letter from the volume name.

To simplify handling, I moved all the code into a user-defined function named *BrowseForFolder*. You can call the function by using the following statement:

```
tmp = BrowseForFolder(Title, flags, dir)
```

The *Title* parameter submits the text shown in the dialog box. The *flags* parameter specifies the code (see Table 12-4) to search for files and folders. The *dir* parameter is a string containing the path that's selected in the dialog box. If you submit the value "", *My Computer* is preselected.

The function returns a string containing the path to the object. If the string contains the value "*-1*", the user clicked the Cancel button. A value of "*-5*" indicates that the user selected a file in the root folder, which Windows 2000 doesn't allow. You can use the following code to determine whether the returned name is valid:

```
file = BrowseForFolder(Title, flags, dir)
If file = "-5" Then
    WScript.Echo "Not possible to select files in root folder"
Else
    If file = "-1" Then
        WScript.Echo "No object selected; Cancel clicked"
    Else
        WScript.Echo "Object: ", file
    End If
End If
```

Listing 12-25 is a small VBScript program that invokes the Browse For Folder dialog box and lets the user select a file or a folder. The result is shown in a dialog box (Figure 12-18).

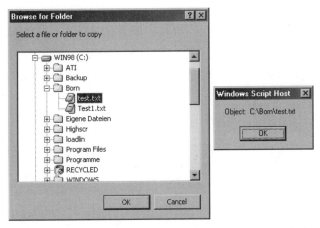

Figure 12-18 *Selecting a file in the Browse For Folder dialog box*

```
'***********************************************************
' File:     FileSelectDialog.vbs (WSH sample in VBScript)
' Author:  (c) G. Born
'
' Using the shell dialog box to select a folder
' or a file
' Warning: A run-time error occurs if the script
' is executed in Windows 2000 and the user selects
' a file in the root folder of a drive.
'***********************************************************
Option Explicit

' Flags for the options parameter
Const BIF_returnonlyfsdirs   = &H0001
Const BIF_dontgobelowdomain  = &H0002
Const BIF_statustext         = &H0004
Const BIF_returnfsancestors  = &H0008
Const BIF_editbox            = &H0010
Const BIF_validate           = &H0020
Const BIF_browseforcomputer  = &H1000
Const BIF_browseforprinter   = &H2000
Const BIF_browseincludefiles = &H4000
```

Listing 12-25 *FileSelectDialog.vbs*   *(continued)*

Listing 12-25 *continued*

```
Dim file

file = BrowseForFolder( _
      "Select a file or folder to copy", _
      BIF_returnonlyfsdirs + BIF_browseincludefiles, _
      "")
If file = "-5" Then
    WScript.Echo "Not possible to select files in root folder"
Else
    If file = "-1" Then
        WScript.Echo "No object selected; Cancel clicked"
    Else
        WScript.Echo "Object: ", file
    End If
End If


' Using the shell's BrowseForFolder method to
' return the full path to the selected object
' title = Text shown in the dialog box
' flag = One of the values for controlling the
'        BrowseForFolder behavior
' dir = Preselected directory (can be "")
Function BrowseForFolder(title, flag, dir)
    On Error Resume Next

    Dim oShell, oItem, tmp

    ' Create WshShell object.
    Set oShell = WScript.CreateObject("Shell.Application")

    ' Invoke Browse For Folder dialog box.
    Set oItem = oShell.BrowseForFolder(&H0, title, flag, dir)
    If Err.Number <> 0 Then
        If Err.Number = 5 Then
            BrowseForFolder= "-5"
            Err.Clear
            Set oShell = Nothing
            Set oItem = Nothing
            Exit Function
        End If
    End If
```

```
    ' Now we try to retrieve the full path.
    BrowseForFolder = oItem.ParentFolder.ParseName(oItem.Title).Path

    ' Handling: Cancel button and selecting a drive
    If Err<> 0 Then
        If Err.Number = 424 Then            ' Handle Cancel button.
            BrowseForFolder = "-1"
        Else
            Err.Clear
            ' Handle situation in which user selects a drive.
            ' Extract drive letter from the title--first search
            ' for a colon (:).
            tmp = InStr(1, oItem.Title, ":")
            If tmp > 0 Then             ' A : is found; use two
                                        ' characters and add \.

                BrowseForFolder = _
                    Mid(oItem.Title, (tmp - 1), 2) & "\"
            End If
        End If
    End If

    Set oShell = Nothing
    Set oItem = Nothing
    On Error GoTo 0
End Function

'*** End
```

NOTE On machines that had only Windows 2000 or Windows 98 installed, the *BrowseForFolder* method failed to return valid filenames during the first attempt to access a folder. An error code reported that the selected file was missing. After I installed Microsoft Office on those machines, the error didn't occur again.

Chapter 13

Controlling Windows and Applications from Scripts

Microsoft Windows Script Host (WSH) 2 offers some notable new features for controlling scripts, such as methods for delaying a script, simulating sending keystrokes to applications, and switching between applications. In this chapter, you'll learn how to use these methods to automate common tasks and to set up your environment during logon. This chapter will also show you how to add logon scripts in Microsoft Windows 2000, and we'll look at new Windows 2000 features for executing scripts during startup, shutdown, logon, and logoff.

DELAYING SCRIPT EXECUTION

To suspend or delay execution of statements in a script, you can use the *Sleep* method, which we already used in previous chapters.

Using the *Sleep* Method to Reduce the CPU Load

Sometimes you must synchronize a script with another process. For example, in Chapter 11 you saw a situation in which a Windows 98 domain logon script tries to read the *UserName* property. When this property returns a blank value, the script must wait until the property is nonblank. The following code solves this problem:

```
Set WshNetwork = WScript.CreateObject("WScript.Network")
User = WshNetwork.UserName   ' Initialize value.
Do While User = ""           ' Loop until user name is returned.
    WScript.Sleep 200            ' Suspend to lower CPU load.
    User = WshNetwork.UserName   ' Read property.
Loop
```

The script uses a loop to poll the *WshNetwork.UserName* property until the returned value is nonblank. You saw a similar technique in Chapter 9, in which a script needed to wait until the user confirmed a Microsoft Internet Explorer form's input by clicking the OK button. We used the following code sequence to poll the state of the form:

```
Do                          ' Wait until the OK button is clicked.
    WScript.Sleep 200 ' Suspend the script for 200 milliseconds.
Loop While (oIE.Document.Script.CheckVal() = 0)
```

The third VBScript statement calls the *CheckVal* method to determine the Internet Explorer form's internal state. If the user clicks the form's OK button, *CheckVal* returns 1 and the loop terminates. Polling has one big disadvantage: it can spike the CPU load to 100 percent. Therefore, I added this statement to the loop:

```
WScript.Sleep 200  ' Suspend the script for 200 milliseconds.
```

The statement calls the *Sleep* method of the *WScript* object. The parameter submitted to the method specifies how long the script's execution will be suspended, in milliseconds. Each time the loop is executed, *Sleep* suspends script execution for 200 milliseconds. During this period, the script incurs no CPU usage.

The consequences of using the *Sleep* method within polling are shown in Figure 13-1. On the Performance tab of the Windows 2000 Task Manager, the CPU Usage History diagram shows the CPU load incurred by two script programs (obtained from the Form sample). Execution of the *Do While* loop without the *WScript.Sleep* statement spikes the CPU load to 100 percent until the user clicks the OK button (Figure 13-1, left). The figure also shows the CPU load incurred by the script if it uses the *WScript.Sleep* statement (Figure 13-1, right). The improved script doesn't incur a heavy CPU load. The small spike visible at the beginning of this time period is caused by mouse clicks that launch the script and load the form in Internet Explorer and by the loop in the script that polls *oIE.Busy* until the browser finishes loading the form.

Without *Sleep*

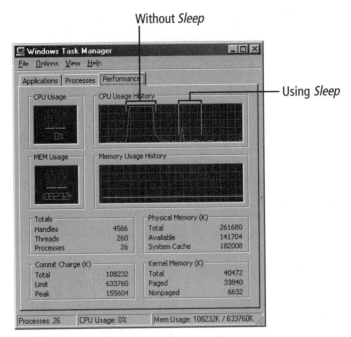

Using *Sleep*

Figure 13-1 *Processor usage during polling*

NOTE You can monitor the CPU usage history in Microsoft Windows NT and Windows 2000 using Task Manager. In Windows 95 and Windows 98, you can use System Monitor (which is also available in Windows NT and Windows 2000).

Using a Delay to Solve a Problem with Asynchronous Processes

Now let's look at how the *Sleep* method can help solve another problem with asynchronous processes. I came across this problem while using the *SendKeys* method (introduced later in this chapter). Let's say that a script launches two external applications, Calculator and Notepad, and shows a dialog box that allows user interaction:

```
oShell.Run "Calc.exe",1      ' Launch Calculator.
oShell.Run "Notepad.exe", 1 ' Launch Notepad.
WScript.Echo "Have applications been launched?"
```

Which window do you think will be shown first, and which one will remain in the foreground? At first glance, you might say that Calculator will be shown first and then the Notepad window will overlap the Calculator window and the Echo dialog box will remain in the foreground. However, on my systems, the Calculator window and the Echo dialog box are hidden by the Notepad window. The user can recognize the Echo dialog box only by its button on the taskbar.

This behavior is the result of how Windows processes these applications. The script shells out two *Run* calls and continues to execute the next instruction. As a result, the Echo dialog box is shown before Windows can launch the external applications. Also, the order of the application windows depends on the amount of time that each application needs for launching.

NOTE In *MsgBox* or *Popup*, you can use the constant *vbSystemModal* to force Windows to show the dialog box in the foreground. However, this constant doesn't work with the *Echo* method.

To specify which application window is shown in the foreground, you can simply open application windows in sequential order and write the script in such a way that it waits until the window is visible. In most cases, you can do this by using a simple delay after executing the *Run* method:

```
oShell.Run "Calc.exe", 1      ' Launch Calculator.
WScript.Sleep 500             ' Wait 0.5 second.
oShell.Run "NotePad.exe", 1   ' Launch Notepad.
WScript.Sleep 500             ' Wait 0.5 second.
WScript.Echo "Please close all application windows"
```

Calling the *Sleep* method with a parameter of *500* causes the script to pause 0.5 seconds until the next instruction is processed. As a result, the application windows and the Echo dialog box are shown in the appropriate order. This behavior is shown in the short VBScript program in Listing 13-1. This program launches Calculator and Notepad and displays a dialog box. In a second step, both applications and an additional dialog box are launched, with a short delay between each statement.

```
'***************************************************
' File:     RunApps.vbs (WSH sample in VBScript)
' Author:   (c) G. Born
'
' Launching Calculator and Notepad by using the
' Run method
'***************************************************
Option Explicit

Dim oShell

' Create the WshShell object.
Set oShell = WScript.CreateObject("WScript.Shell")

oShell.Run "Calc.exe", 1     ' Launch Calculator.
oShell.Run "NotePad.exe", 1  ' Launch Notepad.
```

Listing 13-1 *RunApps.vbs*

```
' Now delay script after launching an application.
WScript.Echo "Second Attempt: Launch Notepad and Calculator"

oShell.Run "Calc.exe", 1      ' Launch Calculator.
WScript.Sleep 500             ' Wait 0.5 second.
oShell.Run "NotePad.exe", 1   ' Launch Notepad.
WScript.Sleep 500             ' Wait 0.5 second.

WScript.Echo "Please close all application windows"

'*** End
```

ACTIVATING AN APPLICATION USING THE *APPACTIVATE* METHOD

You can use the *Run* method of the *WshShell* object as shown earlier to launch external applications, and in WSH 2 you can switch an application to the foreground (activate the application) by using the *AppActivate* method.

Let's look at a simple scenario in which a script launches two applications. One application window gets the focus. If the user clicks on the other window, it receives the focus. To control a window from a WSH script (to send data to it with *SendKeys*, for example), you must ensure that the window keeps the focus.

The *AppActivate* method uses the following syntax:

```
obj.AppActivate title
```

The object variable *obj* contains a reference to the *WshShell* object, and *title* contains the title text shown in the window of the (already running) process that is to be activated. The short script in Listing 13-2 uses the *AppActivate* method. The script launches Calculator and Notepad and then changes the focus from one window to the next. The script asks the user for a window title and transfers the focus to the window containing the given title text.

```
'*************************************************************
' File:   AppActivateWSH2.vbs (WSH 2 sample in VBScript)
' Author: (c) G. Born
'
' Launching Calculator and Notepad and using
' AppActivate to switch between applications
'*************************************************************
Option Explicit
```

Listing 13-2 *AppActivateWSH2.vbs*   *(continued)*

Listing 13-2 *continued*

```
' Define the title strings of the application windows.
' Important: Strings depend on the localized version of Windows.
Const Edit_Title = "Untitled - Notepad"   ' Window title
Const Calc_Title = "Calculator"           ' Window title

Dim Wsh, win_title

' Create the WshShell object, which Run and AppActivate require.
Set Wsh = WScript.CreateObject("WScript.Shell")

' Try to launch two applications. To ensure that the last
' application receives the focus, delay the script.
Wsh.Run "Calc.exe", 1      ' Launch Calculator.
WScript.Sleep 800          ' Delay allows Calculator to get the focus.
Wsh.Run "Notepad.exe", 1 ' Launch Notepad.
WScript.Sleep 800          ' Delay allows Notepad to get the focus.

WScript.Echo "Click OK to set focus to the Calculator window"

' Set the focus back to the Calculator window.
Wsh.AppActivate Calc_Title

' Set the focus to the Notepad window.
WScript.Echo "Click OK to set the focus to Notepad"
Wsh.AppActivate Edit_Title

' Ask user for a window title and set the focus to that window.
win_title = InputBox ("Please enter the window title", _
                      "Ask for window title", Calc_Title)
Wsh.AppActivate win_title

'*** End
```

Let's take a closer look at some of the code in Listing 13-2. First, you define two constants that hold the title strings of the windows:

```
Const Edit_Title = "Untitled - Notepad"   ' Window title
Const Calc_Title = "Calculator"           ' Window title
```

Defining these title strings as constants is handy because both Calculator and Notepad use localized titles. For example, German Windows uses different strings than U.S. Windows does. To adapt this sample to a localized version of Windows, you need only change the title text in the constants. Then you create a reference to *WScript.Shell*, which you need to execute the *Run* method:

```
Set Wsh = WScript.CreateObject("WScript.Shell")
```

After these preliminaries, you're ready to launch the applications by using the *Run* method:

```
Wsh.Run "Calc.exe", 1      ' Launch Calculator.
Wsh.Run "Notepad.exe", 1 ' Launch Notepad.
```

To avoid having the Calculator window get the focus because of a delay during loading, you use the *Sleep* method:

```
Wsh.Run "Calc.exe", 1      ' Launch Calculator.
WScript.Sleep 800          ' Delay allows Calculator to get the focus.
Wsh.Run "Notepad.exe", 1 ' Launch Notepad.
WScript.Sleep 800          ' Delay allows Notepad to get the focus.
```

A delay of 800 milliseconds is sufficient on my system to ensure that the Notepad window gets the focus. The second delay ensures that the script's dialog box is shown in the foreground after both applications are launched, as shown in Figure 13-2. If you omit the delay, one of the applications will probably become visible after the dialog box is shown. In the sample in Listing 13-2, the script's dialog box is hidden in the background and the application window receives the focus.

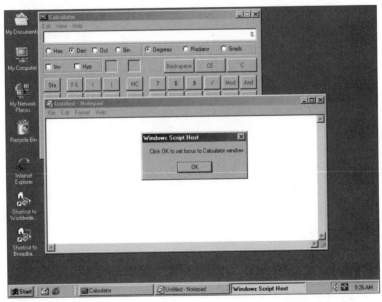

Figure 13-2 *Desktop with application windows and the script's dialog box, which keeps the focus*

The following command transfers the focus to the Calculator window if the user clicks the OK button:

```
Wsh.AppActivate Calc_Title
```

Other dialog boxes the script invokes allow the user to inspect the results of each step. In the last step, the user can enter the title text of any window shown on the Desktop or on the taskbar. The script transfers the focus to this window.

> **IMPORTANT** The *AppActivate* method doesn't affect the window style when it changes the focus to a specified application or window—for example, it doesn't affect whether the window is maximized or minimized. Therefore, a button on the taskbar could receive the focus. WSH 2 doesn't provide a method for changing the window style.

Pitfalls of Using the *AppActivate* Method

To determine which application to activate, *AppActivate* compares the *title* parameter submitted to the method with the title string of each running application. If no exact match exists, any application whose title string begins with the pattern contained in the *title* variable is activated. If no application is found, any application whose title string ends with the pattern contained in the *title* variable is activated.

Although generally useful, the *AppActivate* method has several drawbacks:

- You must know the exact title during design time. If the script runs on a localized version of Windows, you must first specify the constants with the window titles.

- If a program changes its title text, it becomes difficult or impossible to use *AppActivate*.

- If the window is minimized, you can't make the window style normal or maximized.

- If several windows use the same window title, you can't use the title text to detect a specific window. If more than one instance of an application named by title exists, *AppActivate* activates the first instance (as determined by an internal, open window list).

The program shown in Listing 13-3 uses *AppActivate* in JScript and invokes two instances of Calculator. It then tries to switch the focus between the Calculator windows. Because both windows use the same title, no change occurs.

```
//**********************************************************
// File:     AppActivateWSH2.js (WSH 2 sample in JScript)
// Author:   (c) G. Born
//
// Launching Calculator twice and trying to switch
// between the windows
//**********************************************************

// Define the title strings of the application windows.
// Important: Strings depend on the localized version of Windows.
var Calc_Title = "Calculator";            // Window title

// Create the WshShell object, which Run and
// AppActivate require.
var Wsh = WScript.CreateObject("WScript.Shell");

// Try to launch two applications. To ensure that the
// last application receives the focus, delay the script.
Wsh.Run("Calc.exe", 1);     // Launch Calculator.
Wsh.Run("Calc.exe", 1);     // Launch second instance of Calculator.
WScript.Sleep(800);         // Delay until Calculator gets the focus.

// Switch focus between Calculator windows.
WScript.Echo("Click OK to set focus to Calculator window");
Wsh.AppActivate(Calc_Title);

WScript.Echo("Click OK to set focus to second Calculator window");
Wsh.AppActivate(Calc_Title);

//*** End
```

Listing 13-3 *AppActivateWSH2.js*

To summarize, the WSH 2 *AppActivate* method doesn't provide any way to change the window style, and the window title isn't the best means to identify a window. The WSH 2 Programmer's Reference says that *AppActivate* can use the process identifier obtained from the *Shell* function to activate a window, but WSH 2 doesn't support a *Shell* function.

USING THE *SENDKEYS* METHOD TO SIMULATE KEYSTROKES

A script can invoke an application and switch its window to the foreground. All keystrokes that the user enters affect that application window. Sometimes a script needs the ability to mimic user input.

Using *SendKeys* in WSH 2

In WSH 2, you can use the *SendKeys* method of the *WshShell* object. Let's look at a simple example. The following JScript code uses the *Run* method to launch Calculator:

```
var WshShell = WScript.CreateObject("WScript.Shell");
WshShell.Run("Calc.exe");
WScript.Sleep(200);
```

The last statement is required to allow the Calculator window to receive the focus. If this delay is omitted, the script might execute subsequent statements that send keystrokes before Calculator receives the focus; if this happens, all keystrokes will be lost.

After Calculator becomes active, the script sends the expression *10 + 2 =* to the Calculator window. The *SendKeys* method has the following syntax:

```
WshShell.SendKeys keys
```

The *SendKeys* method is part of the *WshShell* object; the *keys* parameter contains the character or characters to send. Each "key" submitted in this parameter is represented by at least one character. Keyboard keys can be represented by a single character. For example, to send the A key, you pass the character *A* in the *key* argument. If the string contains several characters (such as *ABC*), the characters are sent to the application.

The plus sign (+) has a special meaning in the *SendKeys* command. (See Table 13-2 on page 409.) This character must be enclosed within braces in order to be passed to the method. To send a plus sign, for example, you write the string within the *key* parameter as *{+}*.

Thus, you use the following statements to send the commands to the Calculator window:

```
WshShell.SendKeys("10");
WshShell.SendKeys("{+}");
WshShell.SendKeys("2");
WshShell.SendKeys("=");
```

Each *SendKeys* call submits a parameter that contains the string. Calculator evaluates the expression and displays the value *12*. The following commands pause the script and clear the result in Calculator's display:

```
WScript.Sleep(2000);
WshShell.SendKeys("c");
```

Within a loop, the script forces Calculator to add the numbers 1 through 3:

```
for (var i = 1; i <= 3; i++)
{
    WshShell.SendKeys(i); // Add numbers 1 through 3.
    WshShell.SendKeys("{+}");
}
```

The full script sample is shown in Listing 13-4.

```
//*********************************************************
// File:      SendKeysWSH2.js (WSH 2 sample in JScript)
// Author:    (c) G. Born
//
// Using the SendKeys method to launch Calculator
// and make a calculation
//*********************************************************

// Create WshShell object, which the Run method requires.
var WshShell = WScript.CreateObject("WScript.Shell");

// Launch Calculator.
WshShell.Run("Calc.exe");

// Pause until Calculator is ready to receive input;
// otherwise, the "keyboard input" from SendKeys will go
// into the Windows message buffer and will be passed to
// the active window before Calculator gets the focus.
WScript.Sleep(200);          // Just wait a little while.

WshShell.SendKeys("10");
WshShell.SendKeys("{+}");
WshShell.SendKeys("2");
WshShell.SendKeys("=");

WScript.Sleep(2000);         // Wait two seconds.
WshShell.SendKeys("c");      // Clear result.
```

Listing 13-4 *SendKeysWSH2.js*   *(continued)*

Listing 13-4 *continued*

```
for (var i = 1; i <= 3; i++)
{
    WshShell.SendKeys(i);     // Add numbers 1 through 3.
    WshShell.SendKeys("{+}");
}

WScript.Echo("Terminate?");
WScript.Sleep(200);
WshShell.SendKeys("%{F4}");  // Close Calculator using Alt+F4.

//*** End
```

More on the *SendKeys* method

The plus sign (+), the caret (^), the percent sign (%), the tilde (~), and parentheses ( ) have special meanings in the *SendKeys* command. (See Tables 13-1 and 13-2.) These characters must be enclosed within braces for the string to be passed to the method. To send a plus sign, for example, you write the string within the *key* parameter as {+}. Brackets ([and]) must also be enclosed within braces before they're passed to the *SendKeys* method because these characters have a special meaning in applications that use Dynamic Data Exchange (DDE). You send the characters for braces as {{} and {}}.

Some keys on your keyboard, including the Enter key and the Tab key, don't produce visible characters. To pass these keys to the *SendKeys* method, you must code them. Table 13-1 shows the coding of all the special keys.

Table 13-1   CODES FOR SPECIAL KEYS IN THE *SENDKEYS* METHOD

Key	*Code*
Backspace	{BACKSPACE}, {BS}, or {BKSP}
Break	{BREAK}
Caps Lock	{CAPSLOCK}
Delete	{DELETE} or {DEL}
Cursor down	{DOWN}
End	{END}
Enter	{ENTER} or ~
Esc	{ESC}
Help	{HELP}
Home	{HOME}
Insert	{INSERT} or {INS}
Cursor left	{LEFT}
Num Lock	{NUMLOCK}

Key	Code
Page Down	{PGDN}
Page Up	{PGUP}
Print	{PRTSC}
Cursor right	{RIGHT}
Scroll lock	{SCROLLLOCK}
Tab	{TAB}
Cursor up	{UP}
F1	{F1}
F2	{F2}
F3	{F3}
F4	{F4}
F5	{F5}
F6	{F6}
F7	{F7}
F8	{F8}
F9	{F9}
F10	{F10}
F11	{F11}
F12	{F12}
F13	{F13}
F14	{F14}
F15	{F15}
F16	{F16}

To send key combinations that include Shift, Ctrl, or Alt, you must insert a special code in front of the second key code. The special codes for these keys are shown in Table 13-2.

Table 13-2 CODES FOR KEY COMBINATIONS IN THE *SENDKEYS* METHOD

Key	Code Used in Front of Second Key Code
Shift	+
Ctrl	^
Alt	%

Consequently, ^X stands for Ctrl+X. If a key combination contains more than two keys, you must place the characters within parentheses. This arrangement might sound complicated, but it's not. For example, to send the key combination Shift+E+C, you send the string *+(EC)*. The plus sign represents the Shift key, and *(EC)* represents the keys E and C, which must both be pressed while the Shift key is held down. To send a key combination of Shift+E followed by the C key, you use the string *+EC* instead. The plus sign represents the Shift key, which is used in combination with E. After that key combination is processed, the single character C is received. The parentheses in the first example force Windows to interpret the keys within the braces as a key combination with the leading control code for Shift.

To represent a repeating key, you use the format *{keycode number}*. (The blank between *keycode* and *number* is mandatory.) For example, the string *{LEFT 42}* represents 42 presses of the Cursor left key; the string *{H 10}* represents 10 presses of the H key.

> **TIP**   To toggle the Num Lock key automatically, you can write a script that sends the code *{NUMLOCK}* using *SendKeys*. Executing this script from the Startup menu toggles the Num Lock key during each system start. The NumLock.vbs file in the \WSHDevGuide\Chapter13 folder on the companion CD does this for you.

Manipulating Two Applications Using *SendKeys*

Now I'll show you a sample that uses the *SendKeys* method and then show you how to use *SendKeys* in combination with other methods. The sample is written in JScript and launches Calculator and Notepad with the following commands:

```
oWSH.Run("Notepad.exe", 1);    // Launch Notepad with empty window.
WScript.Sleep(500);            // Delay until Notepad gets the focus.
oWSH.Run("Calc.exe", 1);       // Launch Calculator with empty window.
WScript.Sleep(500);            // Delay until Calculator gets the focus.
```

The *Sleep* method ensures that Calculator receives the focus. You can then use *SendKeys* to calculate *10 + 2* using the following commands:

```
oWSH.SendKeys("10");           // Just calculate something.
oWSH.SendKeys("{+}");
oWSH.SendKeys("2");
oWSH.SendKeys("=");
```

The sequence above uses the key codes to force Calculator to evaluate the expression. You can then use the following statement to copy the result to the Clipboard:

```
oWSH.SendKeys("^{c}");         // Copy result to Clipboard.
```

The code *^{c}* represents the Ctrl+C shortcut. The script then displays a dialog box that informs the user that the result will be written to the Notepad window. If the user closes the dialog box, the script transfers the focus to the Notepad window and inserts the Clipboard content by using the following code:

```
oWSH.AppActivate(Edit_Title);
// Write text to Notepad window.
// First insert result from the Clipboard.
oWSH.SendKeys("Calculation Result: ");
oWSH.SendKeys("^{v}");
oWSH.SendKeys("\n\n");
```

The first statement uses the window title to transfer the focus to the application. (This approach isn't reliable if more than one open window uses the same title.) The three calls to the *SendKeys* method write some text into the Notepad window and then paste the calculation result from the Clipboard. The code *\n\n* creates two new lines at the end of the document. The script then uses a simple *for* loop to write more text to the Notepad window:

```
// Now write the text 30 times.
for (var i = 1; i <= 30; i++)
{
    oWSH.SendKeys(i + " Hello, world\n");
}
```

The script then tries to close the Calculator window and the Notepad window. It first tries to close the Calculator window:

```
oWSH.AppActivate(Calc_Title); // Set focus to Calculator.
oWSH.SendKeys("%{F4}");        // Close Calculator using Alt+F4.
```

Using Alt+F4 to close the Notepad window invokes the "Do you want to save the changes?" dialog box, so the script also needs an additional step to "click" the No button.

```
oWSH.AppActivate(Edit_Title);
oWSH.SendKeys("%{F4}");   // Close Notepad using Alt+F4.
oWSH.SendKeys("%{N}");    // "Click" the No button.
```

The full implementation is shown in Listing 13-5.

```
//*************************************************
// File:     SendKeys1.js (WSH 2 sample in JScript)
// Author:   (c) G. Born
//
// Using the SendKeys method and the AppActivate
// method to launch Calculator and Notepad and
// write to the application windows
//*************************************************
```

Listing 13-5 *SendKeys1.js*   *(continued)*

Listing 13-5 *continued*

```
// Define the title strings of the application windows.
// Important: Strings depend on the localized version of Windows.
var Edit_Title = "Untitled - Notepad";   // Window title
var Calc_Title = "Calculator";           // Window title

// Create the WshShell object, which Run and
// AppActivate require.
var oWSH = WScript.CreateObject("WScript.Shell");

// Try to launch two applications. To ensure that the
// last application receives the focus, delay the script.
oWSH.Run("Notepad.exe",1);   // Launch Notepad with empty window.
WScript.Sleep(500);          // Delay until Notepad gets the focus.
oWSH.Run("Calc.exe",1);      // Launch Calculator.
WScript.Sleep(500);          // Delay until Calculator gets the focus.

oWSH.SendKeys("10");         // Just calculate something.
oWSH.SendKeys("{+}");
oWSH.SendKeys("2");
oWSH.SendKeys("=");

oWSH.SendKeys("^{c}");       // Copy result to Clipboard.

WScript.Echo("Write text to Notepad window.");

// Set focus to Notepad window.
oWSH.AppActivate(Edit_Title);
// Write text to Notepad window.
// First insert result from Clipboard.
oWSH.SendKeys("Calculation Result: ");
oWSH.SendKeys("^{v}");
oWSH.SendKeys("\n\n");

// Now write the text 30 times.
for (var i = 1; i <= 30; i++)
{
    oWSH.SendKeys(i + " Hello, world\n");
}

WScript.Echo("Close Calculator window.");

oWSH.AppActivate(Calc_Title); // Set focus to Calculator.
oWSH.SendKeys("%{F4}");        // Close Calculator using Alt+F4.

WScript.Echo("Close Notepad window.");
```

```
// Set focus to Notepad and send terminate command.
oWSH.AppActivate(Edit_Title);

oWSH.SendKeys("%{F4}");  // Close Notepad using Alt+F4.
oWSH.SendKeys("%{N}");   // "Click" the No button.

//*** End
```

You now know a few WSH 2 programming techniques for controlling external applications. For a much deeper discussion and information on additional methods for handling external applications, see *Advanced Development with Microsoft Windows Script Host 2.0.*

CUSTOMIZING WINDOWS USING LOGON SCRIPTS

You learned in previous chapters how to write scripts for mapping network drives or connecting to a network printer. You know also how to use the *FileSystemObject* object and its methods (to back up files, for example), and you've learned the techniques for developing scripts that create shortcuts on the Desktop or on the Start menu. You're therefore aware that you can use scripts to customize user systems and automate tasks. What I haven't discussed yet is how to write scripts that are executed during events such as startup, shutdown, logon, and logoff. Since Windows NT 4 supports logon scripts (as batch files, for example) Microsoft has made the effort in Windows 2000 to provide extended support for scripting during startup, shutdown, logon, and logoff.

Setting Up a Logon Script

In Windows 2000 (and even in Windows NT), an administrator can set up any user account in such a way that a logon script runs automatically whenever the user logs on. (You can use customized scripts from previous chapters for that purpose.) To set up a logon script, you take the following steps:

1. Copy the logon script or scripts to the script path. (See the explanation on pages 414 and 415 regarding the exact location.)

2. Log on as an administrator, and launch the tool to manage user accounts. In Windows 2000, the Microsoft Management Console (MMC) provides the necessary functions. Double-click on Administrative Tools in Control Panel, and then double-click on Computer Management. (In Windows NT 4, you use the User Manager program to administer user accounts.)

3.   Select a user account and show the properties. In MMC, select the branch
     System Tools/Local Users And Groups/Users and double-click on the entry
     with the user's name in the user account list. (In Windows NT 4, double-
     click on the user's name in the list of accounts to open the dialog with
     the user's account properties.)

4.   Select the Profile property page on the user property sheet and enter the
     name of the logon script file in the Logon Script text box (Figure 13-3).
     (In Windows NT 4, click the Profile button to open the dialog box with
     the Logon Script text box.)

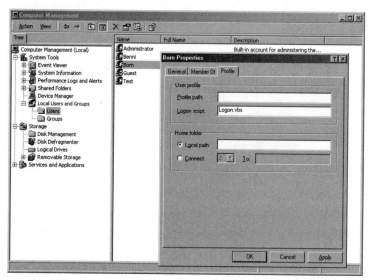

Figure 13-3 *The Microsoft Management Console with the Profile property page*

After you close the property pages and dialog boxes using the OK button, the
settings for this user account are saved. If you haven't done so already, you need to
copy the logon script to the logon script path. This path depends on whether the logon
script is executed when logging on to a domain or when logging on to a local account. To execute the logon script when logging on to a domain, the script is stored
on the primary domain controller. On a Windows NT 4 domain controller, the logon
script path is

   systemroot\system32\repl\import\scripts

where *systemroot* stands for the path to the Windows folder; on a Windows 2000
domain controller, the logon script path is

   sysvol*domainname*\scripts

For local accounts on either Windows 2000 or Windows NT 4, the logon script path is as follows:

systemroot\system32\repl\import\scripts

If the script is in this logon path, you only need to enter the filename (Logon.vbs, for example) in the Logon Script text box. You can also use a subfolder within the script path to store the logon scripts (so that you can group different logon scripts for user groups, for example). In this case, you must precede the filename with the relative path (such as *admins\Logon.vbs*).

The logon script will now run automatically whenever that user logs on. The advantage of this approach is that you can assign an individual logon script to each user.

> **IMPORTANT**   In Windows 2000, you can use WSH script files directly as logon scripts. (You can enter files with the extensions .vbs, .js, and .wsf in the Logon Script text box.) Windows NT 4 supports only logon script files with the extensions .exe, .cmd, and .bat, so you must create a .bat file that launches the WSH logon script, store the .bat file in the script path, and enter the name of the .bat file in the Logon Script text box.

Using Global Logon and Logoff Scripts

Windows 2000 offers an alternative way to run scripts automatically during user logon or user logoff:

1. Write your script with the necessary commands for what you need done during logon or logoff. Store this script in a WSH script file in a local folder.

2. Log on with administrator rights and launch an instance of MMC that supports User and Group policies. (The steps are described in Appendix B.)

3. Select the branch Local Computer Policy/User Configuration/Windows Settings/Scripts (Logon/Logoff) on the Tree tab.

4. MMC shows two icons in the right pane for logon and logoff scripts. Double-click on one of these icons to open the Scripts property page (Figure 13-4).

5. Click Add to invoke the Add A Script dialog box (Figure 13-5). Enter the script filename and the optional script parameters in the dialog box. You can also use the Browse button to select a script file in any folder.

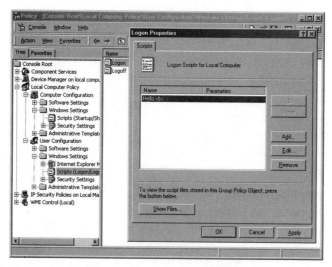

Figure 13-4 *MMC with the Scripts property page*

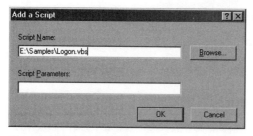

Figure 13-5 *The Add A Script dialog box*

After you close all open dialog boxes using the OK button, the selected script file is executed automatically (independent of the user's account) whenever a user logs on or logs off (depending on which icon you double-clicked).

Using Startup and Shutdown Scripts

Windows 2000 allows execution of startup and shutdown scripts independent of user logon or logoff. This comes in handy for machines running without a user currently logged on (servers, for example). If you need a script to be executed automatically during startup or shutdown, take these steps, which are similar to those in the previous section:

1. Write your script with the necessary commands for what you need done during startup or shutdown. Store this script in a WSH script file in a local folder.

2. Log on with administrator rights and launch an instance of MMC that supports User and Group policies.

3. Connect to a remote machine if necessary (the local policy will be loaded automatically), and click the Local Computer Policy/Computer Configuration/Windows Settings/Scripts (Startup/Shutdown) item on the Tree tab (Figure 13-4).

4. Double-click on the Startup or Shutdown icon in the right pane, and click Add to invoke the Add A Script dialog box (Figure 13-5).

5. Enter the script's filename and path and optional parameters in the Add A Script dialog box. If necessary, use the Browse button to select a script file in any folder.

After you close all open dialog boxes using the OK button, the selected script file is executed automatically during each system startup or shutdown (depending on which icon you double-clicked).

Startup and Logon Scripts in Windows 95 and Windows 98

If Windows 95 or Windows 98 machines are running in a network environment with a Windows NT domain controller, a network administrator can set up logon scripts to be executed in a user or group policy. If the computer is running in a workgroup environment or as a standalone system, you can choose between two approaches for executing scripts automatically during user logon:

■ The simplest way is to add a shortcut to the Startup folder of the Start menu, which contains a command to execute the script. (You can do this in Windows 98 using drag and drop, for example).

■ You can add a command such as *WScript.exe path\scriptfile* to the *Run* key in the Registry in the branch HKEY_LOCAL_MACHINE\SOFTWARE\ Microsoft\Windows. You can use the System Policy Editor or the System Configuration Utility (in Windows 98) to maintain the *Run* key entries. Or you can use the Registry access techniques shown in Chapter 11 to add the command to or remove it from the *Run* Registry key.

Whichever approach you choose, all scripts are executed during each user logon.

Chapter 14

Programming Techniques and Tips

This chapter offers a number of useful techniques and tips for working with Microsoft Windows Script Host (WSH), some of which were introduced in earlier chapters. They're organized by general topic: run-time errors; paths and dates; long filenames, the At command, and system calls; user dialog boxes and output; file handling; playing sound; the Windows shell; and calling a DUN connection.

RUN-TIME ERRORS

Both VBScript and JScript support inline error handling, meaning that your script can intercept and recover from errors that otherwise would cause the script to terminate. In this section, I'll summarize what you need to know about using explicit run-time error handling within scripts.

Handling Run-Time Errors in VBScript

You implement explicit run-time error handling in VBScript by using the *On Error Resume Next* statement, which causes the next statement to be executed after a run-time error. This statement enables inline run-time error handling. (Only syntax errors are still reported by the script engine.)

You can retrieve the error code by using the *Err* object. For example, if *oWSH* is an object variable pointing to the *WshShell* object, you can check a possible error raised while using the *RegRead* method:

```
valx = oWSH.RegRead("....", "xxxx")
If Err <> 0 Then
    ⋮
```

If a run-time error occurs during execution of the first statement, the value of the *Err* object is not equal to 0. You can retrieve the error code by using *Err.Number* and retrieve the error text by using *Err.Description*. I used this technique in several earlier chapters to handle run-time errors.

You use the *On Error GoTo 0* statement to disable run-time error handling. After this statement, the script engine handles run-time errors.

> **WARNING** As I mentioned, enabling inline run-time error handling suppresses all implicit error messages, so your script is responsible for detecting and reporting run-time errors. The danger with this approach is that certain hard-to-find errors could escape detection. Even if the script contains an *Option Explicit* statement, mistyped variables and function or procedure names are not reported as erroneous. Instead, the statement simply fails and the script engine moves on to the next statement. To avoid this risk, I strongly recommend that you disable run-time error handling (using *On Error GoTo 0*) as soon as possible after enabling it.

Handling Run-Time Errors in JScript

JScript supports run-time error handling in script engine versions 5 and later. You use the *try {...} catch (e) {...}* sequence as follows:

```
try
{
    var valx = WSH.RegRead("....", "xxxx");
}
catch (e)
{
    if (e != 0)
        WScript.Echo("Error during Registry access");
}
```

You must set the *try* keyword in front of a statement. You enclose the statement or block of statements in braces. The *catch (e)* statement is called if a run-time error occurs. The variable *e* receives the error object, which can be evaluated in the statements following the *catch* block. (These statements must also be enclosed in braces.)

Raising a Run-Time Error in VBScript

You can raise your own run-time errors by using the methods the script language provides. In VBScript, you use the *Raise* method of the *Err* object. The following code raises a run-time error and displays the error description:

```
On Error Resume Next

Err.Clear
Err.Raise 6     ' Raise an error.

MsgBox "Error code: " & Err.Number & vbCrLf & Err.Description, _
     vbOKOnly, "VBScript-Error-Description"

On Error GoTo 0
```

This code simulates an overflow error (code 6). You can use this snippet to write a short VBScript program that asks for an error code and returns the error description.

> **NOTE** The VBScriptError.vbs file in the \WSHDevGuide\Chapter14 folder on the book's companion CD asks for an error number and shows the description of the error. All error messages are also described in the VBScript Language Reference. But the same can't be said for errors caused by the operating system (or OLE or COM components). You can obtain these error descriptions from internal tables by using the right Windows API calls, but these techniques are beyond the scope of this book.

PATHS AND DATES

To access external files, you need the path to those files. In this section, we'll examine how to obtain the current script file's folder, the default folder, or the drive. I'll also explain a pitfall of using date differences.

Getting the Script's Path

Sometimes it's handy to know the path to your script—for example, when you want to process files in your script's folder. Using the script's path as a working folder is less error-prone than using absolute paths because the script's path is always valid (even after renaming the script folder or moving it to another drive). WSH has no function or method for retrieving a script's path, so in VBScript you can use the *ScriptFullName* property of the *WScript* object to extract the path, as shown here:

```
Function GetPath
    ' Retrieve path to the script file.
    Dim path
    path = WScript.ScriptFullName  ' Script filename
    GetPath = Left(path, InStrRev(path, "\"))
End Function
```

In JScript, you can use the following function to retrieve the path:

```
function GetPath()
{
    // Retrieve the script path.
    var path = WScript.ScriptFullName;  // Script filename
    path = path.substr(0, path.lastIndexOf("\\") + 1);
    return path;
}
```

Both functions assume that the path ends with a backslash character. If WSH is ever ported to other operating systems (such as Macintosh or UNIX), this method of extracting the path might fail. In this case, you can use the following construction instead:

```
path = Left(Wscript.ScriptFullName, _
            Len(Wscript.ScriptFullName) - Len(Wscript.ScriptName))
```

This statement simply subtracts the script filename from the full name, so it's independent of the file-naming convention. If you don't want to use this trick, you can use the *FileSystemObject* object's *GetParentFolderName* method, as shown here:

```
Dim fso
Set fso = CreateObject("Scripting.FileSystemObject")
Path = fso.GetParentFolderName(WScript.ScriptFullName)
```

As long as Microsoft implements *GetParentFolderName* correctly, you get the path (independent of the operating system). However, you must use extra memory to create the file system object and expend extra time to execute the method.

Getting the Current Directory

Microsoft Visual Basic and Microsoft Visual Basic for Applications (VBA) have a function that retrieves the current directory. In a script, the current directory is identical to the directory from which the script is executed, so you can use either the code shown in the previous section or the following statements to retrieve the current directory:

```
Dim fso
Set fso = WScript.CreateObject("Scripting.FileSystemObject")
' CurrentDir = fso.GetAbsolutePathName("")
' Or use the following syntax:
CurrentDir = fso.GetAbsolutePathName(".")
```

In this sequence, the *FileSystemObject* object retrieves the path by using the *GetAbsolutePathName* method with the parameter ".".

NOTE CurrentDir.vbs (in the \WSHDevGuide\Chapter14 folder) shows the current directory and the script path in a message box. Alternatively, you can use the *GetDir* method (which I'm about to explain).

Setting the Default Folder

WSH doesn't provide a way to set the default directory of a program, but a few workarounds are available. The simplest approach is to put the requested files into the folder that contains the script file. You can then use the *GetPath* functions (as you've already seen) to locate the path to the current folder.

The second approach is to create a shortcut file, set its execution path and working directory, and then use the *Run* method to execute the shortcut. The application launched from the shortcut file receives all the parameters set.

The third approach is to create a BAT file that includes *cd* commands and calls the application. You can then use the *Run* method to execute the batch program. (You can find details about creating shortcut files and using the *Run* method in Chapters 7 and 10.)

Getting the Current Drive Name

You can retrieve the current drive name by using the *ScriptFullName* property of the *WScript* object, but this approach is complicated by UNC paths. A much simpler method, which also works for UNC paths, uses the following code:

```
Set oFS = WScript.CreateObject("Scripting.FileSystemObject")
oldDrive = oFS.GetDriveName(WScript.ScriptFullName)
```

You pass the *ScriptFullName* property value to the *FileSystemObject* object's *GetDriveName* method, and the method returns the name of the current drive, as shown in Figure 14-1.

Figure 14-1 *Displaying the name of the current drive (from a UNC path)*

NOTE The code shown above always returns the drive from which the script file is launched. You can't change the current drive from WSH using the methods provided by its object model.

Calculating Date Differences

You can calculate date differences in VBScript by using the *DateDiff* function. According-ing to the VBScript help, you must specify the interval in the first parameter; the other two parameters are the dates used to calculate the difference, as shown here.

```
WScript.Echo DateDiff("d", Now, "1/1/2020") & _
             " days left to 2020..."
```

This statement uses the *"d"* (days) interval to calculate the days left until the year 2020. *Now* submits the current date, and the third parameter sets a fixed date value.

NOTE The date separator you use depends on the local settings of your op-erating system.

Figure 14-2 shows a sequence of date differences and displays the days left until a given date. Something went wrong, as you can see in the last line: the date differ-ence is negative.

Figure 14-2 *Date differences*

Let's take a closer look at the code for calculating date differences. Both the following lines calculate the date difference between now and January 1, 2020:

```
MsgBox DateDiff("d", Now, "1/1/2020") & " days left to 2020..."
MsgBox DateDiff("d", Now, "1/1/20") & " days left to 2020..."
```

Even though the second statement uses a two-digit year value, *20*, both statements return the correct date difference (in days).

However, it's risky to use two-digit dates. The following two statements result in different values:

```
MsgBox DateDiff("d", Now, "1/1/2030") & " days left to 2030..."
MsgBox DateDiff("d", Now, "1/1/30") & " days left to 2030..."
```

The second statement displays a negative value (as shown in Figure 14-3). The date *"1/1/20"* causes *DateDiff* to calculate the days until January 1, 2020, but *"1/1/30"* causes *DateDiff* to calculate the days until January 1, 1930.

This situation is the result of the infamous "Y2K bug." Many programs written in the 20th century used two-digit year values. To enable programs to calculate date differences between 19*xx* and 20*xx*, Windows uses a bias value for two-digit year values. All values between 0 and 29 are interpreted as the years from 2000 to 2029. Values of 30 to 99 are interpreted as 1930 to 1999. Therefore, it's always good programming style to use four-digit date values in your scripts. You can check this behavior by using the DateTest.vbs file in the \WSHDevGuide\Chapter14 folder.

LONG FILENAMES, THE AT COMMAND, AND SYSTEM CALLS

In this section, we'll cover how to work with long filenames, how to use the AT command, and how to invoke system calls by using the *Run* method.

Using the Windows NT Scheduler to Execute WSH Scripts

You can use the Microsoft Windows NT scheduler to execute a script at a specified time:

```
AT 18:00:00 /interactive "C:\WSHDevGuide\Chapter14\RunExit.vbs"
```

On the *AT* command line, you must write the entire path to the script file. You must also set the */interactive* flag if the script requests user interaction.

> NOTE   In Windows 98 and Windows 2000, you can use the Task Scheduler to schedule script execution. (Even though the Task Scheduler provides an API for other programs, it doesn't support a scripting interface; Microsoft Site Server includes a helper DLL that provides the necessary COM interface.)

Using Long Filenames in Scripts

If your scripts contain long filenames or if you use long filenames in the command to execute a script, you must enclose the paths in double quotes, as shown here:

```
WshShell.Run _
    """C:\Programs\Microsoft Office\Office\Excel.exe""", 1, True
```

In VBScript, you must write a double quote in a string as *""*. The first double quote indicates the beginning of the string. The next two double quotes indicate that the double quote must be inserted into the string.

In JScript, you write a double quote in a string as \\":

```
WshShell.Run _
    ("\"C:\\Programs\\Microsoft Office\\Office\\Excel.exe\"",
    1, true);
```

> **NOTE**   If you build the command line by fetching a pathname and then con-
> catenating a string with the specific filename, you must add double quotes around
> the resulting string (because the fetched pathname might have an embedded
> space). An example is *oWSH.Run """" & path & """", 3, True*. The four double
> quotes are required because the two inner double quotes force the language
> engine to recognize one *"*. The outer double quotes mark the inner double quote
> as a string character.

Using the *Run* Method to Execute System Calls

To call Windows API functions from your WSH script, you need an ActiveX control
that provides the right interface. (I explain how to write such controls in *Advanced
Development with Microsoft Windows Script Host 2.0.*) Nevertheless, Windows 95,
Windows 98, Windows NT, and Windows 2000 provide a few backdoor options that
allow you to access system routines from a script by using the *Run* method.

Using RunDll32.exe to shut down Windows 95 or Windows 98

If you don't have an ActiveX control that provides a method to shut down Windows
95 or Windows 98, you can use the following command within the *Run* method:

```
WshShell.Run "%WINDIR%\RunDll32.exe user,ExitWindows", 1, -1
```

The program RunDll32.exe activates several Windows API functions contained
in library (DLL) files. The command shown here launches RunDll32.exe. This helper
program accesses the library User.exe and calls the library's *ExitWindows* API function.

> **TIP**   You can use any Windows DLL library in a RunDll32.exe command, but
> you must keep in mind some restrictions. The names of the functions exported
> from the library are case-sensitive. (For example, *exitwindows* is different from
> *ExitWindows*.) Also, you can't use RunDll32.exe to pass arguments to Windows
> API functions. But there are a few exceptions that allow you to use RunDll32.exe
> to call other functions and submit a string within the command line. These func-
> tions (such as *SHExitWindowsEx*, which is discussed later) examine the com-
> mand line for arguments.

The VBScript program shown in Listing 14-1 contains the command to shut
down Windows 95 or Windows 98 from a WSH script. (This sample, like the others in
this chapter, is in the \WSHDevGuide\Chapter14 folder on the book's companion CD.)

```
'***********************************************
' File:    RunExit.vbs (WSH sample in VBScript)
' Author: (c) G. Born
'
' Using the Run method to call the Windows 95 or
' Windows 98 ExitWindows API function
'***********************************************
```

Listing 14-1 *RunExit.vbs*

```
Option Explicit

Dim WshShell

Set WshShell = WScript.CreateObject("WScript.Shell")

If (MsgBox("Shut down Windows 95 or Windows 98", vbYesNo + vbQuestion, _
    "WSH sample - by G. Born") = vbYes) Then _
    WshShell.Run _
        "%WINDIR%\RunDll32.exe user,ExitWindows", 1, -1

'*** End
```

NOTE   This call won't work in Windows NT or Windows 2000 because the operating system doesn't support the *ExitWindows* function in User.exe. (A shutdown in Windows NT or Windows 2000 requires privileges for the caller.) The ActiveX control WSHExtend.ocx (discussed in *Advanced Development with Microsoft Windows Script Host 2.0*) provides a method for shutting down Windows 95, Windows 98, Windows NT, or Windows 2000.

A trick for shutting down and restarting Windows 95 or Windows 98

The technique I just showed you for shutting down Windows 95 or Windows 98 can't be used to restart the system. However, these versions of Windows support MS-DOS mode (console window mode), which unloads the Windows kernel and loads only the MS-DOS core. Therefore, if you execute an MS-DOS program in MS-DOS mode, Windows terminates. After quitting the MS-DOS application, the Windows kernel is reloaded automatically. This has the same effect as a restart.

You can use this MS-DOS mode behavior to force a Windows restart in Windows 95 or Windows 98. First, you create a BAT file containing only the following command:

```
@Exit
```

Then you right-click on the BAT file icon and choose Properties from the shortcut menu. On the Program property page, check the MS-DOS Mode option and uncheck the Warn Before Entering MS-DOS Mode option. Now, a subsequent double-click on the BAT file launches the batch program in MS-DOS mode. Because the BAT file contains the *Exit* command, this mode quits immediately and Windows reloads. To restart Windows from a WSH script, you simply write a script that uses the *Run* method to execute your BAT file.

This trick works well for Windows 95 and Windows 98 (but not for Windows Millennium Edition). If you want more control over the shutdown and restart process, you must access another Windows API function, named *ExitWindowsEx*. This function is available in Windows 95, Windows 98, and Windows NT. Unfortunately, you can't use the RunDll32.exe program to call this API function because the function requires two parameters: one that defines the exit mode and one that's reserved. Without an ActiveX control, you can't use this API function.

I also discovered another undocumented trick in Windows 98 (and in Windows Millennium Edition) for calling the *ExitWindowsEx* function from the shell with the requested parameter. This trick uses the function *SHExitWindowsEx* in the file Shell32.dll. This function acts as a wrapper for *ExitWindowsEx* and can be called from the Windows shell by using the following command:

```
RunDll32.exe Shell32.dll,SHExitWindowsEx 0x0
```

RunDll32.exe calls the function *SHExitWindowsEx* in Shell32.dll. The function has one argument, which must be submitted as a string. (This is one of the exceptions I mentioned earlier: *SHExitWindowsEx* supports parameter passing from the command line.) The submitted argument specifies a hexadecimal number as a parameter for the exit mode. The string *0x0* specifies the value 0, *0x01* specifies the value 1, and so on. *SHExitWindowsEx* reads this argument, converts it to a hexadecimal number, and calls the original API function *ExitWindowsEx* with the requested parameters. Table 14-1 lists the values you can use for this argument.

Table 14-1 *SHExitWindowsEx* Argument Values

Argument	Result
0x0	Log off
0x1	Shut down
0x2	Restart

Obviously, you can use RunDll32.exe to force Windows 98 to shut down or to restart, or to force a user to log off. Listing 14-2 is a WSH script that does all this.

```
'***************************************************
' File:     RunExitEx.vbs (WSH sample in VBScript)
' Author:   (c) G. Born
'
' Using the Run method to call the undocumented
' Windows 98 SHExitWindowsEx API function to
' shut down, restart, or log off
'
' Shell32.dll,SHExitWindowsEx,0x0 Log off
' Shell32.dll,SHExitWindowsEx,0x1 Shut down
' Shell32.dll,SHExitWindowsEx,0x2 Restart
'***************************************************
Option Explicit
```

Listing 14-2 *RunExitEx.vbs*

```
Dim Shell, Title, obj
Title = "WSH sample - by G. Born"

' Create shell objects.
Set Shell = WScript.CreateObject("Shell.Application")
Set obj = WScript.CreateObject("WScript.Shell")

' Call Logoff mode.
If (MsgBox("Log off?", _
    vbYesNo + vbQuestion, Title) = vbYes) Then
    obj.Run "RunDll32.exe Shell32.dll,SHExitWindowsEx 0x0"
Else
    ' Call Shutdown mode.
    If (MsgBox("Shut down Windows?", _
        vbYesNo + vbQuestion, Title) = vbYes) Then
        obj.Run "RunDll32.exe Shell32.dll,SHExitWindowsEx 0x01"
    Else
        ' Call Restart mode.
        If (MsgBox("Restart Windows?", _
            vbYesNo + vbQuestion, Title) = vbYes) Then
            obj.Run "RunDll32.exe Shell32.dll,SHExitWindowsEx 0x02"
        End If
    End If
End If

'*** End
```

This call won't work in Windows 95, Windows NT, or Windows 2000 because these operating systems don't support the helper function. I'll come back to this topic a bit later when I explain how to access the Windows 98 shell to suspend your machine or invoke the Shutdown Windows dialog box.

Locking a Windows 2000 Workstation

Although you can't use a RunDll32.exe call to exit Windows NT or Windows 2000, you can lock a Microsoft Windows 2000 Professional workstation. In Windows 2000, the module *User32* provides the *LockWorkStation* API call. The code in Listing 14-3 uses RunDll32.exe to call this API function and lock the system.

```
'*********************************************************
' File:    NTLockWorkStation.vbs (WSH sample in VBScript)
' Author:  (c) G. Born
'
' Locking a Windows 2000 workstation
'*********************************************************
Option Explicit
```

Listing 14-3 *NTLockWorkStation.vbs*   *(continued)*

Listing 14-3 *continued*

```
Dim WshShell

' Create WshShell object (for Run).
Set WshShell = WScript.CreateObject("WScript.Shell")

' Ask user to allow lock.
If MsgBox("Lock workstation?", vbYesNo, "WSH Sample") = vbYes Then
    ' Use LockWorkStation API call.
    WshShell.Run "RunDll32.exe user32.dll,LockWorkStation"
End If

'*** End
```

The user can double-click on the file to lock the workstation. After the user enters a password, the desktop with all open windows is restored. This sample isn't very useful by itself (because you can lock your workstation by pressing Ctrl+Alt+Del and then click the Lock Computer button). But the technique it demonstrates can come in handy during script execution.

Invoking the Copy Disk Dialog Box

Windows uses DiskCopy.dll internally to handle a disk copy between two floppy disks. You can call this library to invoke the Copy Disk dialog box (shown in Figure 14-3).

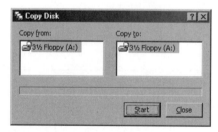

Figure 14-3 *The Copy Disk dialog box*

This DLL exports a function that can be called from other programs. You can use RunDll32.exe to call the *DiskCopyRunDll* entry in DiskCopy.dll from a WSH script by using the following command:

```
RunDll32.exe DiskCopy.dll,DiskCopyRunDll
```

This command invokes the Copy Disk dialog box. Listing 14-4 accesses the Copy Disk dialog box from a WSH script.

```
'***********************************************
' File:   CopyDisk.vbs (WSH sample in VBScript)
' Author: (c) G. Born
'
' Invoking the Copy Disk dialog box
'***********************************************
Option Explicit

Dim WshObj      ' Object for the Run method

Set WshObj = WScript.CreateObject("WScript.Shell")

WshObj.Run _
    "RunDll32.exe DiskCopy.dll,DiskCopyRunDll", _
    1, True ' Launch dialog box.

'*** End
```

Listing 14-4 *CopyDisk.vbs*

Invoking the Format Dialog Box

You can use a similar technique to invoke the Format dialog box to format a floppy disk in Windows. The format function is implemented in the file Shell32.dll; you can invoke it by using the *SHFormatDrive* call, which displays the Format dialog box. The following command accesses this function from a WSH script:

```
RunDll32.exe Shell32.dll,SHFormatDrive
```

The script in Listing 14-5 invokes the Format dialog box.

```
'***************************************************
' File:   Format.vbs (WSH sample in VBScript)
' Author: (c) G. Born
'
' Invoking the Format dialog box for a floppy disk
'***************************************************
Option Explicit

Dim WshObj      ' Object for Run method

Set WshObj = WScript.CreateObject("WScript.Shell")

WshObj.Run "RunDll32.exe Shell32.dll,SHFormatDrive", _
           1, True ' Launch dialog box.

'*** End
```

Listing 14-5 *Format.vbs*

Invoking the Screen Saver Property Page

The Screen Saver property page allows you to install a screen saver. You can invoke this property page from a script or from the Windows shell by using the following command:

```
RunD1l32.exe desk.cpl,InstallScreenSaver
```

Listing 14-6 invokes the property page by using VBScript.

```
'***************************************************
' File:    ScreenSaver.vbs (WSH sample in VBScript)
' Author: (c) G. Born
'
' Installing a screen saver
'***************************************************
Option Explicit

Dim WshObj       ' Object for the Run method

Set WshObj = WScript.CreateObject("WScript.Shell")

WshObj.Run _
    "RunD1l32.exe desk.cpl,InstallScreenSaver", _
    1, True ' Screen saver property page

'*** End
```

Listing 14-6 *ScreenSaver.vbs*

Calling Control Panel Modules

The previous sample introduces a method for invoking the Screen Saver property page using RunDll32.exe. You can also use Control.exe instead of RunDll32.exe within the *Run* method to invoke a Control Panel property page via .cpl files. The following command invokes the Buttons property page of the Mouse Properties property sheet:

```
WshObj.Run "Control.exe main.cpl,@0,0"
```

The parameters following the name of the module (.cpl file) specify which property page of that module is shown in the foreground. Table 14-2 lists some of the modules and their parameters.

Table 14-2 CONTROL PANEL MODULES AND THEIR PARAMETERS

Module	*Name*	*Index*	*Description*	*Examples*
Appwiz.cpl	n/a*	0 to 3	Opens the property page addressed in *index* of the Add/Remove Programs dialog box (or property sheet, depending on the operating system version).	*Control.exe Appwiz.cpl,,1*
Desk.cpl	n/a	0 to 3	Opens a page of the Display property sheet.	*Control.exe Desk.cpl,,1*
Intl.cpl	n/a	0 to 4	Opens the Regional Options property sheet and selects a property page. The second parameter defines the property page.	*Control.exe Intl.cpl,,1*
Main.cpl	@0 to @5	0 to x	Supports the property sheets for mouse, keyboard, energy saving, and PCMCIA. The first parameter specifies the module. You can use a name (such as Mouse or Keyboard) or an index value in the format @x (where *x* is a placeholder for a value from 0 to 5). Names are localized. The second parameter specifies the module's property page.	*Control.exe Main.cpl,@0,1* *Control.exe Main.cpl,Mouse,1*
Mmsys.cpl	@0, @1	0 to x	Opens the property sheet for sound or multimedia. The first parameter specifies the property sheet (0 = Multimedia; 1 = Sounds). The second parameter specifies the property page.	*Control.exe Mmsys.cpl,@0,1*
Sysdm.cpl	n/a	0 to 3	Opens the System property sheet and selects one of the pages.	*Control.exe Sysdm.cpl,,0*
Timedate.cpl	n/a	0, 1	Opens the Date/Time property sheet.	*Control.exe Timedate.cpl,,0*

* "n/a" means "not applicable."

The names of the property sheets vary a bit depending on the version of the operating system. The number of property pages also varies. Table 14-2 shows the options for Windows 98 (most of which can be used in Windows 95, Windows NT, and Windows 2000).

Using the *Run* Method to Handle Network Mappings

You can use the *WshNetwork* object to handle network mappings for drives and printers, but sometimes changing network settings by using this object and its methods can get too complicated. An easier way is to use the *Run* method along with the MS-DOS *Net* command. To delete all network mappings on a machine, for example, you can use the following command in a script:

```
Set objSh = WScript.CreateObject("WScript.Shell")
objSh.Run "NET USE * /DELETE /YES", 0, True
```

The *NET USE* command accesses the network mappings. The wildcard character (*) defines all mappings, and the switch */DELETE* removes these mappings. The option */YES* forces the action without user input.

NOTE   For more information on the *NET* command, open the Command Prompt window and type *NET /?* or *NET USE /?* to see a help page.

USER DIALOG BOXES AND OUTPUT

We've looked at numerous samples showing script output in user dialog boxes. Now I'd like to share a few hints and programming techniques for handling script output in user dialog boxes. I'll also discuss input/output streaming in the Command Prompt window (console) and offer a few hints on printing different document types in WSH scripts.

Using Tabs and Line Feeds

When you submit a string to the dialog box methods (such as *Echo* and *Popup*) and functions (such as *MsgBox*) mentioned in previous chapters, the string is formatted automatically to fit in the dialog box. But you can insert tab and line-feed characters into the string to format the output as you wish. VBScript uses the predefined *vbCrLf* constant to force a line wrap:

```
WScript.Echo "First line " & vbCrLf & "Second line "
```

In JScript, you add the escape characters \n (new line) to the string:

```
WScript.Echo("First line \nsecond line ");
```

To format columns in a dialog box, you can insert tab stop characters into the text. In VBScript, you do this by using the named constant *vbTab* in your string. In JScript, you insert the escape characters \t in the string to force a tab. Tab stop positions are fixed within the dialog box.

Displaying Console Input and Output

To display console input and output in the Command Prompt window, you can use the *StdIn* and *StdOut* stream properties in WSH 2. To use these stream properties, you must run the script in CScript.exe. (WScript.exe causes a run-time error because Windows applications don't support input/output streams.)

The following sample uses the methods of WSH 2 to read user input from the command line and echo the typed string. This script must be executed in CScript.exe. Because there's no guarantee that the user will launch the script with the right host, the script itself forces execution of CScript.exe.

```
If (Not IsCScript()) Then
    Set WshShell = WScript.CreateObject("WScript.Shell")
    WshShell.Run "CScript.exe " & WScript.ScriptFullName
    WScript.Quit              ' Terminate script.
End If
```

If the user-defined function *IsCScript* returns the value *False*, the script executes the *Run* method to launch a second copy of the script. This copy is executed in CScript.exe. The function *IsCScript* uses the following code:

```
Function IsCScript()
    ' Check whether CScript.exe is the host.
    If (InStr(UCase(WScript.FullName), "CSCRIPT") <> 0) Then
        IsCScript = True
    Else
        IsCScript = False
    End If
End function
```

The function checks whether the host returns a string containing *"CSCRIPT"*. This string is returned from the *FullName* property of the *WScript* object.

You can use the following command to write to the output stream:

```
WScript.StdOut.WriteLine "Please enter something"
```

The command uses the *StdOut* property of the *WScript* object and executes the *WriteLine* method. The method shows the submitted parameter in the command prompt window (Figure 14-4).

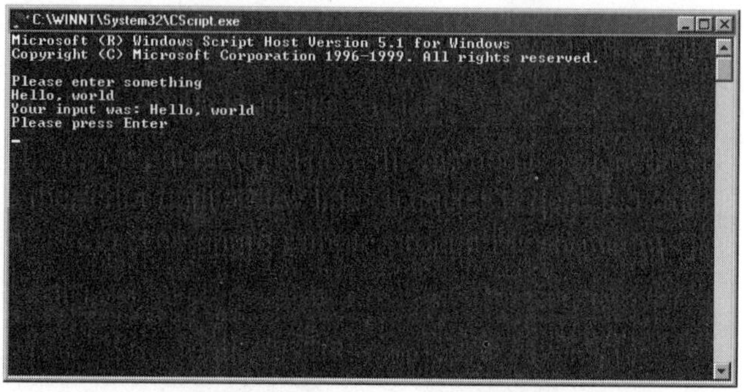

Figure 14-4 *User input at the command prompt*

To read user input from the console input, you use the *ReadLine* method of the *StdIn* property of the *WScript* object, as shown in the following command:

```
tmp = WScript.StdIn.ReadLine
```

The user input returned from the method is assigned to the variable *tmp*. *ReadLine* pauses the script until a new line character is detected (that is, until the user presses the Enter key). The entire sample program is shown in Listing 14-7.

```
'**************************************************
' File:    StdIO.vbs (WSH 2 sample in VBScript)
' Author: (c) G. Born
'
' Using the WSH 2 StdIn and StdOut properties
'**************************************************
Option Explicit

Dim tmp, WshShell

' Test whether the host is CScript.exe.
If (Not IsCScript()) Then
    Set WshShell = WScript.CreateObject("WScript.Shell")
    WshShell.Run "CScript.exe " & WScript.ScriptFullName
    WScript.Quit             ' Terminate script.
End If

WScript.StdOut.WriteLine "Please enter something"
tmp = WScript.StdIn.ReadLine

WScript.StdOut.WriteLine "Your input was: " & tmp

WScript.StdOut.WriteLine "Please press Enter"
tmp = WScript.StdIn.ReadLine ' Wait until key is pressed.
```

Listing 14-7 *StdIO.vbs*

```
Function IsCScript()
    ' Check whether CScript.exe is the host.
    If (InStr(UCase(WScript.FullName), "CSCRIPT") <> 0) Then
        IsCScript = True
    Else
        IsCScript = False
    End If
End Function

'*** End
```

Writing to a Line and Reading from It

The sample above writes a string to the command line, forces a new line, and reads the user input. In most cases, you should write a string and read the user input on the same line. You can do this using the *Write* method instead of the *WriteLine* method:

```
WScript.StdOut.Write("Enter a number> ")
```

The statement above writes text to the command line but doesn't advance the cursor to the next line. The user can then enter something on the same line in the Command Prompt window. This user input can be read using the *Read* method or the *ReadLine* method.

You can use the *Read* method to read a given number of characters. The following command retrieves the first character of input after the user presses Enter:

```
tmp = WScript.StdIn.Read(1)
```

If the user types the string *1234{Enter}*, where *{Enter}* stands for the Enter key, *Read(1)* returns the value *1*. (The *Read* method is especially useful when reading fixed-length fields from a data file.) Listing 14-8 shows how to use *Write* and *Read* to handle user input and messages on one line.

```
'*****************************************************
' File:   StdIO1.vbs (WSH 2 sample in VBScript)
' Author: (c) G. Born
'
' Using the WSH 2 StdIn and Stdout properties
'*****************************************************
Option Explicit

Dim tmp, WshShell
```

Listing 14-8 *StdIO1.vbs*   *(continued)*

Listing 14-8 *continued*

```
' Test whether the host is CScript.exe.
If (Not IsCScript()) Then
    Set WshShell = WScript.CreateObject("WScript.Shell")
    WshShell.Run "CScript.exe " & WScript.ScriptFullName
    WScript.Quit                 ' Terminate script.
End If


' Write a string without a new line.
WScript.StdOut.Write("Type in a three-digit number and press Enter> ")

' Use the Read method to get the first character of input.
tmp = WScript.StdIn.Read(1)

' Echo the data.
WScript.StdOut.WriteLine("The first character was " & tmp)

' Next line
WScript.StdOut.Write("Type in a three-digit number and press Enter> ")

' Use ReadLine to retrieve the data.
tmp = WScript.StdIn.ReadLine()

' Show input using the Echo method.
WScript.Echo "You entered", tmp
WScript.Echo "Please press the Enter key to quit the script"

WScript.Echo WScript.StdIn.Read(1)  ' Wait.

Function IsCScript()
    ' Check whether CScript.exe is the host.
    If (InStr(UCase(WScript.FullName), "CSCRIPT") <> 0) Then
        IsCScript = True
    Else
        IsCScript = False
    End If
End Function

'*** End
```

Piping Program Output

In the Command Prompt window, the piping mechanism allows you to use the output of one program as the input of another program. The following command uses the output of the *dir* command as input for the *more* filter:

```
dir *.* | more
```

You can use a similar command to pipe some input to a script program. Let's say that the program StdIOFilter.vbs reads the default stream as input. We can type this command to cause the command prompt to execute the *dir* command:

```
dir *.* | CScript.exe StdIOFilter.vbs
```

The *dir* output will be piped as input for the script program. It is important to use CScript.exe to call the host. StdIOFilter.vbs can read the standard input stream, process the input, and write the result to the standard output. Listing 14-9 reads the input stream, adds a leading and a trailing line, converts all characters to uppercase, and writes the result to the default output stream.

```vbscript
'*******************************************************
' File:   StdIOFilter.vbs (WSH 2 sample in VBScript)
' Author: (c) G. Born
'
' Reading input data and sending it
' to the output stream
'*******************************************************
Option Explicit

Dim tmp

' Now read the input stream.
tmp = WScript.StdIn.ReadAll()

' Try to write the result to the standard output stream.
WScript.StdOut.WriteLine("*** Output Filter demo ***")
WScript.StdOut.Write(UCase(tmp))
WScript.StdOut.WriteLine("*** End of input data ***")

'*** End
```

Listing 14-9 *StdIOFilter.vbs*

NOTE To launch StdIOFilter.vbs, you must use the command shown above. You cannot use the *IsCScript* function to shell a second copy of CScript.exe because WSH can't handle the input/output streams properly.

Using Files for Streaming

Let's take a look at how a script can use the *TextStream* object to read data from a text file, process the data, and display it. Our sample VBScript program can run under CScript.exe or WScript.exe. It shells a *dir* command, which creates a directory listing of drive C:\ and redirects the output to a temporary file. Then the script reads the temporary file and removes the header with the volume name. Then it strips the date and time columns from the directory listing. The result (including the two summary lines) is shown in a dialog box.

This simple script demonstrates a few new techniques. First it creates a temporary file in the system's temporary folder using the methods of the *FileSystemObject* object:

```
Set fso = CreateObject("Scripting.FileSystemObject")
tmp = fso.GetTempName
```

The variable *tmp* contains a name for a temporary file that is generated by the operating system. Next you find the path of the folder that the operating system uses to store temporary files. You retrieve the location of this folder using the *GetSpecialFolder* method:

```
path = fso.GetSpecialFolder(tmpFolder)
```

The *tmpFolder* parameter must be set to the constant value *2*.

NOTE A value of *0* for the *tmpFolder* parameter returns the path to the Windows folder. The value *1* returns the location of the system folder. In previous chapters, I mentioned that the system folder depends on the operating system. Windows 95 and Windows 98 have the \System folder, and Windows NT and Windows 2000 use \System32. Therefore, you can use *GetSpecialFolder* with a value of *1* to retrieve the location and name of the system folder independent of the operating system.

After retrieving the path of the temporary folder, you can create the absolute path of the temporary file:

```
tmp = path & "\" & tmp
```

The following two statements shell a *dir* command, which creates a temporary file containing the results of the command:

```
Set WshShell = CreateObject("WScript.Shell")
WSHShell.Run "%comspec% /c " & cmd & " >" & tmp, 0, True
```

The variable *%comspec%* contains the name of the command processor. The second parameter is set to *0* (normal window size), and the third parameter is set to *True* to force the script to pause until the command terminates.

The following command opens the temporary file and returns a *TextStream* object associated with the file:

```
Set oFile = fso.OpenTextFile(tmp)
```

You can then use the following loop to skip the first four lines:

```
For i = 1 to 4
    oFile.SkipLine
Next
```

The next statement reads the rest of the temporary file into the string variable *txt*:

```
txt = oFile.ReadAll
```

After the temporary file is read, you can close and delete it using the following commands:

```
oFile.Close
fso.DeleteFile tmp
```

The variable *txt* contains the file's content in a single string. If you want to process this content line by line, you can use the *Split* function:

```
lines = Split(txt, vbCrLf)
```

This function splits the string into an array, using the separator given as a second parameter. You can then access the lines using the array elements *lines(0)*, *lines(1)*, and so on.

Next you can join the array into a single string using the following command:

```
txt = Join(lines, vbCrLf)
```

The *Join* function adds the pattern submitted in the second parameter to each line and stores the result to a string. The entire VBScript sample is shown in Listing 14-10. The script shows two dialog boxes, the first containing the original output of the *dir* command and the second showing the filtered data (with the time and date stripped off).

```
'*****************************************************
' File:    Pipe.vbs (WSH 2 sample in VBScript)
' Author:  (c) G. Born
'
' Exchanging data between MS-DOS
' commands and a script using temporary files
'*****************************************************
Option Explicit
```

Listing 14-10 *Pipe.vbs*   *(continued)*

Listing 14-10 *continued*

```vbscript
Const cmd = "dir c:\*.* /ON"    ' Command to be executed
Const tmpFolder = 2          ' System's temp folder

Dim WshShell, fso, oFile, tmp, path, txt, lines, i

' Create a FileSystemObject.
Set fso = CreateObject("Scripting.FileSystemObject")

' Retrieve a temporary filename.
tmp = fso.GetTempName

' Retrieve the path to the temporary system folder.
path = fso.GetSpecialFolder(tmpFolder)
tmp = path & "\" & tmp        ' Create temporary file path.

' Now we have a temporary file. Create a WshShell object...
Set WshShell = CreateObject("WScript.Shell")
' ...and shell an MS-DOS command that redirects
' the output to the temporary file.
WSHShell.Run "%comspec% /c " & cmd & " >" & tmp, 0, True

' The MS-DOS command is finished. A temporary file
' now exists containing the output of the dir command.
' Read the file's content.
Set oFile = fso.OpenTextFile(tmp)

' Skip the first lines.
For i = 1 to 4
    oFile.SkipLine
Next
txt = oFile.ReadAll               ' The rest of the file
oFile.Close
fso.DeleteFile tmp                ' Delete temp file.

WScript.Echo txt      ' Show content.
' Here we can try to process the content.
' First, split all lines into an array.
lines = Split(txt, vbCrLf)
' Ignore the last 2 lines.
For i = 1 to UBound(lines) - 3
    lines(i) = Mid(lines(i), 40) ' Split off the date and time.
Next

' Join the array data into one string and show it.
MsgBox Join(lines, vbCrLf)

'*** End
```

Logging Script Output

To log the script output to a file, you can use the *LogEvent* method of the *WshShell* object (provided in WSH 2). This method appends the data to a log file. In Windows NT and Windows 2000, the entry goes into the system's log file; you can view it using the Event Viewer (Figure 14-5).

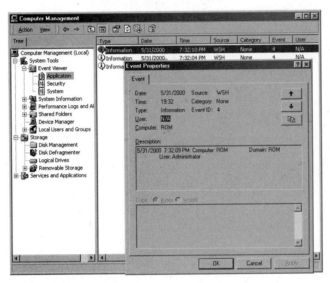

Figure 14-5 *Viewing a log entry in the Event Viewer*

In Windows 95 and Windows 98, the event is appended to the file WSH.log, which is in the user's Windows folder. The entry is written as a record with a date/time stamp, the event type, and the text submitted to the *LogEvent* method. To call this method, you can use the following code:

```
Set WshShell = WScript.CreateObject("WScript.Shell")
flag = WshShell.LogEvent(INFORMATION, Text)
```

The *LogEvent* method of the *WScript.Shell* object requires two parameters. The first parameter defines the event type and has a value between 0 and 16. The second parameter contains the text to be appended to the log file. If the method succeeds, the value *True* is returned; otherwise, *False* is returned.

Let's look at a small VBScript program that records the date, time, computer name, domain name, and user name to a log file each time a user logs on to the machine. It first collects the information that will go into the log file. The information requested is contained in the properties of the *WshNetwork* object, so you can create a text variable that contains the necessary data:

```
Text = Date & "  " & Time & ": Computer: " & _
       WshNetwork.ComputerName & vbTab
Text = Text & "Domain: " & _
       WshNetwork.UserDomain & vbTab

User = WshNetwork.UserName       ' Initialize value.
Do While User = ""               ' Loop until user name is returned.
    WScript.Sleep 200            ' Suspend to lower CPU load.
    User = WshNetwork.UserName    ' Read property.
Loop

Text = Text & "User: " & User & vbTab
```

Because this sample makes sense only in a Windows 95 or Windows 98 system (Windows NT and Windows 2000 record user logins by default), I used the technique mentioned in Chapter 11 to wait until the *UserName* property returns a valid name. You can write this string to a log file by using the following code:

```
WshShell.LogEvent INFORMATION, Text
```

This call doesn't return any value because we're using a procedure call. So how do you force Windows 95 or Windows 98 to execute this script each time a user logs on? You add a command that consists of the script's path and filename to the value *UserLog* of the following Registry key:

```
HKLM\Software\Microsoft\Windows\CurrentVersion\Run
```

The content of this key is processed each time a user logs on. Listing 14-11 shows a script that adds the command to the *Run* key during each execution. The user must launch the script only once to force automatic execution. To remove the entry from the Registry, you can use the System Policy Editor, the Registry Editor, or (in Windows 98) the System Configuration Utility.

```
'**************************************************************
' File:    UserLog.vbs (WSH 2 sample in VBScript)
' Author:  (c) G. Born
'
' Writing the user name using the WSH 2 LogEvent method.
' The script is added to the Run key, so it's handy
' to establish a user log function in Windows 95
' and Windows 98.
'**************************************************************
Option Explicit
```

Listing 14-11 *UserLog.vbs*

```
Const SUCCESS = 0
Const ERROR = 1
Const WARNING = 2
Const INFORMATION = 4
Const AUDIT_SUCCESS = 8
Const AUDIT_FAILURE = 16

Dim Text, User
Dim WshNetwork, WshShell            ' Object variable

' Create reference to the WshShell object.
' (needed for Registry access and EventLog method).
Set WshShell = WScript.CreateObject("WScript.Shell")

' Add script to Run key so that it will
' be executed at each logon.
AddRun

' Create a new WshNetwork object to access network properties.
Set WshNetwork = WScript.CreateObject("WScript.Network")

Text = Date & "  " & Time & ": Computer: " & _
     WshNetwork.ComputerName & vbTab
Text = Text & "Domain: " & _
     WshNetwork.UserDomain & vbTab

User = WshNetwork.UserName        ' Initialize value.
Do While User = ""                ' Loop until user name is returned.
   WScript.Sleep 200              ' Suspend to lower CPU load.
   User = WshNetwork.UserName     ' Read property.
Loop

Text = Text & "User: " & User & vbTab

' Write log file entry. Returns True (success) or False (failed).
If WshShell.LogEvent(INFORMATION, Text) Then
   ' Remove for silent use.
   WScript.Echo "Log Event written" & vbCrLf & Text  ' Show result.
Else
   WScript.Echo "LogEvent method failed in UserLog.vbs"
End If

Sub AddRun()
   ' Add the batch file for launching the script to the
   ' Registry's Run key.
   Dim Command
```

(continued)

445

Listing 14-11 *continued*

```
    Const Root = "HKEY_LOCAL_MACHINE"
    Const key = "\Software\Microsoft\Windows\CurrentVersion\Run\"
    Const valname = "UserLog"

    Command = WScript.ScriptFullName

    WshShell.RegWrite Root & Key & valname, Command, "REG_SZ"
End Sub

'*** End
```

Printing from a WSH Script

WSH has no printing support because printing isn't a simple task in Windows. The only way to print from a script is to force an application to do the job for you. To print a plain text file, you can use Notepad.exe. Notepad supports the /p switch, which allows you to print a text file and then close the editor after printing, as shown here:

```
Notepad /p C:\Test\Text.txt
```

The command forces Windows to load Notepad and submit the parameters of the command line. If Notepad finds a filename in the command line, it tries to load that file. If it detects the /p switch, it sends the file to the default printer. After printing, Notepad quits.

The following code snippet, taken from PrintTxt.vbs, uses this technique to print the source code of the script:

```
Set oWshShell = WScript.CreateObject("WScript.Shell")

' Shell out a command to print using Notepad.
oWshShell.Run "Notepad /p " & WScript.ScriptFullName, 7, True
```

The first line creates an object instance of the *WshShell* object, which is required for the *Run* method. The second statement shells out a command to launch Notepad and print the specified text file. The statement uses the *ScriptFullName* property to insert the script's filename. The second parameter submitted to the *Run* method is set to 7 to force Notepad to run in a minimized window. The last parameter is set to *True* to tell the script to wait until the process launched from the *Run* method terminates.

This solution works well for plain text files, but you can't use it to change the printer. To invoke the Print dialog box (in Windows 2000) so that the user can select a printer and set printer options, you can use this code snippet:

```
Set oWshShell = WScript.CreateObject("WScript.Shell")

' Shell out a command to print source with MSHTML.
oWshShell.Run "RunDll32.exe MSHTML.dll,PrintHTML " & _
              WScript.ScriptFullName, 7, True

' Shell out a command to print HTML documents with MSHTML.
oWshShell.Run "RunDll32.exe MSHTML.dll,PrintHTML " & _
              GetPath() & "TestForm.htm", 7, True
```

The first statement creates the object instance required for the *Run* method. The next two statements execute the *Run* method. The first statement prints the script's source code, and the second prints an HTML document. Both statements use RunDll32.exe to call a helper DLL. The library MSHTML.dll exports several functions that you can use from external programs. One function is *PrintHTML*. (Note the case-sensitive name.) This API function reads a parameter from the command line that contains the document filename. After the function is invoked, the Print dialog box is displayed. The user can select a printer, set the printer options, and print the document.

> **NOTE** The PrintDocs.vbs sample allows you to print text files, HTML documents, and documents in .rtf format. MSHTML can't print other formats, such as .gif graphics and .pdf files. To print Microsoft Office documents, you can use the Office applications. These applications don't support a */p* switch, but they support a COM interface, so you can access the objects and methods instead. All Office applications contain methods for printing a document. I've also written an ActiveX control that provides methods for printing documents using the Windows shell. (For more details, see *Advanced Development with Microsoft Windows Script Host 2.0*.)

FILE HANDLING

In this section, I'll describe a few programming techniques that you'll find useful for handling files and folders.

Checking Whether a File or Folder Exists

To check whether a file exists, you can use the *FileExists* method of the *FileSystemObject* object:

```
Set fso = CreateObject("Scripting.FileSystemObject")
If (fso.FileExists("C:\Autoexec.bat") Then
    ⋮
```

If the file exists, *FileExists* returns the value *True*.

You can check for the presence of a folder by using the *FolderExists* method:

```
Set fso = WScript.CreateObject("Scripting.FileSystemObject")
If (fso.FolderExists(path)) Then
    ⋮
```

For more information, see the section "Accessing Files and Folders" in Chapter 12.

Checking Whether a Folder is Empty

To check whether a folder is empty, you can use the following code sequence:

```
Function FolderEmpty(path)
    ' Check for an empty folder.
    Dim fso, oFolder, oFiles        ' Object variables
    Dim i, flag

    Set fso = CreateObject("Scripting.FileSystemObject")
    Set oFolder = fso.GetFolder(path)   ' Get folder.
    Set oFiles = oFolder.Files          ' Get Files collection.

    flag = True                     ' No files
    For Each i in oFiles            ' A file has been found if
        flag = false                ' the loop is processed.
        Exit For
    Next

    FolderEmpty = flag              ' Return result.
End Function
```

If the folder is empty, *FolderEmpty* returns the value *True*. For more information, see the section titled "Accessing Files and Folders" in Chapter 12.

Checking Whether an Access Database Is in Use

To access a Microsoft Access database and ensure that the .mdb file isn't open in another Access session, you can use the test for an existing file. When Access 97 opens a database, it automatically produces an .ldb file. This file disappears as soon as Access releases the database. You can check for the existence of an .ldb file to determine whether the database is already in use. The program in Listing 14-12 checks whether an .mdb file is available in the folder and then checks whether the .ldb file exists. It displays the result in a dialog box.

```
'*****************************************************
' File:    MDBOpen.vbs (WSH sample in VBScript)
' Author:  (c) G. Born
'
' Checking whether an Access 97 database is in use
'*****************************************************
Option Explicit

Dim fso, path, txt

' Get path to database file.
' Must be stored here in the script's folder.
path = WScript.ScriptFullName
path = Left(path, InStrRev(path, "\"))

txt = "Database file doesn't exist"
Set fso = WScript.CreateObject("Scripting.FileSystemObject")

If (fso.FileExists(path & "Test1.mdb")) Then ' Exists?
    If (fso.FileExists(path & "Test1.ldb")) Then
        txt = "Database locked by Access"
    Else
        txt = "Database not locked"
    End If
End If

WScript.Echo txt

'*** End
```

Listing 14-12 *MDBOpen.vbs*

> **NOTE** You should copy both MDBOpen.vbs and the Access 97 database Test1.mdb from the \WSHDevGuide\Chapter14 folder to a local folder to conduct the test. This test also works with Access 2000.

Copying a File

You use the *File* object to copy a file. After you create the *FileSystemObject* object, you can access the file by using the *GetFile* method and the *Copy* method, as shown here:

```
Set fso = CreateObject("Scripting.FileSystemObject")
Set fi = fso.GetFile(file1)      ' Create file object.
fi.Copy file2                    ' Copy file1 to file2.
```

> **NOTE** For more information about files and folders, see Chapter 12.

Renaming a File or Folder

You can use the *File* object to rename a file by using the following code:

```
Set fso = CreateObject("Scripting.FileSystemObject")
Set oFile = fso.GetFile("C:\Test.txt") ' Create File object.
oFile.Name = "Test1.txt"                ' Assign a new name.
```

After the *File* object is retrieved, the *Name* attribute is set to the new name.

You can rename a folder in a similar way:

```
Set fso = CreateObject("Scripting.FileSystemObject")
Set oFolder = fso.GetFolder("C:\Test") ' Create Folder object.
oFolder.Name = "Test1"                 ' Assign a new name.
```

After the *Folder* object is retrieved, the *Name* attribute is set to the new name. Alternatively, you can use the *Move* method of the *FileSystemObject* object, as shown in the VBScript sample in Listing 14-13. This sample converts the name of a given file system object to lowercase. The user can drag files or folders to the LCase.vbs file. All dragged file system objects are then shown in lowercase.

```
'*********************************************************
' File:    LCase.vbs (WSH sample in VBScript)
' Author:  (c) G. Born
'
' Converting the names of folders or files to lower
' case. The script supports drag and drop.
'*********************************************************
Option Explicit

' Set the case direction for the module. Changing
' the value of xCase to false forces the script to convert
' to lowercase.
'Const xCase = True  ' We want to convert to uppercase.
Const xCase = False ' We want to convert to lowercase.
Const Title = "Lowercase converter - by G. Born"

Dim objArgs, param, i

' Try to retrieve the arguments.
Set objArgs = WScript.Arguments     ' Create object.
If objArgs.Count < 1 Then  ' No argument at all. Quit with a dialog box.
    MsgBox "Sorry, no arguments found!" & vbCRLF & _
           "Please drag file(s) or folder(s) to the script's icon.", _
           vbInformation + vbOKOnly, Title
    WScript.Quit  ' Quit script!!!
End If
```

Listing 14-13 *LCase.vbs*

```
i = 0
' Try to convert the file to lowercase; count each action.
For Each param In objArgs
    If MakeCase(param, xCase) Then i = i + 1
Next

MsgBox i & " object(s) converted", vbInformation + vbOKOnly, Title

Function MakeCase(file, caseFlag)
    Dim fso, oFile, path, name
    Set fso = CreateObject("Scripting.FileSystemObject")

    If fso.FileExists(file) Then
        Set oFile = fso.GetFile(file)
    Else
        If fso.FolderExists(file) Then
            Set oFile = fso.GetFolder(file)
        Else
            MakeCase = False    ' No file system object
            Exit Function
        End If
    End If

    name = fso.GetFileName(file)
    path = fso.GetParentFolderName(file)

    If caseFlag Then
        oFile.Move path & "\" & UCase(name)
    Else
        oFile.Move path & "\" & LCase(name)
    End If
    Set fso = Nothing
    MakeCase = True
End Function

'*** End
```

NOTE   You can convert LCase.vbs to create uppercase file or folder names. You simply change the value for *xCase* from *False* to *True*. For more information about files and folders, see Chapter 12.

Searching for a File

To search for a file, you can use the *FileSystemObject* object and its subobjects and methods to retrieve a folder and its subfolders. You must hand-write code to process the folder's content and search for the requested files. To retrieve a list of the occurrences of a given file, use the *Run* method to execute the MS-DOS *DIR* command, as shown here:

```
DIR filename /s > List.txt
```

You can then access the List.txt file by using the *TextStream* object and its methods.

Listing All Shortcut Files

I've created a small VBScript program to get the names and locations of all shortcut (.lnk) files contained in the special folders (Desktop, Start menu, and so on). It retrieves the names of the special folders by using the *SpecialFolders* property that returns a collection object. You can use the items in this collection object to retrieve the *Files* collection contained in the folder.

To check whether a file is a shortcut, you can use the following statement:

```
InStrRev(UCase(name), ".LNK")
```

The function returns the value *<> 0* if the filename extension is .lnk. The program in Listing 14-14 searches the special folders for .lnk files and lists the results in a browser window (Figure 14-6).

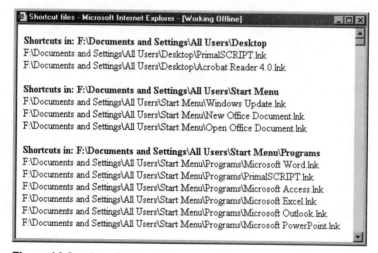

Figure 14-6 *A list of shortcut files*

```vbscript
'****************************************************
' File:    ListShortcuts.vbs (WSH sample in VBScript)
' Author: (c) G. Born
'
' Listing all shortcut files in the special folders
'****************************************************
Option Explicit

Const Title = "Shortcut files"
Dim WshShell
Dim fso, fi, fc, f
Dim text, sysf, fldr

set WshShell = WScript.CreateObject("WScript.Shell")

set fso = WScript.CreateObject("Scripting.FileSystemObject")

text = ""
For Each sysf in WshShell.SpecialFolders
    text = text & "<b>Shortcuts in: " & sysf & "</b><br>"
    Set fldr = fso.getfolder(sysf)
    Set fc = fldr.files
    For Each f In fc
        If IsLnk(f) Then text = text &  f & "<br>"
    Next
    text = text & "<br>"
Next

ShowMSIE text, Title     ' Show item list in browser window.

' Helper function
Function IsLnk(name)
    ' Check whether file is an .lnk file.
    IsLnk = (InStrRev(UCase(name), ".LNK") <> 0)
End Function

Sub ShowMSIE(txt, title)
    Dim oIE, oDoc
    ' Create Internet Explorer Application object.
    Set oIE = WScript.CreateObject("InternetExplorer.Application")
    ' Set browser window properties.
    oIE.left = 20            ' Window position
    oIE.top = 50             ' and other properties
    oIE.height = 380
    oIE.width = 580
```

Listing 14-14 *ListShortcuts.vbs*   *(continued)*

Listing 14-14 *continued*

```
        oIE.menubar = 0                 ' No menu
        oIE.toolbar = 0
        oIE.statusbar = 0
        oIE.navigate("about:blank")     ' Create an empty HTML document.
        oIE.visible = 1                 ' Keep Internet Explorer visible.

        Do While(oIE.Busy): Loop        ' Important: Wait until Internet
                                        ' Explorer is ready.

        Set oDoc = oIE.Document         ' Get Document object.
        oDoc.open                       ' Open document.
                                        ' Write script to the document object.
        oDoc.writeln("<html><head><title>" & title & "</title></head>")
        oDoc.writeln("<body>" & txt & "</body></html>")
        oDoc.close                      ' Close document for write access.
End Sub

'*** End
```

PLAYING SOUND

WSH doesn't support the playing of sound files. In *Advanced Development with Microsoft Windows Script Host 2.0,* I introduce some methods implemented in an ActiveX control for playing sound. However, there are a few other ways that you can play sound in a WSH script. One common approach is to use the Windows ActiveMovie Player. This player installs an ActiveX control called Amovie.ocx that you can use as follows:

```
Set oWSH = WScript.CreateObject("WScript.Shell")
oWSH.Run "RunDll32.exe %WINDIR%\System\Amovie.ocx,RunDll " _
        & "/play /close C:\Test\Sound.wav"
```

The second command shells out a *RunDll32* call that invokes the ActiveMovie Player. The parameters submitted in the command line force the player to play the sound file and close the window automatically.

Amovie.ocx doesn't ship with Windows 2000. Instead, Windows 2000 comes with the file Msdxm.ocx, which does the same thing. So you can use the following command:

```
Set oWSH = WScript.CreateObject("WScript.Shell")
oWSH.Run "RunDll32.exe %WINDIR%\System32\Msdxm.ocx,RunDll " _
        & "/play /close C:\Test\Sound.wav"
```

This command invokes Windows Media Player and plays the specified media file (sound or movie). Note that the .ocx file is located in the \System32 folder in Windows 2000 and in the \System subfolder in Windows 98.

The VBScript sample in Listing 14-15 uses the *GetSpecialFolder* method of the *FileSystemObject* object to retrieve the path to the Windows system folder. It then plays a .wav file.

```
'***************************************************
' File:    PlaySound.vbs (WSH sample in VBScript)
' Author:  (c) G. Born
'
' Playing sound using Msdxm.ocx
'***************************************************
Option Explicit

Dim fso, oWSH
Set fso = WScript.CreateObject("Scripting.FileSystemObject")
Set oWSH = WScript.CreateObject("WScript.Shell")

oWSH.Run "RunDll32.exe " & fso.GetSpecialFolder(1) & _
         "\Msdxm.ocx,RunDll " & _
         "/play /close " & _
         "C:\WSHDevGuide\Chapter14\The Microsoft Sound.wav"

'*** End
```

Listing 14-15 *PlaySound.vbs*

Using Internet Explorer to Play Sound

You can also use Internet Explorer to play a sound file independent of the platform. The sound file is contained in an HTML file and plays in the background as the HTML file loads. The code to process such a sound file is shown here:

```
<html>
    <head>
        <bgsound src="The Microsoft Sound.wav" loop="1">
    </head>
    <body>
    </body>
</html>
```

The *<bgsound>* tag plays a background sound. The sound file is specified in the *src* attribute. To use a script to launch the browser, load the HTML code, and play the sound file, you use the following code:

```
Set oIE = WScript.CreateObject("InternetExplorer.Application")
oIE.Navigate GetPath() & "Sound.htm"  ' HTML page with sound
```

The browser window remains invisible because you don't need it. (*oIE.Visible = 0* is the default setting.) Therefore, you need not set the properties for browser window size and style. The two code lines shown previously are sufficient.

There's just one problem: the script must close the browser, but the browser runs as an independent process, so the script doesn't know when the sound file has been played. In Chapter 13, you learned how to use the *Sleep* method to suspend the script for a given amount of time. You can use this technique to pause the script, during which time Internet Explorer is assumed to have played the sound file. When the script resumes execution, it can call the *Quit* method to terminate the browser. However, if you use the *Sleep* method, the user can't stop playing the sound.

A better solution uses the *Popup* method:

```
oWSH.Popup "Hello, world", 10
```

The second parameter forces *Popup* to close the dialog box after 10 seconds. An open dialog box also suspends script execution, so the program incurs no CPU load during that time.

If the user doesn't want to listen to the sound, he or she can click the OK button to close the dialog box. This causes the script to call the browser's *Quit* method, as shown below, which interrupts the playing of the sound and terminates the browser.

```
oIE.Quit
```

The small VBScript program in Listing 14-16 launches Internet Explorer, loads the Sound.htm file, and suspends script execution for a specified time period. The browser window remains hidden; the user sees only two dialog boxes, one that delays the script and one that reports the end of the program.

```
'****************************************************
' File:    PlaySound1.vbs (WSH sample in VBScript)
' Author:  (c) G. Born
'
' Using Internet Explorer 4 or 5 to play a sound
' file and suspending the script using the Popup
' method
'****************************************************
Option Explicit

Const delay = 10      ' Suspend time in seconds

Dim oIE, oWSH         ' Declare variables.
Dim path
```

Listing 14-16 *PlaySound1.vbs*

```
' Create WshShell object reference (for Popup).
Set oWSH = WScript.CreateObject("WScript.Shell")

' Launch Internet Explorer.
Set oIE = WScript.CreateObject("InternetExplorer.Application")
oIE.Navigate GetPath() & "Sound.htm"  ' HTML page with sound
oIE.Visible = 0          ' Keep invisible.

' Important: Wait until IE is ready.
 Do While (oIE.Busy): Loop

' Delay until the sound is played.
oWSH.Popup "Script suspended for " & delay & " seconds" _
          & vbCrLf & "because we're playing sound." & vbCrLf & _
          "Click OK to cancel sound", delay, _
          "Sound demo", vbInformation + vbSystemModal

oIE.Quit                 ' Close Internet Explorer.

MsgBox "Finished playing sound", vbInformation + vbSystemModal

' Helper function
Function GetPath()
    ' Retrieve script path.
    Dim path
    path = WScript.ScriptFullName
    GetPath = Left(path, InStrRev(path, "\"))
End Function

'*** End
```

THE WINDOWS SHELL

If Internet Explorer 4 or later is installed on your machine, you can access a few functions of the Windows shell. In this section, I'll demonstrate a few neat tricks for using the Windows *Shell* object from a script.

> **NOTE**   The upcoming samples require the Windows shell version 4.71 or later. Version 4.71 is installed with Internet Explorer 4 if the Active Desktop feature is present. Windows 98 comes with Windows shell version 4.72, and Windows 2000 uses version 5. Only users of Windows 95 and Windows NT 4 must check whether Shell32.dll contains the right version. Note that installing Internet Explorer 5 on a machine doesn't update the shell. You must install Internet Explorer 4 with the Active Desktop feature and then upgrade to Internet Explorer 5.

Testing the Shell Version

To test whether your Windows shell is the right version, you can use the small VBScript program in Listing 14-17. The program requires WSH 2. The paths to Shell32.dll are set for Windows NT or Windows 2000. To use the script in Windows 95 or Windows 98, you must uncomment the second statement, which sets the path for Windows 95 and Windows 98.

```
'************************************************************
' File:   GetShellVersion.vbs (WSH 2 sample in VBScript)
' Author: (c) G. Born
'
' Retrieving the file version of the Shell32.dll
' library file
'************************************************************
Option Explicit

Dim fso, oShell              ' Object variables
Dim file, tmp                ' Filename

' Retrieve path to Shell32.dll.
' In Windows NT and Windows 2000, the file is located in
file = "%WINDIR%\System32\Shell32.dll"
' In Windows 95 and Windows 98, the file is located in
'file = "%WINDIR%\System\Shell32.dll"

Set oShell = WScript.CreateObject("WScript.Shell")
file = oShell.ExpandEnvironmentStrings(file)

' Create FileSystemObject object to access the file system.
Set fso = CreateObject("Scripting.FileSystemObject")

' Check whether file exists.
If fso.FileExists(file) Then
    tmp = fso.GetFileVersion(file)     ' Retrieve version.
    If Len(tmp) > 0 Then
        WScript.Echo "File " & file & vbCrLf & _
                     "Version: " & tmp
    Else
        WScript.Echo "File " & file & vbCrLf & _
                     "Version: undefined"
    End if
```

Listing 14-17 *GetShellVersion.vbs*

```
Else
    WScript.Echo "File '" & file & "' not found"
End If

'*** End
```

Arranging the Desktop Windows

If you've ever customized your Desktop to put shortcut menu items such as Minimize All and Tile Windows Horizontally on your taskbar, you know that doing so can be handy—for example, to minimize all open folder windows after a system start. To automate this task using a WSH script, you can use several objects, methods, and properties of the Windows shell.

You first create the *Application* object by using the following statement:

```
Set Shell = WScript.CreateObject("Shell.Application")
```

This object provides the following methods to manipulate windows on your Desktop:

- **MinimizeAll** Minimizes all open windows on your Desktop and shows them as buttons on the taskbar.

- **UndoMinimizeAll** Undoes the last action. Minimized windows are returned to their previous state.

- **TileHorizontally** Tiles all open windows horizontally on the Desktop.

- **TileVertically** Tiles all open windows vertically on the Desktop.

- **CascadeWindows** Cascades all open windows on the Desktop.

The VBScript program in Listing 14-18 shows several dialog boxes that ask the user whether to minimize or tile horizontally or vertically the Desktop windows (Figure 14-7). The script provides an undo function for each step, so you can test how the methods work.

To undo the most recent action, you can use a trick. After arranging the windows by using the *TileVertically* method, for example, you can undo this step by using the *UndoMinimizeAll* method (even though the name suggests a different action).

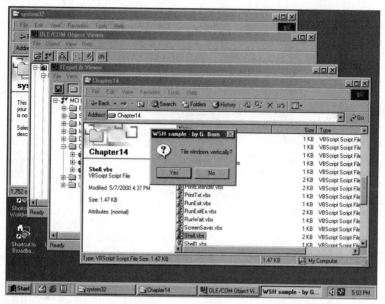

Figure 14-7 *Manipulating Desktop windows using a WSH script*

```
'**************************************************
' File:    Shell.vbs (WSH sample in VBScript)
' Author:  (c) G. Born
'
' Accessing the Windows shell from a WSH script and
' minimizing and aligning horizontally/vertically
' the windows on the Desktop
'**************************************************
Option Explicit

Dim Shell, Title

Title = "WSH sample - by G. Born"

' Create Shell object.
Set Shell = WScript.CreateObject("Shell.Application")

If (MsgBox("Minimize all windows?", _
           vbYesNo + vbQuestion, Title) = vbYes) Then
    Shell.MinimizeAll          ' MinimizeAll method
    WScript.Echo "Undo minimize all. "
    Shell.UndoMinimizeAll      ' Restore windows.
End If
```

Listing 14-18 *Shell.vbs*

```
If (MsgBox("Tile windows vertically?", _
           vbYesNo + vbQuestion, Title) = vbYes) Then
    Shell.TileVertically        ' Vertically
    WScript.Echo "Undo tile vertically."
    Shell.UndoMinimizeAll        ' Restore windows.
End If

If (MsgBox("Tile windows horizontally?", _
           vbYesNo + vbQuestion, Title) = vbYes) Then
    Shell.TileHorizontally
    WScript.Echo "Undo tile horizontally."
    Shell.UndoMinimizeAll          ' Restore windows.
End If

If (MsgBox("Cascade all windows?", _
           vbYesNo + vbQuestion, Title) = vbYes) Then
    Shell.CascadeWindows
    WScript.Echo "Undo cascade windows."
    Shell.UndoMinimizeAll           ' Restore windows.
End If

WScript.Echo "Ready?"

'*** End
```

Opening Folder Windows

You can use the *Run* method to launch Windows Explorer and browse a folder window. Alternatively, you can use the *Open* and *Explore* methods of the *Shell* object from a script to open a folder in Shell mode (single pane) or Explorer mode (two panes). Both methods require the path to the requested folder as an argument. The sample in Listing 14-19 uses these methods to open the Windows folder in Windows Explorer and then open the \System subfolder as a folder window (in Shell mode).

```
'*************************************************
' File:    Shell1.vbs (WSH sample in VBScript)
' Author:  (c) G. Born
'
' Accessing the Windows shell and opening a
' folder window
'*************************************************
Option Explicit
```

Listing 14-19 *Shell1.vbs*

(continued)

Listing 14-19 *continued*

```
Dim Shell, wsh, Title, path

Title = "WSH sample - by G. Born"

' Create WshShell object.
Set wsh = WScript.CreateObject ("WScript.Shell")

' Windows directory
path = wsh.ExpandEnvironmentStrings("%WINDIR%")

' Create Windows shell Application object.
Set Shell = WScript.CreateObject ("Shell.Application")

' Open a folder in the Explorer window.
WScript.Echo "Windows Explorer folder"

' This runs Explorer with the folder tree rooted at the path specified
' (same as wsh.Run "explorer.exe /e,/root," & path).
Shell.Explore path

' Show folder in a shell window.
WScript.Echo "Open Windows folder \System"
Shell.Open path & "\System"

WScript.Echo "Ready?"

'*** End
```

Accessing Windows Shell Dialog Boxes

The Windows shell comes with some integrated dialog boxes, including the Run, Find, and Date/Time dialog boxes, that you can invoke using the taskbar and the Start menu. The shell also provides an Automation interface that you can use from a script. The following command retrieves an object instance of the shell:

```
Set oShell = WScript.CreateObject("Shell.Application")
```

You use methods of the Windows *Shell* object to invoke these dialog boxes or open the Control Panel folder and the property sheets in Control Panel. You can access Control Panel by using the *ControlPanelItem* method:

```
oShell.ControlPanelItem
```

You can submit the name of the requested module (such as Desk.cpl) as a parameter to this method. If you submit an empty string or nothing, the Control Panel folder is opened.

To open the Run dialog box, for example, you simply apply the *FileRun* method to the Windows *Shell* object. The following statement opens the Run dialog box and displays the last command entered:

```
oShell.FileRun
```

To invoke the Find dialog box to search for files and folders, you use this method:

```
oShell.FindFiles
```

To invoke the dialog box to search for a computer, you use this method:

```
oShell.FindComputer
```

If you need the property page to set the current date and time, you use the *SetTime* method:

```
oShell.SetTime
```

I already mentioned several techniques for shutting down Windows 95 or Windows 98. The *Shell* object also has two methods that suspend the PC (activate energy-saving mode) or shut down Windows. The following command initiates Windows *Suspend* mode. (The effect of the *Suspend* method depends on your machine and environment.)

```
oShell.Suspend
```

You can invoke the Shut Down Windows dialog box (Figure 14-8) by using the following command:

```
Shell.ShutdownWindows
```

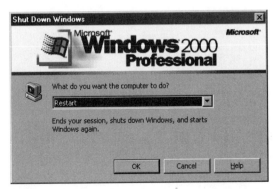

Figure 14-8 *The Shut Down Windows dialog box*

The VBScript program in Listing 14-20 shows several of the dialog boxes just mentioned.

```
'****************************************************
' File:    Shell2.vbs (WSH sample in VBScript)
' Author:  (c) G. Born
'
' Accessing the Windows shell and invoking
' several dialog boxes
'****************************************************
Option Explicit

Dim Shell, wsh, Title, path

Title = "WSH sample - by G. Born"

' Create WshShell object.
Set wsh = WScript.CreateObject ("WScript.Shell")

' Create Windows shell Application object.
Set Shell = WScript.CreateObject ("Shell.Application")

' Invoke the Control Panel folder.
If (MsgBox("Open Control Panel?", _
         vbYesNo + vbQuestion, Title) = vbYes) Then
    Shell.ControlPanelItem ""  ' Without arguments
End If

' Now try to open the module Desk.cpl.
If (MsgBox("Show display properties?", _
         vbYesNo + vbQuestion, Title) = vbYes) Then
    Shell.ControlPanelItem "Desk.cpl"
End If

' Invoke Run dialog box.
If (MsgBox("Open Run dialog box?", _
         vbYesNo + vbQuestion, Title) = vbYes) Then
    Shell.FileRun
End If

' Invoke Search Files dialog box.
If (MsgBox("Open Find: All Files dialog box?", _
         vbYesNo + vbQuestion, Title) = vbYes) Then
    Shell.FindFiles
End If

' Invoke Search Computers dialog box.
If (MsgBox("Open Find: Computer dialog box?", _
         vbYesNo + vbQuestion, Title) = vbYes) Then
    Shell.FindComputer
End If
```

Listing 14-20 *Shell2.vbs*

```
' Invoke Date/Time property sheet.
If (MsgBox("Change date/time?", _
            vbYesNo + vbQuestion, Title) = vbYes) Then
    Shell.SetTime
End If

' Call Suspend method.
If (MsgBox("Suspend Windows?", _
            vbYesNo + vbQuestion, Title) = vbYes) Then
    Shell.Suspend
End If

' Invoke Shut Down Windows dialog box.
If (MsgBox("Open Shut Down Windows dialog box?", _
            vbYesNo + vbQuestion, Title) = vbYes) Then
    Shell.ShutdownWindows
End If

'*** End
```

CALLING A DUN CONNECTION

You can use a WSH script to start a dial-up networking (DUN) connection. WSH doesn't provide an object for direct access, so you must use a trick and call the DUN connection by using the *Run* method of the *Shell* object. You again have to execute RunDll32.exe by using the following Windows 95 or Windows 98 command:

```
%WINDIR%\RunDll32.exe rnaui.dll,RnaDial name
```

%WINDIR% is a placeholder for the Windows folder. The placeholder *name* stands for the requested entry in your DUN folder (*CS3 Connection*, for example). You can check the command by using the Run dialog box. (Choose Run from the Start menu.) The VBScript program shown in Listing 14-21 connects to DUN by using a CompuServe connection.

```
'************************************************
' File:    DUN.vbs (WSH sample in VBScript)
' Author:  (c) G. Born
'
' Invoking dial-up networking (DUN)
'************************************************
Option Explicit

Dim wsh
```

Listing 14-21 *DUN.vbs*   *(continued)*

Listing 14-21 *continued*

```
Set wsh = WScript.CreateObject("WScript.Shell")

wsh.Run "%WINDIR%\RunDll32.exe rnaui.dll,RnaDial CS3 Connection", _
        1, True

WScript.Echo "Ready"

'*** End
```

IMPORTANT   If you use DUN in Windows NT, the command to invoke the connection is a bit different. You create a shortcut to the DUN entry and then use the command *obj.Run "Rasphone.exe -t xxx", 1, True*, where *xxx* is the name of the shortcut file to the DUN entry.

For more control over DUN or the Dial-Up Networking Monitor in Windows NT (for example, to be able to hang up the phone), you can use ActiveX controls that provide objects and methods for accessing Remote Access Service (RAS) or Winsock/TCP/IP. Table 14-3 lists some Web sites from which you can download such ActiveX controls and samples.

Table 14-3   WEB SITES WITH ACTIVEX CONTROLS FOR ACCESSING RAS AND DUN

Web Site	Description
http://www.catalyst.com	Catalyst Development Corporation site. Offers SocketTools, an ActiveX control for Windows Sockets programming and information about TCP/IP programming.
http://www.voidpointer.com	Voidpointer, LLC site. Offers Script Driven Internet (SDI32), a tool for automating Internet-related tasks (such as FTP and e-mail) from a script.
http://cwashington.netreach.net	The download section of C. Washington's site. Contains ActiveX controls and samples for accessing RAS and DUN.
http://factory.glazier.co.nz	Factory Software Components site. Contains helpful ActiveX controls.
http://www.mvps.org/ccrp/	Common Controls Replacement Project site.

Part IV

Appendixes

Appendix A

WSH Resources on the Internet

The following Web sites offer useful information and tools related to Microsoft Windows Script Host (WSH) and script programming.

Address	Description
news://microsoft.public.scripting.wsh *news://microsoft.public.scripting.vbscript* *news://microsoft.public.scripting.jscript*	International newsgroups that deal with WSH, VBScript, and JScript.
msdn.microsoft.com/scripting	Microsoft's scripting Web site, which contains the latest version of WSH and WSH tools as well as documentation for WSH, JScript, VBScript, and much more. This is a must-visit site for script programmers.
www.windows-script.com	A site created by Ian Morrish that contains a WSH FAQ section, a download section, sample code, a discussion group, and more. This is another must-visit site for script programmers. Ian was one of the first contributors to the WSH newsgroups.

(continued)

continued

Address	Description
cwashington.netreach.net	A Win32 scripting page maintained by C. Washington, a frequent participant in WSH newsgroups. The site contains many scripts (in different programming languages) that you can download. This is also a must-visit site for script programmers.
www.borncity.de	The gateway to my WSH Bazaar, which contains samples, FAQs, tutorials on creating ActiveX controls, newsletters, and a list of links to other WSH-related sites.
www.sapien.com	The Web site of SAPIEN Technologies, Inc., which markets the script editor PrimalSCRIPT. You can download a trial version of PrimalSCRIPT from this site.

Appendix B

Script Security

Originally, Microsoft Windows Script Host (WSH) didn't include any mechanism for preventing the execution of WSH scripts from untrusted sources. This led many users to mistakenly assume that you couldn't do anything to protect a system against infection from WSH script viruses. All 32-bit Microsoft Windows operating systems contain mechanisms (albeit not always foolproof or easy to use) to protect the system against accidental infection from e-mail attachments containing viruses. This appendix describes a few strategies for making WSH scripting more secure.

PARTIALLY DISABLING WSH

One solution for Microsoft Windows 95 and Windows 98 (smarter than uninstalling WSH) is to partially disable WSH so that default Windows settings can't be used from a virus to launch WScript.exe or CScript.exe. You can partially disable WSH by renaming WScript.exe and CScript.exe in the system folder (\System or \System32) to something like _CScript.exe and _WScript.exe. If a program tries to execute a .vbs or a .js file, the program fails with an error message stating that the executable isn't found because no EXE file is present.

The advantage of this approach is that an experienced user can still use WSH by explicitly executing a script, using a command such as this:

```
_WScript.exe <path>\script_file
```

As long as _WScript.exe exists and the path to the script file is valid, Windows launches the host and executes the script file.

> **WARNING** This trick works well in Windows 95 and Windows 98. However, in Windows 2000, after the first file is renamed, a dialog box appears, stating that an essential system file is missing and that you can repair the system from the Windows CD. (A copy of the original files is also located in the DLL cache.) In the following section, I describe a better way to protect WSH.

PREVENTING AUTOMATIC EXECUTION OF WSH SCRIPTS

Windows default settings for WSH allow execution of a WSH script file from the shell—that is, the Open command is set to activate the script when the script's file is double-clicked. Another way to prevent the accidental infection of your systems by WSH script viruses is to disable the default Open command. You change the Open action so that the command loads the source code into Notepad instead of executing the script using WSH. If the user accidentally chooses Open to view the attachment in an e-mail reader or in Internet Explorer after clicking a download entry, the script virus isn't executed. Instead, the source code is loaded into Notepad.

> **NOTE** If a user saves a virus-infected attachment and launches it manually, this strategy won't help. But this solution still greatly reduces the risk of accidental infection.

You implement this "redirection" by changing the Registry settings for .vbs, .vbe, .js, .jse, and .wsf file types. You can change these settings in two ways:

- To change the settings for one computer, use the File Types property page (covered later in this section).

- To use an automated procedure that customizes the settings on several computers, create a REG file (as described shortly) and import this file.

Now let's take a look at how the file-type associations are kept in the Registry. All settings for file-type associations are kept in the Registry branch *HKEY-_CLASSES_ROOT*. Each file type owns a key (for example, .vbs) that describes the file extension and a second key (for example, *VBSFile*) that hosts the association. We need to alter the values located in the keys *VBSFile*, *JSFile*, *JSEFile*, *VBEFile*, and *WSFFile*.

> **NOTE** WSH 1 supports only .vbs and .js file types, which have *VBSFile* and *JSFile* entries in the Registry.

The following content of a REG file makes the necessary changes for the .vbs file type (subkey *VBSFile*) in Windows 95 and Windows 98:

```
REGEDIT4

[HKEY_CLASSES_ROOT\VBSFile\Shell\Open\Command]
@="Notepad.exe \"%1\""

[HKEY_CLASSES_ROOT\VBSFile\Shell\Open2\Command]
@="Notepad.exe \"%1\""

[HKEY_CLASSES_ROOT\VBSFile\Shell\Execute]
@="&Execute"

[HKEY_CLASSES_ROOT\VBSFile\Shell\Execute\Command]
@="C:\\Windows\\WScript.exe \"%1\" %*"

[HKEY_CLASSES_ROOT\VBSFile\Shell\ExecuteDOS\Command]
@="C:\\Windows\\COMMAND\\CScript.exe \"%1\" %*"
```

After you import the REG file (double-click on the REG file, and click Yes in the dialog box that asks whether to import the file), the Open command is changed so that a double-click on a VBScript file opens the file in Notepad. To execute the file, right-click on the file and choose Execute from the context menu. The menu command ExecuteDOS executes the script using CScript.exe.

For .js files, you can use a similar REG file. The association is made in the subkey *JSFile*. You use the same code as just shown, but you change the *VBSFile* pattern to *JSFile* and save the result in a second REG file. You can deal with .wsf files in the same way. That file type uses the key *WSFFile* in the Registry, so you must change the *VBSFile* pattern to *WSFFile*.

> **NOTE** You can also use REG files to block associations for encoded versions of script files, which use the filename extensions .vbe and .jse. These file types use the entries *VBEFile* and *JSEFile*, respectively.

To restore the old settings, you can also use a REG file. The following code from a REG file restores the default settings for .vbs and removes the *Execute* and *ExecuteDOS* verbs from the *VBSFile* subkey:

```
REGEDIT4

[HKEY_CLASSES_ROOT\VBSFile\Shell\Open\Command]
@="C:\\WINDOWS\\WScript.exe \"%1\" %*"

[HKEY_CLASSES_ROOT\VBSFile\Shell\Open2\Command]
@="C:\\WINDOWS\\COMMAND\\CScript.exe \"%1\" %*"

[-HKEY_CLASSES_ROOT\VBSFile\Shell\Execute]

[-HKEY_CLASSES_ROOT\VBSFile\Shell\ExecuteDOS]
```

You can create similar REG files for .vbe, .js, .jse, and .wsf files in order to change the default WSH settings for Windows 95 and Windows 98.

> **NOTE**   The same REG file won't work on all platforms. For example, Windows NT 4 and Windows 2000 keep the WSH executables in the system folder \System32, whereas Windows 95 and Windows 98 store the executables in the Windows folder. Also, Windows NT 4 and Windows 2000 store strings in Unicode format; Windows 95 and Windows 98 store strings in ASCII format. Therefore, you must customize the REG files according to what platform is being used. I recommend using the technique I'll describe next for creating the REG files for Windows NT 4 and Windows 2000. Alternatively, you can write a script program that detects the Windows version and the WSH version and alters the necessary Registry settings. For more details about registering file types, see my book *Inside the Microsoft Windows 98 Registry* (Microsoft Press, 1998). The information in that book about registering file types applies to all 32-bit versions of Windows.

If you'd rather not use the REG files just described (or if you want to experiment a bit before you change your system settings or to customize the settings to export into REG files), choose the Folder Options command from the View menu or the Tools menu in a folder window. On the File Types property page, select an entry, such as VBScript Encoded Script File or VBScript Script File, and view the settings by clicking the Edit button (or the Advanced button in Windows 2000). The Edit File Type dialog box will show all the defined verbs for the file type. You can change the settings for the *Open* and *Open2* commands manually and add the old settings for *Open* and *Open2* as *Execute* and *ExecuteDOS*. (Chapter 2 discusses how to add an Edit command for a script file. Repeat the steps described there for other types of script files.)

After changing the settings for script file-type associations, you can fire up the Windows Registry editor Regedit.exe, search for a key (such as *HKEY_CLASSES_ROOT/ JSFile*), and export the key into a REG file by using the Export Registry File command in the Registry menu. Repeat this step for the other file types (such as *VBSFile*, *VBEFile*, *JSEFile*, and *WSFFile*). Then use Notepad to remove unused entries (according to the example shown earlier) and merge the final result of all REG files into one REG file. You can use that final file on other machines to import the Registry settings.

> **WARNING**   Some computer magazines and Web sites advocate removing WSH as a way to protect your system against infection from WSH script viruses. Although this technique is still possible in Windows 95, Windows 98, and Windows NT 4, such an extreme precaution isn't necessary. Furthermore, because WSH is an integral part of the operating system in Windows 2000 and Windows Millennium Edition (Me), stripping out WSH just isn't feasible. Neither do I recommend deleting files such as WScript.exe and CScript.exe in these environments—these are essential system files. Windows 2000 tries to repair the operating system if system files are corrupted or missing (as Windows Me does). Therefore, I recommend that you use one of the strategies described in this appendix.

SECURITY SETTINGS FOR WSH SCRIPTS

Infection of a system by a script virus is always the result of user laziness or ignorance. If users don't open e-mail attachments (and if mail programs are set up so that attachments aren't opened by default, even in preview mode), a virus can't spread. Unfortunately, many inexperienced users open all e-mail attachments that they receive. And most Windows systems are set up so that all security settings are off (which reminds me of some Linux users, who always run their system using *root* user rights).

A system administrator can prevent scripts from being executed without removing WSH. You can also specify that this behavior be valid only for certain users or for the whole system. This option is available in all 32-bit versions of Windows, but you must activate it. The way to block WSH scripts from executing differs a bit between operating systems.

In Windows 2000 and Windows NT 4, you can limit the right to execute a file to specific user groups, so you can block ordinary users from executing WSH EXE files by following these steps:

1. Log on as an administrator, and search for the files CScript.exe and WScript.exe (in the \System32 folder).

2. Right-click on each file, and choose Properties from the context menu.

3. Click on the Security property page (Figure B-1), click Everyone, and uncheck Read & Execute in the Allow column.

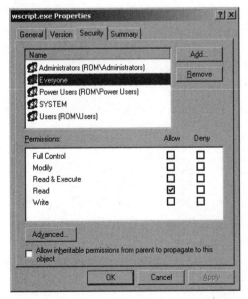

Figure B-1 *Security settings for WScript.exe*

Repeat these steps for all other user groups for which you want to disable WSH. (Only the System and Administrator accounts have the right to execute a script. Also, installing Windows on an NTFS volume is mandatory.)

After you close the Security property page, execution of WSH scripts is blocked for the specified user groups. If you need to execute a script, you can log on as Administrator and execute the file. For online sessions, avoid logging on with Administrator rights.

> **TIP** An administrator might want to allow certain users to execute scripts even though WScript.exe and CScript.exe are disabled for most users. To define a subset of special users, just follow these steps: Create a user account (named Scripter, for example) and add it to a group that allows scripting. In Windows 2000, you can then create a shortcut to files such as WScript.exe or CScript.exe. Within the shortcut file's property page, you can add the path to a script file that can be executed using the shortcut. And you can check the check box Run As Different User. If an ordinary user double-clicks the shortcut file, Windows asks for a username and password. The user can enter the account name (Scripter in this case) and the password to execute the script under this account. By the way, you can also grant special rights to a script with this approach. The trick is to grant the required rights to the user without accidentally lowering system security.

Windows 95 and Windows 98 don't provide individual rights for files, but you can use the System Policy Editor to define system policies by following the steps below. (See the Microsoft Windows Resource Kit for details.) You can also define system policies in this way in Windows NT and Windows 2000.

1. In Windows 95, Windows 98, or Windows NT 4, launch the System Policy Editor (Poledit.exe), load the local Registry (by choosing Open Registry from the File menu), and double-click on Local User.

2. Select the branch Local User/Windows 98 System/Restrictions and select the Only Run Allowed Windows Applications entry.

3. Click the Show button. In the Show Contents dialog box, use the Add button to add all Windows applications that you want to allow a user to execute.

After you close the open windows and restart Windows, the operating system allows the user to run only the applications listed in the Show Contents dialog box. If CScript.exe and WScript.exe aren't in the list, the user can't execute WSH scripts.

NOTE There's a problem with this approach. As a system administrator, you must define all allowed applications, which isn't a simple task. Also, you have to be careful not to disable RegEdit and the System Policy Editor for the Administrator account—otherwise, you can't change Registry entries. For more details about system policies, see the Microsoft Windows Resource Kit or my book *Inside the Microsoft Windows 98 Registry.*

In Windows 2000, defining system policies is much simpler. You can use the Microsoft Management Console (MMC) to specify applications that a user isn't allowed to execute. If you specify WScript.exe and CScript.exe, the user can't execute scripts after the next logon. There's one problem, however: MMC doesn't support system policies by default. You must create your own MMC version that supports local or remote policies. Here are the steps to create your own MMC application:

1. Choose Run from the Start menu.

2. Type *MMC* as a runnable command, and click OK to launch a new instance of MMC with an empty window.

3. Choose Add/Remove Snap-in from the Console menu. On the Add/Remove Snap-in property sheet, click on the Standalone tab.

4. Use the Add button and select the Group Policy snap-in in the Add Standalone Snap-in dialog box.

5. After you close the open dialog boxes, the snap-in (an ActiveX control) is added to MMC. Save the defined page by using the Save As command from the Console menu.

After saving the configuration in an .msc file, you can open this file (as an MMC application) when you want to alter system policies. To change the list of applications not allowed to run, take the following steps:

1. Launch your copy of MMC. Depending on your configuration, you might need to load the settings of a network machine. (The local settings are loaded automatically.)

2. Select the Tree tab in the left pane, and click Local Computer Policy/User Configuration/Administrative Templates/System. The right pane will list the policies defined for your system.

3. Double-click on the Don't Run Specified Windows Applications entry.

4. On the new property sheet, click on the Policy tab, select the Enabled option, and click the Show button.

5. Use the Add button in the Show Contents dialog box to add applications that the user won't be allowed to run, such as WScript.exe and CScript.exe. (See Figure B-2.)

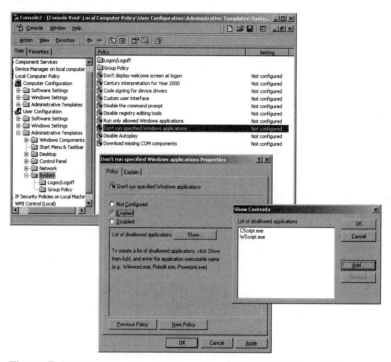

Figure B-2 *Defining system policies using MMC in Windows 2000*

After you close the open dialog box and click the Apply button on the Policy property page, Windows 2000 will block executing WSH scripts on that machine (for the specified user group). Note that a user can still use the Command Prompt window or the Run dialog box to launch WSH scripts, but a double-click at the shell level is disabled. For details on defining system policies for Windows 2000, see the Microsoft Windows 2000 Professional Resource Kit. A resource kit is also available for Windows 2000 Server.

CONCLUDING REMARKS

The strategies mentioned in this appendix should help you prevent the infection of a system by common scripting viruses until Microsoft releases a WSH version that executes only signatured script files.

I should also mention a second concern: security settings in Microsoft Internet Explorer. If script execution is allowed within HTML pages loaded from the Internet, a virus in the form of script code within the HTML document can infect your system. And this virus can use the *CreateObject* method to access WSH methods without using WScript.exe or CScript.exe. You can prevent this situation by disabling script execution in HTML documents viewed from Internet sites. You can apply similar strategies in Microsoft Outlook to disable script executing within HTML pages (sent as e-mail). It's also a good idea to download and install the most recent security patches for Outlook from Microsoft's Web site (*http://officeupdate.microsoft.com*).

Keep in mind that system security isn't only the task of the operating system and software developers. The main responsibility falls on administrators and users. If a user logs on with Administrator rights and if no security settings are set, all doors are open (as in the Linux operating system when users log on as *root*). You can also benefit from using a good virus scanner.

Index

Note: Page numbers in italics refer to figures or tables.

Numbers and Symbols

+ (addition operator), *63, 101*
* (asterisk) as multiplication operator, *63, 101*
\ (backslash)
  as escape character in JScript, 99, 434, 435
  between Registry subkeys in WSH, 288–89, 292
: (colon) in VBScript statements, 52
, (comma) in JScript statements, 94
& (concatenation operator), 56
/ (division operator), *63, 101*
" (double quotes)
  for argument strings, 15
  and long filenames, 425–26
= (equal-to operator), *66, 100*
^ (exponentiation operator), *63*
> (greater-than operator), *66, 100*
>= (greater-than-or-equal-to operator), *66, 100*
< (less-than operator), *66, 100*
<= (less-than-or-equal-to operator), *66, 100*
<> (not-equal-to operator), *66*
% (percent sign) as Modulo operator, *101*
+ (plus sign)
  as addition operator, *63, 101*
  as JScript concatenation operator, 93, 101
; (semicolon) in JScript statements, 93, 94
' (single quote) in VBScript comments, 9, 52–53
– (subtraction operator), *63, 101*

A

About dialog box
  adding Close button, 198
  creating using Internet Explorer, 195–202

About dialog box, *continued*
  displaying in Internet Explorer, *198*
  displaying using JScript, 201–2
  displaying using VBScript, 199–201
  illustrated, *198*
About.htm file, 196, *196–97*, 197, 198
About.js file, 201, *201–2*
About.vbs file, 199–200, *200–201*
ActiveMovie player, 454
ActiveX controls
  installing, 34–35
  licensing, 35
  registering, 34–35
  removing, 35–36
  uninstalling, 35–36
  Web sites for downloading, 466, *466*
  and Windows API functions, 426
addition operator (+), *63, 101*
AddWindowsPrinterConnection method, *WshNetwork* object, 270–71
AllUsersDesktop special folder, *231*
AllUsersPrograms special folder, *231*
AllUsersStartMenu special folder, *231*
AllUsersStartup special folder, *231*
Amovie.ocx file, 454
ampersand (&), 56
And operator, 63, 64, 65
API functions
  ExitWindows, 426–27
  ExitWindowsEx, 427–28
  LockWorkstation, 429–30
  SHExitWindowsEx, 428–29
  using *Run* method to call, 426–27
AppActivate method, 401–5
AppActivateWSH2.js file, 404, 405, *405*
AppActivateWSH2.vbs file, 401, *401–2*, 403–4
Application object, Internet Explorer
  Busy property, 190, 204

Application object, Internet Explorer, *continued*
  in object model, 189–90
  Quit method, 192, 200
  Visible property, 190, 199
applications
  launching more than one, 399–401
  uses for scripts, 4–5
  using *AppActivate* method to activate, 401–5
AppWiz.cpl file, *433*
Args1.vbs file, 150, *150*
Args.js file, 18, *18, 151, 151*
Args.vbs file, 14, *14–15,* 149, *149,* 150
Args.wsh file, 14
arguments
  accessing in scripts using JScript, 151
  accessing in scripts using VBScript, 147–50
  long filenames in, 15
  passing as properties of shortcuts, 16–17
  passing using Command Prompt window, 17–18
  passing using Run dialog box, 16
  problems in passing, 15
  submitting to scripts, 14–18
  using to create shortcuts, 248–53
Arguments property
  WScript object, 147, 148, 151, 253, 254–55
  WshShortcut object, 248
arithmetic operators, JScript, 63
Array function, 131–32
Array object, 112–13
assignment operator (=), 94, 100
asterisk (*) as multiplication operator, *63, 101*
asynchronous processes, 399–401
at sign (@)
Attributes property, *File* object, 347
Autoexec.bat file, 347, 348, 365, 376, 377, 379, 380
AvailableSpace property, drives, 327

B
backing up files
  as use for script, 4
  using *FileSystemObject* object, 359–65
backslash (\)
  as escape character in JScript, 99, 434, 435
  between Registry subkeys in WSH, 288–89, 292

Backup.vbs file, 359–62, *363–64*
batch commands, environment variables in, 162–63
batch files, 3
binary data, and *FileSystemObject* object, 318
BinaryRead.vbs file, 300, *301*
binary values, Windows Registry. *See* *REG_BINARY* Registry data type
bitwise operators, VBScript, 64–66
branches, VBScript, 67–69
Break At Next Statement feature, Microsoft Script Debugger, 42, *43*
break keyword, JScript, 110
breakpoints, 42, 43–44
BrowseForFolder method
  using to select files, 391–95
  using to select folders, 386–91
browsers. *See* Internet Explorer
browser windows, using to read from text files, 365, 368–70
Busy property, Internet Explorer, 190, 204
buttons, dialog box
  using *MsgBox* function to define, 125–27
  using *MsgBox* function to determine which button used for closing, 128–30
  using *MsgBox* function to set focus, 127–28
Buttons property page, 432
ByRef keyword, VBScript, 75–77
ByVal keyword, VBScript, 75–77

C
calculation operators, JScript, 100–101
Calculator program
  launching from Notepad, 174
  using *SendKeys to* manipulate, 410–13
Call Stack feature, Microsoft Script Debugger, 42, *43,* 44
Call statement, 75, 78–79
caret (^) as exponentiation operator, *63*
CascadeWindows method, *Shell* object, 459
case, converting names of files and folders to lowercase, 450–51
case sensitivity, in JScript, 93, 95, 329
ChangeShortcutIcon.vbs file, 259–60, *260–62*
characters. *See* strings
CheckVal method, 398
Choose File dialog box, 209–11, *210*

classes, VBScript
  ClassSample1.vbs file, 88, *88–89*
  ClassSample.vbs example, 86, *86–87*
  extending, 87–89
  overview, 85–86
ClassSample1.vbs file, 88, *88–89*
ClassSample.vbs file, 86, *86–87*
Clear All Breakpoints feature, Microsoft Script
    Debugger, 42, *43*
Close button, adding to About dialog box
    code, 198
collections, 47–48, 107, 112
colon (:) in VBScript statements, 52
columns, formatting in dialog boxes, 435
comma (,) in JScript statements, 94
Command Prompt window
  displaying console input and output, 435–37
  displaying environment variables, 152, *152*
  executing scripts, 12–13
  passing arguments to scripts, 17–18, *18*
  piping program output, 439
  using *Echo* method in, 119–20
Command Window feature, Microsoft Script
    Debugger, 42, 43–44, *43*
comments
  adding to JScript files, 10, 93
  adding to VBScript files, 9, 52–53
comparison operators
  in JScript, 100
  in VBScript, 66–67
component-based programming, 45–50
Component Object Model (COM), and
    CreateObject method, 166–67
ComputerName property, *WshNetwork* object,
    268
computer names, retrieving from networks,
    267–70
concatenation
  in JScript, 93, 101
  in VBScript, 56–57
concatenation operators, 56, 93, 101
conditional operator, 105
console applications. *See* CScript.exe file
constants
  in JScript, 94
  in VBScript, 54–55
continued lines
  in JScript, 93

continued lines, *continued*
  in VBScript, 52
continue keyword, JScript, 110
Control.exe file, 432–34
Control Panel
  invoking property pages, 432–34
  list of modules and parameters, *433*
  opening folder in Windows shell, 462
ControlPanelItem method, *Shell* object, 462
control structures, JScript. *See also* loops,
    JScript
  break keyword, 110
  conditional operator, 105
  continue keyword, 110
  If statement, 104–5
  overview, 104
  switch statement, 109–10
control structures, VBScript. *See also* loops,
    VBScript
  If...Then...ElseIf statements, 68
  If...Then...Else statements, 68
  If...Then statements, 67–68
  Select Case statements, 68–69
Copy Disk dialog box, 430–31, *430*
CopyDisk.vbs file, 430, *431*
CopyFile method, *FileSystemObject* object,
    361, 362
CopyFolder method, *FileSystemObject* object,
    337–38
copying files
  using *File* object, 356, 449
  using *FileSystemObject* object, 361, 362
Copy method, *File* object, 356, 449
Count property, *WshArguments* object, *147,*
    148
CPU usage history, 398–99
CreateFolder method, *FileSystemObject* object,
    243, 319
CreateObject method
  vs. *GetObject* method, 167–68
  vs. JScript native method, 169, 319
  and type libraries, 166–67
  VBScript native function, 169, 319
  WScript object, 134–35, 166
CreateShortcut method, *WshShell* object,
    226–30, 238, 242, 243, 253, 263
CreateShortcut object, 253–55

CreateTextFile method, *FileSystemObject*
    object, 319
CScript.exe file, 10, 11, *11–12*, 12, 16, 17,
    119–20, 435, 440, 471
CStr function, 56
CurrentDir.vbs file, 423

D

databases. *See* Microsoft Access
data types
    in JScript, 97–98
    in VBScript, 54, 55
    in Windows Registry, 287–88, 299–300
DateCreated property
    File object, 347, 348, 353
    Folder object, 347, 348, 353
DateDiff function, 424–25
DateLastAccessed property
    File object, 347
    Folder object, 347
DateLastModified property
    File object, 347
    Folder object, 347
Date object, 112
dates
    calculating differences, 424–25
    retrieving file information, 347–55
    undefined file creation dates, 352–55
Day function, 360
debugging
    JS files, 21, 39–40
    script file overview, 36
    tracing programs, 37–39
    using Microsoft Script Debugger, 39–44
    VBS files, 21, 39–40
    WSF files, 21, 41–42
decrement operators, JScript, 101–2
default directory, setting, 423
DefaultPrinter.vbs file, 279–80, *280–81*
DeleteFile method, *FileSystemObject* object,
    319, 356
DeleteFolder method, *FileSystemObject* object,
    319, 339
Description property, *WshShortcut* object, 253
Desk.cpl file, *433*
Desktop
    creating shortcuts for accessing, 238–42
    creating shortcuts to Web sites, 263–65
    methods for arranging windows, 459–61

Desktop special folder, *231*
dialog boxes
    Browse For Folder dialog box, 385–95
    Choose File dialog box, 209–11, *210*
    Copy Disk dialog box, 430–31, *430*
    creating custom welcome messages using
        Popup method, 138–40
    creating custom welcome message using
        MsgBox function, 130–33
    creating in WSH, 117–40
    defining icon and buttons using *MsgBox*
        function, 125–27
    for displaying list of all special folders,
        232–34
    Echo method vs. *MsgBox* function, 122–23
    Edit FileType dialog box, 28, *28*
    for file selection, 209–10, 209–11
    Folder Options dialog box, 27, *27*
    Format dialog box, 431
    formatting tips, 434–35
    input, 183–93
    modal, 196–98
    for reading from text files, 365–76
    using Internet Explorer to create About
        dialog box, 195–202
    using *MsgBox* function to create, 122–33
    in Windows shell, 462–65
Dialog.vbs file, 386–89, *390–91*
Dim statement, 60–62
directories. *See also* folders
    current, retrieving, 422–23
    default, setting, 423
DisconnectObject method, *WScript* object,
    168–70
Disconnect.vbs file, 169, *169–70*
DiskCopy.dll file, 430–31
DiskCopyRunDll function, 430
disk drives. *See* drives, disk
division operator (/), *63, 101*
Document object, Internet Explorer, 189–90,
    199
Do...Loop Until loop, VBScript, 70
Do...Loop While loop, VBScript, 70
domain names, retrieving from networks,
    267–70
double quotes (")
    for argument strings, 15
    and long filenames, 425–26

Do Until loop, VBScript, 69–70
do...while loop, JScript, 108–9
Do While loop, VBScript, 69, 383, 398
DriveExists method, *FileSystemObject* object,
    326
DriveLetter property, *Drive* object, 324
Drive object
    defined, *317*
    DriveLetter property, 324
    DriveType property, 321, 324
    ShareName property, 322, 324
    VolumeName property, 321, 324
drives, disk
    current, retrieving name, 423
    listing, 320–25
    showing properties, 325–31
    using *FileSystemObject* object to access,
        320–31
Drives collection, *317*, 320, 323
DriveType property, *Drive* object, 321, 324
DUN (dial-up networking) connections,
    calling, 465–66
DUN.vbs file, 465, *465–66*

E
Echo.js file, 121, *121*
Echo method, *WScript* object
    in Args.js example, 18, *18*
    forcing line feed, 121–22
    and I/O redirection, 18
    vs. *MsgBox* function, 122–23, 368
    simple example, 49
    syntax overview, 117–18
    use in tracing scripts, 38
    using in Command Prompt window,
        119–20
    using in JScript, 120–21
    using in VBScript, 118–19
    using to create dialog boxes, 117–22
Echo.vbs file, 118, *118*, 119
ECMAScript, 5, 91
Edit FileType dialog box, 28, *28*
editor programs, as replacements for Notepad,
    29–34
EditPad, 33
EditPlus, 33
End Function statement, 72
Engine.js file, *147*

Engine.vbs file, *146*
Enumerate.vbs file, 305, *306–7*
Enumerator object, 107, 323
EnumPrinterConnections property,
    WshNetwork object, 278, 279
Environment1.vbs file, 159, *160–61*
Environment2.vbs file, 161, *161–62*
Environment3.js file, 165, *165*
Environment3.vbs file, 164, *164*
Environment.js file, 157, *157–58*
Environment property, *WshShell* object, 153
environment variables
    accessing in JScript, 157–58
    accessing in VBScript, 156–57
    creating in VBScript, 159–60
    deleting in VBScript, 161–62
    displaying in Command Prompt window,
        152, *152*
    expanding using
        ExpandEnvironmentalStrings method,
        164–65
    how to access, 152–53
    list by operating system, *154–55*
    overview, 152
    setting in Command Prompt window,
        158–59
    using in batch commands, 162–63
Environment.vbs file, 156, *156–57*
equal sign (=), *66, 100*
Eqv operator, 63
Err object, 82, 273, 420
errors. *See* debugging; run-time errors;
    syntax errors
ErrorTest1.js file, 41
ErrorTest1.vbs file, 41
ErrorTest2.js file, 41
ErrorTest2.vbs file, 38, 41, 58, *58*
ErrorTest.vbs file, 36
ErrorTest.wsf file, 41, *41, 42*
escape sequences, JScript, 98–99, 434, 435
event handling, 6, 205, 214
Event viewer, 443
Execute method, regular expression objects,
    83, 84
EXE files, 6
Exit Do loop, VBScript, 70
Exit For loop, VBScript, 71
Exit Function statement, 73

ExitWindows API function, 426–27
ExitWindowsEx API function, 427–28
ExpandEnvironmentalStrings method,
    WshShell object, 164–65, 238, 344
Explore method, *Shell* object, 461
exponentiation operator (^), *63*
expressions, regular, 82–85, 370–76
external files
    including, 20–21
    role of path, 421

F

Favorites special folder, *232*
File1.js file, 350, *351–52*
File1.vbs file, 347–48, *349–50*
File2.wsf file, 353, *354–55*
File3.js file, 358, *358–59*
File3.vbs file, 355–57, *357–58*
FileExists method, *FileSystemObject* object,
    355, 367, 447–48
filename extensions, 8
filenames
    in argument strings, 15
    converting to lowercase, 450–51
    long, using in scripts, 425–26
File object
    Attributes property, 347
    Copy method, 356, 449
    DateCreated property, 347, 348, 353
    DateLastAccessed property, 347
    DateLastModified property, 347
    defined, *318*
    Move method, 356
    Name property, 347, 450
FileRun method, *Shell* object, 463
files
    checking existence, 447–48
    retrieving attributes and dates, 347–55
    searching for, 452
    undefined creation dates, 352–55
    uses for scripts, 4–5
    using *BrowseForFolder* method to select,
        391–95
    using *File* object to copy, 356, 449
    using *File* object to rename, 450
    using *FileSystemObject* object to access,
        331–65

files, *continued*
    using *FileSystemObject* object to copy, 361,
        362
    using *FileSystemObject* object to delete,
        355–59
    using *FileSystemObject* object to list all files
        in a folder, 343–46
Files collection, *318, 347*
FileSelectDialog.vbs file, 391–93, *393–95*
Files.js file, *346*
Files.vbs file, 343–45, *345*
FileSystemObject object
    CopyFile method, 361, 362
    CopyFolder method, 337–38
    CreateFolder method, 243, 319
    CreateTextFile method, 319
    creating, 318–19, 320, 323
    defined, *318*
    DeleteFile method, 319, 356
    DeleteFolder method, 319, 339
    DriveExists method, 326
    FileExists method, 355, 367, 447–48
    FolderExists method, 246, 336, 361, 362, 448
    GetAbsolutePathName method, 422–23
    GetDrive method, 319, 327
    GetDriveName method, 423
    GetFile method, 319, 355, 449
    GetFolder method, 319, 332, 344
    GetParentFolderName method, 336–37, 422
    GetSpecialFolder method, 334, 440, 455
    methods of, 319–20
    MoveFolder method, 338–39
    Move method, 450
    object model, *317–18,* 318–20
    OpenTextFile method, 365, 366, 367, 377,
        383
    using to access drives, 320–31
    using to access files and folders, 331–65
    using to access text files, 365–85
    using to append new text to existing text
        files, 380–82
    using to back up folders, 359–65
    using to list all drives on a machine, 320–25
    using to list all files in a folder, 343–46
    using to read from text files, 365–76
    using to rename folders, 337–39
    using to write to text files, 376–85

file types, registering, 28
File Types property page, 474
Filter function, 383
Folder1.js file, 341, *341–43*
Folder1.vbs file, 335–39, *339–41*
FolderEmpty function, 361, 448
FolderExists method, *FileSystemObject* object,
    246, 336, 361, 362, 448
Folder object
   DateCreated property, 347, 348, 353
   DateLastAccessed property, 347
   DateLastModified property, 347
   defined, *318*
   using to rename folders, 450
Folder Options dialog box, 27, *27*
folders
   checking existence, 447–48
   checking whether empty, 448
   opening windows, 461–62
   using *BrowseForFolder* method to select,
     386–91
   using *FileSystemObject* object to access,
     331–65
   using *FileSystemObject* object to back up,
     359–65
   using *FileSystemObject* object to copy,
     337–39
   using *FileSystemObject* object to create,
     335–36
   using *FileSystemObject* object to delete
     folders, 339
   using *FileSystemObject* object to list
     subfolders, 332–35
   using *FileSystemObject* object to move,
     337–39
   using *FileSystemObject* object to rename,
     337–39
   using *Folder* object to rename, 450
Folders collection, *318,* 332
Folders.js file, 334, *334–35*
Folders.vbs file, 332–33, *333*
Fonts special folder, *232*
For Each...In loop, VBScript, 150, 233, 305
For Each...Next loop, VBScript, 71
for...in loop, JScript, 107
for loop, JScript, 105–6, 324
Form1.js file, 207, *208–9*
Form1.vbs file, 203–5, *206–7*

Form2.js file, 209–10, *210–11*
Form3.htm file, 212–15, *215–16,* 217
Form3.js file, 220, *220–21*
Form3.vbs file, 217–18, *218–19*
Format dialog box, 431
FormatNumber function, 327
Format.vbs file, *431*
<form> HTML tag, 198, 203, 213
forms, user input
   creating, 202–21
   example, *202*
   file selection dialog box, 209–11
   HTML code for, 202, *202,* 203
   improving, 212–21
   storing as templates, 217
   using JScript WSH script to display, 207,
     208–9, 220–21
   using VBScript WSH script to display,
     203–5, *206–7,* 217–19
For...Next loop, VBScript, 70–71, 84–85
FreeSpace property, drives, 327
Function keyword, VBScript, 72
functions, JScript
   built-in, 111
   user-defined, 110–11
functions, VBScript
   built-in, 73
   declaring, 71–72
   Function.vbs example, 72–73, *72*
   passing parameters, 75–77
   vs. procedures, 74
   user-defined, 73
   when to use, 71
Function.vbs file, 72–73, *72*

G

GetAbsolutePathName method,
   FileSystemObject object, 422–23
GetDomain.js file, 314, *315–16*
GetDomain.vbs file, 313, *313–14*
GetDrive method, *FileSystemObject* object,
   319, 327
GetDriveName method, *FileSystemObject*
   object, 423
GetDriveXJS.wsf file, 329, *330–31*
GetDriveX.wsf file, 325–27, *328–29*
GetFile method, *FileSystemObject* object, 319,
   355, 449

GetFolder method, *FileSystemObject* object, 319, 332, 344

GetObject method vs. *CreateObject* method, 167–68

GetParentFolderName method, *FileSystemObject* object, 336–37, 422

GetPath function, 177, 382, 423

GetShellVersion.vbs file, 458, *458–59*

GetShortcut function, 253

GetShortcutProperties.js file, 257, *258–59*

GetShortcutProperties.vbs file, 253–56, *256–57*

GetSpecialFolder method, *FileSystemObject* object, 334, 440, 455

Global property, regular expression objects, 83, 84, 370

greater-than operator (>), *66, 100*

greater-than-or-equal-to-operator (>=), *66, 100*

H

"Hello, world" program
  creating, 7–10
  creating in JScript, 9–10
  creating in VBScript, 7–9

Hello.vbs file
  creating in Notepad, 8, 9
  listing, 8, *8*

HideUserName.js file, 311, *311–12*

host options, 11, *11–12,* 12, 13

Hotkey property, 243

hot keys, 243, 244

HTAs. *See* HTML applications (HTAs)

HTML applications (HTAs), 198

HTML files
  creating for forms, 212–17, 217
  and JScript programs, 92
  sound files in, 455–56
  using *showModalDialog* method in Internet Explorer to display, 196–98
  using with Internet Explorer and WSH to create forms, 202–21
  VBScript programs within, 53

I

IconLocation property, 239, 260

icons
  for shortcuts, changing, 259–63
  using *MsgBox* function to define in dialog boxes, 125–26

If statement, JScript, 104–5

If...Then...ElseIf statement, VBScript, 68

If...Then...Else statement, VBScript, 68

If...Then statement, VBScript, 67–68

Imp operator, 63

increment operators, JScript, 101–2

inline error handling, VBScript, 80

Input1.js file, 192, *192–93*

InputBox function
  list of parameters, 184
  in VBScript, 183–85, 326
  vs. *WSHInputBox method,* 186, 335, 385

input dialog boxes
  invoking in JScript, 186–93
  invoking in VBScript, 183–85

<*input*> HTML tag, 198, 203, 209

Input.vbs file, 184–85, *185*

installing ActiveX controls, 34–35

Internet Explorer
  accessing from WSH scripts, 188–93
  Application object, 189–90, 192, 199, 200, 204
  JScript example, 189–93
  and language engine versions, 7
  object model, 189–90, 204
  and *prompt* method, 189–93
  relationship to WSH, 7
  showModalDialog method, 196–98, 199
  using to create About dialog boxes, 195–202
  using to play sounds, 455–56
  using with WSH to create forms, 202–21

Intl.cpl file, *433*

intrinsic constants, 55

I/O redirection, using *Echo* method, 18

IsLnk function, 255

IsReady property, drives, 327

IsWinNT function, 260

J

JavaScript, 4. *See also* JScript

<*job*> element, 187

Join function, 441

JScript. *See also* .js files
  accessing files and folders, 334–35
  accessing Windows Registry, 292–93
  activating applications using *AppActivate* method, 404, 405

JScript, *continued*
  appending new text to existing text files,
    381–82
  built-in objects, 111–12
  vs. C++, 92
  combining with VBScript in single WSF file,
    186–88
  comments in, 10, 93
  constants in, 94
  continued lines in, 93
  copying and deleting files, 358–59
  and *CreateShortcut* method, 229–30
  creating "Hello, world" program in, 9–10
  creating objects using *CreateObject*
    method, 134–37, 166
  creating shortcuts to Web sites, 264–65
  creating welcome messages using *Popup*
    method, 138–40
  defined, 5
  displaying About dialog box, 201–2
  displaying drive properties, 329–31
  and *Echo* method, 120–21, 122
  and environment variables, 157-58, 165
  forcing line wraps in dialog boxes, 434–35
  handling run-time errors, 420
  hiding last user name at Windows logon,
    311–12
  Internet Explorer example, 189–93
  invoking input dialog boxes, 186–93
  language engines, 7, 113, 146, 147
  launching Calculator from, 174
  listing all drives on a machine, 323–25
  listing all files in a folder, 346
  listing mapped printers, *279*
  long filenames in, 425
  mapping network drives, 284–86
  and Microsoft Script Debugger, 39–40, 44
  and *MsgBox* function, 123, 134, 341
  new keyword, 169, 319
  operators in, 99–103
  overview, 91–92
  porting VBScript programs to, 207
  printer mapping example, 275, *276*
  program structure, 92–99
  reading from text files, 374–76
  relationship of WSH to, 4, 5
  retrieving script path, 422

JScript, *continued*
  retrieving workgroup names in Windows
    98, 314–16
  retrieving *WScript* properties in, 144–45
  and *SendKeys* method, 406–13
  statements in, 93–94
  variables in, 94
  vs. VBA, 6
  vs. VBScript, 92
  vs. Visual Basic, 6
  writing to text files, 379–80
  WSH script for displaying user-input forms,
    207, *208–9,* 220–21
  for WSH vs. for HTML documents, 92
JScript.js template file, 9, 24
.js files. *See also* JScript
  About.js file, 201, *201–2*
  AppActivateWSH2.js file, 404, 405, *405*
  Args.js file, 18, *18,* 151, *151*
  building using template file, 9, 24
  changing association in Registry, 473
  debugging, 21, 39–40
  Echo.js file, 121, *121*
  Engine.js file, *147*
  Environment3.js file, 165, *165*
  Environment.js file, 157, *157-58*
  ErrorTest1.js file, 41
  ErrorTest2.js file, 41
  File1.js file, 350, *351–52*
  File3.js file, 358, *358–59*
  Files.js file, *346*
  Folder1.js file, 341, *341–43*
  Folders.js file, 334, *334–35*
  Form1.js file, 207, *208–9*
  Form2.js file, 209–10, *210–11*
  Form3.js file, 220, *220–21*
  GetDomain.js file, 314, *315–16*
  GetShortcutProperties.js file, 257, *258–59*
  HideUserName.js file, 311, *311–12*
  including references in new scripts, 20
  Input1.js file, 192, *192–93*
  JScript.js template file, 9, 24
  ListPrinterMapping.js file, *279*
  MapDrives.js file, 284, *284–86*
  MapPrinter.js file, 275, *276*
  Network.js file, *269-70*
  OKCancel.js file, 92, *92*
  overview, 5, 6

.js files, *continued*
    Popup.js file, *136,* 137
    Properties.js file, 144, *144–45*
    ReadText.js file, 374, *374–76*
    registering file type, 28
    Registry.js file, 292, *292–93*
    RunDOS.js file, 181, *181–82*
    SendKeys1.js file, 410–11, *411–13*
    SendKeysWSH2.js file, 406–7, *407–8*
    Shortcut1.js file, *241–42*
    SpecialFolder1.js file, *237*
    SpecialFolder.js file, *234–35*
    Startmenu1.js file, *251–53*
    Startmenu.js file, 246, *246–47*
    URLShortcut.js file, *264–65*
    Welcome.js file, 138–39, *139–40*
    WriteTxt1.js file, 381, *381–82*
    Write.Txt.js file, 379, *379–80*
    WSHDemo.js file, 106, *106*

K

KeyExists function, 296–99
keys, Windows Registry, 286–87, *287,* 296–99
keystrokes, using *SendKeys* method to
    simulate, 406–13

L

language engines, 7, 145–47. *See also* JScript;
    VBScript
LCase.vbs file, 450, *450–51*
Length property, *WshArguments* object, *147,*
    151
less-than operator (<), *66, 100*
less-than-or-equal-to operator (<=), *66, 100*
licensing ActiveX controls, 35
line feeds, forcing with *Echo* method, 121–22
ListDrives.vbs file, 321–22, *322–23*
ListDrives.wsf file, 323–24, *324–25*
ListPrinterMapping.js file, *279*
ListPrinterMapping.vbs file, 278, *278,* 279
ListShortcuts.vbs file, 452, *453–54*
literal constants, 55
LNK files, 225, 452
LockWorkstation API function, 429–30
LogEvent method, *WshShell* object, 443–46
logging script output to files, 443–46
logical operators
    in JScript, 102–3

logical operators, *continued*
    in VBScript, 63–66
logo, displaying, 14
logon, Windows, hiding last user name,
    311–12
logon scripts
    setting up, 413–15
    using to customize Windows, 413–16
long filenames, 425–26
loops, JScript
    do...while loop, 108–9
    for...in loop, 107
    for loop, 105–6
    while loop, 107–8
loops, VBScript, 69–71
LPT port, specifying, 270, 271, 272, 273

M

Main.cpl file, *433*
MapAddPrinterConnection.vbs file, 272–74,
    274–75
MapDrives.js file, 284, *284–86*
MapDrives.vbs file, 282, *283–84*
MapNetworkDrive method, *WshNetwork*
    object, 282
mapping, printer. *See* printer mapping
mapping network drives, 281–86
MapPrinter1.vbs file, 271, *271–72*
MapPrinter.js file, 275, *276*
Math object, 112
MDBOpen.vbs file, 448, *449*
Media Player, invoking, 455
methods
    defined, 48
    native, 169, 318, 319
    vs. VBScript procedure calls, 49
Microsoft Access
    checking whether database is in use, 448–49
    testing for existing files, 448–49
Microsoft JScript. *See* JScript
Microsoft Script Debugger
    Command window, 44, *44*
    debugger window, 42–43, *43*
    invoking in WSH version 1, 39
    invoking in WSH version 2, 39–40
    list of commands, 42
    obtaining, 39
    overview, 39

Microsoft Script Editor, 30–33
MinimizeAll method, *Shell* object, 459
minus sign (–) as subtraction operator, *63, 101*
Mmsys.cpl file, *433*
modal dialog boxes, 196–98
Modulo operator, *63, 101*
Month function, 132, 360
Mouse Properties property sheet, 432
MoveFolder method, *FileSystemObject* object, 338–39
Move method, *File* object, 356
Move method, *FileSystemObject* object, 450
MS-DOS applications, network printing support for, 270, 271
MS-DOS batch files, 3
MS-DOS commands, 180–82, 356, 440–42
MS-DOS mode, using to force Windows restarts, 427
MsgBox1.vbs file, 126, *126–27*
MsgBox2.vbs file, 129, *129–30*, 130
MsgBox function. *See also* buttons, dialog box
   creating welcome message, 130–33
   vs. *Echo method,* 122–23
   list of optional parameters, 123
   vs. *Popup* function, 134, 135, 341
   problem with length text files, 368
   using, 122–33
   using to define dialog box icon and buttons, 125–27
MsgBox.vbs file, 124–25, *124*
MSHTML.dll file, 447
multiplication operator (*), *63, 101*
MultiStrRead.vbs file, 301, *302*
MyDocuments special folder, *232*

N

Name property, collection items, 305, 332, 347, 450
names. *See* user names; workgroups, retrieving names in Windows 98
naming
   JScript variables, 95–97
   scripts, 8
   VBScript variables, 62
native methods, 169, 318, 319
Navigate property, Internet Explorer, 199
NetHood special folder, *232*
network drives, mapping, 281–86

Network.js file, *269–70*
Network Neighborhood property sheets, 267–70
networks
   connecting to printers, 270–81
   mapping drives, 281–86
   retrieving information from, 267–70
   retrieving workgroup names in Windows 98, 312–16
Network.vbs file, 269, *269*
new keyword, JScript, 169, 319
Notepad. *See also* script editors
   creating script files in, 8
   creating shortcut using arguments, 248–53
   launching from VBScript, 173
   limitations as script editor, 26
   replacement programs for, 29–34
   using *SendKeys* to manipulate, 410–13
   using to print from scripts, 446
not-equal-to operator (<>), *66*
Not operator, 63, 64, 65
NTLockWorkstation.vbs file, 429, *429–30*, 430
Number property, *Err* object, 273
numbers, in JScript, 98
numerical constants, 54–55

O

object models
   FileSystemObject object, *317–18,* 318–20
   Internet Explorer, 189–90, 204
   overview, 46–47
object-oriented programming (OOP). *See* component-based programming
objects
   availability of, 49–50
   collections of, 47–48
   creating using native methods, 169, 318, 319
   Internet Explorer example, 189–93
   JScript, 111–12
   methods for, 48–49
   object model, 46–47
   overview, 45–46
   programming overview, 45–50
   properties of, 48–49
   simple example, 46
   for Windows Script Host, 49
   and *With* statement in VBScript, 89–90

OCX files. *See also* ActiveX controls
  registering, 34–35
  removing, 35–36
OKCancel.js file, 92, *92*
onclick event, 214
On Error GoTo statement, 420
On Error Resume Next statement, 80, 243, 273,
  274, 294, 353, 419
opening
  folder windows, 461–62
  scripts in Notepad, 26
Open method, *Shell* object, 461
OpenTextFile method, *FileSystemObject*
  object, 365, 366, 367, 377, 383
operators, JScript
  assignment, 94, 100
  calculation, 100–101
  comparison, 100
  increment and decrement, 101–2
  logical, 102–3
  order of precedence, 103
  overview, 99
operators, VBScript
  arithmetic, 63
  bitwise, 64–66
  comparison, 66–67
  logical, 63–66
  order of precedence, 67
Option Explicit statement, 57–59, 420
Or operator, 63, 65, 66

P

ParentFolder method, 392
parentheses
  and operator order of precedence, 67, 103
  in VBScript procedure calls, 75, 78–79
ParseName method, 392
path
  blanks in, 175–76
  changing in Windows Registry, 309–11
  and Folders.js file, 334
  and HTML file location, 199
  passing to methods, 199
  relative vs. absolute, 14
  retrieving for scripts, 421–22
  role in accessing external files, 421
Path property, 392

Pattern property, regular expression objects,
  83, 84
patterns, searching for using VBScript, 82–85
percent sign (%) as Modulo operator, *101*
Pipe.vbs file, 440–41, *441–42*
piping mechanism, Command Prompt
  window, 439
PlaySound1.vbs file, 455–56, *456–57*
PlaySound.vbs file, 455, *455*
plus sign (+)
  as addition operator, *63, 101*
  as JScript concatenation operator, 93, 101
Popup.js file, *136*, 137
Popup method, *WshShell* object
  list of parameters, 135
  vs. *MsgBox* function, 134, 135, 341
  in PlaySound1.vbs, 456
  using in JScript, 134, 135–36
  using to create dialog box in VBScript,
    137–38
  using to create welcome dialog box in
    JScript, 138–40
Popup.vbs file, 137, *137–38*
PrimalSCRIPT, 29–30
Print dialog box, 446–47
PrintDocs.vbs file, 447
printer mapping
  displaying list of mapped printers, 278–79
  overview, 270–71
  removing, 276–77
  run-time error handling, 273
  specifying default printer, 279–81
  using *AddPrinterConnection* method,
    272–76
  using *AddWindowsPrinterConnection*
    method, 271–72
printers, network, connecting to, 270–81
PrintHood special folder, *232*
PrintHTML function, 447
printing from WSH scripts, 446–47
PrintTxt.vbs file, 446
Private keyword, VBScript, 60, 87
Procedure1.vbs file, 75, *75–76*, 76
Procedure2.vbs file, 76, *76–77*, 77
procedures, VBScript
  declaring, 74
  vs. functions, 74
  passing parameters, 75–77

procedures, VBScript, *continued*
   problems calling, 77–79
   and run-time error handling, 80
Procedure.vbs example, 74–75, *74*
Programs special folder, *232*
prompt method, Internet Explorer, 189–93
properties
   arguments as, 16–17
   defined, 48
   setting for scripts, 13–14
Properties.js file, 144, *144–45*
Properties.vbs file, 143, *143–44*
Public keyword, VBScript, 60, 87

Q

Quit method, Internet Explorer, 192, 200
Quit method, *WScript* object, 176–80
quotes, double (")
   for argument strings, 15
   and long filenames, 425–26
quotes, single (') in VBScript comments, 9,
   52–53

R

ReadLine method, 367, 436
Read method, 437
ReadShortcut function, 253
ReadText.js file, 374, *374–76*
ReadTxt.vbs file, 365–72, *372–74*
Recent special folder, *232*
reference element, 20, 21
RegAccessTest.vbs file, 302, *303–4*
REG_BINARY Registry data type, 287, 300,
   301
RegDelete method, *WshShell* object, 288, 289
REG_DWORD Registry data type, 287, 300
REG_EXPAND_SZ Registry data type, 300
RegExp object, 84, 370. *See also* regular
   expression objects
RegExpression.vbs file, 84–85, *84*
RegExpTest function, 84–85
REG files, 472–74
REG_FULL_RESSOURCE_DESCRIPTION
   Registry data type, 305
registering ActiveX controls, 34–35
registering file types, 28
Registry. *See* Windows Registry

Registry1.vbs file, 294, *294–96*
Registry2.vbs file, 296, *297–98*
Registry2.wsf file, 298, *298–99*
Registry Editor, 286–87, *287*
Registry.js file, 292, *292–93*
Registry.vbs file, 290, *291–92*
RegKeyFromString method, *RegObj* object,
   305, 307
REG_MULTI_SZ Registry data type, 299, 301,
   302
Regobj.dll file, 305, 307
RegObj object, 305, 307
RegRead method, *WshShell* object, 288, 289,
   297, 300, 301, 302, 420
RegSvr32.exe file
   using to install OCX files, 34–35
   using to uninstall OCX files, 36
REG_SZ Registry data type, 287, 299
regular expression objects, 82–85, 370–76
RegWrite method, *WshShell* object, 287,
   288–89, 300
RemoteRegistry method, *RegObj* object, 307
RemoteReg.vbs file, 307, *307–8*
RemoveNetworkDrive method, *WshNetwork*
   object, 284
RemovePrinterConnection method,
   WshNetwork object, 276–77
removing ActiveX controls, 35–36
removing printer mapping, 276–77
REM statement, 52
renaming files and folders, 337–39, 450–51
Replace method, regular expression objects,
   83, 370, 383
ReplaceTxt.vbs file, 382–84, *384–85*
replacing text in text files, 382–85
root keys, Windows Registry, 286–87, *287,*
   288
Run1.vbs file, 177, *178*
Run2.vbs file, 178, 179–80, *179*
RunApps.vbs file, 399–400, *400–401*
Run dialog box, using to pass arguments to
   scripts, 16
RunDll32.exe file, 426–27, 432, 447, 465
RunDOS.js file, 181, *181–82*
RunExitEx.vbs file, 428, *428–29,* 429
RunExit.vbs file, *426–27,* 427
Run feature, Microsoft Script Debugger, 42,
   43

Run method
    and Control.exe file, 432–34
    and RunDll32.exe file, 432
    using to execute MS-DOS commands,
        180–82
    using to execute system calls, 426–29
    using to launch applications from scripts,
        170–73, 176, 177, 400
RunTest.vbs file, 175, *175,* 176
run-time errors
    in accessing Windows Registry, 293–96
    handling in JScript, 420
    handling in VBScript, 80, *81,* 82, 419–20,
        421
    and Microsoft Script Debugger, 39–44
    overview, 419
    in printer mapping, 273
    raising, 421
RunTimeError.vbs file, 80, *81*
Run.vbs file, 173, *173*

S

Save method, 251
scope
    JScript variables, 95
    VBScript variables, 60
Screen Saver property page, invoking, 432
screen savers, installing, 432
ScreenSaver.vbs file, 432, *432*
script debuggers
    invoking in JS files, 21, 39–40
    invoking in VBS files, 21, 39–40
    invoking in WSF files, 21, 41–42
    troubleshooting, 22
script editors
    creating custom shortcut commands for,
        26–28
    EditPad, 33
    EditPlus, 33
    limitations of Notepad as, 26
    other than Notepad, 29–34
    PrimalSCRIPT, 29–30
    UltraEdit 32 program, 33
<script> element
    including external files in, 20
    overview, 19, 20
    in WSH2Input.wsf file, 187
script files. *See* scripts

ScriptFullName property, *WScript* object,
    421–22, 423
Script object, Internet Explorer
    in object model, 189–91
    showModalDialog method, 196–98, 199
Script property page, 13–14, *13*
scripts. *See also* JScript; VBScript
    accessing environment variables, 152–65
    adding comments to, 9–10, 52–53, 93
    building using template files, 9, 26
    creating from scratch, 7–10, 23
    creating shortcuts to, 16–17
    debugging, 36–44
    delaying execution, 397–401
    editing, 26–34
    executing in Windows, 10–11
    executing using Command Prompt window,
        12–13
    executing using Windows NT scheduler,
        425
    including external files in, 20
    launching applications from, 170–82
    loading, 26
    logging output to files, 443–46
    logon, using to customize Windows,
        413–17
    long filenames in, 425–26
    naming, 8
    opening in Notepad, 26
    passing arguments in, 14–18
    playing sound files in, 454–57
    preventing automatic execution, 472–74
    printer support, 446–47
    removing syntax errors, 36
    retrieving current directory, 422–23
    retrieving path, 421–22
    saving, 8, 23, *24*
    security settings, 475–78
    setting properties, 13–14
    shutdown, 416–17
    startup, 416–17
    tracing, 37–39
    type libraries in, 20–21
    uses for, 4–5
    using long filenames in, 425
script templates
    configuring Windows for, 24–26
    JScript.js, 9, 24

script templates, *continued*
    loading, 9, 26
    registering using Tweak UI, 25
    using to create new script files, 9, 26
    VBScript.vbs, 9, 24
    WSHfile.wsf, 24
Scrrun.dll file, 318
security
    partially disabling WSH, 471–72
    preventing automatic execution of WSH
        scripts, 472–74
    settings for WSH scripts, 475–78
Select Case statement, 68–69
semicolon (;) in JScript statements, 93, 94
SendKeys1.js file, 410–11, *411–13*
SendKeys method, *WSHShell* object
    codes for key combinations, 409, *409,* 410
    codes for special keys, 408, *408–9*
    using to manipulate two applications,
        410–13
    using to simulate keystrokes, 406–13
    in Windows Script Host 2, 406–10
SendKeysWSH2.js file, 406–7, *407–8*
SendTo special folder, *232*
SetDefaultPrinter method, *WshNetwork*
    object, 279–80
SetInstPath.vbs file, 309, *310–11*
Set statement, 62
ShareName property, *Drive* object, 322, 324
shareware replacements for Notepad, 29–34
sharing network resources. *See* network
    drives, mapping; printers, network,
    connecting to
Shdocvw.dll file, 391
Shell1.vbs file, 461, *461–62*
Shell2.vbs file, 462–63, *464–65*
Shell32.dll file, 259, 428, 431, 458
Shell object
    CascadeWindows method, 459
    ControlPanelItem method, 462
    Explore method, 461
    FileRun method, 463
    MinimizeAll method, 459
    Open method, 461
    TileHorizontally method, 459
    TileVertically method, 459
    UndoMinimizeAll method, 459
    using from scripts, 457–66

Shell.vbs file, 459, *460–61*
SHExitWindowsEx API function, 428–29
ShFormatDrive function, 431
Shortcut1.js file, *241–42*
Shortcut1.vbs file, 238–39, *239–40*
shortcuts
    changing icons, 259–63
    creating for access to Desktop, 238–42
    creating for script editors, 26–28
    creating for script files, 16–17
    creating on Start menu, 242–48
    creating to Web sites, 263–65
    listing file names and locations, 452–54
    overview, 225, *226*
    reading properties, 253–59
    setting arguments as properties, 16–17
    updating files, 259–63
    using arguments to create, 248–53
    using *CreateShortcut* method to create,
        226–30
showModalDialog method, Internet Explorer,
    196–98, 199
shutdown scripts, 416–17
Shut Down Windows dialog box, 463–64
shutting down Windows, 426–29
single quotes (') in VBScript comments, 9,
    52–53
slash (/). *See also* backslash (\)
    and command line arguments, 18
    in JScript comments, 10, 93
    preceding host options, 11
Sleep method, *WScript* object, 199, 397–401,
    456
sound files, playing in scripts, 454–57
SpecialFolder1.js file, *237*
SpecialFolder1.vbs file, 235, *236*
SpecialFolder.js file, *234–35*
special folders
    displaying list in dialog box, 232–34
    finding, 231, *232*
    list of names, *231–32*
    overview, 231
    retrieving path to, 235–37
SpecialFolders property, *WshShell* object,
    231–37, 238, 242, 452
SpecialFolder.vbs file, 232–33, *234*
Split function, 441
Start menu, creating shortcuts on, 242–48

Startmenu1.js file, *251–53*
Startmenu1.vbs file, 248, *249–50,* 251
Startmenu.js file, 246, *246–47*
StartMenu special folder, *232*
Startmenu.vbs file, 242–44, *244–45*
startup scripts, 416–17
Startup special folder, *232*
statements
    in JScript, 93–94
    in VBScript, 52
StdIO1.vbs file, 437, *437–38*
StdIOFilter.vbs file, 439, *439*
StdIO.vbs file, 435–36, *436–37*
StdIn stream property, WSH 2, 435
StdOut stream property, WSH 2, 435
Step Into feature, Microsoft Script Debugger,
    42, 43, *43*
Step Out feature, Microsoft Script Debugger,
    42, 43, *43*
Step Over feature, Microsoft Script Debugger,
    42, 43, *43*
Stop Debugging feature, Microsoft Script
    Debugger, 42, *43*
Stop statement, 39
String object, 111
strings
    concatenation, 56–57, 93, 101
    enclosing in double quotes, 15
    escape sequences in JScript, 98–99, 434,
        435
    as JScript data subtype, 98
Subfolders property, 334
subkeys, Windows Registry, 287, *287,* 305–7
subtraction operator (–), *63, 101*
switch statement, 109–10
syntax errors, 36
Sysdm.cpl file, *433*

T

TargetPath property, *WshShell* object, 253, 263
template files. *See* script templates
Templates special folder, *232*
temporary files, 440–42
Test1.wsf file, 21
Test.htm file, 196, *196*
Test method, regular expression objects, 83
Test.vbs file, 176, *177*

Test.wsf file, 20
text, replacing in text files, 382–85
<textarea> HTML tag, 213
text editors. *See* Notepad; script editors
text files
    appending new text to, 380–82
    reading from, 365–76
    replacing text, 382–85
    writing to, 376–85
TextStream object, *318,* 440–42, 452
TileHorizontally method, *Shell* object, 459
TileVertically method, *Shell* object, 459
Timedate.cpl file, *433*
time-out value, setting, *13,* 14
<title> HTML tag, 197, 203
Toggle Breakpoint feature, Microsoft Script
    Debugger, 42, 43–44, *43*
TotalSize property, drives, 327
toUpperCase method, in JScript, 329
tracing scripts, 37–39
troubleshooting
    procedure calls in VBScript, 77–79
    script debugger, 22
try...catch statement, 246, 275, 420
Tweak UI, 24, *25,* 26
type libraries, 21–22

U

UCase function, 329
UltraEdit 32 program, 33
UNC (Universal Naming Convention), 14, 270,
    271, 272
UndoMinimizeAll method, *Shell* object, 459
uninstalling ActiveX controls, 35–36
Universal Naming Convention (UNC), 14, 270,
    271, 272
UnMapPrinter.vbs file, 276–77, *277*
updating shortcut files, 259–63
URLShortcut.js file, *264–65*
URLShortcut.vbs file, 263, *263–64*
user-defined functions
    JScript, 110–11
    VBScript, 73
UserDomain property, *WshNetwork* object,
    268
UserLog.vbs file, 443–44, *444–46*
UserName property, *WshNetwork* object, 268,
    398, 444

user names
  hiding at Windows logon, 311–12
  retrieving from networks, 267–70

V

variables, JScript
  and data types, 97–98
  naming, 95–97
  overview, 94–95
  scope rules, 95
variables, VBScript
  declaring scope, 60, 61
  naming, 62
  and *Option Explicit* statement, 57–58
  overview, 55
  script-level, 55–62
Variant data type
  in JScript, 97–98
  in VBScript, 54, 55
variant subtypes, 55–57
VarType function, 57 .
VBScript. *See also* .vbs files
  accessing files and folders, 332, 333
  accessing script arguments, 147–50
  accessing Windows Registry, 288–92
  accessing Windows Registry remotely,
    307–9
  activating applications using *AppActivate*
    method, 401–4
  advanced features, 80–90
  backing up folders using *FileSystemObject*
    object, 359–64
  calculating date differences, 424–25
  calling *ExitWindows* API function, 426–27
  changing Windows 98 installation path in
    Windows Registry, 309–11
  checking for existence of Windows Registry
    keys, 296–99
  combining with JScript in single WSF file,
    186–88
  comments in, 9, 52–53
  constants in, 54–55
  continued lines in, 52
  control structures in, 67–69
  copying and deleting files, 355–58
  and *CreateShortcut* method, 226–29
  creating "Hello, world" program in, 7–9

VBScript, *continued*
  creating objects using *CreateObject*
    method, 165–66
  creating shortcuts to Web sites, 263–64
  defined, 5, 51
  Dim statement, 60–62
  displaying About dialog box, 199–201
  displaying drive properties, 325–29
  displaying list of special folders, 232–34
  Echo method in, 118–19, 122
  enumerating Windows Registry keys and
    values, 305–7
  and environment variables, 156–57, 159–64
  forcing line wraps in dialog boxes, 434
  formatting columns in dialog boxes, 435
  Function keyword, 72
  handling run-time errors, 80, *81, 82,*
    419–20, 421
  installing screen savers, 432
  invoking Command window in Microsoft
    Script Debugger, 44
  invoking input dialog boxes, 183–85
  launching Notepad from, 173
  listing all drives on a machine, 321–23
  listing all files in a folder, 343–45
  listing mapped printers, 278–79
  long filenames in, 425
  loops in, 69–71
  mapping network drives, 281–84
  and Microsoft Script Debugger, 39–40
  and *MsgBox* function, 122–33
  operators in, 63–67
  piping program output, 439
  porting programs to JScript, 207
  printer mapping examples, 270, 271,
    271–72, 272–74, 274–75
  Private keyword, 60, 87
  program structure, 53
  programs within HTML documents, 53
  Public keyword, 60, 87
  reading from text files, 365–74
  relationship of WSH to, 4, 5
  removing printer mapping, 276–77
  replacing text in text files, 382–85
  retrieving language engine properties, 146,
    146
  retrieving script path, 421

VBScript, *continued*
 retrieving workgroup names in Windows
  98, 313–14
 retrieving *WScript* properties, 143–44
 run-time errors when accessing Windows
  Registry, 294–96
 sample code listing, 53
 selecting files using *BrowseForFolder*
  method, 391–95
 selecting folders using *BrowseForFolder*
  method, 386–91
 Set statement, 62
 setting default printer, 279–81
 statements in, 52
 support for regular expressions, 82–85
 syntax, 9
 updating shortcut files, 259–62
 using files for streaming, 440–42
 version 5 features, 82–90
 vs. Visual Basic, 6
 vs. Visual Basic for Applications (VBA), 6
 With statement, 89–90
 writing to text files, 376–78
 WSH script for displaying user-input forms,
  203–5, *206–7*, 217–19
VBScriptError.vbs file, 421
VBScript.vbs template file, 9, 24
.vbs files. *See also* VBScript
 About.vbs file, 199–200, *200–201*
 AppActivateWSH2.vbs file, 401, *401–2,*
  403–4
 Args1.vbs file, 150, *150*
 Args.vbs file, 14, *14–15,* 149, *149,* 150
 Backup.vbs file, 359–62, *363–64*
 BinaryRead.vbs file, 300, *301*
 building using template file, 9, 24
 ChangeShortcutIcon.vbs file, 259–60,
  260–62
 changing association in Registry, 472–73
 ClassSample1.vbs file, 88, *88–89*
 ClassSample.vbs file, 86, *86–87*
 CopyDisk.vbs file, 430, *431*
 CurrentDir.vbs file, 423
 debugging, 21, 39–40
 DefaultPrinter.vbs file, 279–80, *280–81*
 Dialog.vbs file, 386–89, *390–91*
 Disconnect.vbs file, 169, *169–70*
 DUN.vbs file, 465, *465–66*

.vbs files, *continued*
 Echo.vbs file, 118, *118,* 119
 Engine.vbs file, *146*
 Enumerate.vbs file, 305, *306–7*
 Environment1.vbs file, 159, *160–61*
 Environment2.vbs file, 161, *161–62*
 Environment3.vbs file, 164, *164*
 Environment.vbs file, 156, *156–57*
 ErrorTest1.vbs file, 41
 ErrorTest2.vbs file, 38, 41, 58, *58*
 ErrorTest.vbs file, 36
 File1.vbs file, 347–48, *349–50*
 File3.vbs file, 355–57, *357–58*
 FileSelectDialog.vbs file, 391–93, *393–95*
 Files.vbs file, 343–45, *345*
 Folder1.vbs file, 335–39, *339–41*
 Folders.vbs file, 332–33, *333*
 Form1.vbs file, 203–5, *206–7*
 Form3.vbs file, 217–18, *218–19*
 Format.vbs file, *431*
 Function.vbs file, 72–73, *72*
 GetDomain.vbs file, 313, *313–14*
 GetShellVersion.vbs file, 458, *458–59*
 GetShortcutProperties.vbs file, 253–56,
  256–57
 Hello.vbs file, 8, 9
 including references in new scripts, 20
 Input.vbs file, 184–85, *185*
 LCase.vbs file, 450, *450–51*
 ListDrives.vbs file, 321–22, *322–23*
 ListPrinterMapping.vbs file, 278, *278,* 279
 ListShortcuts.vbs file, 452, *453–54*
 MapAddPrinterConnection.vbs file, 272–74,
  274–75
 MapDrives.vbs file, 282, *283–84*
 MapPrinter1.vbs file, 271, *271–72*
 MDBOpen.vbs file, 448, *449*
 MsgBox1.vbs file, 126, *126–27*
 MsgBox2.vbs file, 129, *129–30,* 130
 MsgBox.vbs file, 124–25, *124*
 MultiStrRead.vbs file, 301, *302*
 Network.vbs file, 269, *269*
 NTLockWorkstation.vbs file, 429, *429–30,*
  430
 overview, 5, 6, 8
 Pipe.vbs file, 440–41, *441–42*
 PlaySound1.vbs file, 455–56, *456–57*
 PlaySound.vbs file, 455, *455*

.vbs files, *continued*
Popup.vbs file, 137, *137–38*
PrintDocs.vbs file, 447
PrintTxt.vbs file, 446
Procedure1.vbs file, 75, *75–76, 76*
Procedure2.vbs file, 76, *76–77, 77*
Procedure.vbs file, 74–75, *74*
Properties.vbs file, 143, *143–44*
ReadTxt.vbs file, 365–72, *372–74*
RegAccessTest.vbs file, 302, *303–4*
RegExpression.vbs file, 84–85, *84*
registering file type, 28
Registry1.vbs file, 294, *294–96*
Registry2.vbs file, 296, *297–98*
Registry.vbs file, 290, *291–92*
RemoteReg.vbs file, 307, *307–8*
ReplaceTxt.vbs file, 382–84, *384–85*
Run1.vbs file, 177, *178*
Run2.vbs file, 178, 179–80, *179*
RunApps.vbs file, 399–400, *400–401*
RunExitEx.vbs file, 428, *428–29, 429*
RunExit.vbs file, *426–27*, 427
RunTest.vbs file, 175, *175*, 176
RunTimeError.vbs file, 80, *81*
Run.vbs file, 173, *173*
ScreenSaver.vbs file, 432, *432*
SetInstPath.vbs file, 309, *310–11*
Shell1.vbs file, 461, *461–62*
Shell2.vbs file, 462–63, *464–65*
Shell.vbs file, 459, *460–61*
Shortcut1.vbs file, 238–39, *239–40*
SpecialFolder1.vbs file, 235, *236*
SpecialFolder.vbs file, 232–33, *234*
Startmenu1.vbs file, 248, *249–50*, 251
Startmenu.vbs file, 242–44, *244–45*
StdIO1.vbs file, 437, *437–38*
StdIOFilter.vbs file, 439, *439*
StdIO.vbs file, 435–36, *436–37*
Test.vbs file, 176, *177*
UnMapPrinter.vbs file, 276–77, *277*
URLShortcut.vbs file, 263, *263–64*
UserLog.vbs file, 443–44, *444–46*
VBScriptError.vbs file, 421
VBScript.vbs template file, 9, 24
Welcome.vbs file, 133, *133*
WriteTxt.vbs file, 376–77, *378*
WSHDemo.vbs file, *37*, 37–38, 39, 53, *53*

viruses. *See* security
Visible property, Internet Explorer, 190, 199
Visual Basic for Applications (VBA), 4, 6, 51
Visual Basic vs. VBScript, 6
Visual Studio, 7
VolumeName property, *Drive* object, 321, 324

W
Web sites
creating Desktop shortcuts to, 263–65
list of Internet resources for WSH, 469–70
Weekday function, 132
Welcome.js file, 138–39, *139–40*
welcome messages
creating in JScript using *Popup* method,
138–40
creating in VBScript using *MsgBox* function,
130–33
Welcome.vbs file, 133, *133*
while loop, JScript, 107–8
While...Wend loop, VBScript, 71
window object, Internet Explorer, 196–98
Window_OnLoad event, 214
windows
and asynchronous processes, 399–401
methods for arranging on Desktop, 459–61
Windows 95 and 98
changing installation path in Windows
Registry, 309–11
hiding last user name at logon, 311–12
list of environment variables, *154–55*
and network printer connections, 270
retrieving workgroup names, 312–16
security settings, 476–77
uses for scripts, 4–5
using MS-DOS mode to force Windows
restarts, 427
using RunDll32.exe to shut down, 426–27
using startup and shutdown scripts, 417
and WSH 2, 5–6
Windows 2000
invoking Print dialog box, 446–47
list of environment variables, *154–55*
locking workstations, 429–30
and network printer connections, 270–71
playing sound files in scripts, 454–55
security settings, 475–78

Windows 2000, *continued*
setting up logon scripts to run automatically, 415–16
uses for scripts, 4–5
using startup and shutdown scripts, 416–17
Windows API functions. *See* API functions
Windows Editor, 238–42
Windows Media Player, invoking, 455
Windows NT
installing WSH 2, 6–7
list of environment variables, *154–55*
locking workstations, 429–30
and network printer connections, 270–71
security settings, 475–78
setting up logon scripts to run automatically, 413–15
uses for scripts, 4–5
using scheduler to execute scripts, 425
Windows Registry
accessing remotely, 307–9
changing file-type associations in, 472–74
checking for existence of keys, 296–99
enumerating keys and values, 305–7
run-time errors when accessing, 293–96
using *WshShell* object to access, 286–316
Windows Script Host (WSH)
accessing Windows Registry, 288–96
background, 3–4
creating dialog boxes, 117–40
determining whether installed, 5–6
executing scripts, 10–14
installing version 2, 6–7
and language engine versions, 7, 113, 145–47
list of Internet resources, 469–70
overview, 3–4
partially disabling, 471–72
preventing automatic execution of scripts, 472–74
printing from scripts, 446–47
security settings for scripts, 475–78
upgrading to WSH 2, 5–7
using Internet Explorer from scripts, 188–93
using with Internet Explorer to create forms, 202–21
working with objects, 141–82
Windows Scripting Host. *See* Windows Script Host (WSH)

Windows shell
accessing dialog boxes, 462–65
arranging Desktop windows, 459–61
opening folder windows, 461–62
overview, 457
testing version, 458–59
WindowStyle property, 238–39
With statement, 89–90
workgroups, retrieving names in Windows 98, 312–16
WriteLine method, 377, 435
Write method, 437
WriteTxt1.js file, 381, *381–82*
WriteTxt1.wsf file, 380, *380–81*
Write.Txt.js file, 379, *379–80*
WriteTxt.vbs file, 376–77, *378*
WScript.exe file, 10, 11, *11–12,* 12, *13,* 16, 17, 440, 471
WScript object
Arguments property, 147, 148, 151, 253, 254–55
CreateObject method, 134–35, 166
DisconnectObject method, 168–70
Echo method (*see* Echo method, *WScript* object)
list of properties, *142*
overview, 49, 142
Quit method, 176–80
retrieving properties in JScript, 144–45
retrieving properties in VBScript, 143–44
ScriptFullName property, 421–22, 423
Sleep method, 397–401, 456
.wsf files
combining multiple scripts in, 186–88
debugging, 21, 41–42
Option Explicit statement in, 59
overview, 5, 6, 19
registering file type, 28
structure of, 19
using template file to build, 24
variable scope in, 61
as XML documents, 19–20
WSH2Input.wsf file, 187, *187–88*
WshArguments object
accessing properties, 147–51
as collection, 148, 149
Count property, *147,* 148
Item property, *147,* 148

WshArguments object, *continued*
  Length property, *147,* 151
  list of properties, *147*
WSHDemo3.wsf file, 61
WSHDemo.js file, 106, *106*
WSHDemo.vbs file, 37–38, *37, 39,* 53, *53*
WSH files, 14–15
WSHfile.wsf template file, 24
WSHInputBox function, 186, 329, 335, 385
WSH.log file, 443
WshNetwork object
  accessing properties, 268
  AddPrinterConnection method, 270, 271,
    272–74
  AddWindowsPrinterConnection method,
    270–71
  ComputerName property, 268
  creating, 267
  EnumPrinterConnections property, 278, 279
  instantiating, 270
  MapNetworkDrive method, 282
  RemoveNetworkDrive method, 284
  RemovePrinterConnection method, 276–77
  SetDefaultPrinter method, 279–80
  UserDomain property, 268
  UserName property, 268, 398, 444
WshShell object
  CreateShortcut method, 226–30, 238, 242,
    243, 253, 263
  Environment property, 153
  instantiating, 134–35
  list of methods, *163*
  LogEvent method, 443–46
  Popup method (*see Popup* method,
    WshShell object)
  RegDelete method, 288, 289
  RegRead method, 288, 289, 297, 300, 301,
    302, 420
  RegWrite method, 287, 288–89, 300
  Run method, 170–73, 176, 177
  SendKeys method, 406–13
  SpecialFolders property, 231–37, 238, 242,
    452
  TargetPath property, 253, 263
  using methods to create Windows
    shortcuts, 225–65
  using to access Windows Registry, 286–316

WshShortcut object, 226, 227–28, 238, 242,
  243, 244, 248, 256
WshSpecialFolders collection, 232, 233, 235

X
XML documents, WSF files as, 19–20
Xor operator, 63, 66

Y
Year function, 360

GÜNTER BORN

Günter Born holds a degree in physics and has studied information science and electrical engineering. He began work as a software developer and project engineer in 1979 in the German spacecraft and chemical industries. His work involved managing software development groups and consulting on several international projects with Japan, Thailand, and European countries. Since 1993, he has worked as an independent writer and translator.

Born began working with computers as a student, when one of his professors encouraged him to work through a series of equations for mechanical systems. Too poor to buy a pocket calculator and too lazy to do the calculations by hand, he turned to an IBM 370 computer, which had to be fed with punched cards. An incorrect FORTRAN statement resulted in a long listing and wasted time, but after he finally got the program running it saved him a lot of time and provided a lot of free paper, which he used for classroom notes.

Later he programmed Digital Equipment PDP 11 and VAX computers and Intel microprocessors in FORTRAN, PL/M, and assembly language. In 1983 he joined a project that used one of the first IBM PC/XT computers shipped to Europe.

Born's publishing career started inauspiciously. In 1987, he failed to publish an article about an 8085/Z80 disassembler implemented in BASIC because no one wanted to read about BASIC. So he decided to learn Pascal. He borrowed an old IBM PC/XT with a Borland Pascal compiler, spent a weekend porting his disassembler to Pascal, replaced the BASIC listings with Pascal source code, and succeeded in getting his article published in a computer magazine. Born wrote his first book to earn the money to buy a PC. (However, the royalties barely covered the cost of the machine.)

Born has since published many articles and over 90 books and CD titles, from computer books for children to books about applications to high-end programming titles. His book *The File Formats Handbook* became a standard in the programming community. He is also the author of *Inside the Registry for Microsoft Windows 95* and *Inside the Microsoft Windows 98 Registry*. Born contributed to the *Microsoft Windows 98 Resource Kit* and has authored, translated, and acted as technical editor on several books published by Microsoft Press Germany.

The manuscript for this book was prepared using Microsoft Word 2000. Pages were composed by Microsoft Press using Adobe PageMaker 6.52 for Windows, with text in Garamond and display type in Helvetica Black. Composed pages were delivered to the printer as electronic prepress files.

Cover Graphic Designer
Girvin | Strategic Branding & Design

Cover Illustrator
Glenn Mitsui

Interior Graphic Artist
Michael Kloepfer

Principal Compositor
Paula Gorelick

Principal Proofreaders/Copy Editors
Melissa Bryan, Roger LeBlanc

Technical Copy Editor
Shawn Peck

Indexer
Julie Kawabata

MICROSOFT LICENSE AGREEMENT
Book Companion CD

IMPORTANT—READ CAREFULLY: This Microsoft End-User License Agreement ("EULA") is a legal agreement between you (either an individual or an entity) and Microsoft Corporation for the Microsoft product identified above, which includes computer software and may include associated media, printed materials, and "online" or electronic documentation ("SOFTWARE PRODUCT"). Any component included within the SOFTWARE PRODUCT that is accompanied by a separate End-User License Agreement shall be governed by such agreement and not the terms set forth below. By installing, copying, or otherwise using the SOFTWARE PRODUCT, you agree to be bound by the terms of this EULA. If you do not agree to the terms of this EULA, you are not authorized to install, copy, or otherwise use the SOFTWARE PRODUCT; you may, however, return the SOFTWARE PRODUCT, along with all printed materials and other items that form a part of the Microsoft product that includes the SOFTWARE PRODUCT, to the place you obtained them for a full refund.

SOFTWARE PRODUCT LICENSE

The SOFTWARE PRODUCT is protected by United States copyright laws and international copyright treaties, as well as other intellectual property laws and treaties. The SOFTWARE PRODUCT is licensed, not sold.

1. **GRANT OF LICENSE.** This EULA grants you the following rights:

    a. **Software Product.** You may install and use one copy of the SOFTWARE PRODUCT on a single computer. The primary user of the computer on which the SOFTWARE PRODUCT is installed may make a second copy for his or her exclusive use on a portable computer.

    b. **Storage/Network Use.** You may also store or install a copy of the SOFTWARE PRODUCT on a storage device, such as a network server, used only to install or run the SOFTWARE PRODUCT on your other computers over an internal network; however, you must acquire and dedicate a license for each separate computer on which the SOFTWARE PRODUCT is installed or run from the storage device. A license for the SOFTWARE PRODUCT may not be shared or used concurrently on different computers.

    c. **License Pak.** If you have acquired this EULA in a Microsoft License Pak, you may make the number of additional copies of the computer software portion of the SOFTWARE PRODUCT authorized on the printed copy of this EULA, and you may use each copy in the manner specified above. You are also entitled to make a corresponding number of secondary copies for portable computer use as specified above.

    d. **Sample Code.** Solely with respect to portions, if any, of the SOFTWARE PRODUCT that are identified within the SOFTWARE PRODUCT as sample code (the "SAMPLE CODE"):

      i. **Use and Modification.** Microsoft grants you the right to use and modify the source code version of the SAMPLE CODE, *provided* you comply with subsection (d)(iii) below. You may not distribute the SAMPLE CODE, or any modified version of the SAMPLE CODE, in source code form.

      ii. **Redistributable Files.** Provided you comply with subsection (d)(iii) below, Microsoft grants you a nonexclusive, royalty-free right to reproduce and distribute the object code version of the SAMPLE CODE and of any modified SAMPLE CODE, other than SAMPLE CODE, or any modified version thereof, designated as not redistributable in the Readme file that forms a part of the SOFTWARE PRODUCT (the "Non-Redistributable Sample Code"). All SAMPLE CODE other than the Non-Redistributable Sample Code is collectively referred to as the "REDISTRIBUTABLES."

      iii. **Redistribution Requirements.** If you redistribute the REDISTRIBUTABLES, you agree to: (i) distribute the REDISTRIBUTABLES in object code form only in conjunction with and as a part of your software application product; (ii) not use Microsoft's name, logo, or trademarks to market your software application product; (iii) include a valid copyright notice on your software application product; (iv) indemnify, hold harmless, and defend Microsoft from and against any claims or lawsuits, including attorney's fees, that arise or result from the use or distribution of your software application product; and (v) not permit further distribution of the REDISTRIBUTABLES by your end user. Contact Microsoft for the applicable royalties due and other licensing terms for all other uses and/or distribution of the REDISTRIBUTABLES.

2. **DESCRIPTION OF OTHER RIGHTS AND LIMITATIONS.**

    • **Limitations on Reverse Engineering, Decompilation, and Disassembly.** You may not reverse engineer, decompile, or disassemble the SOFTWARE PRODUCT, except and only to the extent that such activity is expressly permitted by applicable law notwithstanding this limitation.

    • **Separation of Components.** The SOFTWARE PRODUCT is licensed as a single product. Its component parts may not be separated for use on more than one computer.

    • **Rental.** You may not rent, lease, or lend the SOFTWARE PRODUCT.

    • **Support Services.** Microsoft may, but is not obligated to, provide you with support services related to the SOFTWARE PRODUCT ("Support Services"). Use of Support Services is governed by the Microsoft policies and programs described in the user manual, in "online" documentation, and/or in other Microsoft-provided materials. Any supplemental software code provided to you as part of the Support Services shall be considered part of the SOFTWARE PRODUCT and subject to the terms and conditions of this EULA. With respect to technical information you provide to Microsoft as part of the Support Services, Microsoft may use such information for its business purposes, including for product support and development. Microsoft will not utilize such technical information in a form that personally identifies you.

- **Software Transfer.** You may permanently transfer all of your rights under this EULA, provided you retain no copies, you transfer all of the SOFTWARE PRODUCT (including all component parts, the media and printed materials, any upgrades, this EULA, and, if applicable, the Certificate of Authenticity), **and** the recipient agrees to the terms of this EULA.

- **Termination.** Without prejudice to any other rights, Microsoft may terminate this EULA if you fail to comply with the terms and conditions of this EULA. In such event, you must destroy all copies of the SOFTWARE PRODUCT and all of its component parts.

3. **COPYRIGHT.** All title and copyrights in and to the SOFTWARE PRODUCT (including but not limited to any images, photographs, animations, video, audio, music, text, SAMPLE CODE, REDISTRIBUTABLES, and "applets" incorporated into the SOFTWARE PRODUCT) and any copies of the SOFTWARE PRODUCT are owned by Microsoft or its suppliers. The SOFTWARE PRODUCT is protected by copyright laws and international treaty provisions. Therefore, you must treat the SOFTWARE PRODUCT like any other copyrighted material **except** that you may install the SOFTWARE PRODUCT on a single computer provided you keep the original solely for backup or archival purposes. You may not copy the printed materials accompanying the SOFTWARE PRODUCT.

4. **U.S. GOVERNMENT RESTRICTED RIGHTS.** The SOFTWARE PRODUCT and documentation are provided with RESTRICTED RIGHTS. Use, duplication, or disclosure by the Government is subject to restrictions as set forth in subparagraph (c)(1)(ii) of the Rights in Technical Data and Computer Software clause at DFARS 252.227-7013 or subparagraphs (c)(1) and (2) of the Commercial Computer Software—Restricted Rights at 48 CFR 52.227-19, as applicable. Manufacturer is Microsoft Corporation/One Microsoft Way/Redmond, WA 98052-6399.

5. **EXPORT RESTRICTIONS.** You agree that you will not export or re-export the SOFTWARE PRODUCT, any part thereof, or any process or service that is the direct product of the SOFTWARE PRODUCT (the foregoing collectively referred to as the "Restricted Components"), to any country, person, entity, or end user subject to U.S. export restrictions. You specifically agree not to export or re-export any of the Restricted Components (i) to any country to which the U.S. has embargoed or restricted the export of goods or services, which currently include, but are not necessarily limited to, Cuba, Iran, Iraq, Libya, North Korea, Sudan, and Syria, or to any national of any such country, wherever located, who intends to transmit or transport the Restricted Components back to such country; (ii) to any end user who you know or have reason to know will utilize the Restricted Components in the design, development, or production of nuclear, chemical, or biological weapons; or (iii) to any end user who has been prohibited from participating in U.S. export transactions by any federal agency of the U.S. government. You warrant and represent that neither the BXA nor any other U.S. federal agency has suspended, revoked, or denied your export privileges.

DISCLAIMER OF WARRANTY

NO WARRANTIES OR CONDITIONS. MICROSOFT EXPRESSLY DISCLAIMS ANY WARRANTY OR CONDITION FOR THE SOFTWARE PRODUCT. THE SOFTWARE PRODUCT AND ANY RELATED DOCUMENTATION ARE PROVIDED "AS IS" WITHOUT WARRANTY OR CONDITION OF ANY KIND, EITHER EXPRESS OR IMPLIED, INCLUDING, WITHOUT LIMITATION, THE IMPLIED WARRANTIES OF MERCHANTABILITY, FITNESS FOR A PARTICULAR PURPOSE, OR NONINFRINGEMENT. THE ENTIRE RISK ARISING OUT OF USE OR PERFORMANCE OF THE SOFTWARE PRODUCT REMAINS WITH YOU.

LIMITATION OF LIABILITY. TO THE MAXIMUM EXTENT PERMITTED BY APPLICABLE LAW, IN NO EVENT SHALL MICROSOFT OR ITS SUPPLIERS BE LIABLE FOR ANY SPECIAL, INCIDENTAL, INDIRECT, OR CONSEQUENTIAL DAMAGES WHATSOEVER (INCLUDING, WITHOUT LIMITATION, DAMAGES FOR LOSS OF BUSINESS PROFITS, BUSINESS INTERRUPTION, LOSS OF BUSINESS INFORMATION, OR ANY OTHER PECUNIARY LOSS) ARISING OUT OF THE USE OF OR INABILITY TO USE THE SOFTWARE PRODUCT OR THE PROVISION OF OR FAILURE TO PROVIDE SUPPORT SERVICES, EVEN IF MICROSOFT HAS BEEN ADVISED OF THE POSSIBILITY OF SUCH DAMAGES. IN ANY CASE, MICROSOFT'S ENTIRE LIABILITY UNDER ANY PROVISION OF THIS EULA SHALL BE LIMITED TO THE GREATER OF THE AMOUNT ACTUALLY PAID BY YOU FOR THE SOFTWARE PRODUCT OR US$5.00; PROVIDED, HOWEVER, IF YOU HAVE ENTERED INTO A MICROSOFT SUPPORT SERVICES AGREEMENT, MICROSOFT'S ENTIRE LIABILITY REGARDING SUPPORT SERVICES SHALL BE GOVERNED BY THE TERMS OF THAT AGREEMENT. BECAUSE SOME STATES AND JURISDICTIONS DO NOT ALLOW THE EXCLUSION OR LIMITATION OF LIABILITY, THE ABOVE LIMITATION MAY NOT APPLY TO YOU.

MISCELLANEOUS

This EULA is governed by the laws of the State of Washington USA, except and only to the extent that applicable law mandates governing law of a different jurisdiction.

Should you have any questions concerning this EULA, or if you desire to contact Microsoft for any reason, please contact the Microsoft subsidiary serving your country, or write: Microsoft Sales Information Center/One Microsoft Way/Redmond, WA 98052-6399.

OWNER REGISTRATION CARD

Register Today!

0-7356-0931-4

Return the bottom portion of this card to register today.

Microsoft® Windows® Script Host 2.0 Developer's Guide

FIRST NAME

MIDDLE INITIAL

LAST NAME

INSTITUTION OR COMPANY NAME

ADDRESS

CITY

STATE

ZIP

( )

E-MAIL ADDRESS

PHONE NUMBER

U.S. and Canada addresses only. Fill in information above and mail postage-free.
Please mail only the bottom half of this page.

For information about Microsoft Press®
products, visit our Web site at
mspress.microsoft.com

Microsoft®